The Reading Teacher's BOOK OF LISTS

FOURTH EDITION

Edward Bernard Fry, Ph.D.
Jacqueline E. Kress, Ed.D.
Dona Lee Fountoukidis, Ed.D.

JOSSEY-BASS
A Wiley Imprint
www.josseybass.com

KH

Published by Jossey-Bass
A Wiley Imprint
989 Market Street, San Francisco, CA 94103-1741 www.josseybass.com

Jossey-Bass books and products are available through most bookstores. To contact Jossey-Bass directly call our Customer Care Department within the U.S. at (800) 956-7739, outside the U.S. at (317) 572-3986 or fax (317) 572-4002.

Jossey-Bass also publishes its books in a variety of electronic formats. Some content that appears in print may not be available in electronic books.

Library of Congress Cataloging-in-Publication Data

Fry, Edward Bernard
    The reading teacher's book of lists / Edward Bernard Fry,
Jacqueline E. Kress, Dona Lee Fountoukidis.—4th ed.
        p. cm.
    Includes bibliographical references and index.
    ISBN 0-13-028185-9 (paperback)
    ISBN 0-13-088406-5 (spiral wire)
    ISBN 0-13-040586-8 (w/CD)
    1. Reading—Miscellanea.   2. Curriculum planning—Miscellanea.
3. Tutors and tutoring—Miscellanea.   4. Handbooks, vade-mecums,
etc.   I. Title: Book of Lists.   II. Kress, Jacqueline E.   III. Fountoukidis, Dona.
IV. Title.
LB1050.2.F79   2000
428.4—dc20   00-026222
                                                                CIP

Printed in the United States of America
FIRST EDITION
PB Printing 10 9 8 7

12/13/05

This book is dedicated to the many teachers, professors, volunteers, and editors who are actively engaged in the struggle against illiteracy in their schools, colleges, church basements, and publishing houses.

About the Authors

Edward B. Fry, Ph.D. is Professor Emeritus of Education at Rutgers University (New Brunswick, NJ) where, for 24 years, he was director of the Reading Center. At Rutgers, Dr. Fry taught graduate and undergraduate courses in Reading, curriculum, and other educational subjects, and served as mentor and dissertation committee member for doctoral candidates in Reading and Educational Psychology. As the Reading Center director, he provided instruction for children with reading problems, trained teacher candidates, and conducted statewide reading conferences. Dr. Fry is known internationally for his Readability Graph which is used by teachers, publishers, and others to judge the reading difficulty of books and other materials. He is also well known for his Instant Words, a high-frequency word list, and for reading, spelling, and secondary curriculum materials. He works as a curriculum author and reading consultant.

Jacqueline E. Kress, Ed.D. is Associate Dean and Director of Graduate Studies at Fordham University's Graduate School of Education (New York, NY) and works with university and school faculty in the preparation and professional development of teachers, administrators, and other educators. She is an experienced reading teacher and teacher educator, having taught developmental and remedial reading in urban elementary schools, and reading skills and methods courses at the undergraduate and graduate levels. Dr. Kress has designed numerous educational programs, including programs for at-risk students, students with special instructional needs, and standards-based K–12 and college-level curricula. She is the author of *The ESL Teacher's Book of Lists* and co-author of *The Readability Machine* (both published by Prentice Hall).

Dona L. Fountoukidis, Ed.D. is Director of Planning, Research, and Evaluation at William Paterson University (Wayne, NJ) where she conducts research on student learning. Dr. Fountoukidis has held a variety of teaching positions. In Japan, she taught English as a second language to Japanese junior and senior high school students. In the United States, she has taught college courses in developmental reading and study skills, reading methods and reading methods for the content areas, as well as courses in statistics and educational psychology.

Preface
to the Fourth Edition

It is surprising to us, and also a great pleasure, that hundreds of thousands of teachers, publishers, tutors, home schoolers, and other individuals have used previous editions of this book. Part of its popularity is due to word of mouth where one teacher tells another, or one editor tells an author, that there is a wealth of creative ideas and helpful information in *The Reading Teacher's Book of Lists*. We are sure that you, too, will find many useful lists in this new fourth edition.

We thought a good deal about the extraordinary changes in reading and literacy education that have occurred since the first edition was published in 1984 while developing the lists for this fourth edition. In just fifteen years, the long-running argument about the best way to teach beginning reading seems to have been fairly settled. Most now agree that a balanced approach is best, employing a broad range of phonics and word recognition skills and using authentic reading materials to further teach and reinforce these skills.

In even less time, the Internet, World Wide Web, and other technologies have entered our business and daily life, and are now in many classrooms across the nation. In addition, as we reviewed each list, we marveled at the rapidity of change in the English language itself. We found, for example, that some words were no longer relevant—the compound word "flashcube"—while many new words, like "keypad," needed to be added to keep teachers and students abreast of developments at the beginning of the new millennium.

The Reading Teacher's Book of Lists, Fourth Edition reflects these changes and more while preserving a great deal of the material that has made the earlier editions so recognized and well-used. It contains substantially updated versions of most of the lists found in the third edition, plus many new ones. For example, our phonics section includes many new lists that will help you balance your reading and literacy programs, beginning with the sounds of our alphabet (*Consonant* and *Vowel Sounds*) to a systematic phonics skill development component (*Suggested Phonics Teaching Order*). In this section, you'll also find updated lists that are the cornerstone of our earlier editions (*Phonograms, Phonically Irregular Words,* and *Syllabication Rules*).

New lists abound throughout this resource. In Useful Words, you'll find *Mass Nouns* and *Nonreversible Word Pairs* . . . *Reading Math* is an important addition for reading success across the curriculum . . . the Writing section boasts brand new *Story Starters* . . . the Literature section has been significantly updated and now includes *Coretta Scott King Awards, Books for Reluctant and Developing Readers*, and *Books Without Words* . . . and Assessment contains *Rubrics* at the primary and elementary levels. Other new lists include *Teaching with Newspapers, Comprehension Strategies, Oxymorons, Activities for Tutors, Search Engines for Educators, Fifty Reading Tips for Parents*, and *Anagrams*. And whether you are a new or expert web-surfer, be sure to check out web sites for *Children's Literature, Writers and Word Lovers*, and for *Reading Instruction*.

You'll also find that many of the lists you've referred to over and over again have been expanded and updated, like *Analogies, Prefixes, Suffixes, Graphic Organizers, 100 Ways to Praise, Games and Methods for Teaching, Acronyms and Initializations, Sentence Tunes*, and *Sound Awareness Books*, to name just a few. Of course, we have the "classics" that have stood the test of time, such as *Phonics Example Words, Homophones, The First 1,000 Instant Words, The Readability Graph, Greek and Latin Roots, Interest Inventories, Metaphors and Similes, Homographs and Heteronyms*, and more. And to make your search for any list easier, the fourth edition is organized into fifteen convenient sections and includes a handy index.

We'd like to thank our families, friends, colleagues, and dear readers for all their suggestions and help. We are continually delighted and motivated by your enthusiasm for *The Reading Teacher's Book of Lists*. We hope you enjoy this edition as much as we have enjoyed writing it for you. We welcome your comments.

Edward Bernard Fry
Jacqueline E. Kress
Dona Lee Fountoukidis

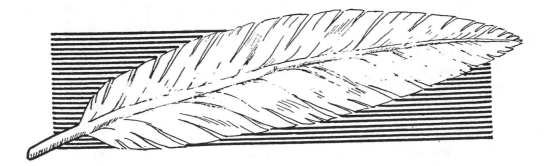

A User's Guide

The wide diversity of lists in this book makes it possible for teachers to pick and choose those that meet specific classroom and teaching needs. Some lists may be appropriate for different types of teaching (*writing*) or for various grade levels (*primary*). The following list suggestions are designed to help you and to make this book of lists even more useful.

Contents

6   WRITING   197

7   INSTRUCTION   225

8   COMPREHENSION AND STUDY SKILLS   261

9 ASSESSMENT 295

10 SPELLING 315

11 THE INTERNET 335

12 ESL/LANGUAGE 355

13 WORD PLAY FUN 389

14 ABBREVIATIONS, SYMBOLS, AND SIGNS   417

15 REFERENCE   443

INDEX   457

1
PHONICS

List 1. CONSONANT SOUNDS

The following are all the beginning consonant sounds for either words or syllables (except for final consonant blends). They constitute what some linguists call the "onset" for the syllable. The rest of the syllables must have a vowel or a vowel plus consonant (a vowel plus a consonant is called a phonogram or rime).

Single Consonants

b	h	n	v
c	j	p	w
d	k	r	y
f	l	s	z
g	m	t	

Consonant Digraphs

ch as in "chin"   ph as in "phone"
sh as in "shut"   gh as in "rough"
th (voiced) as in "thin"
th (voiceless) as in "this"
wh (hw blend) as in "which"

Important Exceptions

qu = /kw/ as in "quick"
(the letter "q" is never used without "u")
ph = /f/ as in "phone"
c = /s/ before e, i, or y as in "cent," "city,"
   or "cycle"
c = /k/ before a, o, or u as in "can," "cot," or "cub"
g = /j/ before e, i, or y as in "gem," "giraffe,"
   or "gym"
x = /ks/ blend as in "fox"
s = /z/ sound at the end of some words as in "is"
ng = /ng/ phoneme as in "sing"
ck = /k/ often at the end of a word as in "luck"

Rare Exceptions

ch = /k/ as in "character"
ch = /sh/ as in "chef"
ti = /sh/ as in "attention"
s = /sh/ as in "sure"
x = /gz/ as in "exact"
x = /z/ as in "xylophone"
s = /zh/ as in "measure"
si = /zh/ as in "vision"

Silent Consonants

gn = /n/ as in "gnat"
kn = /n/ as in "knife"
wr = /r/ as in "write"
gh = /silent/ as in "high"
mb = /m/ as in "lamb"
if = /f/ as in "calf"
lk = /k/ as in "walk"
tle = /l/ as in "castle"

Initial Consonant Blends

r family	l family	s family	3-letter s family	no family
br as in "bride"	bl as in "blend"	sc as in "scare"	sch as in "school"	dw as in "dwell"
cr as in "crop"	cl as in "clay"	sk as in "skunk"	scr as in "scrub"	tw as in "twin"
dr as in "drive"	fl as in "fly"	sm as in "smile"	squ as in "squall"	thr as in "threw"
fr as in "free"	gl as in "glass"	sn as in "snack"	str as in "strong"	
gr as in "grand"	pl as in "plug"	sp as in "spell"	spr as in "sprout"	
pr as in "prize"	sl as in "slow"	st as in "sting"	spl as in "splash"	
tr as in "trust"		sw as in "swipe"	shr as in "shrank"	
wr as in "write"				

Final Consonant Blends

(Note: These are usually learned best with rhymes.)

ct as in "act"	lt as in "salt"	nk as in "think"	sk as in "tusk"
ft as in "lift"	mp as in "jump"	nt as in "hunt"	sp as in "lisp"
ld as in "old"	nc(e) as in "since"	pt as in "kept"	st as in "lost"
lm as in "calm"	nch as in "lunch"	rd as in "word"	
lp as in "pulp"	nd as in "band"	rt as in "art"	

See also List 7, Suggested Phonics Teaching Order; List 8, Phonics Example Words.

List 2. VOWEL SOUNDS

There are about 21 vowel sounds in English (the actual number is dialect dependent), including vowel sounds affected by the consonant "r." For words that use these vowel sounds, refer to List 8—Phonics Example Words.

Short Vowels

a = /ă/ as in "cat"
e = /ĕ/ as in "end"
i = /ĭ/ as in "sip"
o = /ŏ/ as in "hot"
u = /ŭ/ as in "cup"

Vowel Y

y = /ī/ as in "try," "cycle"
y = /ē/ as in "funny"

Schwa

a = /ə/ as in "ago"
e = /ə/ as in "happen"
o = /ə/ as in "other"

Dipthongs

oi = /oi/ as in "oil"
oy = /oi/ as in "boy"
ou = /ou/ as in "out"
ow = /ou/ as in "how"

Long Vowels—Final E Rule

a = /ā/ as in "make"
e = /ē/ as in "these"
i = /ī/ as in "five"
o = /ō/ as in "hope"
u = /ū/ as in "cube"

Long Vowels— Open Syllable Rule

a = /ā/ as in "baby"
e = /ē/ as in "we"
i = /ī/ as in "tiger"
o = /ō/ as in "open"

Double O

oo = /o͞o/ as in "soon"
oo = /o͝o/ as in "good"
u = /o͞o/ as in "truth"
u = /o͝o/ as in "put"

Long Vowel Digraphs

ai = /ā/ as in "aid"
ay = /ā/ as in "say"
ea = /ē/ as in "eat"
ee = /ē/ as in "see"
oa = /ō/ as in "oat"
ow = /ō/ as in "own"

Vowel Plus R

ar = /är/ as in "far"
er = /ər/ as in "her"
ir = /ər/ as in "sir"
or = /ôr/ as in "for"
ur = /ər/ as in "fur"

Broad O

o = /ô/ as in "long"
a(l) = /ô/ as in "also"
a(w) = /ô/ as in "saw"
a(u) = /ô/ as in "auto"

Vowel Exceptions

ea = /ĕ/ as in "bread" or /ē/ as in "seat"

e = /silent/ as in "come" and "make"

y = /y/ as in "yes"

le = /əl/ as in "candle"
al = /əl/ as in "pedal"
ul = /əl/ as in "awful"

"ea" makes both a long and short E sound.

E at the end of a word is usually silent, and often makes the preceding vowel long.

Y is a consonant at the beginning of a word (yes), but is a vowel in the middle or end of other words. See Vowel Y shown above.

Final le makes a schwa plus l sound.
Final al makes a schwa plus l sound.
Final ul makes a schwa plus l sound.

See also List 3, The Final "E" Rule; List 4, Double Vowels; List 7, Suggested Phonics Teaching Order; List 8, Phonics Example Words.

The Reading Teacher's Book of Lists, Fourth Edition, © 2000 by John Wiley & Sons, Inc.

List 3. THE FINAL "E" RULE

Often, an "e" at the end of a word makes the preceding vowel long. Here are some short vowel words contrasted with long vowel words that illustrate this rule.

A Words

fad—fade	rag—rage	wag—wage
stag—stage	cam—came	dam—dame
tam—tame	sham—shame	ban—bane
can—cane	pan—pane	Sam—same
cap—cape	gap—gape	fat—fate
tap—tape	scrap—scrape	rat—rate
hat—hate	mat—mate	

I words

hid—hide	rid—ride	slid—slide
dim—dime	rim—rime	Tim—time
grim—grime	prim—prime	slim—slime
din—dine	fin—fine	pin—pine
shin—shine	spin—spine	tin—tine
twin—twine	win—wine	rip—ripe
grip—gripe	snip—snipe	strip—stripe
bit—bite	kit—kite	lit—lite
quit—quite	spit—spite	sit—site

O words

lob—lobe	rob—robe	glob—globe
cod—code	nod—node	rod—rode
cop—cope	hop—hope	mop—mope
pop—pope	slop—slope	tot—tote

U words

cub—cube	tub—tube	cut—cute

Exceptions to the final e rule. The letter "e" is nearly always silent at the end of a word. Here are some words that have a silent final "e," but *do not* follow the final e rule.

- most words ending in -le: circle, cattle, middle, apple, single
- most words ending in -ce: since, notice, voice, force, dance, office
- most words ending in -se: house, else, horse, course, praise, sense
- most words ending in -re: before, sure, figure, are, measure, square
- most words ending in -ve: give, love, believe
- others: come, some, one, there, large, eye, edge, gone

See also List 7, Suggested Phonics Teaching Order; List 8, Phonics Example Words.

The Reading Teacher's Book of Lists, Fourth Edition, © 2000 by John Wiley & Sons, Inc.

List 4. DOUBLE VOWELS

The following are long vowel digraphs contrasted with short vowels in closed syllables.
The old double vowel rule has too many exceptions like "oo" or "ou" to be generalized.

Short a /ă/	Long a /ā/	Short e /ĕ/	Long e /ē/	Short i /ĭ/	Long i /ī/	Short o /ŏ/	Long o /ō/
lad	laid	red	reed	did	died	crock	croak
mad	maid	bed	bead	lid	lied	clock	cloak
pad	paid	fed	feed			rod	road
clam	claim	led	lead			sop	soap
man	main	Ned	need			cot	coat
pan	pain	wed	weed			got	goat
ran	rain	bled	bleed				
van	vain	bred	breed				
bran	brain	Fred	freed				
plan	plain	sped	speed				
span	Spain	stem	steam				
pant	paint	Ben	bean				
bat	bait	Ken	keen				
		men	mean				
		ten	teen				
		fend	fiend				
		pep	peep				
		rep	reap				
		step	steep				
		bet	beet				
		bet	beat				
		met	meet				
		met	meat				
		net	neat				
		pet	peat				
		set	seat				
		den	dean				
		best	beast				

The Reading Teacher's Book of Lists, Fourth Edition, © 2000 by John Wiley & Sons, Inc.

See also List 7, Suggested Phonics Teaching Order; List 8, Phonics Example Words.

List 5. SOUND DETERMINED BY LETTER POSITION

Another way of teaching phonics is to show how the sound of the letter or grapheme is determined by its position or environment within a word. For example, 1 shows that many consonants make the same sound no matter where they are, but 2 shows that the position in a syllable or other factors change the sound.

1. Position-independent letter correspondences (doesn't matter where the letter is)

Single Consonants

t	/t/	top	f	/f/	fish
n	/n/	nut	v	/v/	valentine
r	/r/	ring	h	/h/	hand
m	/m/	man	k	/k/	kite
d	/d/	dog	w	/w/	window
l	/l/	letter	j	/j/	jar
p	/p/	pen	z	/z/	zebra
b	/b/	book			

2. Position-dependent letter correspondences (position changes sound)

Closed Syllable Rule (syllable ends in a consonant)

a	/a/	at
e	/e/	end
i	/i/	is
o	/o/	hot
u	/u/	pup

Second Sounds

s	/s/	saw	(at the beginning)
s	/z/	his	(frequently at the end)
y	/y/	yes	(at the beginning)
y	/e/	funny	(at the end)
y	/i/	my	(middle or end)
e	/silent/	come	(at the end)

Open Syllable Rule (syllable ends in a vowel)

a	/ā/	table	o	/ō/	donut
e	/ē/	before	u	/ū/	music
i	/ī/	tiny			

Schwa (always in unaccented syllable when word has two or more syllables)

a	/ə/	principal	o	/ə/	canyon
e	/ə/	happen	u	/ə/	radium
i	/ə/	pencil			

Letter X (always at end)

x	/ks/	box

3. Marker-dependent letter correspondences (marker is another letter in the word)

Final E Rule (always "VCe")

a	/ā/	cake	o	/ō/	home
e	/ē/	these	u	/ū/	use
i	/ī/	ice			

Consonant Second Sounds

c	/k/	cake	(followed by a, o, u)
c	/s/	city	(followed by i, e, y)
g	/g/	gate	(followed by a, o, u)
g	/j/	gem	(followed by i, e, y)

R Modified Vowels (always where "r" follows)

a	/är/	far	o	/or/	for
e	/ûr/	her	u	/ûr/	fur
i	/ûr/	fir			

4. Digraph correspondences (two letters positioned together)

Consonant Digraphs

sh	/sh/	shoe
ch	/ch/	church
th	/th/	this
th	/th/	thing
wh	/hw/	white
mb	/m/	bomb

Long Vowel Digraphs

ea	/ē/	eat
ee	/ē/	see
ai	/ā/	aid
ay	/ā/	say
oa	/ō/	oat
ow	/ō/	know

Broad O Digraphs

au	/o/	auto
aw	/o/	saw

Double O

oo	/oo/	moon
oo	/oo/	look

Exceptions

qu	/kw/	quick
ea	/e/	bread
ph	/f/	phone
ng	/ng/	sing

Silent Consonants

gn	/n/	gnat
kn	/n/	knife
wr	/r/	write
gh	/silent/	right
ck	/k/	back

Diphthongs

ou	/ou/	out
ow	/ou/	now
oy	/oi/	boy
oi	/oi/	boil
ew	/ew/	few

List 6. PHONICS AWARENESS

The English language uses 26 alphabetic letters in more than 100 combinations to represent between 44 to 45 speech sounds. Phonics helps new as well as experienced readers make connections between letter patterns and the speech sounds for which they stand. It begins with an awareness and recognition of letters and sounds, then builds connections between them, starting with the most frequent and distinct correspondences.

Letter Knowledge

Recognize, name, and distinguish upper- and lower-case letters.

Word Segmentation

Recognize individual words within a sentence. Example: "I went to the store." (5 words)

Syllable Segmentation

Recognize and separate syllables within words. Examples: Bill-y, Ton-ya, a-bout, talk-ing

Syllable Blending

Can listen to simple polysyllabic words spoken in separate syllables and can say the complete blended word. Example: let-ter → letter

Phonemic Awareness— Consonants

Upon hearing two similar words with different initial consonants, tell whether the initial sounds are the same or different. Examples: mat—sat; big—beg

Upon hearing two similar words with different final consonants, tell whether the final sounds are the same or different. Examples: sat—sad; met—mat

Phonemic Awareness— Vowels

Upon hearing two similar words with different vowel sounds, tell whether the vowel (medial) is the same or different. Examples: mane—cane; pin—pen

Phonemic Blending

Upon hearing separate phonemes, blend them and say the complete word. Example: /t/ /o/ /m/ → Tom

Phonemic Segmentation

Upon hearing a complete word, separate and pronounce the individual sounds. Example: cat → /c/ /a/ /t/

Rhyming

Recognize and produce rhyming pairs. Examples: tan/pan; big/pig; get/set; sap/tap

Upon hearing a series of onset consonants and a phonogram, blend them to produce rhyming words. Examples: /k/ /ab/ → cab; /d/ /ab/ → dab; /g/ /ab/ → gab; /j/ /ab/ → jab

Upon hearing a series of rhymes, break the rhyme into onset and rime. Examples: set → / s / / et /; bet → /b/ /et/ ; let → /l/ /et/

The Reading Teacher's Book of Lists, Fourth Edition, © 2000 by John Wiley & Sons, Inc.

List 7. SUGGESTED PHONICS TEACHING ORDER

The Reading Teacher's Book of Lists, Fourth Edition, © 2000 by John Wiley & Sons, Inc.

	Letter(s)	Sound	Example	Letter(s)	Sound	Example
Easy Consonants (high frequency / high contrast)	t	/t/	tap	l	/l/	lap
	n	/n/	nap	c	/k/	cat
	r	/r/	rat	p	/p/	pat
	m	/m/	mat	b	/b/	bat
	d	/d/	dog	f	/f/	fat
	s	/s/	sat	v	/v/	vet
Short Vowels	a	/ă/	cat	o	/ŏ/	hot
	e	/ĕ/	let	u	/ŭ/	cut
	i	/ĭ/	hit			
Long Vowels (final e rule)	a_e	/ā/	make	o_e	/ō/	bone
	e_e	/ē/	these	u_e	/ū/	use
	i_e	/ī/	nine			
Long Vowels (open syllable rule- end of word)	e	/ē/	me	o	/ō/	go
Other Single Consonants	g	/g/	get	x	/ks/	box
	h	/h/	hot	qu	/kw/	quit
	k	/k/	kit	z	/z/	zip
	w	/w/	wet	y	/y/	yes
	j	/j/	jet			
Initial Consonant Digraphs	th	/t̶h̶/	thin	sh	/sh/	ship
	th	/th/	these	wh	/hw/	when
	ch	/ch/	chin			
Y Vowels	-y	/ī/	my	y	/ē/	funny
Consonant Second Sounds	c	/s/	city	g	/j/	gym
	s	/z/	his	x	/gs/	exam
Long Vowel Digraphs	ea	/ē/	meat	ay	/ā/	day
	ee	/ē/	feet	oa	/ō/	boat
	ai	/ā/	pain	ow	/ō/	tow
Initial Consonant Blends	pr	/pr/	prize	fr	/fr/	free
	tr	/tr/	trip	st	/st/	step
	gr	/gr/	greet	sp	/sp/	spin
	br	/br/	Brad	sk	/sk/	skip
	cr	/cr/	crib	sc	/sc/	scan
	dr	/dr/	drive	sw	/sw/	swim

	Letter(s)	Sound	Example	Letter(s)	Sound	Example
Initial Consonant Blends (cont.)	sm	/sm/	smell	fl	/fl/	flip
	sn	/sn/	snap	sl	/sl/	slap
	pl	/pl/	play	gl	/gl/	glow
	cl	/cl/	clip	tw	/tw/	twin
	bl	/bl/	blip	str	/str/	street
Final Consonant Blends	ld	/ld/	cold	nt	/nt/	ant
	lf	/lf/	elf	mb	/mb/	lamb
	sk	/sk/	ask	mp	/mp/	camp
	st	/st/	pest	ng	/ng/	sing
	nk	/nk/	ink			
R-Vowels	ar	/är/	far	air	/âr/	fair
	er	/ûr/	her	are	/âr/	bare
	ir	/ûr/	fir	ear	/ēr/	tear
	or	/ôr/	for	eer	/ēr/	beer
	ur	/ûr/	fur			
Broad O Vowels	aw	/aw/	awful	al	/aw/	also
	au	/aw/	auto	o	/aw/	off
Other Vowels— Diphthongs	ow	/ou/	owl	oi	/oi/	boil
	ou	/ou/	out	oy	/oi/	boy
Double O Vowels	oo	/o͞o/	pool	u	/o͞o/	truth
	oo	/o͝o/	foot	u	/o͝o/	push
Schwa in Unaccented Syllable	a	/ə/	about	o	/ə/	onion
	e	/ə/	letter	u	/ə/	circus
	i	/ə/	holiday			
Other Spellings / Silent Letters	gn	/n/	gnu	kn	/n/	knew
	ph	/f/	phone	wr	/r/	write
Other Vowel Spellings	ough	/aw/	ought	igh	/ī/	sight
	ea	/ea/	head			

The Reading Teacher's Book of Lists, Fourth Edition, © 2000 by John Wiley & Sons, Inc.

See also List 8, Phonics Example Words.

List 8. PHONICS EXAMPLE WORDS

This is an important list at the heart of phonics instruction. It alphabetically lists 99 single phonemes (speech sounds) and consonant blends (usually two phonemes), and it gives example words for each of these, often for their use in the beginning, middle, and end of words. These example words are also common English words, many taken from the list of Instant Words. This list solves the problem of coming up with a good common word to illustrate a phonics principle for lessons and worksheets.

/a/ SHORT A, CLOSED SYLLABLE RULE

Initial			Medial		
and	add	am	that	has	began
at	act	animal	can	than	stand
as	adjective	ant	had	man	black
after	answer	ax	back	hand	happen
an	ask	Africa	last	plant	fast

apple

/ā/ LONG A, OPEN SYLLABLE RULE

Initial	Medial			
able	paper	lazy	label	vibration
acre	lady	flavor	equator	basis
agent	baby	tomato	relation	hazy
apron	radio	navy	vapor	potato
Asia	crazy	station	enable	ladle
apex	labor	basic	volcano	vacation
April				tablecloth

table

/ā/ LONG A, FINAL E RULE

Initial		Medial			
ate	ape	make	late	gave	baseball
age	ace	made	tale	base	spaceship
ache		face	place	plane	racetrack
ale		same	name	game	shapeless
		came	wave	shape	
		state	space		

cake

/ā/ LONG A, AI DIGRAPH

Initial	Medial				
aim	rain	mail	claim	obtain	faint
aid	train	pain	detail	paid	grain
ailment	wait	sail	explain	remain	rail
ail	tail	strait	fail	wait	
	chain	afraid	gain	plain	
	jail	brain	main	laid	

nail

11

/ā/ LONG A, AY DIGRAPH

Medial

always	gayly	jaywalk
mayor	haystack	player
layer	wayside	daylight
maybe	payment	
	Rayon	

Final

day	pay	repay
say	gray	anyway
away	bay	way
play	stay	pray
may	birthday	lay
today	highway	gay
		hay

crayon

/ə/ SCHWA, A SPELLING

Initial

about	appear
above	away
ago	again
alone	ahead
America	another
alike	agree

Medial

several	canvass
national	familiar
senator	career
thousand	purchase
magazine	compass
breakfast	diagram

Final

antenna	china
algebra	comma
alfalfa	idea
banana	

announce

/aw/ AL DIGRAPH SPELLING

Initial

all	altogether
always	alternate
also	altar
already	albeit
almost	almanac
although	almighty

Medial

talk	scald
walk	walnut
chalk	fallen
salt	
false	
falter	

Final

call	baseball
tall	wall
fall	stall
overall	recall
hall	
small	

ball

/aw/ AU DIGRAPH SPELLING

Initial

August	Australia	audible
author	autoharp	authentic
autumn	auction	auditor
auditorium	auburn	
autograph	auxiliary	
audience	automatic	

Medial

because	cause	sausage
caught	dinosaur	overhaul
laundry	sauce	launch
haul	caution	faucet
daughter	exhaust	
fault	fraud	

auto

/aw/ AW DIGRAPH SPELLING

Initial

awful
awkward
awning
awe
awl
awfully

Medial

lawn	yawn	crawl
drawn	tawny	squawk
lawyer	drawer	scrawl
hawk	shawl	
lawful	bawl	

Final

law	paw
jaw	claw
draw	flaw
straw	gnaw
thaw	caw
taw	

saw

The Reading Teacher's Book of Lists, Fourth Edition, © 2000 by John Wiley & Sons, Inc.

/air/ AIR VOWEL, AR AND ARE SPELLINGS

Initial	Medial			Final		
area	January	February	declare	care	fare	
	dictionary	tiara	beware	rare	stare	
	vary	parent	flare	aware	glare	
	primary	wary		share	welfare	
	secretary	careful		spare	hare	
	canary	scare		bare	square	
	daring	scarcely		dare		

library

/ar/ AR VOWEL, AR SPELLING

Initial		Medial		Final		
are	argument	card	garden	car	mar	
arm	article	March	start	far	par	
army	arch	farm	dark	bar	scar	
art	armor	hard	yard	jar		
artist	ark	part	party	tar		
arctic	arbor	large				

star

/b/ REGULAR B CONSONANT SOUND

Initial		Medial		Final		
be	back	number	subject	tub	job	
by	but	problem	baby	cab	club	
boy	because	remember		rob	rub	
been	below	object		cub	grab	
box	before	probably		rib	adverb	
big	better			verb	bulb	

book

/bl/ CONSONANT BLEND

Initial				Medial		
black	blame	blank	blink	oblige	obliterate	
blue	bloom	blast	blur	emblem	grumbling	
bleed	blossom	blend	blow	tumbler	oblivious	
blood	blond	blue	blanket	nosebleed	gambler	
blind	blade	blot	bleach	ablaze	rambling	
				nimbly		

block

/br/ CONSONANT BLEND

Initial			Medial		
bread	bring	brush	library	daybreak	algebra
break	breath	breeze	umbrella	cobra	embrace
brick	branch	bridge	celebrate	membrane	lubricate
broad	bright	brain	vibrate	outbreak	
brother	broken	brass	abroad	zebra	
brown	brave	breakfast			

broom

/k/ HARD C, REGULAR CONSONANT K SOUND

Initial

can   call
come   country
came   cut
camp   car
color   cold
could   carry

Medial

because   across
picture   become
American   quickly
second

Final

back   check
rock   stick
sick   black
lock   pick
kick   thick
music   electric

cat

/s/ SOFT C, REGULAR CONSONANT S SOUND

Initial

cent   certain   cigar
circle   civil   cyclone
cycle   ceiling   cellar
circus   celebrate cease
center   cereal
cell   cinder

Medial

pencil   decide
fancy   Pacific
concert   percent
acid   precise
dancing   process
peaceful   sincere

Final

face
since
ice

city

/ch/ CH CONSONANT DIGRAPH SOUND

Initial

children   chief
church   chart
change   chin
chance   chest
cheer   chain
check   chase

Medial

pitcher   searching
attached   stretched
purchase   exchange
merchant

Final

which   catch
each   branch
much   touch
such   inch
teach   reach
rich   watch

chair

/cl/ CONSONANT BLEND

Initial

clean   clear   clever   climb
cloth   class   cliff   click
clay   clap   close
claim   claws   cloud
club   clerk   clues

clock

Medial

enclose   eclipse
include   acclaim   disclose
cyclone   conclude   decline
exclaim   reclaim   proclaim
exclude   declare   incline

/cr/ CONSONANT BLEND

Initial

cry   crew   cried   cruel
crack   crazy   crops   credit
crowd   cross   crayon
crash   crow   creek
cream   create   crown

Medial

across   aircraft   recruit
secret   sacred   scarecrow
increase   concrete   screen
microscope disease
democrat   decree

crab

14

/d/ REGULAR D CONSONANT SOUND

Initial		Medial		Final	
do	does	study	order	and	find
day	door	under	Indians	good	need
did	done	idea	didn't	had	did
dear	different	body		said	old
down	during			red	around
deep	don't			would	end

dog

/dr/ CONSONANT BLEND

Initial		Medial			
dry	dream	drift	address	undress	hydrogen
draw	dragon	drama	hundred	withdraw	laundress
drug	drill	drain	children	daydream	redress
drove	drink	drip	dandruff	eardrum	dewdrop
drop	drive	drench	cathedral	laundry	
dress	drew	droop			

drum

/e/ SHORT E, CLOSED SYLLABLE RULE

Initial		Medial				
end	empty	ever	when	let	set	men
egg	energy	edge	then	them	went	spell
every	explain	enter	get	very	help	next
extra	enjoy	elf	left	tell	well	red
enemy	engine	else				

elephant

/ē/ LONG E, OPEN SYLLABLE RULE

Initial	Medial			Final	
even	cedar	meter	being	me	we
equal	demon	prefix	recent	he	be
ether	secret	react	legal	she	maybe
evil	zebra	area	really		
ecology		female	depot		

Egypt

/ē/ LONG E, EE DIGRAPH

Initial	Medial		Final		
eel	sleep	seem	see	bee	fee
eerie	green	teeth	three	degree	spree
	keep	sweet	tree	flee	referee
	street	week	free	knee	
	feet	screen	agree	glee	
	wheel	fifteen			
	feel				

deer

The Reading Teacher's Book of Lists, Fourth Edition, © 2000 by John Wiley & Sons, Inc.

/ē/ LONG E, EA DIGRAPH

Initial

eat   eager
each   easel
east   Easter
easy   eaten
eagle   eastern

ease   **Medial**
eaves   neat   leaf
easily   read   feast
           least   peach
           beat   meat
           clean   weak
           deal   peanut

Final
sea
tea
flea
plea
pea

peach

/e/ SHORT E, EA SPELLING

Medial

head   breath   feather   meadow   threaten   heaven
heavy   dear   death   pleasant   treasure   dread
ready   ahead   measure   spread   weapon   pleasure
thread   breakfast instead   heading   weather   widespread
steady   already   leather   sweat   overhead   gingerbread
dead

bread

/ə/ SCHWA, E SPELLING

Initial

efface   effective
effect   efficient
efficiency
erratic
essential
erroneous

Medial

happen   scientist fuel   label
problem   item   given   absent
hundred   united   level   agent
arithmetic quiet   heaven   hundred
children   diet   even   often
calendar   different happen

eleven

/er/ ER VOWEL, ER SPELLING

Medial

camera   afternoon
allergy   liberty
bakery   operate
wonderful federal
dangerous battery

Final

her   better   another   river
mother   sister   baker   winter
over   under   wonder   liver
other   after   ever   shower
were   water   offer   lower

letter

/f/ REGULAR F CONSONANT SOUND

Initial

for   father
first   face
find   family
four   follow
funny   far
food   few

Medial

after   different
before   Africa
often   beautiful
careful

Final

if   chief
half   stuff
myself   brief
off   cliff
leaf   itself
himself   wolf

fish

/fl/ CONSONANT BLEND

Initial

flower	floor	fleet	flea
flat	flavor	flow	fluffy
flight	flood	flap	
flew	flute	flock	
fly	flame	fling	
float	flash	flip	

Medial

afflict	inflame
inflict	afloat
conflict	reflect
influence	inflate
aflame	inflexible
snowflake	

flag

/fr/ CONSONANT BLEND

Initial

free	frost	fruit	frisky
from	frank	freedom	freighter
front	freshman	frozen	fragile
friend	frame	France	
Friday	fresh		
fry	fraction		

Medial

afraid	defraud
affront	infringe
befriend	leapfrog
bullfrog	refrain
carefree	refresh
confront	infrequent

frog

/g/ REGULAR G CONSONANT SOUND

Initial

go	gun
good	game
got	gas
gave	gift
girl	gone
get	garden

Medial

again	segment
ago	regular
began	figure
sugar	
wagon	
signal	

Final

dog	frog
big	pig
egg	log
lcg	bag
fig	
flag	

gate

/j/ SOFT G, REGULAR CONSONANT J SOUND

Initial

gem	gym
gentlemen	gypsy
geography	ginger
generous	gelatin
gently	germ
	general

Medial

gesture	danger
genius	energy
genuine	region
generate	engine
giant	original
	vegetable
	oxygen

Final

change	page
large	village
bridge	huge
age	strange

giraffe

/gl/ CONSONANT BLEND

Initial

glad	glisten	glare	glider
glass	gloom	glade	glimpse
glow	glue	gleam	glitter
glory	glum	glee	glance
glove	glamour		glaze

Medial

eyeglass	hourglass
jingling	bugler
spyglass	angler
smuggling	mangling
wiggling	singly

globe

/gr/ CONSONANT BLEND

Initial

grade	grand				
great	green				
grow	ground				
grew	group				
grass	grab				
gray	grain				

Medial

grant	hungry	program	disgrace	
grin	angry	regret	fragrant	
gradual	congress	degrade	outgrow	
grandfather	agree	engrave	engross	
gravity	degree			

grapes

/h/ REGULAR H CONSONANT SOUND

Initial

he	help	half	high	
had	here	his	hit	
have	happy	hen	house	
her	home	hero		
him	hard	hide		
how	has	hill		

Medial

behind	rehearse
ahead	behold
unhappy	unhook
behave	ahoy
overheard	
autoharp	

hand

/i/ SHORT I, CLOSED SYLLABLE RULE

Initial

in	it	ill
is	invent	include
if	important	isn't
into	insect	inside
inch	instead	

Medial

with	will	different
did	big	until
this	still	miss
little	give	begin
which	his	city
	him	

INDIA

India

/ī/ LONG I, OPEN SYLLABLE RULE

Initial

I	icy
idea	Irish
I'll	iodine
iris	Iowa
I'm	ivory
item	

Medial

bicycle	pilot	variety	title
tiny	quiet	dinosaur	spider
silent	triangle	giant	diagram
rifle	climate	lion	China

iron

/ī/ LONG I, Final E RULE

Initial / **Medial**

Initial	Medial				
idle	five	fire	nine	mile	drive
ire	white	write	bite	size	wire
isle	ride	life	like	wide	mine
I've	time	side	line	describe	wife

ice

The Reading Teacher's Book of Lists, Fourth Edition, © 2000 by John Wiley & Sons, Inc.

/er/ ER VOWEL, IR SPELLING

Medial

girl	skirt	thirteen	shirk	circuit	
first	birthday	girth	mirth	girdle	
third	thirsty	birth	confirm	stirrup	
shirt	affirm	circus	Virginia	dirty	
dirt	circle	thirty	firm		

Final

fir
sir
stir
tapir
whir
astir

girl

/j/ REGULAR J CONSONANT SOUND

Initial

just	jet
jump	job
January	joke
jaw	joy
July	juice

Medial

June	object	project	unjust
jungle	enjoy	adjust	majesty
junior	subject	dejected	majority
jacket	major	overjoyed	rejoice
join	banjo	adjoin	
	adjective	reject	

jar

/k/ REGULAR K CONSONANT SOUND

Initial

kind	kiss
key	kitten
kill	kid
king	kettle
keep	kick
kin	keen

Medial

monkey	market
broken	packing
turkey	stroking
worker	

Final

like	work
make	mark
book	speak
look	milk
cake	bank
cook	break

kite

/n/ SOUND, KN SPELLING

Initial

knee	knelt
knew	knit
know	knock
knowledge	knight
knife	knuckle

knack	knockout	knell
kneel	knickers	kneecap
knapsack	knothole	knotty
knob	knoll	known
knead	knave	

Medial

unknown
doorknob
penknife
acknowledge
knickknack
knock-kneed

knot

/l/ REGULAR L CONSONANT SOUND

Initial

little	large
like	last
long	line
look	learn
live	left
land	light

Medial

only	really
below	follow
along	family
children	

Final

will	oil
all	tell
girl	until
school	spell
shall	well
small	vowel

letter

/m/ REGULAR M CONSONANT SOUND

Initial		**Medial**		**Final**	
me	more	number	important	from	farm
my	mother	American	example	them	room
make	move	something	family	am	arm
much	must	complete		seem	team
many	made			warm	form
may	men			him	bottom

man

/n/ REGULAR N CONSONANT SOUND

Initial		**Medial**		**Final**	
not	name	many	until	in	man
no	number	under	any	on	even
new	need	answer	animal	can	own
night	never	country		when	open
next	near			an	been
now	next			then	than

nut

/ng/ CONSONANT DIGRAPH SOUND

Medial		**Final**			
slingshot	gangster	sing	long	bang	spring
lengthen	singer	bring	song	lung	strong
longing	hanger	thing	gang	wing	fang
kingdom	gangplank	going	hang	ring	hung
youngster	gangway	swing	young	fling	string
					wrong

king

/o/ SHORT O, CLOSED SYLLABLE RULE

Initial		**Medial**			
odd	opera	not	fox	follow	rock
olive	oxygen	hot	drop	got	bottom
oxen	operate	body	pop	problem	copy
October	occupy		clock	product	cannot
opportunity					

box

/ō/ LONG O, OPEN SYLLABLE RULE

Initial		**Medial**	**Final**		
open	odor	October	go	zero	echo
over	omit	program	no	cargo	volcano
obey	oboe	Roman	so	piano	
ocean	okra	moment	hello	potato	
Ohio		poem	ago	hero	
		total	also		
		broken	auto		

radio

The Reading Teacher's Book of Lists, Fourth Edition, © 2000 by John Wiley & Sons, Inc.

/ō/ LONG O, Final E RULE

Initial	Medial				
owe	home	rode	whole	rose	stove
	those	nose	slope	spoke	awoke
	hope	stone	bone	smoke	phone
	note	joke	tone	drove	
	along	globe	pole	vote	

rope

/ō/ LONG O, OA DIGRAPH

Initial	Medial				
oak	coat	toast	approach	croak	coal
oat	soap	goat	loaf	soak	toad
oath	road	goal	groan	cloak	moan
oatmeal	coast	loan	foam	roach	throat
oaf	load	float	roast	boast	coach

boat

/ō/ LONG O, OW DIGRAPH

Initial	Medial		Final		
own	bowl	crowbar	show	follow	mow
owe	stowaway	bowling	low	tomorrow	glow
owing	snowball	mower	slow	throw	know
owner	towboat		snow	blow	crow
			row	grow	arrow
			yellow	flow	borrow

window

/ow/ OW DIPHTHONG, OW SPELLING

Medial			Final		
down	crown	towel	how	somehow	endow
town	cowboy	powder	now	eyebrow	vow
brown	power	tower	cow	bow	prow
flower	vowel	chowder	plow	scow	avow
crowd	downward	shower	allow	sow	snowplow

owl

/oi/ OI DIPHTHONG, OY SPELLING

Initial	Medial		Final		
oyster	royal	joyous	toy	decoy	convoy
	voyage	disloyal	joy	newsboy	envoy
	loyal	loyalty	enjoy	annoy	corduroy
	boycott	enjoyment	employ	soy	
	annoying	joyful	destroy	viceroy	
	employer	boyish	coy	Troy	
	boyhood		cowboy	alloy	

boy

/ə/ SCHWA, O SPELLING

Initial

other	oblige	
original	obstruct	
official	oppose	
observe	occasion	
opinion	oppress	
objection	opossum	

Medial

mother	action
money	canyon
atom	weapon
second	period
nation	mission
method	riot

Final

kimono

violin

/oi/ OI DIPHTHONG, OI SPELLING

Initial

oilcloth
oilwell
oily
ointment

Medial

join	broil	coil	sirloin	joint	
point	spoil	moisture	disappoint	embroider	
voice	avoid	exploit	toil	typhoid	
coin	poison	doily	void		
choice	boil	soil	broiler		
noise	turmoil	rejoice			

oil

/ow/ OW DIPHTHONG, OU SPELLING

Initial

out	outer
our	outline
ounce	outside
oust	outlook
ourselves	outcry
outdoors	outfield
ouch	

Medial

hour	aloud	doubt
sound	found	count
about	council	boundary
around	ground	
round	loud	
scout	cloud	
amount	mountain	

Final

thou

house

/aw/ O SPELLING

Initial

off	onto
office	offset
officer	offspring
often	onward
on	onset
offer	oncoming

Medial

offhand	soft	wrong	moth
offshore	long	cloth	frost
ostrich	along	toss	cross
	cost	coffee	belong
	across	strong	
		song	

dog

/or/ OR VOWEL, OR SPELLING

Initial

or	Oregon
order	organ
ore	ordinary
orbit	oral
orchestra	orchard
	orchid

Medial

short	score	corner
horn	form	store
forget	before	north
born	horse	force
cord	story	
	important	

Final

for
more
nor

fork

The Reading Teacher's Book of Lists, Fourth Edition, © 2000 by John Wiley & Sons, Inc.

/oo/ SHORT DOUBLE O, OO SPELLING

hook

Medial

look	took	foot	shook	brook	cook
good	wood	stood	goodbye	wool	dogwood
book	rook	soot	lookout	notebook	rookie
afoot	hoof	cookie	football	understood	handbook
hood	crook	nook	wooden	neighborhood	overlook
motherhood					

/oo/ LONG DOUBLE O, OO SPELLING

Initial	Medial			Final	
ooze	soon	tooth	mood	too	bamboo
	school	cool	roof	zoo	cuckoo
	room	goose	loose	shampoo	boo
	food	troop	balloon	woo	igloo
	shoot	fool	noon	coo	
	smooth	boot		tattoo	
	pool	took		kangaroo	

moon

/p/ REGULAR P CONSONANT SOUND

Initial		Medial		Final	
put	point	open	perhaps	up	ship
people	piece	example	happy	sleep	top
page	pass	paper		jump	step
pair	person	important		help	map
part	paper	upon		stop	deep
picture	pull			group	drop

pencil

/f/ SOUND, PH SPELLING

Initial		Medial		Final	
photo	phase	alphabet	cellophane	photograph	telegraph
phonics	phantom	orphan	emphasis	phonograph	graph
phrase	phonetic	nephew	gopher	autograph	triumph
physical	pharmacy	sulphur	graphic	paragraph	
physician	phoenix	geography	trophy		
pheasant	phenomenon	sophomore			

telephone

/pl/ CONSONANT BLEND

Initial			Medial		
play	place	player	supply	display	applaud
plant	plan	pleasant	multiply	explain	apply
plain	plane	plot	employ	supplying	complain
please	planets	plank	reply	surplus	
plow	plastic	plug	perplex		
plus	platform	plate	imply		

airplane

The Reading Teacher's Book of Lists, Fourth Edition, © 2000 by John Wiley & Sons, Inc.

/pr/ CONSONANT BLEND

Initial

pretty	president	present	probably
price	prince	problem	prove
press	program	produce	pray
print	program	property	products
	practice	provide	propeller
	prepare		

Medial

surprise	approach
April	approximate
improve	appropriate
apron	impression
express	

prize

/kw/ QU CONSONANT BLEND SOUND

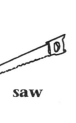

Initial

quart	quiet
quite	quack
question	quail
quick	quake
quit	quilt
queer	quiz

Medial

quote	square	liquid	squirm
quill	equal	equipment	sequence
quality	squirrel	equator	squeak
	frequent	equivalent	inquire
	require	squash	
	equation	earthquake	

queen

/r/ REGULAR R CONSONANT SOUND

Initial

run	rest
red	ride
right	road
ran	rock
read	room
rat	rod

Medial

very	large
part	story
word	form
around	

Final

our	other
their	over
for	water
year	her
dear	after
your	near

ring

/s/ REGULAR S CONSONANT SOUND

Initial

some	sound
so	say
see	sentence
said	side
soon	same
set	sea

Medial

also	question
person	inside
answer	system
himself	

Final

this	less
us	across
likes	its
makes	gas
yes	bus
miss	perhaps

saw

/z/ Z CONSONANT SOUND, S SPELLING

Medial

music	observe	please
easy	museum	cheese
busy	present	wise
those	result	these
because	season	
desert	poison	

Final

is	odds	news
as	says	hers
was	suds	does
his	yours	
has	tongs	
ours	days	

eyes

/sc/ CONSONANT BLEND

Initial

score	scatter	scream	scoop
school	scholar	scallop	scrub
screen	scout	screw	
scratch	scare	scared	
scarf	scramble	scab	
scar	scrape		

Medial

describe	inscribe
telescope	unscramble
description	microscopic
microscope	unscrupulous
nondescript	telescoping
unscrew	descriptive

scale

/sh/ CONSONANT BLEND

Initial

she	shot
shall	shirt
show	shell
ship	sheet
short	shop
shape	shut

Medial

dashed	ashes
splashing	friendship
sunshine	
worship	
fisherman	

Final

wish	rush
wash	dish
fish	crash
push	bush
finish	flash
fresh	establish

shoe

/sk/ CONSONANT BLEND

Initial

sky	skeleton	skillet
skin	skull	skirmish
skill	skid	skinny
skunk	sketch	skylark
skirt	ski	skeptic
skip	skim	skate

Medial

outskirts
askew
muskrat
rollerskate
muskmelon
masked

Final

desk	mask
task	husk
ask	dusk
brisk	

desk

/sl/ CONSONANT BLEND

Initial

slow	sled	slope	sly
sleep	slave	slam	slash
slept	sleeve	slate	slab
slip	slant	slipper	sleek
slid	slice	sleet	slimy
slap	slight	slim	

Medial

asleep	oversleep
landslide	snowslide
onslaught	grandslam
enslave	nonslip
bobsled	
manslaughter	

slide

/sm/ CONSONANT BLEND

Initial

smile	smash	smock	smote	smuggler
smooth	smear	smoky	smokestack	smelt
smell	smith	smudge	smattering	smite
small	smolder	smuggle	smorgasbord	
smart	smack	smug	smithy	
smother	smog	smitten	smoker	

Medial

blacksmith
gunsmith
silversmith
locksmith

smoke

The Reading Teacher's Book of Lists, Fourth Edition, © 2000 by Prentice Hall

/sn/ CONSONANT BLEND

Initial

snow	snuggle	snapshot	sniff	snooze	snuff
snowball	snip	sneak	sniffle	snorkel	snowman
snare	snarl	snatch	snipe	snort	sniper
sneeze	snap	sneakers	snob	snout	snowy
snore	snack	sneer	snoop	snub	
snug	snail				

snake

/sp/ CONSONANT BLEND

Initial   Medial   Final

sports	speed	spider	inspect	despair	clasp
space	spell	spend	respect	inspire	crisp
speak	spot	spark	respond	despite	gasp
spring	spin		despise		grasp
spread	spoke		unspeakable		wasp
special	spare		respectful		lisp
					wisp

spoon

/st/ CONSONANT BLEND

Initial   Medial   Final

stop	story	stick	instead	restless	best
step	street	stone	destroy	poster	cast
stay	stand	stood	restore	tasty	dust
state	star		westward		fast
still	study		haystack		least
store	strong		destruction		past
					west

stamp

/sw/ CONSONANT BLEND

Initial

swim	switch	sweet	swollen	swampy	swarthy
swell	swallow	swift	sway	swirl	swat
swept	swung	swan	swine	swarm	swerve
sweat	swam	swagger	swoop	swear	sworn
swing	swamp	swap	swindle	swelter	swish
sweep					

sweater

/t/ REGULAR T CONSONANT SOUND

Initial   Medial   Final

to	took	city	later	not	what
two	top	into	sentence	at	set
take	ten	water	until	it	part
tell	talk	after		out	got
too	today			get	put
time	told			but	want

table

/th/ VOICELESS TH CONSONANT DIGRAPH SOUND

Initial		**Medial**		**Final**	
thank	thought	something	toothbrush	with	truth
think	thread	author	python	both	death
thing	threw	nothing		ninth	south
third	thumb	athlete		worth	fifth
thirty	thunder	faithful		cloth	bath
thick	threat	bathtub		teeth	

three

/th/ VOICED TH CONSONANT DIGRAPH SOUND

Initial		**Medial**		**Final**
the	though	mother	weather	smooth
that	thus	other	gather	
them	thy	brother	breathing	
they	thence	father	rhythm	
this	their	although	farther	
there	then	bother	leather	
than	thou	clothing	northern	
these		either		

feather

/tr/ CONSONANT BLEND

Initial		**Medial**			
track	trick	trouble	extra	control	country
tractor	travel	trap	electric	sentry	patrol
train	tree	trail	central	waitress	
trade	trim	triangle	attract	contract	
truly	trip	traffic	entry	patron	
try	true		subtract	contrast	

truck

/tw/ CONSONANT BLEND

Initial					**Medial**
twelve	twirl	twinkle	twinge	twelfth	between
twenty	twine	twist	twang	twill	entwine
twice	tweed	twitter	twentieth	twiddle	untwist
twig	twilight	twitch	tweet		intertwine

twins

/u/ SHORT U, CLOSED SYLLABLE RULE

Initial			**Medial**		
up	unhappy	unless	but	number	such
us	upon	umpire	run	must	hunt
under	usher		much	study	summer
until	unusual		just	hundred	jump
ugly	uproar		cut	sudden	gun
uncle	upset		funny	sun	

umbrella

The Reading Teacher's Book of Lists, Fourth Edition, © 2000 by John Wiley & Sons, Inc.

/ū/ LONG U, OPEN SYLLABLE RULE

Initial		**Medial**		**Final**	
unit	unify	future	humid	fugitive	menu
united	unique	human	museum	funeral	
Utah	utilize	valuable	continuous	beautiful	
uniform		humor	fuel	unusual	
universe		January	bugle	musician	
usual		pupil	cubic	puny	
university		community	communicate		

music

/o͝o/ SHORT DOUBLE O, U SPELLING

Medial

bullet	bush	cushion	bull's-eye	pulpit	bulldog
full	bushel	ambush	bushy	fully	armful
pull	sugar	bulletin	pullet	bullfrog	bully
push	pudding	handful	pushcart	fulfill	bullfight
put	butcher	pulley	bulldozer	bulwark	output

bull

/o͞o/ LONG DOUBLE O, U, AND U_E SPELLINGS

Medial

June	flute	tune	punctuation	revolution	tuna
July	prune	conclusion	constitution	ruby	influence
truth	cruel	tube	duty	prudent	solution
junior	numeral	February	nutrition	situation	rhubarb
rule	parachute	aluminum	reduce	ruin	truly
crude					

ruler

/er/ ER VOWEL, UR SPELLING

Initial	**Medial**			**Final**	
urn	turn	purple	further	fur	spur
urban	burn	hurt	purpose	sulfur	cur
urchin	hurry	turkey	burst	murmur	bur
urge	curl	curb	surf	concur	
urgent	Thursday	nurse	church	occur	
	purse	surface		slur	

turtle

/v/ REGULAR V CONSONANT SOUND

Valentine

Initial		**Medial**		**Final**	
very	vowel	over	however	give	live
visit	van	even	cover	five	move
voice	verb	never	several	love	above
vote	vase	river		gave	leave
view	violin			twelve	wave
vest	valley			have	believe

The Reading Teacher's Book of Lists, Fourth Edition, © 2000 by John Wiley & Sons, Inc.

/w/ REGULAR W CONSONANT SOUND

Initial

		Medial			
we	water	would	away	awake	halfway
with	way	wave	reward	aware	sidewalk
will	were	win	forward	unwind	upward
was	word	woman	want	highway	midway
work	week	wait	sandwich	backward	tapeworm

window

/wh/ WH CONSONANT BLEND SOUND

Initial

				Medial	
when	white	whip	whiskey	awhile	buckwheat
what	while	whisper	whack	bobwhite	cartwheel
which	why	whistle	whiff	overwhelm	somewhere
whether	wheat	wheeze	whimper	somewhat	anywhere
where	whale	wharf	whiz	everywhere	nowhere
					meanwhile

wheel

/r/ SOUND, WR SPELLING

Initial

				Medial	
write	wrestle	wretch	wrung	awry	typewriter
writing	wrist	wrinkle	wry	rewrite	typewritten
written	wreath	wrapper	wrangle	handwriting	
wrote	wring	wrathful		unwrap	
wrong	wreck	wreckage		playwright	
wrap	wren	wriggle		shipwreck	

wrench

/ks/ REGULAR X CONSONANT SOUND

Medial

		Final			
Mexico	explain	fox	fix	complex	vex
Texas	axis	ax	relax	index	wax
mixture	oxen	six	mix	lax	sex
extremely	extra	tax	prefix	hex	perplex
sixty	excuse	ox		lox	
expert	exclaim				

box

/y/ REGULAR Y CONSONANT SOUND

Initial

				Medial	
you	youth	yam	yew	lawyer	vineyard
year	yawn	yank	yeast	canyon	papaya
yellow	yard	yak	yen	beyond	dooryard
yes	yet	yodel	yolk	courtyard	stockyard
yell	your	yacht	yonder	barnyard	backyard
young					

yarn

/ē/ LONG E, Y SPELLING

Medial	Final			
anything	very	happy	country	early
babysit	any	lady	city	money
everyone	many	story	really	quickly
ladybug	pretty	family	body	heavy
bodyguard	only	study	usually	ready
copying	funny	every	easy	energy
everything				

baby

/ī/ LONG I, Y SPELLING

Medial		Final			
myself	type	my	sky	shy	reply
nylon	lying	by	July	defy	sly
cycle	rhyme	why	fry	dry	deny
dying	python	buy	apply	ally	
style	hyena	cry	pry	spy	

fly

/z/ REGULAR Z CONSONANT SOUND

Initial		Medial		Final	
zero	zipper	lazy	citizen	size	quiz
zoo	zoom	crazy	frozen	freeze	whiz
zone		puzzle	grazing	prize	buzz
zest		dozen		realize	fizz
zenith		magazine		breeze	fuzz
zigzag				organize	jazz
zinc				seize	adz

zebra

The Reading Teacher's Book of Lists, Fourth Edition, © 2000 by John Wiley & Sons, Inc.

See also List 1, Consonant Sounds; List 7, Suggested Phonics Teaching Order; List 9, Phonograms; List 11, Phonically Irregular Words.

List 9. PHONOGRAMS

As teachers, we found it difficult to find a complete list of phonograms, so we developed our own using many available lists and a rhyming dictionary. We think this is the most complete one in existence. These are useful for all kinds of games and drills in reading and spelling. Phonograms, or rimes, have been used in the teaching of reading since Colonial times and are currently used in regular classrooms, remedial/corrective reading instruction, English as a Second Language classes, and in adult literacy instruction. Because syllable rimes also include just vowel endings like -ay in "say" or -ea in "tea," we have included some of them in this list. These phonograms are all one-syllable words; however, the same phonograms appear in many polysyllabic words.

The Reading Teacher's Book of Lists, Fourth Edition, © 2000 by John Wiley & Sons, Inc.

-ab	quack	glad	jag	fail	paint	rake
/a/	rack	shad	lag	Gail	saint	take
cab	sack		nag	hail	taint	wake
dab	tack	**-ade**	rag	jail	quaint	brake
gab	black	**/ā/**	sag	mail		drake
jab	clack		tag	nail	**-air**	flake
lab	crack	bade	wag	pail	**/air/**	shake
nab	knack	fade	brag	quail		snake
tab	shack	jade	crag	rail	fair	stake
blab	slack	made	drag	sail	hair	
crab	smack	wade	flag	tail	lair	**-ale**
drab	snack	blade	shag	wail	pair	**/ā/**
flab	stack	glade	slag	flail	chair	
grab	track	grade	snag	snail	flair	bale
scab	whack	shade	stag	trail	stair	dale
slab		spade	swag			gale
stab	**-act**	trade		**-ain**	**-aise**	hale
	/a/		**-age**	**/ā/**	**/ā/**	male
-ace		**-aff**	**/ā/**			pale
/ā/	fact	**/a/**		lain	raise	sale
	pact		cage	main	braise	tale
face	tact	gaff	gage	pain	chaise	scale
lace	tract	chaff	page	rain	praise	shale
mace		quaff	rage	vain		stale
pace	**-ad**	staff	sage	wain	**-ait**	whale
race	**/a/**		wage	brain	**/ā/**	
brace		**-aft**	stage	chain		**-alk**
grace	bad	**/a/**		drain	bait	**/aw/**
place	cad		**-aid**	grain	gait	
space	dad	daft	**/ā/**	plain	wait	balk
trace	fad	raft		slain	strait	calk
	gad	waft	laid	Spain	trait	talk
-ack	had	craft	maid	sprain		walk
/a/	lad	draft	paid	stain	**-ake**	chalk
	mad	graft	raid	strain	**/ā/**	stalk
back	pad	shaft	braid	train		
hack	sad		staid		bake	**-all**
Jack	tad	**-ag**		**-aint**	cake	**/ô/**
lack	Brad	**/a/**	**-ail**	**/ā/**	fake	
Mack	Chad		**/ā/**		Jake	ball
pack	clad	bag		faint	lake	call
		gag	bail		make	fall
		hag			quake	

31

gall
hall
mall
pall
tall
wall
small
squall
stall

-alt
/aw/

halt
malt
salt

-am
/a/

cam
dam
ham
jam
Pam
ram
Sam
tam
yam
clam
cram
dram
gram
scam
scram
sham
slam
swam
tram

-ame
/ā/

came
dame
fame
game
lame
name
same
tame
blame
flame
frame
shame

-amp
/a/

camp
damp
lamp
ramp
tamp
vamp
champ
clamp
cramp
scamp
stamp
tramp

-an
/a/

ban
can
Dan
fan
man
pan
ran
tan
van
bran
clan
flan
plan
scan
span
than

-ance
/a/

dance
lance
chance
France
glance
prance
stance
trance

-anch
/a/

ranch
blanch
branch
stanch

-and
/a/

band
hand
land
sand
bland
brand
gland
stand
strand

-ane
/ā/

bane
cane
Jane
lane
mane
pane
sane
vane
wane
crane
plane

-ang
/ā/

bang
fang
gang
hang
pang
rang
sang
tang
clang
slang
sprang
twang

-ank
/ā/

bank
dank
hank
lank
rank
sank
tank
yank
blank
clank

crank
drank
flank
Frank
plank
prank
shank
stank
thank

-ant
/a/

can't
pant
rant
chant
grant
plant
scant
slant

-ap
/a/

cap
gap
lap
map
nap
pap
rap
sap
tap
yap
chap
clap
flap
scrap
slap
snap
strap
trap
wrap

-ape
/ā/

cape
gape
nape
rape
tape
drape
grape

scrape
shape

-ar
/ar/

bar
car
far
jar
mar
par
tar
char
scar
spar
star

-ard
/ar/

bard
card
guard
hard
lard
yard
shard

-are
/air/

bare
care
dare
fare
hare
mare
pare
rare
ware
blare
flare
glare
scare
share
snare
spare
square
stare

-arge
/ar/

barge

large
charge

-ark
/ar/

bark
dark
hark
lark
mark
park
Clark
shark
spark
stark

-arm
/ar/

farm
harm
charm

-arn
/ar/

barn
darn
yarn

-arp
/ar/

carp
harp
tarp
sharp

-art
/ar/

cart
dart
mart
part
tart
chart
smart
start

-ase
/ā/

base
case
vase
chase

-ash
/a/

bash
cash
dash
gash
hash
lash
mash
rash
sash
brash
clash
flash
slash
smash
stash
thrash
trash

-ask
/a/

ask
cask
mask
task
flask

-asm
/a/

chasm
plasm
spasm

-asp
/a/

gasp
hasp
rasp
clasp
grasp

-ast
/a/

cast
fast
last
mast
past
vast
blast

The Reading Teacher's Book of Lists, Fourth Edition, © 2000 by John Wiley & Sons, Inc.

-aste
/ā/

baste
haste
paste
taste
waste
chaste

-ass
/a/

bass
lass
mass
pass
brass
class
glass
grass

-at
/a/

bat
cat
fat
gnat
hat
mat
pat
rat
sat
tat
vat
brat
chat
drat
flat
scat
slat
spat
that

-atch
/a/

batch
catch
hatch
latch
match
patch
scratch
thatch

-ate
/ā/

date
fate
gate
hate
Kate
late
mate
rate
crate
grate
plate
skate
state

-ath
/ǎ/

bath
lath
math
path
wrath

-aught
/aw/

caught
naught
taught
fraught

-aunch
/aw/

haunch
launch
paunch

-aunt
/aw/

daunt
gaunt
haunt
jaunt
taunt
flaunt

-ave
/ā/

cave
Dave
gave
pave

rave
save
wave
brave
crave
grave
shave
slave
stave

-aw
/aw/

caw
gnaw
jaw
law
paw
raw
saw
claw
draw
flaw
slaw
squaw
straw

-awl
/aw/

bawl
brawl
crawl
drawl
shawl
scrawl
trawl

-awn
/aw/

dawn
fawn
lawn
pawn
yawn
brawn
drawn
prawn
spawn

-ax
/a/

lax
Max
tax

wax
flax

-ay
/ā/

bay
day
gay
hay
jay
lay
may
nay
pay
quay
ray
say
way
bray
clay
cray
fray
gray
play
pray
slay
spray
stay
stray
sway
tray

-aze
/ā/

daze
faze
gaze
haze
maze
raze
blaze
craze
glaze
graze

-ea
/ē/

pea
sea
tea
flea
plea

-each
/ē/

beach
leach
peach
reach
teach
bleach
breach
preach
screech

-ead
/e/

dead
head
lead
read
bread
dread
spread
thread
tread

-ead
/ē/

bead
lead
read
knead
plead

-eak
/ē/

beak
leak
peak
teak
weak
bleak
creak
freak
sneak
speak
squeak
streak
tweak

-eal
/ē/

deal
heal
meal

peal
real
seal
teal
veal
zeal
squeal
steal

-ealth
/e/

health
wealth
stealth

-eam
/ē/

beam
ream
seam
cream
dream
gleam
scream
steam
stream
team

-ean
/ē/

bean
dean
Jean
lean
mean
wean
clean
glean

-eap
/ē/

heap
leap
reap
cheap

-ear
/ē/

dear
fear
gear
hear
near

rear
sear
tear
year
clear
shear
smear
spear

-ear
/e/

bear
pear
wear
swear

-east
/ē/

beast
feast
least
yeast

-eat
/ē/

beat
feat
heat
meat
neat
peat
seat
bleat
cheat
cleat
pleat
treat
wheat

-eave
/ē/

heave
leave
weave
cleave
sheave

-eck
/e/

deck
heck
neck
peck

check
fleck
speck
wreck

-ed
/e/

bed
fed
led
Ned
red
Ted
wed
led
bred
fled
Fred
shed
shred
sled
sped

-edge
/e/

hedge
ledge
wedge
dredge
pledge
sledge

-ee
/ē/

bee
fee
knee
lee
see
tee
wee
flee
free
glee
tree

-eech
/ē/

beech
leech
breech
screech
speech

-eed
/ē/

deed
feed
heed
kneed
need
reed
seed
weed
bleed
breed
creed
freed
greed
speed
steed
treed
tweed

-eek
/ē/

leek
meek
peek
reek
seek
week
cheek
creek
Greek
sleek

-eel
/ē/

feel
heel
keel
peel
reel
creel
steel
wheel

-eem
/ē/

deem
seem
teem

-een
/ē/

keen

queen
seen
teen
green
preen
screen
sheen

-eep
/ē/

beep
deep
Jeep
keep
peep
seep
weep
cheep
creep
sheep
sleep
steep
sweep

-eer
/ē/

beer
deer
jeer
leer
peer
queer
seer
sneer
steer

-eet
/ē/

beet
feet
meet
fleet
greet
sheet
skeet
sleet
street
sweet
tweet

-eeze
/ē/

breeze

freeze
sneeze
squeeze
tweeze
wheeze

-eft
/e/

deft
heft
left
cleft
theft

-eg
/e/

beg
keg
leg
meg
peg

-eigh
/ā/

neigh
weigh
sleigh

-eld
/e/

held
meld
weld

-ell
/e/

bell
cell
dell
fell
hell
jell
knell
Nell
sell
tell
well
yell
dwell
quell
shell
smell
spell
swell

-elp
/e/

help
kelp
yelp

-elt
/e/

belt
felt
knelt
melt
pelt
welt
dwelt
smelt

-em
/e/

gem
hem
stem
them

-en
/e/

Ben
den
hen
Ken
men
pen
ten
yen
glen
then
when
wren

-ence
/e/

fence
hence
whence

-ench
/e/

bench
wench
clench
drench
French
quench

stench
trench
wrench

-end
/e/

bend
end
fend
lend
mend
rend
send
tend
vend
wend
blend
spend
trend

-ense
/e/

dense
sense
tense

-ent
/e/

bent
cent
dent
gent
Kent
lent
rent
sent
tent
vent
went
scent
spent

-ep
/e/

pep
rep
prep
step

-ept
/e/

kept
wept

crept
slept
swept

-erge
/er/

merge
serge
verge

-erk
/er/

jerk
clerk

-erm
/er/

berm
germ
term
sperm

-ern
/er/

fern
tern
stern

-erve
/er/

nerve
serve
verve
swerve

-esh
/e/

mesh
flesh
fresh

-ess
/e/

Bess
guess
less
mess
bless
chess
dress
press
stress
tress

34

The Reading Teacher's Book of Lists, Fourth Edition, © 2000 by John Wiley & Sons, Inc.

-est
/e/

best
guest
jest
lest
nest
pest
rest
test
vest
west
zest
blest
chest
crest
quest
wrest

-et
/e/

bet
get
jet
let
met
net
pet
set
wet
yet
Chet
fret
whet

-etch
/e/

fetch
retch
sketch
wretch

-ew
/o͞o/

dew
few
hew
Jew
knew
new
pew
blew

brew
chew

-ex
/e/

hex
sex
vex
flex

-ey
/ā/

hey
gray
prey
they
whey

-ib
/i/

bib
fib
jib
rib
crib
glib

-ibe
/ī/

jibe
bribe
scribe
tribe

-ice
/ī/

dice
lice
mice
nice
rice
vice
price
slice
splice
thrice
twice

-ick
/i/

Dick
hick
kick

lick
Nick
pick
quick
Rick
sick
tick
wick
brick
chick
click
flick
slick
stick
thick
trick

-id
/i/

bid
did
hid
kid
lid
mid
quid
rid
grid
skid
slid

-ide
/ī/

bide
hide
ride
side
tide
wide
bride
chide
glide
pride
slide
snide
stride

-ie
/ī/

die
fie
lie
pie

tie
vie

-ied
/ī/

died
lied
dried
fried
tried

-ief
/ē/

brief
chief
grief
thief

-ield
/ē/

field
yield
shield

-ier
/ī/

brier
crier
drier
flier

-ies
/ī/

dies
lies
pies
ties
cries
dries
flies
fries
skies
tries

-ife
/ī/

fife
knife
life
rife
wife
strife

-iff
/i/

miff
tiff
cliff
skiff
sniff
whiff

-ift
/i/

gift
lift
rift
sift
drift
shift
swift
thrift

-ig
/i/

big
dig
fig
gig
jig
pig
rig
wig
brig
sprig
swig
twig

-igh
/ī/

high
nigh
sigh
thigh

-ight
/ī/

knight
light
might
night
right
sight
tight
blight
bright

flight
fright
plight
slight

-ike
/ī/

bike
dike
hike
like
Mike
pike
spike
strike

-ild
/ī/

mild
wild
child

-ile
/ī/

bile
file
mile
Nile
pile
tile
vile
smile
stile
while

-ilk
/i/

bilk
milk
silk

-ill
/i/

bill
dill
fill
gill
hill
ill
Jill
kill
mill
pill
quill

rill
sill
till
will
chill
drill
frill
grill
skill
spill
still
swill
thrill
trill
twill

-ilt
/i/

gilt
jilt
hilt
kilt
tilt
wilt
quilt
stilt

-im
/i/

dim
him
Jim
Kim
rim
Tim
vim
brim
grim
prim
slim
swim
trim
whim

-ime
/ī/

dime
lime
mime
time
chime
clime
crime

35

grime
prime
slime

-imp
/i/

limp
chimp
crimp
primp
skimp
blimp

-in
/i/

bin
din
fin
gin
kin
pin
sin
tin
win
chin
grin
shin
skin
spin
thin
twin

-ince
/i/

mince
since
wince
prince

-inch
/i/

cinch
finch
pinch
winch
clinch
flinch

-ind
/ī/

bind
find
hind

kind
mind
rind
wind
blind
grind

-ine
/ī/

dine
fine
line
mine
nine
pine
tine
vine
wine
brine
shine
shrine
spine
swine
whine

-ing
/i/

bing
ding
king
ping
ring
sing
wing
zing
bring
cling
fling
sling
spring
sting
string
swing
thing
wring

-inge
/i/

binge
hinge
singe
tinge
cringe

fringe
twinge

-ink
/i/

kink
link
mink
pink
rink
sink
wink
blink
brink
chink
clink
drink
shrink
slink
stink
think

-int
/i/

hint
lint
mint
tint
glint
print
splint
sprint
squint
stint

-ip
/i/

dip
hip
lip
nip
quip
rip
sip
tip
zip
blip
chip
clip
drip
flip
grip
ship

skip
slip
snip
strip
trip
whip

-ipe
/ī/

pipe
ripe
wipe
gripe
snipe
stripe
swipe
tripe

-ir
/er/

fir
sir
stir
whir

-ird
/er/

bird
gird
third

-ire
/ī/

fire
hire
tire
wire
spire

-irk
/er/

quirk
shirk
smirk

-irt
/er/

dirt
flirt
shirt
skirt
squirt

-irth
/er/

birth
firth
girth
mirth

-ise
/ī/

guise
rise
wise

-ish
/i/

dish
fish
wish
swish

-isk
/i/

disk
risk
brisk
frisk
whisk

-isp
/i/

lisp
wisp
crisp

-iss
/i/

hiss
kiss
miss
bliss
Swiss

-ist
/i/

fist
list
mist
wrist
grist
twist

-it
/i/

bit

fit
hit
kit
knit
lit
pit
quit
sit
wit
flit
grit
skit
slit
spit
split
twit

-itch
/i/

ditch
hitch
pitch
witch
switch

-ite
/ī/

bite
kite
mite
quite
rite
site
white
write
sprite

-ive
/ī/

dive
five
hive
jive
live
chive
drive
strive
thrive

-ix
/i/

fix
mix
six

-o
/ōō/

do
to
who

-o
/ō/

go
no
so
pro

-oach
/ō/

coach
poach
roach
broach

-oad
/ō/

goad
load
road
toad

-oak
/ō/

soak
cloak
croak

-oal
/ō/

coal
foal
goal
shoal

-oam
/ō/

foam
loam
roam

-oan
/ō/

Joan
loan
moan
groan

-oar
/or/

boar
roar
soar

-oast
/ō/

boast
coast
roast
toast

-oat
/ō/

boat
coat
goat
moat
gloat
float
throat

-ob
/o/

Bob
cob
fob
gob
job
knob
lob
mob
rob
sob
blob
glob
slob
snob

-obe
/ō/

lobe
robe
globe
probe

-ock
/o/

dock
hock
knock
lock

mock
rock
sock
tock
block
clock
crock
flock
frock
shock
smock
stock

-od
/o/

cod
God
mod
nod
pod
rod
sod
Tod
clod
plod
prod
shod
trod

-ode
/ō/

code
lode
mode
node
rode
strode

-oe
/ō/

doe
foe
hoe
Joe
toe
woe

-og
/o/

bog
cog
dog
fog
hog

jog
log
tog
clog
flog
frog
grog
slog
smog

-ogue
/ō/

brogue
rogue
vogue

-oil
/oi/

boil
coil
foil
soil
toil
spoil
broil

-oin
/oi/

coin
join
loin
groin

-oist
/oi/

foist
hoist
joist
moist

-oke
/ō/

coke
joke
poke
woke
yoke
broke
choke
smoke
spoke
stoke
stroke

-old
/ō/

bold
cold
fold
gold
hold
mold
old
sold
told
scold

-ole
/ō/

dole
hole
mole
pole
role
stole
whole

-oll
/ō/

poll
roll
toll
droll
knoll
scroll
stroll
troll

-oll
/o/

doll
loll
moll

-olt
/ō/

bolt
colt
jolt
molt
volt

-om
/o/

Mom
Tom
prom

-ome
/ō/

dome
home
Nome
Rome
tome
gnome
chrome

-ome
/u/

come
some

-omp
/o/

pomp
romp
chomp
stomp

-on
/u/

son
ton
won

-ond
/o/

bond
fond
pond
blond
frond

-one
/ō/

bone
cone
hone
lone
tone
zone
clone
crone
drone
phone
prone
shone
stone

-ong
/aw/

bong

dong
gong
long
song
tong
prong
strong
thong
wrong

-oo
/ōō/

boo
coo
goo
moo
poo
too
woo
zoo
shoo

-ood
/o͝o/

good
hood
wood
stood

-ood
/ōō/

food
mood
brood

-oof
/ōō/

goof
roof
proof
spoof

-ook
/o͝o/

book
cook
hook
look
nook
took
brook
crook
shook

-ool
/ōō/

cool
fool
pool
tool
drool
school
spool
stool

-oom
/ōō/

boom
doom
loom
room
zoom
bloom
broom
gloom
groom

-oon
/ōō/

coon
loon
moon
noon
soon
croon
spoon
swoon

-oop
/ōō/

coop
hoop
loop
droop
scoop
sloop
snoop
stoop
swoop
troop

-oor
/oo/

poor
boor
moor
spoor

The Reading Teacher's Book of Lists, Fourth Edition, © 2000 by John Wiley & Sons, Inc.

-oose
/ōō/

goose
loose
moose
noose

-oot
/ōō/

boot
hoot
loot
moot
root
toot
scoot
shoot

-op
/o/

bop
cop
hop
mop
pop
sop
top
chop
crop
drop
flop
plop
prop
shop
slop
stop

-ope
/ō/

cope
dope
hope
lope
mope
nope
pope
rope
grope
scope
slope

-orch
/or/

porch
torch
scorch

-ord
/or/

cord
ford
lord
chord
sword

-ore
/or/

bore
core
fore
gore
more
pore
sore
tore
wore
chore
score
shore
snore
spore
store
swore

-ork
/or/

cork
fork
pork
York
stork

-orm
/or/

dorm
form
norm
storm

-orn
/or/

born

corn
horn
morn
torn
worn
scorn
shorn
sworn
thorn

-ort
/or/

fort
Mort
port
sort
short
snort
sport

-ose
/ō/

hose
nose
pose
rose
chose
close
prose
those

-oss
/aw/

boss
loss
moss
toss
cross
floss
gloss

-ost
/ô/

cost
lost
frost

-ost
/ō/

host
most

post
ghost

-ot
/o/

cot
dot
got
hot
jot
knot
lot
not
pot
rot
tot
blot
clot
plot
shot
slot
spot
trot

-otch
/o/

botch
notch
blotch
crotch
Scotch

-ote
/ō/

note
quote
rote
vote
wrote

-oth
/aw/

moth
broth
cloth
froth
sloth

-ouch
/ow/

couch

pouch
vouch
crouch
grouch
slouch

-oud
/ow/

loud
cloud
proud

-ough
/u/

rough
rough
slough

-ought
/aw/

bought
fought
ought
sought
brought
thought

-ould
/oo/

could
would
should

-ounce
/ow/

bounce
pounce
flounce
trounce

-ound
/ow/

bound
found
hound
mound
pound
round
sound

wound
ground

-oup
/ōō/

soup
croup
group
stoup

-our
/ow/

hour
sour
flour
scour

-ouse
/ow/

douse
house
louse
mouse
rouse
souse
blouse
grouse
spouse

-out
/ow/

bout
gout
lout
pout
rout
tout
clout
flout
grout
scout
shout
snout
spout
sprout
stout
trout

-outh
/ow/

mouth
south

-ove
/ō/

cove
wove
clove
drove
grove
stove
trove

-ove
/u/

dove
love
glove
shove

-ow
/ō/

bow
know
low
mow
row
sow
tow
blow
crow
flow
glow
grow
show
slow
snow
stow

-ow
/ow/

bow
cow
how
now
row
sow
vow
brow
chow
plow
prow
scow

-owl
/ow/

fowl
howl
jowl
growl
prowl
scowl

-own
/ow/

down
gown
town
brown
clown
crown
drown
frown

-own
/ō/

known
mown
sown
blown
flown
grown
shown
thrown

-owse
/ow/

dowse
browse
drowse

-ox
/o/

box
fox
lox
pox

-oy
/oi/

boy
coy
joy
Roy
soy

toy
ploy

-ub
/u/

cub
dub
hub
nub
pub
rub
sub
tub
club
drub
flub
grub
scrub
shrub
snub
stub

-ube
/ōō/

cube
rube
tube

-uck
/u/

buck
duck
luck
muck
puck
suck
tuck
Chuck
cluck
pluck
shuck
stuck
struck
truck

-ud
/u/

bud
cud
dud
mud

spud
stud
thud

-ude
/ōō/

dude
nude
rude
crude
prude

-udge
/u/

budge
fudge
judge
nudge
drudge
grudge
sludge
smudge
trudge

-ue
/ōō/

cue
due
hue
Sue
blue
clue
flue
glue
true

-uff
/u/

buff
cuff
huff
muff
puff
ruff
bluff
fluff
gruff
scuff
sluff
snuff
stuff

-ug
/u/

bug
dug
hug
jug
lug
mug
pug
rug
tug
chug
drug
plug
shrug
slug
smug
snug
thug

-uke
/ōō/

duke
nuke
puke
fluke

-ule
/ū/

mule
pule
rule
yule

-ulk
/u/

bulk
hulk
sulk

-ull
/u/

cull
dull
gull
hull
lull
mull
skull

-ull
/o͝o/

bull

full
pull

-um
/u/

bum
gum
hum
mum
rum
sum
chum
drum
glum
plum
scum
slum
strum
swum

-umb
/u/

dumb
numb
crumb
plumb
thumb

-ume
/ōō/

fume
flume
plume
spume

-ump
/u/

bump
dump
hump
jump
lump
pump
rump
chump
clump
frump
grump
plump
slump
stump

thump
trump

-un
/u/

bun
fun
gun
nun
pun
run
sun
shun
spun
stun

-unch
/u/

bunch
hunch
lunch
munch
punch
brunch
crunch

-une
/ū/

June
tune
prune

-ung
/u/

dung
hung
lung
rung
sung
clung
flung
sprung
stung
strung
swung
wrung

-unk
/u/

bunk
dunk

funk
hunk
junk
punk
sunk
chunk
drunk
flunk
plunk
shrunk
skunk
slunk
spunk
stunk
trunk

-unt
/u/

bunt
hunt
punt
runt
blunt
grunt
shunt
stunt

-up
/u/

cup
pup
sup

-ur
/er/

cur
fur
blur
slur
spur

-ure
/ū/

cure
lure
pure
sure

-url
/er/

burl
curl

furl
hurl
purl
churl
knurl

-urn
/er/

burn
turn
churn
spurn

-urse
/er/

curse
nurse
purse

-urt
/er/

curt
hurt
blurt
spurt

-us
/u/

bus
pus
plus
thus

-use
/ū/

fuse
muse
ruse

-ush
/u/

gush
hush
lush
mush
rush
blush
brush
crush
flush

plush
slush
thrush

-uss
/u/

buss
cuss
fuss
muss
truss

-ust
/u/

bust
dust
gust
just
lust
must
rust
crust
thrust
trust

-ut
/u/

but
cut
gut
hut
jut
nut
rut
Tut
glut
shut
smut
strut

-utch
/u/

Dutch
hutch
clutch
crutch

-ute
/ū/

cute
jute
lute
mute
brute
chute
flute

-utt
/u/

butt
mutt
putt

-y
/ī /

by
my
cry
dry
fly
fry
ply
pry
shy
sky
sly
spy
spry

try
why

-ye
/ī /

aye
dye
eye
lye
rye

The Reading Teacher's Book of Lists, Fourth Edition, © 2000 by John Wiley & Sons, Inc.

See also List 1, Consonant Sounds; List 2, Vowel Sounds.

List 10. THE MOST COMMON PHONOGRAMS

A phonogram, or rime, is usually a vowel sound plus a consonant sound, but it is often less than a syllable and therefore less than a word. When a consonant sound is added at the beginning, or at the onset, the two form many recognizable words. Adding single consonants or consonant blends to common phonograms is an excellent way to quickly build reading and spelling vocabulary. This list includes the most common phonograms ranked in the order of the number of words they can form.

The Reading Teacher's Book of Lists, Fourth Edition, © 2000 by John Wiley & Sons, Inc.

Rime	Example Words				Rime	Example Words			
-ay	jay	say	pay	day	play	-ug	rug	bug	hug	dug	tug
-ill	hill	Bill	will	fill	spill	-op	mop	cop	pop	top	hop
-ip	dip	ship	tip	skip	trip	-in	pin	tin	win	chin	thin
-at	cat	fat	bat	rat	sat	-an	pan	man	ran	tan	Dan
-am	ham	jam	dam	ram	Sam	-est	best	nest	pest	rest	test
-ag	bag	rag	tag	wag	sag	-ink	pink	sink	rink	link	drink
-ack	back	sack	Jack	black	track	-ow	low	slow	grow	show	snow
-ank	bank	sank	tank	blank	drank	-ew	new	few	chew	grew	stew
-ick	sick	Dick	pick	quick	chick	-ore	more	sore	tore	store	score
-ell	bell	sell	fell	tell	yell	-ed	bed	red	fed	led	Ted
-ot	pot	not	hot	dot	got	-ab	cab	dab	jab	lab	crab
-ing	ring	sing	king	wing	thing	-ob	cob	job	rob	Bob	knob
-ap	cap	map	tap	clap	trap	-ock	sock	rock	lock	dock	block
-unk	bunk	sunk	junk	skunk	trunk	-ake	cake	lake	make	take	brake
-ail	pail	jail	nail	sail	tail	-ine	line	nine	pine	fine	shine
-ain	rain	pain	main	chain	plain	-ight	light	night	right	fight	sight
-eed	feed	seed	weed	need	freed	-im	him	Kim	rim	grim	brim
-y	my	by	dry	try	fly	-uck	duck	luck	buck	truck	stuck
-out	pout	trout	scout	shout	spout	-um	gum	bum	hum	drum	plum

See also List 9, Phonograms.

41

List 11. PHONICALLY IRREGULAR WORDS

As every reading teacher knows, there are many words that do not follow regular phonics or spelling rules. This list contains common words that are not pronounceable using regular phonics rules. Students need to learn to recognize them on sight and to memorize their spellings. See also words with silent letters in Consonant Sounds, List 1.

a	does	listen	said	usually
adjective	door	live	science	want
again	earth	many	should	was
although	enough	measure	sign	watch
answer	example	most	some	water
any	eyes	mother	something	where
are	father	mountain	stretch	were
become	feather	move	subtle	what
been	find	of	sure	who
both	four	off	the	woman
bread	friends	often	their	women
brought	from	old	there	words
climbed	give	on	they	work
cold	great	once	though	world
color	group	one	thought	would
come	have	only	through	you
could	heard	other	to	young
country	island	people	today	your
design	kind	picture	two	youth
do	learn	piece		

List 12. STANDALONES

Words in the English language often follow patterns—similar sounds and/or spellings. Just take a look at the number of phonograms in List 9. Or think about how easy it is to rhyme most longer words. The list below contains words that have no "close cousins" or rhymes. Can you think of any other words for which there is no true rhyme?

bulb	hundred	nothing	tablet
dreamt	hungry	orange	wasp
druggist	infant	purple	Wednesday
exit	month	silver	zebra
film	noisy	sixth	

The Reading Teacher's Book of Lists, Fourth Edition, © 2000 by John Wiley & Sons, Inc.

List 13. SYLLABICATION RULES[*]

The teaching of syllabication rules is somewhat controversial. Some say you should, and some say it is not worth the effort. Syllables sometimes are part of phonics lessons because syllabication affects vowel sounds (for example, an open vowel rule), and sometimes they are part of spelling or English lessons. There is no close agreement on various lists of syllabication rules, and some of the rules have plenty of exceptions. We are not urging you to teach them, but neither are we urging you to refrain from doing so.

Rule 1. VCV[†]   A consonant between two vowels tends to go with the second vowel unless the first vowel is accented and short.
Examples: *bro'-ken, wag'-on,* **e-vent'**

Rule 2 . VCCV   Divide two consonants between vowels unless they are a blend or digraph. (See List 1.)
Examples: *pic-ture, ush-er*

Rule 3. VCCCV   When there are three consonants between two vowels, divide between the blend or the digraph and the other consonant.
Example: *an-gler*

Rule 4. Affixes   Prefixes always form separate syllables (*un-hap-py*), and suffixes form separate syllables if they contain a vowel and in the following cases:
a.   The suffix *-y* tends to pick up the preceding consonant to form a separate syllable.
Example: *fligh-ty*
b.   The suffix *-ed* tends to form a separate syllable only when it follows a root that ends in *d* or *t*.
Example: *plant-ed* (not in stopped)
c.   The suffix *-s* never forms a syllable except sometimes when it follows an *e*.
Examples: *at-oms, cours-es*

Rule 5. Compounds   Always divide compound words.
Example: *black-bird*

Rule 6. Final *le*   Final *le* picks up the preceding consonant to form a syllable.
Example: *ta-ble*

The Reading Teacher's Book of Lists, Fourth Edition, © 2000 by John Wiley & Sons, Inc.

[*]Source: P. Costigan, *A Validation of the Fry Syllabification Generalization.* Unpublished master's thesis. Rutgers University, New Brunswick, NJ, 1977. Available from ERIC.

[†]V = vowel: C = consonant.

NOTE: These rules tend to give phonetic (sound) division of syllables that is in harmony with phonics instruction. Dictionaries tend to favor morphemic (meaning) division for main entries. Often, this does not conflict with the phonetic (pronunciation) division but sometimes it does; for example, "skat-er" morphemic versus "ska-ter" phonetic. The "er" is a morphemic (meaning) unit meaning "one who."

Rule 7. Vowel Clusters	Do not split common vowel clusters, such as:
	a. *R*-controlled vowels (*ar, er, ir, or,* and *ur*). Example: *ar-ti-cle*
	b. Long vowel digraphs (*ea, ee, ai, oa,* and *ow*). Example: *fea-ture*
	c. Broad *o* clusters (*au, aw,* and *al*). Example: *au-di-ence*
	d. Diphthongs (*oi, oy, ou,* and *ow*). Example: *thou-sand*
	e. Double *o* like *oo*. Examples: *moon, look*
Rule 8. Vowel Problems	Every syllable must have one and only one vowel sound.
	a. The letter *e* at the end of a word is silent. Example: *come*
	b. The letter *y* at the end or in the middle of a word operates as a vowel. Examples: *ver-y, cy-cle*
	c. Two vowels together with separate sounds form separate syllables. Example: *po-li-o*

The Reading Teacher's Book of Lists, Fourth Edition, © 2000 by John Wiley & Sons, Inc.

See also List 23, Prefixes; List 24, Suffixes.

2

USEFUL
WORDS

List 14. INSTANT WORDS

These are the most common words in English, ranked in frequency order. The first 25 make up about a third of all printed material. The first 100 make up about half of all written material, and the first 300 make up about 65 percent of all written material. Is it any wonder that all students must learn to recognize these words instantly and to spell them correctly also?

FIRST HUNDRED

WORDS 1–25	WORDS 26–50	WORDS 51–75	WORDS 75–100
the	or	will	number
of	one	up	no
and	had	other	way
a	by	about	could
to	word	out	people
in	but	many	my
is	not	then	than
you	what	them	first
that	all	these	water
it	were	so	been
he	we	some	call
was	when	her	who
for	your	would	oil
on	can	make	its
are	said	like	now
as	there	him	find
with	use	into	long
his	an	time	down
they	each	has	day
I	which	look	did
at	she	two	get
be	do	more	come
this	how	write	made
have	their	go	may
from	if	see	part

Common suffixes: *-s, -ing, -ed, -er, -ly, -est*

The Reading Teacher's Book of Lists, Fourth Edition, © 2000 by John Wiley & Sons, Inc.

SECOND HUNDRED

WORDS 101–125	WORDS 126–150	WORDS 151–175	WORDS 176–200
over	say	set	try
new	great	put	kind
sound	where	end	hand
take	help	does	picture
only	through	another	again
little	much	well	change
work	before	large	off
know	line	must	play
place	right	big	spell
year	too	even	air
live	mean	such	away
me	old	because	animal
back	any	turn	house
give	same	here	point
most	tell	why	page
very	boy	ask	letter
after	follow	went	mother
thing	came	men	answer
our	want	read	found
just	show	need	study
name	also	land	still
good	around	different	learn
sentence	form	home	should
man	three	us	America
think	small	move	world

Common suffixes: *-s, -ing, -ed, -er, -ly, -est*

The Reading Teacher's Book of Lists, Fourth Edition, © 2000 by John Wiley & Sons, Inc.

THIRD HUNDRED

WORDS 201–225	WORDS 226–250	WORDS 251–275	WORDS 275–300
high	saw	important	miss
every	left	until	idea
near	don't	children	enough
add	few	side	eat
food	while	feet	facet
between	along	car	watch
own	might	mile	far
below	close	night	Indian
country	something	walk	really
plant	seem	white	almost
last	next	sea	let
school	hard	began	above
father	open	grow	girl
keep	example	took	sometimes
tree	begin	river	mountain
never	life	four	cut
start	always	carry	young
city	those	state	talk
earth	both	once	soon
eye	paper	book	list
light	together	hear	song
thought	got	stop	being
head	group	without	leave
under	often	second	family
story	run	later	it's

Common suffixes: *-s, -ing, -ed, -er, -ly, -est*

The Reading Teacher's Book of Lists, Fourth Edition, © 2000 by John Wiley & Sons, Inc.

FOURTH HUNDRED

WORDS 301–325

body
music
color
stand
sun
question
fish
area
mark
dog
horse
birds
problem
complete
room
knew
since
ever
piece
told
usually
didn't
friends
easy
heard

WORDS 326–350

order
red
door
sure
become
top
ship
across
today
during
short
better
best
however
low
hours
black
products
happened
whole
measure
remember
early
waves
reached

WORDS 351–375

listen
wind
rock
space
covered
fast
several
hold
himself
toward
five
step
morning
passed
vowel
true
hundred
against
pattern
numeral
table
north
slowly
money
map

WORDS 376–400

farm
pulled
draw
voice
seen
cold
cried
plan
notice
south
sing
war
ground
fall
king
town
I'll
unit
figure
certain
field
travel
wood
fire
upon

FIFTH HUNDRED

WORDS 401–425

done
English
road
halt
ten
fly
gave
box
finally
wait
correct
oh
quickly
person
became
shown
minutes
strong
verb
stars
front
feel
fact
inches
street

WORDS 426–450

decided
contain
course
surface
produce
building
ocean
class
note
nothing
rest
carefully
scientists
inside
wheels
stay
green
known
island
week
less
machine
base
ago
stood

WORDS 451–475

plane
system
behind
ran
round
boat
game
force
brought
understand
warm
common
bring
explain
dry
though
language
shape
deep
thousands
yes
clear
equation
yet
government

WORDS 476–500

filled
heat
full
hot
check
object
am
rule
among
noun
power
cannot
able
six
size
dark
ball
material
special
heavy
fine
pair
circle
include
built

The Reading Teacher's Book of Lists, Fourth Edition, © 2000 by John Wiley & Sons, Inc.

SIXTH HUNDRED

WORDS 501–525

can't
matter
square
syllables
perhaps
bill
felt
suddenly
test
direction
center
farmers
ready
anything
divided
general
energy
subject
Europe
moon
region
return
believe
dance
members

WORDS 526–550

picked
simple
cells
paint
mind
love
cause
rain
exercise
eggs
train
blue
wish
drop
developed
window
difference
distance
heart
sit
sum
summer
wall
forest
probably

WORDS 551–575

legs
sat
main
winter
wide
written
length
reason
kept
interest
arms
brother
race
present
beautiful
store
job
edge
past
sign
record
finished
discovered
wild
happy

WORDS 576–600

beside
gone
sky
glass
million
west
lay
weather
root
instruments
meet
third
months
paragraph
raised
represent
soft
whether
clothes
flowers
shall
teacher
held
describe
drive

SEVENTH HUNDRED

WORDS 601 625

cross
speak
solve
appear
metal
son
either
ice
sleep
village
factors
result
jumped
snow
ride
care
floor
hill
pushed
baby
buy
century
outside
everything
tall

WORDS 626–650

already
instead
phrase
soil
bed
copy
free
hope
spring
case
laughed
nation
quite
type
themselves
temperature
bright
lead
everyone
method
section
lake
consonant
within
dictionary

WORDS 651–675

hair
age
amount
scale
pounds
although
per
broken
moment
tiny
possible
gold
milk
quiet
natural
lot
stone
act
build
middle
speed
count
cat
someone
sail

WORDS 676–700

rolled
bear
wonder
smiled
angle
fraction
Africa
killed
melody
bottom
trip
hole
poor
let's
fight
surprise
French
died
beat
exactly
remain
dress
iron
couldn't
fingers

The Reading Teacher's Book of Lists, Fourth Edition, © 2000 by John Wiley & Sons, Inc.

EIGHTH HUNDRED

WORDS 701–725	WORDS 726–750	WORDS 751–775	WORDS 776–800
row	president	yourself	caught
least	brown	control	fell
catch	trouble	practice	team
climbed	cool	report	God
wrote	cloud	straight	captain
shouted	lost	rise	direct
continued	sent	statement	ring
itself	symbols	stick	serve
else	wear	party	child
plains	bad	seeds	desert
gas	save	suppose	increase
England	experiment	woman	history
burning	engine	coast	cost
design	alone	bank	maybe
joined	drawing	period	business
foot	east	wire	separate
law	pay	choose	break
ears	single	clean	uncle
grass	touch	visit	hunting
you're	information	bit	flow
grew	express	whose	lady
skin	mouth	received	students
valley	yard	garden	human
cents	equal	please	art
key	decimal	strange	feeling

NINTH HUNDRED

WORDS 801–825	WORDS 826–850	WORDS 851–875	WORDS 876–900
supply	guess	thick	major
corner	silent	blood	observe
electric	trade	lie	tube
insects	rather	spot	necessary
crops	compare	bell	weight
tone	crowd	fun	meat
hit	poem	loud	lifted
sand	enjoy	consider	process
doctor	elements	suggested	army
provide	indicate	thin	hat
thus	except	position	property
won't	expect	entered	particular
cook	flat	fruit	swim
bones	seven	tied	terms
tail	interesting	rich	current
board	sense	dollars	park
modern	string	send	sell
compound	blow	sight	shoulder
mine	famous	chief	industry
wasn't	value	Japanese	wash
fit	wings	stream	block
addition	movement	planets	spread
belong	pole	rhythm	cattle
safe	exciting	eight	wife
soldiers	branches	science	sharp

The Reading Teacher's Book of Lists, Fourth Edition, © 2000 by John Wiley & Sons, Inc.

TENTH HUNDRED

WORDS 901–925

company
radio
we'll
action
capital
factories
settled
yellow
isn't
southern
truck
fair
printed
wouldn't
ahead
chance
born
level
triangle
molecules
France
repeated
column
western
church

WORDS 926–950

sister
oxygen
plural
various
agreed
opposite
wrong
chart
prepared
pretty
solution
fresh
shop
suffix
especially
shoes
actually
nose
afraid
dead
sugar
adjective
fig
office
huge

WORDS 951–975

gun
similar
death
score
forward
stretched
experience
rose
allow
fear
workers
Washington
Greek
women
bought
led
march
northern
create
British
difficult
match
win
doesn't
steel

WORDS 976–1000

total
deal
determine
evening
nor
rope
cotton
apple
details
entire
corn
substances
smell
tools
conditions
cows
track
arrived
located
sir
seat
division
effect
underline
view

See also List 15, Picture Nouns; List 92, Games and Methods for Teaching; List 126, Spelling Teaching Methods.

List 15. PICTURE NOUNS

Combined with the first hundred Instant Words, these picture words make a powerful beginning reading and writing vocabulary.

1. People
boy
girl
man
woman
baby

2. Toys
ball
doll
train
game
skateboard

3. Numbers
one
two
three
four
five

4. Clothing
shirt
pants
dress
shoes
hat

5. Pets
cat
dog
rabbit
bird
fish

6. Furniture
table
chair
sofa
chest
desk

7. Eating Objects
cup
plate
bowl
fork
spoon

8. Transportation
bicycle
truck
bus
plane
boat

9. Food
bread
meat
soup
fruit
cereal

10. Drinks
water
milk
juice
soda
malt

11. Zoo Animals
elephant
giraffe
bear
lion
monkey

12. Fruit
fruit
orange
grape
pear
banana

13. Plants
bush
flower
grass
tomatoes
tree

14. Sky Things
sun
moon
star
cloud
rain

15. Earth Things
water
rock
dirt
field
hill

16. Farm Animals
horse
cow
pig
chicken
duck

17. Workers
farmer
police officer
cook
doctor
nurse

18. Entertainment
television
radio
movie
ball game
band

19. Writing Tools
pen
pencil
crayon
typewriter
computer

20. Reading Things
book
newspaper
magazine
sign
letter

The Reading Teacher's Book of Lists, Fourth Edition, © 2000 by John Wiley & Sons, Inc.

See also List 14, Instant Words; List 92, Games and Methods for Teaching.

List 16. HOMOPHONES

Homophones are words that sound the same but have different meanings and usually different spellings. We think this is one of the most complete lists of homophones available. Recognizing homophones is particularly important because computer "spell check" programs do not recognize them as spelling errors. There are many ways to teach homophones, including reading and spelling games, jokes and riddles, and workbook exercises. See List 92, Games and Methods for Teaching, for suggestions.

This list contains only homophones that have different spellings. If a pair has the same spelling (for example, *bat* meaning a flying animal and *bat* meaning a club), they are included in the homograph list. The term *homonym* can include both homophones (same sound) and homographs (same spelling).

Easy Homophones

add	close	hi	need	rain
ad	clothes	high	knead	reign
	cloze			rein
air		hole	new	
heir	creek	whole	knew	read
	creak		gnu	reed
already		horse		
all ready	dear	hoarse	night	real
	deer		knight	reel
ant		I		
aunt	die	eye	no	red
	dye	aye	know	read
ate				
eight	fair	in	oh	right
	fare	inn	owe	write
ball				
bawl	feet	its	one	road
	feat	it's	won	rode
bare				rowed
bear	find	led	or	
	fined	lead	oar	sale
be			ore	sail
bee	flower	loan		
	flour	lone	our	see
beat			hour	sea
beet	for	made		
	four	maid	pair	seem
been	fore		pare	seam
bin		meet	pear	
	great	meat		sell
blue	grate		peace	cell
blew		might	piece	
	heard	mite		sent
brake	herd		plane	cent
break		missed	plain	scent
	here	mist		
by	hear		principal	shoe
bye		morn	principle	shoo
buy		mourn		

55

side
sighed

steal
steel

to
two
too

we
wee

wood
would

so
sew
sow

tail
tale

toe
tow

weather
whether

you
you're

some
sum

their
there
they're

told
tolled

week
weak

son
sun

through
threw

way
weigh

where
wear
ware

Homophone Master List

acts (deeds)
ax (tool)

ad (advertisement)
add (addition)

ads (advertisements)
adz (axlike tool)

aid (assistance)
aide (a helper)

ail (be sick)
ale (beverage)

air (oxygen)
heir (successor)

aisle (path)
I'll (I will)
isle (island)

all (everything)
awl (tool)

all together (in a group)
altogether (completely)

already (previous)
all ready (all are ready)

allowed (permitted)
aloud (audible)

altar (in a church)
alter (change)

ant (insect)
aunt (relative)

ante (before)
anti (against)

arc (part of a circle)
ark (boat)

ascent (climb)
assent (agree)

assistance (help)
assistants (those who help)

ate (did eat)
eight (number)

attendance (presence)
attendants (escorts)

aural (by ear)
oral (by mouth)

away (gone)
aweigh (clear anchor)

awful (terrible)
offal (entrails)

aye (yes)
eye (organ of sight)
I (pronoun)

bail (throw water out)
bale (bundle)

bait (lure)
bate (to decrease)

ball (round object)
bawl (cry)

band (plays music)
banned (forbidden)

bard (poet)
barred (having bars)

bare (nude)
bear (animal)

bark (dog's sound)
barque (ship)

baron (nobleman)
barren (no fruit)

base (lower part)
bass (deep tone)

based (at a base)
baste (cover with liquid)

bases (plural of *base*)
basis (foundation)

bask (warm feeling)
Basque (country)

bazaar (market)
bizarre (old)

be (exist)
bee (insect)

beach (shore)
beech (tree)

bearing (manner)
baring (uncovering)

beat (whip)
beet (vegetable)

beau (boyfriend)
bow (decorative knot)

been (past participle of *be*)
bin (box)

beer (drink)
bier (coffin)

bell (something you ring)
belle (pretty woman)

berry (fruit)
bury (put in ground)

berth (bunk)
birth (born)

better (more good)
bettor (one who bets)

bight (slack part of rope)
bite (chew)
byte (computer unit)

billed (did bill)
build (construct)

blew (did blow)
blue (color)

block (cube)
bloc (group)

boar (hog)
bore (drill; be tiresome)

boarder (one who boards)
border (boundary)

boll (cotton pod)
bowl (dish; game)

bolder (more bold)
boulder (big stone)

born (delivered at birth)
borne (carried)

borough (town)
burro (donkey)
burrow (dig)

bough (of a tree)
bow (of a ship)

bouillon (clear broth)
bullion (uncoined gold or silver)

boy (male child)
bouy (floating object)

brake (stop)
break (smash)

bread (food)
bred (cultivated)

brewed (steeped)
brood (flock)

brews (steeps)
bruise (bump)

bridal (relating to bride)
bridle (headgear for horse)

Britain (country)
Briton (Englishman)

broach (bring up)
brooch (pin)

but (except)
butt (end)

buy (purchase)
by (near)
bye (farewell)

cache (hiding place)
cash (money)

callous (unfeeling)
callus (hard tissue)

cannon (big gun)
canon (law)

canvas (cloth)
canvass (survey)

capital (money; city)
Capitol (building of U.S. Congress)

carat (weight of precious stones)
caret (proofreader's mark)
carrot (vegetable)

carol (song)
carrel (study space in library)

cast (throw; actors in a play)
caste (social class)

cause (origin)
caws (crow calls)

cede (grant)
seed (part of a plant)

ceiling (top of room)
sealing (closing)

cell (prison room)
sell (exchange for money)

cellar (basement)
seller (one who sells)

censor (ban)
sensor (detection device)

cent (penny)
scent (odor)
sent (did send)

cereal (relating to grain)
serial (of a series)

cession (yielding)
session (meeting)

chance (luck)
chants (songs)

chased (did chase)
chaste (modest)

cheap (inexpensive)
cheep (bird call)

chews (bites)
choose (select)

chic (style)
sheik (Arab chief)

chilly (cold)
chili (hot pepper)

choral (music)
coral (reef)
chorale (chorus)
corral (pen for livestock)

chord (musical notes)
cord (string)

chute (slide)
shoot (discharge gun)

cite (summon to court)
sight (see)
site (location)

57

claws (nails on animal's feet)
clause (part of a sentence)

click (small sound)
clique (group of friends)

climb (ascend)
clime (climate)

close (shut)
clothes (clothing)
cloze (test)

coal (fuel)
cole (cabbage)

coarse (rough)
course (path; school subject)

colonel (military rank)
kernel (grain of corn)

complement (complete set)
compliment (praise)

coop (chicken pen)
coupe (car)

core (center)
corps (army group)

correspondence (letters)
correspondents (writers)

council (legislative body)
counsel (advise)

cousin (relative)
cozen (deceive)

creak (grating noise)
creek (stream)

crews (groups of workers)
cruise (sail)
cruse (small pot)

cruel (hurting)
crewel (stitching)

cue (prompt)
queue (line up)

currant (small raisin)
current (recent, fast part of a stream)

curser (one who curses)
cursor (moving pointer)

cymbal (percussion instrument)
symbol (sign)

deer (animal)
dear (greeting; loved one)

desert (abandon)
dessert (follows main course of meal)

die (expire)
dye (color)

dine (eat)
dyne (unit of force)

disburse (pay out)
disperse (scatter)

discreet (unobtrusive)
discrete (noncontinuous)

doe (female deer)
dough (bread mixture)
do (musical note)

do (shall)
dew (moisture)
due (owed)

done (finished)
dun (demand for payment; dull color)

dual (two)
duel (formal combat)

duct (tube)
ducked (did duck)

earn (work for)
urn (container)

ewe (female sheep)
yew (shrub)
you (personal pronoun)

eyelet (small hole)
islet (small island)

fain (gladly)
feign (pretend)

faint (weak)
feint (pretend attack)

fair (honest; bazaar)
fare (cost of transportation)

fawn (baby deer)
faun (mythical creature)

faze (upset)
phase (stage)

feat (accomplishment)
feet (plural of *foot*)

find (discover)
fined (penalty of money)

fir (tree)
fur (animal covering)

flair (talent)
flare (flaming signal)

flea (insect)
flee (run away)

flew (did fly)
flu (influenza)
flue (shaft)

flour (milled grain)
flower (bloom)

for (in favor of)
fore (front part)
four (number 4)

foreword (preface)
forward (front part)

forth (forward)
fourth (after third)

foul (bad)
fowl (bird)

franc (French money)
frank (honest)

friar (brother in religious order)
fryer (frying chicken)

gate (fence opening)
gait (foot movement)

gilt (golden)
guilt (opposite of innocence)

gnu (antelope)
knew (did know)
new (opposite of *old*)

gorilla (animal)
guerrilla (irregular soldier)

grate (grind)
great (large)

groan (moan)
grown (cultivated)

guessed (surmised)
guest (company)

hail (ice; salute)
hale (healthy)

hair (on head)
hare (rabbit)

hall (passage)
haul (carry)

handsome (attractive)
hansom (carriage)

hangar (storage building)
hanger (to hang things on)

halve (cut in half)
have (possess)

hart (deer)
heart (body organ)

hay (dried grass)
hey (expression to get attention)

heal (make well)
heel (bottom of foot)
he'll (he will)

hear (listen)
here (this place)

heard (listened)
herd (group of animals)

heed (pay attention)
he'd (he would)

hertz (unit of wave frequency)
hurts (pain)

hew (carve)
hue (color)

hi (hello)
hie (hasten)
high (opposite of *low*)

higher (above)
hire (employ)

him (pronoun)
hymn (religious song)

hoarse (husky voice)
horse (animal)

hole (opening)
whole (complete)

holey (full of holes)
holy (sacred)
wholly (all)

horde (crowd)
hoard (hidden supply)

hostel (lodging for youth)
hostile (unfriendly)

hour (sixty minutes)
our (possessive pronoun)

hurdle (jump over)
hurtle (throw)

idle (lazy)
idol (god)
idyll (charming scene)

in (opposite of *out*)
inn (hotel)

insight (self knowledge)
incite (cause)

instance (example)
instants (short periods of time)

insure (protect against loss)
ensure (make sure)

intense (extreme)
intents (aims)

its (possessive pronoun)
it's (it is)

jam (fruit jelly)
jamb (window part)

knit (weave with yarn)
nit (louse egg)

lam (escape)
lamb (baby sheep)

lain (past participle of *lie*)
lane (narrow way)

lay (recline)
lei (necklace of flowers)

lead (metal)
led (guided)

leak (crack)
leek (vegetable)

lean (slender; incline)
lien (claim)

leased (rented)
least (smallest)

lessen (make less)
lesson (instruction)

levee (embankment)
levy (impose by legal authority)

liar (untruthful)
lyre (musical instrument)

lichen (fungus)
liken (compare)

lie (falsehood)
lye (alkaline solution)

lieu (instead of)
Lou (name)

lightening (become light)
lightning (occurs with thunder)

load (burden)
lode (vein or ore)

loan (something borrowed)
lone (single)

locks (plural of lock)
lox (smoked salmon)

loot (steal)
lute (musical instrument)

low (not high; cattle sound)
lo (interjection)

made (manufactured)
maid (servant)

mail (send by post)
male (masculine)

main (most important)
Maine (state)
mane (hair)

maize (Indian corn)
maze (confusing network of passages)

mall (courtyard)
maul (attack)

manner (style)
manor (estate)

mantel (over fireplace)
mantle (cloak)

marry (join together)
merry (gay)
Mary (name)

marshal (escort)
martial (militant)

massed (grouped)
mast (support)

maybe (perhaps, adj.)
may be (is possible, v.)

meat (beef)
meet (greet)
mete (measure)

medal (award)
meddle (interfere)

might (may; strength)
mite (small insect)

miner (coal digger)
minor (juvenile)

missed (failed to attain)
mist (fog)

moan (groan)
mown (cut down)

mode (fashion)
mowed (cut down)

morn (early day)
mourn (grieve)

muscle (flesh)
mussel (shellfish)

naval (nautical)
navel (depression on abdomen)

nay (no)
neigh (whinny)

need (require)
knead (mix with hands)

new (not old)
knew (remembered)
gnu (animal)

night (evening)
knight (feudal warrior)

no (negative)
know (familiar with)

none (not any)
nun (religious sister)

not (in no manner)
knot (tangle)

oar (of a boat)
or (conjunction)
ore (mineral deposit)

ode (poem)
owed (did owe)

oh (exclamation)
owe (be indebted)

one (number)
won (triumphed)

overdo (go to extremes)
overdue (past due)

overseas (abroad)
oversees (supervises)

pail (bucket)
pale (white)

pain (discomfort)
pane (window glass)

pair (two of a kind)
pare (peel)
pear (fruit)

palate (roof of mouth)
palette (board for paint)
pallet (tool)

passed (went by)
past (former)

patience (composure)
patients (sick persons)

pause (brief stop)
paws (feet of animals)

peace (tranquility)
piece (part)

peak (mountaintop)
peek (look)
pique (offense)

peal (ring)
peel (pare)

pearl (jewel)
purl (knitting stitch)

pedal (ride a bike)
peddle (sell)

peer (equal)
pier (dock)

per (for each)
purr (cat sound)

pi (Greek letter)
pie (kind of pastry)

plain (simple)
plane (flat surface)

plait (braid)
plate (dish)

pleas (plural of *plea*)
please (to be agreeable)

plum (fruit)
plumb (lead weight)

pole (stick)
poll (vote)

pore (ponder; skin gland)
pour (flow freely)

pray (worship)
prey (victim)

presents (gifts)
presence (appearance)

principal (chief)
principle (rule)

profit (benefit)
prophet (seer)

rack (framework; torture)
wrack (ruin)

rain (precipitation)
reign (royal authority)
rein (harness)

raise (put up)
raze (tear down)
rays (of sun)

rap (hit; talk)
wrap (cover)

read (peruse)
reed (plant)

read (perused)
red (color)

real (genuine)
reel (spool)

reek (give off strong odor)
wreak (inflict)

rest (relax)
wrest (inflict)

review (look back)
revue (musical)

right (correct)
rite (ceremony)
write (inscribe)

rime (ice, or rhyme)
rhyme (same end sound)

ring (circular band)
wring (squeeze)

road (street)
rode (transported)
rowed (used oars)

roe (fish eggs)
row (line; use oars)

role (character)
roll (turn over; bread)

root (part of a plant)
route (highway)

rose (flower)
rows (lines)

rote (by memory)
wrote (did write)

rude (impolite)
rued (was sorry)

rumor (gossip)
roomer (renter)

rung (step on a ladder; past of *ring*)
wrung (squeezed)

rye (grain)
wry (twisted)

sail (travel by boat)
sale (bargain)

scene (setting)
seen (viewed)

scull (boat; row)
skull (head)

sea (ocean)
see (visualize)

seam (joining mark)
seem (appear to be)

sear (singe)
seer (prophet)

serf (feudal servant)
surf (waves)

sew (mend)
so (in order that)
sow (plant)

shear (cut)
sheer (transparent)

shoe (foot covering)
shoo (drive away)

shone (beamed)
shown (exhibited)

side (flank)
sighed (audible breath)

sign (signal)
sine (trigonometric function)

slay (kill)
sleigh (sled)

sleight (dexterity)
slight (slender)

slew (killed)
slue (swamp)

soar (fly)
sore (painful)

sole (only)
soul (spirit)

some (portion)
sum (total)

son (male offspring)
sun (star)

staid (proper)
stayed (remained)

stair (step)
stare (look intently)

stake (post)
steak (meat)

stationary (fixed)
stationery (paper)

steal (rob)
steel (metal)

step (walk)
steppe (prairie of Europe
or Asia)

stile (gate)
style (fashion)

straight (not crooked)
strait (channel of water)

suite (connected rooms)
sweet (sugary)

surge (sudden increase)
serge (fabric)

tacks (plural of *tack*)
tax (assess; burden)

tail (animal's appendage)
tale (story)

taught (did teach)
taut (tight)

tea (drink)
tee (holder for golf ball)

teas (plural of *tea*)
tease (mock)

team (crew)
teem (be full)

tear (cry)
tier (level)

tern (sea bird)
turn (rotate)

their (possessive pronoun)
there (at that place)
they're (they are)

theirs (possessive pro-
noun)
there's (there is)

threw (tossed)
through (finished)

throne (king's seat)
thrown (tossed)

thyme (herb)
time (duration)

tic (twitch)
tick (insect; sound of
clock)

tide (ebb and flow)
tied (bound)

to (toward)
too (also)
two (number)

toad (frog)
towed (pulled)

toe (digit on foot)
tow (pull)

told (informed)
tolled (rang)

trussed (tied)
trust (confidence)

vain (conceited)
vane (wind indicator)
vein (blood vessel)

vale (valley)
veil (face cover)

vary (change)
very (absolutely)

vice (bad habit)
vise (clamp)

vile (disgusting)
vial (small bottle)

wade (walk in water)
weighed (measured heav-

iness)

wail (cry)
whale (sea mammal)

waist (middle)
waste (trash)

wait (linger)
weight (heaviness)

waive (forgive)
wave (swell)

want (desire)
wont (custom)

ware (pottery)
wear (have on)
where (what place)

way (road)
weigh (measure heavi-
ness)
whey (watery part of
milk)

ways (plural of *way*; ship-
yard)
weighs (heaviness)

we (pronoun)
wee (small)

weak (not strong)
week (seven days)

weal (prosperity)
we'll (we will)
wheel (circular frame)

weather (interlace)
whether (if)

weave (interlace)
we've (we have)

we'd (we would)
weed (plant)

weir (dam)
we're (we are)

wet (moist)
whet (sharpen)

The Reading Teacher's Book of Lists, Fourth Edition, © 2000 by John Wiley & Sons, Inc.

which (what one)
witch (sorceress)

while (during)
wile (trick)

whine (complaining sound)
wine (drink)

who's (who is)
whose (possessive of *who*)

wood (of a tree)
would (is willing to)

worst (most bad)
wurst (sausage)

yoke (harness)
yolk (egg center)

you (pronoun)
ewe (female sheep)
yew (evergreen tree)

you'll (you will)
yule (Christmas)

your (possessive pronoun)
you're (you are)

See also List 17, Homophone Teaching Suggestions; List 18, Homographs and Heteronyms; List 21, Easily Confused Words.

List 17. HOMOPHONE
TEACHING SUGGESTIONS

Have some fun. Both you and the students can develop jokes and riddles.

What is a large animal without its fur? (**a bare bear**)
What is an insect's relative? (**an aunt ant**)

Proofread and correct sentences.

Please drink sum milk.
Turn write at the end of the street.

Make flash cards.

Write one of a homophone pair on each side. Student sees one side, and tries to spell the other. Then discuss the meanings or use the words in a sentence.

Make playing cards for a "Go Fish" or "Rummy"-type game.

Use the same cards for a "Concentration"-type game.

You or the students can *make some worksheets.*

Write the homophone pair: "sell— ___ ___ ___ ___ "
Select the correct word: "Dogs have (for—four) legs."

Make a game in which half of a pair of homophones is provided.

Bingo cards
Crossword puzzles

Make teaching devices.

Spinner games
Board games (example: racetrack and shake dice)

Old-fashioned *spelling tests or spelling bees* using homophones.

Find homophones in other materials: social studies, math, art.

Have classroom teams compete for three days.

Have a word wall or corner of a chalkboard with a pair of homophones.

Discuss the words for two minutes and change them periodically.

See also List 16, Homophones; List 92, Games and Methods for Teaching.

The Reading Teacher's Book of Lists, Fourth Edition, © 2000 by John Wiley & Sons, Inc.

List 18. HOMOGRAPHS
AND HETERONYMS

Homographs are words that are spelled the same but have different meanings and different origins. Many other words have multiple meanings, but according to dictionary authorities, what makes these words homographs is that they have different origins as well. Some homographs are also heteronyms, which means that they have a different pronunciation—these are marked with an asterisk (*).

The Reading Teacher's Book of Lists, Fourth Edition, © 2000 by John Wiley & Sons, Inc.

*affect (influence)
 affect (pretend)

 alight (get down from)
 alight (on fire)

 angle (shape formed by two connected lines)
 angle (to fish with hook and line)

 arch (curved structure)
 arch (chief)

 arms (body parts)
 arms (weapons)

*august (majestic)
 August (eighth month of the year)

*axes (plural of *ax*)
 axes (plural of *axis*)

 bail (money for release)
 bail (handle of a pail)
 bail (throw water out)

 ball (round object)
 ball (formal dance)

 band (group of musicians)
 band (thin strip for binding)

 bank (mound)
 bank (place of financial business)
 bank (row of things)
 bank (land along a river)

 bark (tree covering)
 bark (sound a dog makes)
 bark (sailboard)

 base (bottom)
 base (morally low)

*bass (low male voice)
 bass (kind of fish)

 baste (pour liquid on while roasting)
 baste (sew with long stitches)

 bat (club)
 bat (flying animal)
 bat (wink)

 batter (hit repeatedly)
 batter (liquid mixture used for cakes)
 batter (baseball player)

 bay (part of a sea)
 bay (aromatic leaf used in cooking)
 bay (reddish brown)
 bay (alcove between columns)
 bay (howl)

 bear (large animal)
 bear (support; carry)

 bill (statement of money owed)
 bill (beak)

 bit (small piece)
 bit (tool for drilling)
 bit (did bite)

 blaze (fire)
 blaze (mark a trail or a tree)
 blaze (make known)

 blow (hard hit)
 blow (send forth a stream of air)

 bluff (steep bank or cliff)
 bluff (fool or mislead)

 bob (weight at the end of a line)
 bob (move up and down)
 Bob (nickname for Robert)

 boil (bubbling of hot liquid)
 boil (red swelling on the skin)

 boom (deep sound)
 boom (long beam)
 boom (sudden increase in size)

 boon (benefit)
 boon (merry)

65

bore (make a hole)
bore (make weary)
bore (did bear)

bound (limit)
bound (obliged)
bound (spring back)
bound (on the way)

*bow (weapon for shooting arrows)
bow (forward part of a ship)
bow (bend in greeting or respect)

bowl (rounded dish)
bowl (play the game of bowling)

box (four-sided container)
box (kind of evergreen shrub)
box (strike with the hand)

bridge (way over an obstacle)
bridge (card game)

brush (tool for sweeping)
brush (bushes)

buck (male deer)
buck (slang for *dollar*)

buffer (something that softens)
buffer (pad for polishing)

*buffet (cabinet for dishes and linens)
buffet (self-serve meal)
buffet (strike)

butt (thicker end of a tool)
butt (object of ridicule)

can (able to)
can (metal container)

capital (money)
capital (punishable by death)

carp (complain)
carp (kind of fish)

case (condition)
case (box or container)

chap (crack or become rough)
chap (boy or man)

chop (cut with something sharp)
chop (jaw)

chop (irregular motion)
chop (cut of meat)

chord (two or more musical notes)
chord (together)
chord (an emotional response)

Chow (breed of dog)
chow (slang for *food*)

chuck (throw or toss)
chuck (cut of beef)

cleave (cut)
cleave (hold on to)

clip (cut)
clip (fasten)

*close (shut)
close (near)

clove (fragrant spice)
clove (section of a bulb)

cobbler (one who mends shoes)
cobbler (fruit pie with one crust)

cock (rooster)
cock (tilt upward)

colon (mark of punctuation)
colon (lower part of the large intestine)

*commune (talk intimately)
commune (group of people living together)

*compact (firmly packed together)
compact (agreement)

con (swindle)
con (against)

*console (cabinet)
console (ease grief)

*content (all things inside)
content (satisfied)

*converse (talk)
converse (opposite)

corporal (of the body)
corporal (low-ranking officer)

The Reading Teacher's Book of Lists, Fourth Edition, © 2000 by John Wiley & Sons, Inc.

count (name numbers in order)
count (nobleman)

counter (long table in a store or restaurant)
counter (one who counts)
counter (opposite)

crow (loud cry of a rooster)
crow (large black bird)
Crow (tribe of Native American Indians)

cue (signal)
cue (long stick used in a game of pool)

curry (rub and clean a horse)
curry (spicy seasoning)

date (day, month, and year)
date (sweet dark fruit)

defer (put off)
defer (yield to another)

demean (lower in dignity)
demean (humble oneself)

*desert (dry barren region)
desert (go away from)
desert (suitable reward or punishment)

die (stop living)
die (tool)

*do (act; perform)
do (first tone on the musical scale)

dock (wharf)
dock (cut some off)

*does (plural of doe)
does (present tense of to do)

*dove (pigeon)
dove (did dive)

down (from a higher to a lower place)
down (soft feathers)
down (grassy land)

dredge (dig up)
dredge (sprinkle with flour or sugar)

dresser (one who dresses)
dresser (bureau)

drove (did drive)
drove (flock; herd; crowd)

dub (give a title)
dub (add voice or music to a film)

duck (large wild bird)
duck (lower suddenly)
duck (type of cotton cloth)

ear (organ of hearing)
ear (part of certain plants)

egg (oval or round body laid by a bird)
egg (encourage)

elder (older)
elder (small tree)

*entrance (going in)
entrance (delight; charm)

*excise (tax)
excise (remove)

fair (beautiful; lovely)
fair (just; honest)
fair (showing of farm goods)
fair (bazaar)

fan (devise to stir up the air)
fan (admirer)

fast (speedy)
fast (go without food)

fawn (young deer)
fawn (try to get favor by slavish acts)

fell (did fall)
fell (cut down a tree)
fell (deadly)

felt (did feel)
felt (type of cloth)

file (drawer; folder)
file (steel tool to smooth material)
file (material)

fine (high quality)
fine (money paid as punishment)

firm (solid; hard)
firm (business; company)

fit (suitable)
fit (sudden attack)

flag (banner)
flag (get tired)

flat (smooth)
flat (apartment)

fleet (group of ships)
fleet (rapid)

flight (act of flying)
flight (act of fleeing)

flounder (struggle)
flounder (kind of fish)

fluke (lucky stroke in games)
fluke (kind of fish)

fly (insect)
fly (move through the air with wings)

foil (prevent carrying out plans)
foil (metal sheet)
foil (long narrow sword)

fold (bend over on itself)
fold (pen for sheep)

forearm (part of the body)
forearm (prepare for trouble ahead)

forge (blacksmith shop)
forge (move ahead)

*forte (strong point)
forte (loud)

found (did find)
found (set up; establish)

founder (sink)
founder (one who establishes)

frank (hotdog)
frank (bold talk)
Frank (man's name)

fray (become ragged)
fray (fight)

fresh (newly made, not stale)
fresh (impudent, bold)

fret (worry)
fret (ridges on a guitar)

fry (cook in shallow pan)
fry (young fish)

fuse (slow-burning wick)
fuse (melt together)

gall (bile)
gall (annoy)

game (pastime)
game (lame)

gauntlet (challenge)
gauntlet (protective glove)

gin (alcoholic beverage)
gin (apparatus for separating seeds from cotton)
gin (card came)

gore (blood)
gore (wound from a horn)
gore (three-sided insert of cloth)

grate (framework for burning fuel in a fireplace)
grate (have an annoying effect)

grave (place of burial)
grave (important, serious)
grave (carve)

graze (feed on grass)
graze (touch lightly in passing)

ground (soil)
ground (did grind)

grouse (game bird)
grouse (grumble; complain)

gull (water bird)
gull (cheat; deceive)

gum (sticky substance from certain trees)
gum (tissue around teeth)

guy (rope; chain)
guy (fellow)

hack (cut roughly)
hack (carrier or car for hire)

hail (pieces of ice that fall like rain)
hail (shouts of welcome)

hamper (hold back)
hamper (large container or bucket)

The Reading Teacher's Book of Lists, Fourth Edition, © 2000 by John Wiley & Sons, Inc.

hatch (bring forth young from an egg)
hatch (opening in a ship's deck)

hawk (bird of prey)
hawk (peddle goods)

haze (mist; smoke)
haze (bully)

heel (back of the foot)
heel (tip over to one side)

hide (conceal; keep out of sight)
hide (animal skin)

hinder (stop)
hinder (rear)

hold (grasp and keep)
hold (part of ship or place for cargo)

husky (big and strong)
husky (sled dog)

impress (have a strong effect on)
impress (take by force)

*__incense__ (substance with a sweet smell when burned)
incense (make very angry)

*__intern__ (force to stay)
intern (doctor in training at a hospital)

*__intimate__ (very familiar)
intimate (suggest)

*__invalid__ (disabled person)
invalid (not valid)

jam (fruit preserve)
jam (press or squeeze)

jerky (with sudden starts and stops)
jerky (strips of dried meat)

jet (stream of water, steam, or air)
jet (hard black soil)
jet (type of airplane)

jig (dance)
jig (fishing lure)

*__job__ (work)
Job (Biblical man of patience)

jumper (person or thing that jumps)
jumper (type of dress)

junk (trash)
junk (Chinese sailing ship)

key (instrument for locking and unlocking)
key (low island)

kind (friendly; helpful)
kind (same class)

lap (body part formed when sitting)
lap (drink)
lap (one course traveled)

lark (small songbird)
lark (good fun)

lash (cord part of a whip)
lash (tie or fasten)

last (at the end)
last (continue; endure)

launch (start out)
launch (type of boat)

*__lead__ (show the way)
lead (metallic element)

league (measure of distance)
league (group of persons or nations)

lean (stand slanting)
lean (not fat)

leave (go away)
leave (permission)

left (direction)
left (did leave)

lie (falsehood)
lie (place oneself in a flat position; rest)

light (not heavy)
light (not dark)
light (land on)

like (similar to)
like (be pleased with)

lime (citrus fruit)
lime (chemical substance)

limp (lame walk)
limp (not stiff)

line (piece of cord)
line (place paper or fabric inside)

list (series of words)
list (tilt to one side)

*live (exist)
live (having life)

loaf (be idle)
loaf (shaped as bread)

lock (fasten door)
lock (curl of hair)

long (great measure)
long (wish for)

loom (frame for weaving)
loom (threaten)

low (not high)
low (cattle sound)

lumber (timber)
lumber (move along heavily)

mace (club; weapon)
mace (spice)

mail (letters)
mail (flexible metal armor)

maroon (brownish red color)
maroon (leave helpless)

mat (woven floor covering)
mat (border for picture)

match (stick used to light fires)
match (equal)

meal (food served at a certain time)
meal (ground grain)

mean (signify; intend)
mean (unkind)
mean (average)

meter (unit of length)
meter (poetic rhythm)
meter (device that measures flow)

might (past of *may*)
might (power)

mine (belonging to me)
mine (hole in the earth to get ores)

*minute (sixty seconds)
minute (very small)

miss (fail to hit)
miss (unmarried woman or girl)

mold (form; shape)
mold (fungus)

mole (brown spot on the skin)
mole (small underground animal)

mortar (cement mixture)
mortar (short cannon)

mount (high hill)
mount (go up)

mule (cross between donkey and horse)
mule (type of slipper)

mum (silent)
mum (chrysanthemum)

nag (scold)
nag (old horse)

nap (short sleep)
nap (rug fuzz)

net (open-weave fabric)
net (remaining after deductions)

nip (small drink)
nip (pinch)

*object (a thing)
object (to protest)

pad (cushion)
pad (walk softly)

page (one side of a sheet of paper)
page (youth who runs errands)

palm (inside of hand)
palm (kind of tree)

patent (right or privilege)
patent (type of leather)

patter (rapid taps)
patter (light, easy walk)

pawn (leave as security for loan)
pawn (chess piece)

*****peaked** (having a point)
peaked (looking ill)

peck (dry measure)
peck (strike at)

pen (instrument for writing)
pen (enclosed yard)

pile (heap or stack)
pile (nap on fabrics)

pine (type of evergreen)
pine (yearn or long for)

pitch (throw)
pitch (tar)

pitcher (container for pouring liquid)
pitcher (baseball player)

poach (trespass)
poach (cook an egg)

poker (card game)
poker (rod for stirring a fire)

pole (long piece of wood)
pole (either end of the earth's axis)

policy (plan of action)
policy (written agreement)

pool (tank with water)
pool (game played with balls on a table)

pop (short, quick sound)
pop (dad)
pop (popular)

post (support)
post (job or position)
post (system for mail delivery)

pound (unit of weight)
pound (hit hard again and again)
pound (pen)

*****present** (not absent)
present (gift)
present (to introduce formally)

press (squeeze)
press (force into service)

*****primer** (first book)
primer (something used to prepare another)

prune (fruit)
prune (cut; trim)

pry (look with curiosity)
pry (lift with force)

pump (type of show)
pump (machine that forces liquid out)

punch (hit)
punch (beverage)

pupil (student)
pupil (part of the eye)

quack (sound of a duck)
quack (phony doctor)

racket (noise)
racket (paddle used in tennis)

rail (bar of wood or metal)
rail (complain bitterly)

rank (row or line)
rank (having a bad odor)

rare (unusual)
rare (not cooked much)

rash (hasty)
rash (small red spots on the skin)

ream (500 sheets of paper)
ream (clean a hole)

rear (the back part)
rear (bring up)

*****record** (music disk)
record (write down)

recount (count again)
recount (tell in detail)

reel (spool for winding)
reel (sway under a blow)
reel (lively dance)

refrain (hold back)
refrain (part repeated)

*refuse (say no)
refuse (waste; trash)

rest (sleep)
rest (what is left)

rifle (gun with a long barrel)
rifle (ransack; search through)

ring (circle)
ring (bell sound)

root (underground part of a plant)
root (cheer for someone)

*row (line)
row (use oars to move a boat)
row (noisy fight)

sage (wise person)
sage (herb)

sap (liquid in a plant)
sap (weaken)

sash (cloth worn around the waist)
sash (frame of a window)

saw (did see)
saw (tool for cutting)
saw (wise saying)

scale (balance)
scale (outer layer of fish and snakes)
scale (series of steps)

school (place for learning)
school (group of fish)

scour (clean)
scour (move quickly over)

scrap (small bits)
scrap (quarrel)

seal (mark of ownership)
seal (sea mammal)

second (after the first)
second (one-sixtieth of a minute)

*sewer (one who sews)
sewer (underground pipe for wastes)

shark (large meat-eating fish)
shark (dishonest person)

shed (small shelter)
shed (get rid of)

shingles (roofing materials)
shingles (viral disease)

shock (sudden violent disturbance)
shock (thick bushy mass)

shore (land near water's edge)
shore (support)

shot (fired a gun)
shot (worn out)

size (amount)
size (preparation of glue)

*slaver (dealer in slaves)
slaver (salivate)

sledge (heavy sled)
sledge (large hammer)

slip (go easily)
slip (small strip of paper)
slip (undergarment)

*slough (swamp)
slough (shed old skin)

slug (small slow-moving animal)
slug (hit hard)

smack (slight taste)
smack (open lips quickly)
smack (small boat)

snare (trap)
snare (string on bottom of a drum)

snarl (growl)
snarl (tangle)

sock (covering for foot)
sock (hit hard)

soil (ground; dirt)
soil (make dirty)

sole (type of fish)
sole (only)

*sow (scatter seeds)
sow (female pig)

The Reading Teacher's Book of Lists, Fourth Edition, © 2000 by John Wiley & Sons, Inc.

spar (mast of a ship)
spar (argue)
spar (mineral)

spell (say the letters of a word)
spell (magic influences)
spell (period of work)

spray (sprinkle liquid)
spray (small branch with leaves and flowers)

spruce (type of evergreen)
spruce (neat or trim)

squash (press flat)
squash (vegetable)

stable (building for horses)
stable (unchanging)

stake (stick or post)
stake (risk or prize)

stalk (main stem of a plant)
stalk (follow secretly)

stall (place in a stable for one animal)
stall (delay)

staple (metal fastener for paper)
staple (principal element)

stay (remain)
stay (support)

steep (having a sharp slope)
steep (soak)

steer (guide)
steer (young male cattle)

stem (part of a plant)
stem (stop, dam up)

stern (rear part of a ship)
stern (harsh, strict)

stick (thin piece of wood)
stick (pierce)

still (not moving)
still (apparatus for making alcohol)

stoop (bend down)
stoop (porch)

story (account of a happening)
story (floor of a building)

strain (pull tight)
strain (group with an inherited quality)

strand (leave helpless)
strand (thread or string)

strip (narrow piece of cloth)
strip (remove)

stroke (hit)
stroke (pet, soothe)
stroke (an illness)

stunt (stop growth)
stunt (bold action)

sty (pen for pigs)
sty (swelling on eyelid)

swallow (take in)
swallow (small bird)

tap (strike lightly)
tap (faucet)

***tarry** (delay)
tarry (covered with tar)

tart (sour but agreeable)
tart (small fruit-filled pie)

***tear** (drop of liquid from the eye)
tear (pull apart)

temple (building for worship)
temple (side of forehead)

tend (incline to)
tend (take care of)

tender (not tough)
tender (offer)
tender (one who cares for)

tick (sound of a clock)
tick (small insect)
tick (pillow covering)

till (until)
till (plow the land)
till (drawer for money)

tip (end point)
tip (slant)
tip (present of money for services)

tire (become weary)
tire (rubber around a wheel)

toast (browned bread slices)
toast (wish for good luck)

toll (sound of a bell)
toll (fee paid for a privilege)

top (highest point)
top (toy that spins)

troll (ugly dwarf)
troll (method of fishing)

unaffected (not influenced)
unaffected (innocent)

vault (storehouse for valuables)
vault (jump over)

wake (stop sleeping)
wake (trail left behind a ship)

wax (substance made by trees)
wax (grow bigger)

well (satisfactory)
well (hole dug for water)

whale (large sea mammal)
whale (whip)

will (statement of desire for distribution of property after one's death)
will (is going to)
will (deliberate intention or wish)

*wind (air in motion)
wind (turn)

*wound (hurt)
wound (wrapped around)

yak (long-haired ox)
yak (talk endlessly)

yard (enclosed space around a house)
yard (thirty-six inches)

yen (strong desire)
yen (unit of money in Japan)

The Reading Teacher's Book of Lists, Fourth Edition, © 2000 by John Wiley & Sons, Inc.

See also List 16, Homophones; List 19, Easily Confused Words; List 156, Words with Multiple Meanings.

List 19. EASILY CONFUSED WORDS

The following groups of words are frequently used incorrectly. Some are confused because they sound the same but have different meanings; others look and sound different from each other but have meanings that are related. To teach them effectively will require many different strategies and frequent repetitions. Even those of us who understand these words make mistakes when we are in a hurry.

The Reading Teacher's Book of Lists, Fourth Edition, © 2000 by John Wiley & Sons, Inc.

accede (v.)—to comply with
exceed (v.)—to surpass

accent (n.)—stress in speech or writing
ascent (n.)—act of going up
assent (v., n.)—consent

accept (v.)—to agree or take what is offered
except (prep.)—leaving out or excluding

access (n.)—admittance
excess (n., adj.)—surplus

adapt (v.)—to adjust
adept (adj.)—proficient
adopt (v.)—to take by choice

adverse (adj.)—opposing
averse (adj.)—disinclined

affect (v.)—to influence
affect (n.)—feeling

alley (n.)—narrow street
ally (n.)—supporter

allusion (n.)—indirect reference
delusion (n.)—mistaken belief
illusion (n.)—mistaken vision

all ready (adj.)—completely ready
already (adv.)—even now or by this time

all together (pron., adj.)—everything or everyone in one place
altogether (adv.)—entirely

anecdote (n.)—short amusing story
antidote (n.)—something to counter the effect of poison

angel (n.)—heavenly body
angle (n.)—space between two lines that meet in a point

annul (v.)—to make void
annual (adj.)—yearly

ante—prefix meaning before
anti—prefix meaning against

any way (adj., n.)—in whatever manner
anyway (adv.)—regardless

appraise (v.)—to set a value on
apprise (v.)—to inform

area (n.)—surface
aria (n.)—melody

biannual (adj.)—occurring twice per year
biennial (adj.)—occurring every other year

bibliography (n.)—list of writings on a particular topic
biography (n.)—written history of a person's life

bizarre (adj.)—odd
bazaar (n.)—market, fair

breadth (n.)—width
breath (n.)—respiration
breathe (v.)—to inhale and exhale

calendar (n.)—a chart of days and months
colander (n.)—a strainer

casual (adj.)—informal
causal (adj.)—relating to cause

catch (v.)—to grab
ketch (n.)—type of boat

cease (v.)—to stop
seize (v.)—to grasp

click (n.)—short, sharp sound
clique (n.)—small exclusive subgroup

collision (n.)—a clashing
collusion (n.)—a scheme to cheat

coma (n.)—an unconscious state
comma (n.)—a punctuation mark

command (n.,v.)—an order, to order
commend (v.)—to praise, to entrust

comprehensible (adj.)—understandable
comprehensive (adj.)—extensive

confidant (n.)—friend or advisor
confident (adj.)—sure

confidentially (adv.)—privately
confidently (adv.)—certainly

conscience (n.)—sense of right and wrong
conscious (adj.)—aware

contagious (adj.)—spread by contact
contiguous (adj.)—touching or nearby

continual (adj.)—repeated, happening again and again
continuous (adj.)—uninterrupted, without stopping

cooperation (n.)—the art of working together
corporation (n.)—a business organization

costume (n.)—special way of dressing
custom (n.)—usual practice of habit

council (n.)—an official group
counsel (v.)—to give advice
counsel (n.)—advice

credible (adj.)—believable
creditable (adj.)—deserving praise

deceased (adj.)—dead
diseased (adj.)—ill

decent (adj.)—proper
descent (n.)—way down
dissent (n., v)—disagreement, to disagree

deference (n.)—respect
difference (n.)—dissimilarity

deposition (n.)—a formal written document
disposition (n.)—temperament

depraved (adj.)—morally corrupt
deprived (adj.)—taken away from

deprecate (v.)—to disapprove
depreciate (v.)—to lessen in value

desert (n.)—arid land
desert (v.)—to abandon
dessert (n.)—course served at the end of a meal

desolate (adj.)—lonely, sad
dissolute (adj.)—loose in morals

detract (v.)—to take away from
distract (v.)—to divert attention away from

device (n.)—a contrivance
devise (v.)—to plan

disapprove (v.)—to withhold approval
disprove (v.)—to prove something to be false

disassemble (v.)—to take something apart
dissemble (v.)—to disguise

disburse (v.)—to pay out
disperse (v.)—to scatter

discomfort (n.)—distress
discomfit (v.)—to frustrate or embarrass

disinterested (adj.)—impartial
uninterested (adj.)—not interested

effect (n.)—result of a cause
effect (v.)—to make happen

elapse (v.)—to pass
lapse (v.)—to become void
relapse (v.)—to fall back to previous condition

elicit (v.)—to draw out
illicit (adj.)—unlawful

eligible (adj.)—ready
illegible (adj.)—can't be read

elusive (adj.)—hard to catch
illusive (adj.)—misleading

eminent (adj.)—well known
imminent (adj.)—impending

emerge (v.)—rise out of
immerge (v.)—plunge into

emigrate (v.)—to leave a country and take up residence elsewhere
immigrate (v.)—to enter a country for the purpose of taking up residence

envelop (v.)—to surround
envelope (n.)—a wrapper for a letter

erasable (adj.)—capable of being erased
irascible (adj.)—easily provoked to anger

expand (v.)—to increase in size
expend (v.)—to spend

expect (v.)—to suppose; to look forward
suspect (v.)—to mistrust

extant (adj.)—still existing
extent (n.)—amount

facility (n.)—ease
felicity (n.)—happiness

farther (adj.)—more distant (refers to space)
further (adj.)—extending beyond a point (refers to time, quantity, or degree)

finale (n.)—the end
finally (adv.)—at the end
finely (adv.)—in a fine manner

fiscal (adj.)—relating to finance
physical (adj.)—relating to the body

formally (adv.)—with rigid ceremony
formerly (adv.)—previously

human (adj.)—relating to mankind
humane (adv.)—kind

hypercritical (adj.)—very critical
hypocritical (adj.)—pretending to be virtuous

imitate (v.)—to mimic
intimate (v.)—to hint or make known; familiar, close

incredible (adj.)—too extraordinary to be believed
incredulous (adj.)—unbelieving, skeptical

indigenous (adj.)—native
indigent (adj.)—needy
indignant (adj.)—angry

infer (v.)—to arrive at by reason
imply (v.)—to suggest meaning indirectly

ingenious (adj.)—clever
ingenuous (adj.)—straightforward

later (adj.)—more late
latter (adj.)—second in a series of two

lay (v.)—to set something down or place something
lie (v.)—to recline

least (adj.)—at the minimum
lest (conj.)—for fear that

lend (v.)—to give for a time
loan (n.)—received to use for a time

loose (adj.)—not tight
lose (v.)—not win; misplace

magnet (n.)—iron bar with power to attract iron
magnate (n.)—person in prominent position in large industry

message (n.)—communication
massage (v.)—rub body

moral (n., adj.)—lesson; ethic
morale (n.)—mental condition

morality (n.)—virtue
mortality (n.)—the state of being mortal; death rate

of (prep.)—having to do with; indicating possession
off (adv.)—not on

official (adj.)—authorized
officious (adj.)—offering services where they are neither wanted nor needed

oral (adj.)—verbal
aural (adj.)—listening

pasture (n.)—grass field
pastor (n.)—minister

perfect (adj.)—without fault
prefect (n.)—an official

perpetrate (v.)—to be guilty of; to commit
perpetuate (v.)—to make perpetual

perquisite (n.)—a privilege or profit in addition to salary
prerequisite (n.)—a preliminary requirement

persecute (v.)—to harass, annoy, or injure
prosecute (v.)—to press for punishment of crime

personal (adj.)—private
personnel (n.)—a body of people, usually employed in some organization

peruse (v.)—to read
pursue (v.)—to follow in order to overtake

picture (n.)—drawing or photograph
pitcher (n.)—container for liquid; baseball player

precede (v.)—to go before
proceed (v.)—to advance

preposition (n.)—a part of speech
proposition (n.)—a proposal or suggestion

pretend (v.)—to make believe
portend (v.)—to give a sign of something that will happen

quiet (adj.)—not noisy
quit (v.)—to stop
quite (adv.)—very

recent (adj.)—not long ago
resent (v.)—to feel indignant

respectably (adv.)—in a respectable manner
respectively (adv.)—in order indicated
respectfully (adv.)—in a respectful manner

restless (adj.)—constantly moving, uneasy
restive (adj.)—contrary, resisting control

suppose (v.)—assume or imagine
supposed (adj.)—expected

than (conj.)—used in comparison
then (adv.)—at that time; next in order of time

through (prep.)—by means of; from beginning to end
thorough (adj.)—complete

use (v.)—employ something
used (adj.)—secondhand

veracious (adj.)—truthful
voracious (adj.)—greedy

The Reading Teacher's Book of Lists, Fourth Edition, © 2000 by John Wiley & Sons, Inc.

See also List 16, Homophones; List 18, Homographs and Heteronyms.

List 20. COLLECTIVE NOUNS

The word that names groups or collections of people, animals, and things is called a collective noun. Some collective nouns are very familiar (like a **deck** of cards); others are much less so. These words are often substituted for the person, animal, or object they name. For example: The Marines were on parade; the corps marched with the drumbeat.

The Reading Teacher's Book of Lists, Fourth Edition, © 2000 by John Wiley & Sons, Inc.

academy of scholars
agenda of tasks
armada of ships
army of ants (caterpillars, frogs, soldiers)
array of numbers
association of professionals
assortment of items
audience of listeners
aurora of polar bears
bale of cotton (turtles)
band of gorillas (jays, musicians, robbers)
bank of monitors
barren of mules
bask of crocodiles
batch of biscuits (cookies, bread)
bed of clams (flowers, oysters, snakes, vegetables)
belt of asteroids
bevy of ladies (quail, swans)
block of houses (stamps)
brood of children (hens)
bundle of clothes (money, sticks)
cast of actors
cavalcade of horsemen
chain of islands
chapter of a book (verse)
chest of drawers
chorus of singers
class of students
club of members
clump of dirt (earth, grass)
cluster of diamonds (grapes, stars)
clutch of chicks
collection of stamps (books, coins, art)
colony of ants (artists, writers)
committee of people
company of firefighters (soldiers, workers)
conglomeration of businesses
congregation of worshipers
congress of delegates
constellation of stars
convention of professionals
convocation of eagles

corps of marines
council of advisors (chiefs)
couple of people
coven of witches
covey of doves (partridges)
crew of sailors (workers)
crowd of people
culture of bacteria
deck of cards
draught of fish
drove of cattle
exultation of larks
faculty of teachers
family of colors (languages, people)
field of racehorses
fleet of ships
flock of believers (birds, sheep, tourists)
flood of complaints (emotion, money)
flotilla of ships
flush of ducks
gaggle of geese
galaxy of stars
gang of hoodlums
group of things
grove of trees
herd of buffalo (cows, reindeer)
hive of bees
horde of enemies (gnats)
host of angels
huddle of lawyers
knot of toads
league of nations (teams)
line of people
litter of kittens (pigs, puppies)
mob of kangaroos (people, radicals)
mound of dirt (earth)
multitude of followers
murder of crows
nest of bowls (mice, snakes, spies, vipers)
network of computers
pack of dogs (gum, hounds, lies, wolves)
panel of experts
parliament of owls

party of diners (fishermen)
patch of flowers
peep of chickens
people of a city (nation)
pile of things
plague of locusts
pod of whales
portfolio of pictures (stocks, work)
posse of deputies
pride of lions
rag of colts
range of mountains
rookery of penguins
school of fish (porpoises)
set of dishes (teeth)
shelf of books
shock of hair (wheat)

slew of homework
spread of cattle (food, horses)
squad of police (cheerleaders)
stack of pancakes (paper)
staff of employees
string of ponies
swarm of bees (flies, reporters)
team of athletes (horses)
tribe of Indians (natives, peoples)
troop of baboons (kangaroos, police, scouts, soldiers)
troupe of performers
union of workers
wave of emotion (insects, water)
wealth of information
wing of aircraft

The Reading Teacher's Book of Lists, Fourth Edition, © 2000 by John Wiley & Sons, Inc.

List 21. MASS NOUNS

Mass nouns (sometimes called noncountable nouns) are not countable in the usual sense. That is, while we can have "one book" or "two books," "one pen" or "two pens," we do not usually have "one bread" or "two breads," "one money" or "two moneys." Bread and money are mass nouns. There are many such nouns in the English language and most can be grouped into categories. Some of these categories are listed below, along with examples. In teaching these nouns, remember that the adjectives "much" and "a little" can be used only with mass nouns, whereas "a few," "several," and "many" can be used only with countable nouns.

Liquids

blood
gasoline
juice
milk
oil
shampoo
soup
syrup
water

Gases

air
hydrogen
oxygen
pollution
smog
smoke

Solids and Semi-Solids

beef
bread
butter
chicken
cotton
gold
jelly
paper
peanut butter
rayon
silk
silver
soap
toast
toothpaste

Items with Small Parts

corn
grass
pollen
rice
salt
sand
sugar
wheat

Collections of Diverse Things

clothing
equipment
furniture
garbage
jewelry
machinery
mail
silverware

Abstract Nouns

beauty
good
honesty
intelligence
literacy
love
peace
sadness
wealth

Miscellaneous

dissent
history
information
land
momentum
news
psychology
scenery
slang

List 22. NONREVERSIBLE WORD PAIRS

The following are examples of pairs of words that always appear in the same order. Native speakers of English will probably use the correct order automatically; nonnative speakers, however, will need to learn these through practice.

Adam and Eve
bacon and eggs
back and forth
bread and water
bride and groom
business and pleasure
cause and effect
coffee and doughnuts
cream and sugar
crime and punishment
cup and saucer
dead or alive
fish and chips
front and center
fun and games
ham and eggs
hammer and nail
husband and wife
in and out
Jack and Jill
knife and fork
ladies and gentlemen
law and order
life or death
lock and key
lost and found
man and wife

name and address
nice and easy
peaches and cream
pen and pencil
pork and beans
pots and pans
profit and loss
rain or shine
read and write
right and wrong (right or wrong)
rise and fall
salt and pepper
shirt and tie
shoes and socks
short and fat
slip and slide
soap and water
sooner or later
stars and stripes
suit and tie
supply and demand
sweet and sour
tall and thin
trial and error
up and down (up or down)
war and peace
wine and cheese

The Reading Teacher's Book of Lists, Fourth Edition, © 2000 by John Wiley & Sons, Inc.

3

VOCABULARY

List 23. PREFIXES

Prefixes are small but meaningful letter groups added in front of a base word or root that contribute to the meaning of a word. Knowing the meaning of these prefixes—together with the meaning of common base words and Greek and Latin roots—will give students the tools for unlocking the meanings of hundreds of words. In addition to teaching these prefixes directly, it is a good idea to explain prefixes and their meanings when students encounter them in new vocabulary words throughout the year. Beginning prefixes are among the most common prefixes in the English language and tend to form easier words than those in Intermediate to Advanced. You may wish to use the special list of prefixes expressing numbers (many of which also appear in Intermediate to Advanced) to form the basis of a lesson on number words.

BEGINNING PREFIXES

Prefix	Meaning	Examples
anti-	against	antiwar, antisocial, antislavery, antifreeze
dis-	not, opposite	disappear, disagree, disarm, dishonest, discontinue
ex-	former	ex-president, ex-student, ex-athlete, ex-teacher, ex-king
im-, in-	not	impossible, impassable, immobilize, immature, imbalance
		inaccurate, invisible, inactive, indecisive, independent
inter-	among, between	Internet, international, intermission, intervene, interrupt
intra-	within	intramural, intrastate, intravenous, intranet, intramuscular
micro-	small, short	microphone, microscope, microwave, microbe, microfilm
mis-	wrong, not	misbehave, misconduct, misfortune, mistake, miscount
multi-	many, much	multiply, multicolored, multimillionaire, multitude
non-	not	nonsense, nonfiction, nonresistant, nonstop, nonviolent
over-	too much	overdue, overdo, overpriced, overbearing, overactive
post-	after	postpone, postdate, postscript, postmeridian, postwar
pre-	before	prefix, precaution, preamble, prenatal, prelude
pro-	favor	pro-war, Pro-American, pro-education, pro-trade, pro-union
pro-	forward	proceed, produce, progress, project, prognosis, prophet
re-	again	redo, rewrite, reappear, repaint, reheat, relive

The Reading Teacher's Book of Lists, Fourth Edition, © 2000 by John Wiley & Sons, Inc.

Prefix	Meaning	Examples
re-	back	recall, recede, repay, reflect, retract, rebate
sub-	under, below	submarine, subzero, submerge, subordinate, subhuman
super-	above, beyond	superman, supernatural, superior, superpower, supervise
tele-	distant	telephone, telescope, television, telegram, telepathy
trans-	across	transport, transfer, translate, transatlantic, transcribe
un-	not	unhappy, unable, uncomfortable, uncertain, unbeaten
under-	below, less than	underpaid, undercover, underground, underneath, underage

INTERMEDIATE TO ADVANCED PREFIXES

Prefix	Meaning	Examples
after-	after	afternoon, afterward, aftershock, aftereffect, afterthought
ambi-, amphi-	both, around	ambidextrous, ambiguous, ambivalent, ambience
		amphibian, amphitheater, amphora
auto-	self	automobile, automatic, autograph, autobiography, autonomy
be-	make	befriend, bewitch, beguile, bejewel, becalm
bene-	good	benefit, benefactor, benediction, beneficial, benevolent
bi-, bin-	two	bicycle, binocular, bifocal, biannual, bimonthly
cent-, centi-	hundred, hundredth	century, centigrade, centimeter, centennial
circu-	around	circulate, circumference, circus, circumspect, circumstance
co-	together	cooperate, collaborate, coordinate, coincide, co-chair
com-, con-	with	combine, commune, combat, compare, command
		concert, concur, connect, confer, concede, confident
contra-	against, opposite	contrary, contradict, contrast, contraband, contraception
counter-	against, opposite	counteract, countermand, counterproposal, counteroffensive
de-	down, away	deduct, descend, decrease, degrade, depart
de-	not, opposite	deform, deplete, deactivate, defuse, dehumidify
dec-	ten	decade, decathlon, December, decennial
deci-	tenth	decimeter, decimate, decibel, decile, decimal

The Reading Teacher's Book of Lists, Fourth Edition, © 2000 by John Wiley & Sons, Inc.

Prefix	Meaning	Examples
di-	two, double	dilemma, dioxide, dichotomy, diploma, digraph
dia-	through, across	diameter, dialogue, diagonal, diagnose, dialect
du-, duo-	two	duo, duet, dual, duplex, duplicate
dys-	bad	dysfunctional, dysentery, dysphasia, dystrophy
e-	out, away	evict, eject, erupt, emigrate, edict, emancipate
equi-	equal	equator, equation, equilibrium, equidistant, equinox
eu-	good	eulogy, euphoria, euphemism, Eucharist, euthanasia
giga-	billion	gigawatt, gigahertz, gigabyte
hemi-	half	hemisphere, hemistich, hemiplegia, hemicycle
hept-	seven	heptagon, heptameter, heptarchy
hetero-	different	heteronym, heterodoz, heterogenous, heterosexual
hex-	six	hexagon, hexameter, hexagram, hexadecimal
homo-	same	homogeneous, homogenize, homosexual, homophone
hyper-	excessive	hyperactive, hypersensitive, hyperbole, hypercritical
hypo-	under, too little	hypodermic, hypothesis, hypothermia, hypoxia
il-	not	illegal, illegible, illiterate, illogical, illegitimate
ir-	not	irregular, irreconcilable, irrevocable, irresponsible
kilo-	thousand	kilometer, kilogram, kilobyte, kilowatt, kiloliter
macro-	large, long	macroeconomics, macron, macrobiotic, macrocosm
magni-	great, large	magnify, magnificent, magnitude, magnanimous
mal-	bad	maladjusted, malfunction, malice, malevolent
mega-	large, million	megaphone, megalith, megacycle, megawatt, megaton, megabuck, megahertz
meta-	change	metamorphosis, metaphor, metastasis
mid-	middle	midnight, midway, midsummer, midyear, midshipman
milli-	thousand	million, milligram, millimeter, millennium, millibar
mon-, mono-	one	monk, monarch, monocular, monorail, monogamy
neo-	new	neoclassical, neologism, neonatal, neophyte, neon
omni-	all	omnibus, omnificent, omnipotent, omnivorous, omniscient
pan-	all	panorama, panacea, pandemonium, pandemic, Pan-American

Prefix	Meaning	Examples
para-	almost	paramedic, paralegal, paraprofessional, parasail
per-	through	perennial, permeate, permit, pervade, percolate
peri-	around	perimeter, periscope, peripatetic, periphery, periodontist
poly-	many	polysyllabic, polyglot, polyester, polyandry, polygamy
prot-	first, chief	protagonist, proton, prototype, protocol, protoplasm
pseudo-	false	pseudonym, pseudoclassical, pseudointellectual
quadr-	four	quadrangle, quadrant, quadriplegic, quadruple
quint-	five	quintuplet, quintet, quintessential, quintuple
self-	self	selfish, self-denial, self-respect, self-taught
semi-	half	semiannual, semicircle, semiconscious, semiautomatic
sept-	seven	September, septet, septuagenarian
syn-	together	synchronize, syndrome, synergy, synonym, synthesis
tri-	three	triangle, tricycle, trillion, triplet, tripartite, triumvirate
ultra-	beyond	ultramodern, ultraconservative, ultranationalist
uni-	one	unicorn, uniform, unite, universe, unique, unison

PREFIXES EXPRESSING NUMBER

Prefix	Meaning	Examples
deci-	tenth	decimeter
centi-	hundredth	centimeter
milli-	thousandth	millimeter
micro-	millionth	micrometer
nano-	billionth	nanometer
pico-	trillionth	picometer
femto-	quadrillionth	femtometer
atto-	quintillionth	attometer
demi-	half	demigod, demitasse
hemi-	half	hemisphere, hemicycle
semi-	half	semiannual, semicircle, semiclassic
prot-	first	protagonist, protein, proton, prototype
mon-, mono-	one	monk, monarch, monocular, monogamy
uni-	one	unicorn, unicycle, uniform, unify, unite
di-	two	digraph, dioxide, diphthong
tri-	three	triangle, tricycle, trillion, triplet
quadr-	four	quadrangle, quadrant, quadruple

The Reading Teacher's Book of Lists, Fourth Edition, © 2000 by John Wiley & Sons, Inc.

Prefix	Meaning	Examples
tetra-	four	tetrahedron, tetrameter
pent-	five	pentagon, pentathalon, Pentecost
quint-	five	quintet, quintuplets
hex-	six	hexagon, hexameter
sex-	six	sextant, sextet, sextuple
hept-	seven	heptagon, heptameter
sept-	seven	September, septuagenarian
oct-	eight	October, octagon, octane, octopus
ennea-	nine	enneagon, enneahedron, ennead
non-	nine	nonagenarian
nove-	nine	November, novena
deca-, dec-	ten	December, decade, decathlon, decameter
cent-	hundred	century (*note:* cent- is a shortened form of centi, which usually means one hundredth)
hect-	hundred	hectogram, hectometer, hectare
milli-	thousand	million, millipede (*note:* in metric system, milli- means thousandth)
kilo-	thousand	kilometer, kilogram, kilowatt, kiloliter
myria-	ten thousand	myriameter
mega-	million	megawatt, megabyte
giga-	billion	gigabyte
tera-	trillion	terameter
peta-	quadrillion	petameter
exa-	quintillion	exameter

PREFIXES THAT DESCRIBE SIZE

Prefix	Meaning	Examples
macro-	large, long	macrocosm, macron, macroscopic
magni-	great	magnify, magnitude, magnificent
mega-	large	megacycle, megalith, megalomania
micro-	small, short	microbe, microphone, microcosm

PREFIXES THAT DESCRIBE WHEN

Prefix	Meaning	Examples
after-	after	afterglow, afternoon, aftertaste, afterward
ante-	before	antebellum, antecedent, antedate, antediluvian
epi-	after	epilogue, epitaph, epidermis
post-	after	postdate, postdoctoral, posterior, postpone, postscript
pre-	before	preamble, precaution, prefix, prejudice
pro-	before	prognosis, progeny, program, prologue

PREFIXES THAT DESCRIBE WHERE

Prefix	Meaning	Examples
a-	on	aboard, afire, afoot, ashore, atop
ab-	from	abnormal, abhor, abolish, abstain
ac-	to	accent, accept, access, accident, acquire
ad-	to	adapt, add, addict, adhere, admit

Prefix	Meaning	Examples
af-	to	affair, affect, affiliate, affirm, afflict
ag-	to	agglomeration, aggrandize, aggravate
an-	to	annex, annihilate, annotate, announce
as-	to	ascend, ascertain, aspect, aspire, assert
by-	near, side	bypass, byplay, bystander, byway
circu-	around	circulate, circumference, circumspect
de-	from, down	debate, decay, deceive, decide, deform
dia-	through, across	diagnose, diagonal, dialogue, diameter
e-	out, away	effect, effort, eject, emigrate, erupt
em-	in	embalm, embed, embezzle, embrace
en-	in	enchant, enclose, encounter, encourage
enter-	among, between	enterprise, entertain
epi-	upon	epicenter, epidemic, epidermis, epithet
ex-	out	excel, exalt, exceed, exhaust, exit
extra-	outside	extracurricular, extraordinary
hypo-	under	hypochondria, hypodermic, hypothesis
im-	into	immediate, immerse, immigrate, implant
in-	into	incision, include, induce, inhale, infect
inter-	among, between	intercede, interpret, interrupt
intra-	within	intramural, intrastate, intravenous
intro-	inside	introduce, introspect, introject, introvert
mid-	middle	midriff, midshipman, midsummer
off-	from	offset, offshoot, offshore, offspring
on-	on	oncoming, ongoing, onrush, onshore
para-	beside	paradigm, paragraph, parallel, paraphrase
per-	throughout	perceive, percolate, perfect, perform
peri-	all around	perimeter, periscope, peripatetic
pro-	forward	proceed, produce, proficient, progress
pro-	in front of	proclaim, profane, profess
re-	back	recall, recede, reflect, repay, retract
retro-	back	retroactive, retrogress, retro-rocket
sub-	under	subcontract, subject, submerge
super-	over	superimpose, superscript, supersede
tele-	distant	telegram, telekinesis, telephone
through-	through	thoroughbred, thoroughfare
trans-	across	transatlantic, transcend, transcribe
under-	below	undercover, underground, underneath
with-	back, away	withdraw, withhold, within, without

PREFIXES THAT DESCRIBE AMOUNT OR EXTENT OF

Prefix	Meaning	Examples
equi-	equal	equal, equilibrium, equidistant, equator
extra-	beyond	extraordinary, extravagant
hyper-	excessive	hyperactive, hyperbole, hypercritical
hypo-	too little	hypoactive, hypoglycemic
is-	equal	isometric, isomorph, isosceles, isotope
multi-	many, much	multicolored, multifarious, multiply
olig-	few	oligarchy, oligopoly, oligophagous
omni-	all	omnibus, omnificent, omnipotent
out-	surpassing	outbid, outclass, outdo, outlive

The Reading Teacher's Book of Lists, Fourth Edition, © 2000 by John Wiley & Sons, Inc.

Prefix	Meaning	Examples
over-	too much	overactive, overbearing, overblown
pan-	all	panacea, pandemonium, Pandora
pene-	almost	peneplain, peninsula, penultimate
poly-	many	polyandry, polyester, polygamy, polyglot
super-	more than	superfine, superhuman, supernatural
ultra-	beyond	ultraconservative, ultramodern
under-	less than	underage, underdone, underripe

PREFIXES THAT EXPRESS TOGETHERNESS AND SEPARATENESS

Prefix	Meaning	Examples
ab-	away from	abdicate, abduct, aberrant, absent
co-	together	coauthor, cognate, coincide, cooperate
col-	with	collaborate, collateral, colleague, collect
com-	with	combat, combine, comfort, commune
con-	with	concede, concur, concert, confident
syl-	together	syllable, syllogism
sym-	together	symbiosis, symbol, symmetry, sympathy
syn-	together	synchronize, syndrome, synergy

PREFIXES THAT EXPRESS NEGATION

Prefix	Meaning	Examples
a-	not	apathy, atheist, atrophy, atypical
an-	not	anemia, anarchy, anesthesia, anorexia
counter-	opposite	counteract, countermand
de-	opposite	deactivate, deform, degrade, deplete
for-	prohibit	forbid, forget, forgo, forsake, forswear
il-	not	illegal, illegible, illegitimate, illiterate
im-	not	imbalance, immaculate, immature
in-	not	inaccurate, inactive, inadvertent
ir-	not	irrational, irreconcilable, irredeemable
ne-	not	nefarious, never
neg-	not	negative, neglect, negotiate
non-	not	nonchalant, nonconformist, nondescript
un-	opposite	unable, undo, unbeaten, uncertain

PREFIXES THAT MAKE A JUDGMENT

Prefix	Meaning	Examples
anti-	against	antinuclear, antisocial, antislavery
bene-	good	benediction, benefactor, beneficial
contra-	against	contraband, contraception, contradict
dys-	bad	dysentery, dysfunction, dyspepsia
eu-	good	Eucharist, eugenic, euphoria, eulogy
mal-	bad	maladjusted, malaise, malevolent
mis-	bad	misanthrope, misbehave, miscarriage
pro-	for	pro-American, pro-education

MISCELLANEOUS PREFIXES

Prefix	Meaning	Examples
ambi-	both, around	ambidextrous, ambience, ambiguous
amphi-	both, around	amphibian, amphitheater, amphora

Prefix	Meaning	Examples
auto-	self	autobiography, autocratic, autograph
be-	make	becalm, befriend, beguile, bewitch
hetero-	different	heterodox, heteronym, heterosexual
homo-	same	homogeneous, homogenize, homograph
meta-	change	metabolism, metamorphosis, metaphor
neo-	new	neoclassic, neologism, neon, neonatal
para-	almost	paralegal, paramedic
pseudo-	false	pseudoclassic, pseudonym, pseudopod
re-	again	reappear, reclassify, recopy, redo, repaint
self-	self	self-denial, self-respect, selfish

See also List 24, Suffixes; List 27, Greek and Latin Roots; List 28, -Ology Word Family; List 29, -Phobia and -Cide Word Families; List 127, Double-Letter Spelling Patterns.

List 24. SUFFIXES

Suffixes are letter groups that are added to the end of a base word or root. They frequently signify the part of speech and sometimes add meaning. There are two types of suffixes: derivational and inflectional.

Derivational suffixes are more numerous. When added to a base word, this type of suffix creates a new word that is "derived" from the base word but has a different meaning. For example, the addition of -less to hope creates hopeless, a word related to but different in meaning. The following is a list of derivational suffixes. The most frequently occurring suffixes are listed at the beginning level. Suffixes that are somewhat less frequent but still quite common are listed in Intermediate to Advanced.

BEGINNING SUFFIXES

Suffix	Meaning	Examples
-able, -ible	is, can be	comfortable, learnable, walkable, climbable, perishable, durable, gullible, combustible
-ar, -er, -or	one who	beggar, liar, teacher, painter, seller, shipper, doctor, actor, editor
-en	to make	strengthen, fasten, lengthen, frighten, weaken
-er	more	smarter, closer, lighter, quicker, softer, luckier
-ess	one who (female)	princess, waitress, countess, hostess, actress
-est	most	smartest, closest, lightest, quickest, softest, luckiest
-ette	small	dinette, diskette, majorette, barrette
-ful	full of	joyful, fearful, careful, thoughtful, cheerful
-ish	relating to	childish, fiftyish, bookish, selfish
-less	without	thoughtless, tireless, joyless, ageless, careless
-like	resembling	lifelike, homelike, childlike, computerlike
-ly	resembling	fatherly, scholarly, motherly, sisterly, brotherly
-ment	action or process	government, development, experiment
-ness	state or quality of	kindness, happiness, goodness, darkness, fullness
-ship	state or quality of	friendship, hardship, citizenship, internship

INTERMEDIATE TO ADVANCED SUFFIXES

Suffix	Meaning	Examples
-a, -ae	plural	data, criteria, memoranda, alumnae, algae, formulae
-acious	inclined to	loquacious, mendacious, audacious, fallacious
-ade	action or process	blockade, promenade, escapade
-age	action or process	marriage, voyage, pilgrimage, blockage, rummage
-an	relating to	urban, American, veteran, Hawaiian, metropolitan
-ance, -ence	state or quality of	repentance, annoyance, resistance, violence, absence, reticence

Suffix	Meaning	Examples
-ancy, -ency	state or quality of	buoyance, truancy, vacancy, vagrancy, frequency, clemency, expediency, consistency
-ant, -ent	one who	servant, immigrant, assistant, merchant, regent, superintendent, resident
-ant	inclined to	vigilant, pleasant, defiant, buoyant, observant
-arian	one who	librarian, humanitarian, libertarian
-arium, -orium	place for	aquarium, planetarium, solarium, auditorium
-ary, -ory	place for	library, mortuary, sanctuary, infirmary, laboratory, conservatory
-ation, -ion, -sion, -tion	state or quality of	desperation, starvation, inspiration, tension, caution, suspicion, attention, fascination, companion
-ative	inclined to	demonstrative, pejorative, talkative
-ble	repeated action	stumble, squabble, mumble, tumble, fumble
-dom	state or quality of	freedom, boredom, martyrdom, wisdom
-ectomy	surgical removal of	tonsillectomy, appendectomy, mastectomy
-ee	object of action	payee, lessee, employee
-ence	state or quality of	violence, absence, reticence, abstinence
-ency	state or quality of	frequency, clemency, expediency, consistency
-enne	female	comedienne, equestrienne, tragedienne
-er	action or process	murder, plunder, waiver, flounder, thunder
-ern	direction	eastern, western, northern, postern
-ery	state or quality of	bravery, savagery, forgery, slavery
-ese	state or quality of	Japanese, Chinese, Portuguese, Siamese
-esque	relating to	statuesque, picturesque, Romanesque
-etic	relating to	alphabetic, dietetic, frenetic, athletic, sympathetic
-hood	state or quality of	childhood, adulthood, falsehood, nationhood
-ial, -ian	relating to	filial, commercial, remedial, barbarian, Christian
-ic, ical	relating to	comic, historic, poetic, public, rhetorical, economical
-ics	scientific or social	physics, economics, politics, statistics, system demographics
-ide, -ine	chemical compound	fluoride, peroxide, sulfide, iodine, chlorine, quinine
-ina, ine	female	czarina, ballerina, Wilhelmina, heroine, Josephine
-ify	to make	satisfy, terrify, falsify, beautify, villify
-ious	state or quality of	gracious, ambitious, religious, nutritious, delicious
-ism	doctrine of	capitalism, socialism, communism, patriotism
-ist	one who practices	biologist, capitalist, communist, philanthropist
-itis	inflammation of	laryngitis, arthritis, bronchitis, appendicitis

The Reading Teacher's Book of Lists, Fourth Edition, © 2000 by John Wiley & Sons, Inc.

Suffix	Meaning	Examples
-ity, ty	state or quality of	necessity, civility, parity, loyalty, honesty, amnesty, unity
-ive	inclined to	active, passive, negative, restive, positive
-ization	state or quality of	civilization standardization, organization
-ize	to make	standardize, computerize, popularize, pulverize, pasteurize
-ling	small	duckling, yearling, suckling, fledgling
-most	most	utmost, westernmost, innermost, foremost
-oid	resembling	humanoid, asteroid, paranoid, planetoid
-ose	sugars	glucose, sucrose, fructose, dextrose
-ous	full of	joyous, virtuous, nervous, wondrous
-phobia	fear of	claustrophobia, acrophobia (see List 29, -Phobia and -Cide Word Families)
-some	inclined to	meddlesome, awesome, tiresome, fulsome
-th, -eth	numbers	fifth, twelfth, twentieth, fiftieth
-ulent	full of	turbulent, corpulent, fraudulent, truculent
-und	state or quality of	rotund, fecund, moribund, jocund
-uous	state or quality of	contemptuous, tempestuous, sensuous, vacuous
-ure	action or process	censure, procure, endure, inure, secure
-ward	direction	forward, backward, eastward, upward, onward
-ways	manner	sideways, longways, crossways
-wise	manner, direction	clockwise, lengthwise, counterclockwise
-y	being or having	fruity, sunny, rainy, funny, gooey, chewy

Inflectional suffixes indicate the grammatical form of words such as the tense or case of verbs, whether a word is an adjective or adverb, and whether a noun is plural or singular. While this sounds complicated, most native speakers of English are already using most of these suffixes in their speech prior to the beginning of formal reading instruction. Therefore, your primary task is to help them translate endings they already know into sounds. If students are reading for meaning, this may happen almost automatically.

Noun Suffix
-*s* indicates that a noun is plural: books, boys, pencils, dogs, shoes, hands, desks, teachers, students

Adjective Suffixes
Many nouns and/or verbs are changed to adjectives using suffixes. Here are some examples:
-*y* (milk—milky; trick—tricky; boss—bossy)
-*like* (child—childlike; boy—boylike; life—lifelike)
-*ful* (care—careful; thought—thoughtful; fear—fearful)
-*ish* (tickle—ticklish; child—childish; Scot—Scottish)
-*ic* (scene—scenic; history—historic; metal—metallic)
-*ese* (Japan—Japanese; Siam—Siamese; China—Chinese)
-*ward* (east—eastward; west—westward; south—southward)
-*en* (stole—stolen; chose—chosen; write—written)

These suffixes are used to compare adjectives:
  -*er* (fatter, shorter, crazier, smarter, faster)
  -*est* (fattest, shortest, craziest, smartest, fastest)

Verb Suffixes

  -*ed* indicates past tense: walked, cooked, studied, dressed, jumped, cried, typed, tried
  -*ing* indicates a present participle: eating, singing, freezing, studying, dressing, going
  -*en* indicates past participle: eaten, frozen, stolen, written, hidden, forgotten, spoken
  -*s* indicates third-person singular: walks, cooks, studies, dresses, plays, runs, teaches

Adverb Suffix

-*ly* (or -*ily* if the base word ends in y) indicates an adverb. Many adjectives can be changed to adverbs by adding *ly*. Examples: quick—quickly, clear—clearly, beautiful—beautifully, slow—slowly, skillful—skillfully, neat—neatly, plain—plainly, loud—loudly, soft—softly, clumsy—clumsily, hungry—hungrily, greedy—greedily

NOUN SUFFIXES

Suffix	Meaning	Examples
-a	plural	data, criteria, memoranda
-ade	action or process	blockage, escapade, parade, promenade
-ade	product or thing	lemonade, marmalade
-ae	plural (feminine)	alumnae, formulae, larvae, algae
-age	action or process	marriage, voyage, pilgrimage
-ance	state or quality of	repentance, annoyance, resistance
-ancy	state or quality of	buoyancy, truancy, vacancy, vagrancy
-ant	one who	servant, immigrant, assistant, merchant
-ar	one who	beggar, liar
-ard	one who	drunkard, steward, coward, wizard
-arian	one who	librarian, humanitarian, libertarian
-arium	place for	aquarium, planetarium, solarium
-ary	place for	library, mortuary, sanctuary, infirmary
-ation	state or quality of	desperation, starvation, inspiration
-ation	action or process	emancipation, narration, computation
-cle	small	corpuscle, particle, icicle, cubicle
-cule	small	minuscule, molecule
-crat	person of power	democrat, autocrat
-cy	state or quality of	accuracy, bankruptcy, conspiracy
-cy	action or process	truancy, diplomacy, vagrancy, piracy
-dom	state or quality of	freedom, boredom, martyrdom, wisdom
-ectomy	surgical removal of	tonsillectomy, appendectomy, mastectomy
-ee	object of action	payee, lessee, employee
-ence	state or quality of	violence, absence, reticence, abstinence
-ency	state or quality of	frequency, clemency, expediency, consistency
-enne	female	comedienne, equestrienne, tragedienne
-ent	one who	superintendent, resident, regent
-er	one who	teacher, painter, seller, shipper
-er	action or process	murder, thunder, plunder, waiver

The Reading Teacher's Book of Lists, Fourth Edition, © 2000 by John Wiley & Sons, Inc.

Suffix	Meaning	Examples
-ery, -ry	trade or occupation	surgery, archery, sorcery, dentistry
-ery	establishment	bakery, grocery, fishery, nunnery
-ery, -ry	goods or products	pottery, jewelry, cutlery
-ery, -ry	state or quality of	bravery, savagery, forgery, butchery
-ess	one who (female)	waitress, actress, countess, hostess
-et	small	midget, sonnet, bassinet, cygnet
-ette	small (female)	dinette, cigarette, majorette
-eur	one who	chauffeur, connoisseur, masseur
-eur	state or quality of	hauteur, grandeur
-hood, -fy	state or quality of, cause to be	childhood, adulthood, falsehood, beautify, solidify
-i	plural	alumni, foci
-ics	scientific or social system	physics, economics, politics, statistics
-ier, -yer	one who	cashier, financier, gondolier, lawyer
-ide	chemical	fluoride, bromide, peroxide compound
-ina	female	czarina, Wilhelmina, ballerina
-ine	chemical or basic substance	iodine, chlorine, caffeine, quinine
-ine	female	heroine, Josephine, Pauline
-ing	material	bedding, roofing, frosting, stuffing
-ion	state or quality of	champion, companion, ambition, suspicion
-ish	near or like	pinkish, sevenish
-ism	state or quality of	baptism, heroism, racism, despotism
-ism	doctrine of	capitalism, socialism, hedonism
-ist	one who practices	biologist, capitalist, communist
-ite	mineral or rock	granite, anthracite, bauxite
-itis	inflammation of	laryngitis, arthritis, bronchitis
-ity, ty	state or quality of	necessity, felicity, civility, parity
-ization	state or quality of	civilization, standardization, organization
-kin	small	lambkin, napkin, manikin, Munchkin
-let	small	owlet, rivulet, starlet, leaflet, islet
-ling	small	duckling, yearling, suckling, fledgling
-man	one who works with	cameraman, mailman, doorman
-mat	automatic machine	laundromat, vendomat
-ment	action or process	embezzlement, development, government
-ment	state or quality of	amusement, predicament, amazement
-ment	product or thing	instrument, ornament, fragment
-mony	product or thing	testimony, matrimony, ceremony, alimony
-ness	state or quality of	happiness, kindness, goodness, darkness
-ol	alcohols	methanol, ethanol, glycol
-ology	study or science of	biology, psychology (see List 28, -Ology Word Family)
-or	one who	actor, doctor, donor, auditor
-or	state or quality of	error, stupor, candor, fervor, pallor
-orium	place for	auditorium, emporium

Suffix	Meaning	Examples
-ory	place for	laboratory, conservatory, purgatory
-ose	sugars	glucose, sucrose, fructose, dextrose
-osis	abnormal increase	tuberculosis, fibrosis
-phobia	fear of	claustrophobia, acrophobia (see List 29, -Phobia and -Cide Word Families)
-s, -es	plural	pens, books, boxes, parentheses
-'s	possession	John's, dog's
-ship	skill or art of	penmanship, showmanship, horsemanship
-ship	state or quality of	friendship, hardship, citizenship
-sion	state or quality of	tension, compulsion
-th	state or quality of	strength, warmth, filth, depth, length
-tion	state or quality of	attention, caution, fascination
-trix	female	aviatrix, executrix
-tude	state or quality of	gratitude, fortitude, beatitude
-ty	state or quality of	loyalty, honesty, amnesty, unity
-ure	action or process	censure, failure, enclosure, exposure
-wright	one who works with	playwright, shipwright, wheelwright

ADJECTIVE SUFFIXES

Suffix	Meaning	Examples
-acious	inclined to	loquacious, mendacious, audacious, fallacious
-al	relating to	natural, royal, maternal, suicidal
-an	relating to	urban, American, Alaskan, veteran
-ant	inclined to	vigilant, pleasant, defiant, buoyant
-ary	relating to	honorary, military, literary, ordinary
-ate	state or quality of	fortunate, desperate, passionate
-ative	inclined to	demonstrative, pejorative, talkative
-ble	inclined to	gullible, perishable, voluble, durable
-en	relating to	golden, ashen, wooden, earthen
-ent	inclined to	competent, different, excellent
-er	more (comparative)	fatter, smaller, crazier, smarter
-ern	direction	eastern, western, northern, postern
-ese	state or quality of	Japanese, Portuguese, Chinese, Siamese
-esque	relating to	statuesque, picturesque, Romanesque
-est	most (comparative)	fattest, smallest, smartest, fastest
-etic	relating to	alphabetic, dietetic, frenetic
-ful	full of	thoughtful, joyful, careful, fearful
-ial	relating to	filial, commercial, remedial
-ian	relating to	barbarian, physician, Christian
-ic	relating to	comic, historic, poetic, public
-ical	relating to	comical, rhetorical, economical
-ide	state or quality of	candid, sordid, lucid, splendid, rigid
-ile	state or quality of	virile, agile, volatile, docile, fragile
-ine	relating to	feminine, bovine, feline, marine

The Reading Teacher's Book of Lists, Fourth Edition, © 2000 by John Wiley & Sons, Inc.

Suffix	Meaning	Examples
-ious	state or quality of	gracious, ambitious, religious
-ish	relating to	childish, whitish, fiftyish, Scottish
-ive	inclined to	active, passive, negative, affirmative
-less	without	thoughtless, tireless, ageless, careless
-like	resembling	childlike, homelike, lifelike, boylike
-ly	resembling	fatherly, motherly, scholarly
-ly	every	daily, weekly, monthly, yearly
-most	most	utmost, westernmost, innermost
-oid	resembling	humanoid, asteroid, paranoid, planetoid
-ose	full of	verbose, morose, bellicose, comatose
-ous	full of	joyous, virtuous, nervous, wondrous
-some	inclined to	meddlesome, awesome, tiresome
-th, -eth	numbers	fifth, twelfth, twentieth, fiftieth
-ular	relating to	granular, cellular, circular, popular
-ulent	full of	turbulent, corpulent, fraudulent
-und	state or quality of	rotund, fecund, moribund, jocund
-uous	state or quality of	contemptuous, tempestuous, sensuous
-ward	direction	forward, backward, eastward, upward
-y	state or quality of	fruity, sunny, rainy, funny, gooey

VERB SUFFIXES

Suffix	Meaning	Examples
-ade	action or process	blockade, promenade, parade
-age	action or process	ravage, pillage
-ate	to make	activate, fascinate, annihilate, liberate
-ble	repeated action	stumble, squabble, mumble, tumble, fumble
-ed, -d	past tense	talked, walked, baked, raised
-en	past completed action	taken, eaten, proven, stolen
-en	to make	strengthen, fasten, lengthen, frighten, weaken
-er	action or process	discover, murder, conquer, deliver
-fy	to make	satisfy, terrify, falsify, beautify
-ing	continuous action	singing, talking, jumping, eating
-ish	action or process	finish, flourish, nourish, punish
-ize	to make	standardize, computerize, popularize
-s, -es	form third person	runs, finishes
-ure	action or process	censure, procure, endure, inure

ADVERB SUFFIXES

Suffix	Meaning	Examples
-ly	forms adverb from adjective	slowly, beautifully, happily, largely
-ways	manner	sideways, always, longways, crossways
-wise	manner, direction	clockwise, lengthwise

See also List 23, Prefixes; List 27, Greek and Latin Roots; List 128, Spelling Rules for Adding Suffixes; List 129, Plurals; List 150, Parts of Speech.

The Reading Teacher's Book of Lists, Fourth Edition, © 2000 by John Wiley & Sons, Inc.

List 25. SYNONYMS

Synonyms are words that have similar meanings. Dictionaries often use synonyms in their definitions. There are whole books of synonyms and special reference works, such as the thesaurus, that have clusters of words or phrases, all with similar meanings. These are particularly useful in finding just the right word when writing. **Caution:** A synonym may be for only one meaning of a word with several meanings.

able—capable—competent
abrupt—sudden—hasty
achieve—accomplish—attain
add—total—sum up
after—following—subsequent
aim—purpose—goal
all—every—entire
allow—permit—grant
anger—rage—fury
answer—response—reply
arrive—reach—get to
ask—question—interrogate
astonish—surprise—amaze

back—rear—behind
bear—endure—tolerate
before—prior to—in front of
begin—start—initiate
below—under—beneath
birth—origin—genesis
border—edge—margin
bother—annoy—pester
boy—lad—youth
brave—courageous—daring
bulge—swell—portrude
busy—occupied—engaged

call—shout—yell
calm—composed—serene
car—auto—vehicle
carry—tote—lug
careful—cautious—prudent
change—vary—alter
charm—fascinate—enchant
cheat—deceive—swindle
children—youngsters—tots
city—borough—town
close—shut—seal
consent—agree—acquiesce
continue—persevere—persist
country—nation—state
cure—heal—restore

danger—peril—hazard
decrease—lessen—diminish
defect—flaw—blemish
delay—postpone—procrastinate
different—varied—diverse
disaster—calamity—catastrophe
divide—separate—split
during—while—at the same time
dwell—live—reside

eat—consume—devour
effort—exertion—endeavor
end—finish—complete
energy—power—strength
enough—adequate—sufficient
error—mistake—fallacy
explain—expound—elucidate

faith—trust—reliance
fat—plump—stout
fetch—bring—retrieve
find—locate—discover
fix—repair—mend
flat—level—flush
food—nourishment—sustenance
form—shape—make up
fragile—delicate—breakable
freedom—independence—liberty
frequent—often—many times

gay—lively—vivacious
gift—present—donation
give—grant—hand over
glum—morose—sullen
go—leave—depart
grateful—appreciative—thankful
great—grand—large
grow—mature—develop

happy—glad—joyous
hard—difficult—troublesome
hate—detest—despise

The Reading Teacher's Book of Lists, Fourth Edition, © 2000 by John Wiley & Sons, Inc.

have—own—possess
heal—mend—cure
help—aid—assist
hide—conceal—secrete
high—tall—lofty
hold—grasp—clutch
hurry—rush—accelerate

idea—thought—concept
ill—sick—indisposed
income—revenue—earnings
injure—wound—hurt

job—work—occupation
junk—rubbish—waste
just—fair—right

keep—hold—retain
key—answer—solution
kind—considerate—helpful
kill—slaughter—murder

large—big—enormous
last—endure—persist
late—tardy—delayed
learn—acquire—understand
leave—depart—go away
like—enjoy—be fond of
listen—hear—attend
little—small—petite
long—lengthy—drawn out
look—glance—see

mad—crazy—insane
make—build—construct
many—multitudinous—numerous
marvelous—wonderful—extraordinary
mean—stand for—denote
mend—repair—restore
method—way—manner
might—may—perhaps
mistake—error—blunder
move—transport—propel

name—title—designation
near—close by—in the vicinity
need—require—want
new—fresh—recent
noise—uproar—clamor
novice—beginner—learner

occur—happen—take place
often—frequently—repeatedly
old—aged—ancient
omit—delete—remove
one—single—unit
open—unlock—unseal
ornament—decoration—adornment
outlive—survive—outlast

page—sheet—leaf
pain—ache—hurt
pair—couple—duo
pardon—forgive—excuse
part—portion—piece
peak—summit—top
people—public—populace
play—frolic—romp
praise—acclaim—applaud
primary—chief—principal
prohibit—forbid—restrict
put—place—locate

raid—attack—invade
reckless—careless—rash
remote—distant—secluded
renew—restore—revive
respect—honor—revive
revise—alter—correct
right—correct—proper

say—state—remark
seem—appear—look
sell—vend—market
shame—humiliation—mortification
show—demonstrate—display
sorry—regretful—penitent
speed—haste—hurry
start—begin—commence
still—unmoving—silent
stop—halt—end
story—tale—account
strength—power—energy
supply—provide—furnish
surpass—exceed—outdo

take—grab—seize
tense—taut—rigid
terrify—frighten—alarm
thanks—gratitude—appreciation
thaw—melt—dissolve

thief—robber—crook
thin—slender—slim
think—reflect—comtemplate
time—period—season
timid—fearful—cowardly
tiny—small—diminutive
trial—test—experiment
true—faithful—loyal
try—attempt—endeavor
turn—revolve—pivot

ugly—homely—plain
understand—comprehend—discern
unify—consolidate—combine
uproar—tumult—pandemonium
urge—press—exhort

use—operate—employ
vacant—empty—unoccupied
value—worth—price
vast—huge—immense
verify—confirm—substantiate
victor—winner—champion

walk—stroll—saunter
want—desire—crave
waver—fluctuate—vaccillate
weak—feeble—impotent
wealth—riches—fortune
word—term—expression
work—labor—toil
world—globe—earth
write—record—draft

The Reading Teacher's Book of Lists, Fourth Edition, © 2000 by John Wiley & Sons, Inc.

See also List 60, Descriptive Words; List 62, He Said/She Said; List 63, Similes; List 64, Metaphors; List 114, Analogies.

List 26. ANTONYMS

Antonyms are words that mean the opposite or nearly the opposite of each other for one meaning. Both synonyms and antonyms are often used in tests and language drills.
Caution: An antonym may be for only one meaning of a word with several meanings.

The Reading Teacher's Book of Lists, Fourth Edition, © 2000 by John Wiley & Sons, Inc.

above—below
absent—present
accident—intent
accomplishment—failure
achieve—fail
add—subtract
adjacent—distant
admire—detest
admit—reject
adore—hate
advance—retreat
affirm—deny
afraid—confident
after—before
aid—hinder
alarm—comfort
alert—asleep
alive—dead
allow—forbid
alone—together
amateur—professional
amuse—bore
ancient—modern
annoy—soothe
answer—question
apparent—obscure
argue—agree
arrive—depart
arrogant—humble
ascend—descend
attack—defend
attract—repel
awake—asleep
awkward—graceful

back—front
bad—good
bare—covered
beautiful—ugly
before—after
bent—straight
better—worse
big—little
birth—death

bitter—sweet
black—white
blunt—sharp
body—soul
bold—timid
bottom—top
boy—girl
brave—cowardly
break—repair
brief—long
bright—dull
bring—remove
busy—idle
buy—sell

capture—release
cause—effect
cautious—careless
center—edge
change—remain
cheap—expensive
child—adult
chilly—warm
clean—dirty
close—open
cold—hot
command—obey
complex—simple
compliment—insult
constant—variable
continue—interrupt
cool—warm
copy—original
countrymen—foreigner
crazy—sane
crooked—straight
cruel—kind
cry—laugh
curse—bless

damage—improve
dark—light
dawn—sunset
day—night

deep—shallow
destroy—create
difficult—easy
dim—bright
divide—unite
doubt—trust
drunk—sober
dull—sharp
dumb—smart

earth—sky
east—west
easy—hard
elementary—advanced
end—begin
even—odd
evening—morning
evil—good
exceptional—common
expand—shrink

fail—pass
failure—success
false—true
famous—unknown
fancy—plain
fast—slow
fat—thin
fiction—fact
find—lose
finish—start
firm—flabby
fix—break
follow—lead
forgive—blame
forward—backward
free—restricted
fresh—stale
friend—enemy
funny—sad
full—empty

gain—lose
generous—stingy

103

gentle—harsh
get—give
give—receive
glad—sad
gloomy—cheerful
glossy—dull
go—come
gorgeous—ugly
great—small
greed—generous
grief—joy
ground—sky
guard—attack
guess—know

handsome—ugly
happy—sad
hard—soft
hate—love
he—she
head—foot
heal—infect
healthy—sick
heaven—hell
heavy—light
height—depth
help—hinder
hero—coward
high—low
hill—valley
him—her
hire—fire
his—hers
hot—cold
horrible—pleasant
huge—tiny
hurry—slow
hurt—help

idle—active
in—out
individual—group
innocent—guilty
inside—outside
intelligent—stupid

jolly—serious
joy—sadness

keep—lose
kind—cruel
knowledge—ignorance

large—small
last—first
laugh—cry
leading—following
leave—arrive
left—right
less—more
let—prevent
level—uneven
lie—truth
life—death
like—dislike
likely—unlikely
liquid—solid
little—big
lively—inactive
lonely—crowded
long—short
loose—tight
lost—found
loud—soft
love—hate

maintain—discontinue
major—minor
make—destroy
male—female
man—woman
many—few
marvelous—terrible
mature—immature
melt—freeze
mess—tidiness
miscellaneous—specific
mistake—accuracy
mix—separate
moist—dry
more—less
most—least
mother—father
move—stay

naive—sophisticated
nasty—nice
near—far
never—always
new—old
no—yes
nobody—everybody
noise—quiet
none—all

north—south
nothing—something
now—then

obese—thin
obvious—hidden
odd—even
offend—please
offer—refuse
often—seldom
old—young
on—off
one—several
ordinary—uncommon
other—same
over—under

pacify—agitate
pain—pleasure
panic—calm
part—whole
partial—complete
particular—general
pass—fail
passive—active
peace—disturbance
perceive—ignore
permanent—unstable
permit—refuse
pessimistic—optimistic
physical—spiritual
place—misplace
plain—fancy
play—work
plentiful—sparse
plump—thin
polish—dull
polite—rude
pollute—purify
poor—rich
positive—negative
powerful—weak
praise—criticism
preceding—following
present—absent
pretty—ugly
prevent—encourage
pride—modesty
private—public
problem—solution

The Reading Teacher's Book of Lists, Fourth Edition, © 2000 by John Wiley & Sons, Inc.

profit—loss
prohibit—allow
pupil—teacher
push—pull

quality—inferiority
quick—slow
quiet—noise
quit—start

raise—lower
random—specific
rapid—slow
rare—common
raw—cooked
ready—unprepared
rear—front
reduce—increase
regret—rejoice
relax—tighten
remember—forget
repair—destroy
retain—lose
revenge—forgiveness
ridiculous—sensible
right—wrong
rigid—flexible
rise—sink
rough—smooth
rude—polite

sad—happy
same—different
satisfy—displease
secluded—public
segregate—integrate
seldom—often
sell—buy
send—receive
sensational—dull
servant—master
shack—palace
shade—light
shame—honor
sharp—dull
she—he
short—long

show—hide
shy—trusting
sick—healthy
silence—sound
single—married
single—plural
sit—stand
slave—master
slender—fat
slow—fast
small—large
soak—dry
sober—drunk
some—none
something—nothing
sorrow—gladness
sour—sweet
speechless—talkative
spend—earn
stale—fresh
start—stop
started—finished
stay—leave
steal—provide
sterile—fertile
stiff—flexible
still—moving
stingy—generous
stop—go
stranger—friend
strength—weakness
student—teacher
sturdy—weak
sunrise—sunset
superb—inferior
supple—rigid
survive—die
suspect—trust

take—give
tall—short
tame—wild
teach—learn
temporary—permanent
thaw—freeze
there—here
thin—thick

thorough—incomplete
thrifty—wasteful
tidy—messy
tie—loosen
timid—bold
to—from
together—apart
told—asked
top—bottom
toward—away
tragic—comic
transform—retain
transparent—opaque
triumph—defeat
true—false
truth—lie

ultimate—primary
union—separation
unique—common
up—down
upset—stabilize
urge—deter

vacant—full
vague—definite
vanish—appear
vast—limited
vertical—horizontal
villain—hero
visitor—host/hostess

waive—require
wake—sleep
wealth—poverty
weep—laugh
well—badly
wet—dry
white—black
wild—tame
win—lose
with—without
worship—detest
worth—uselessness
wreck—create

See also List 25, Synonyms.

List 27. GREEK AND LATIN ROOTS

Most modern English words originated in other languages. The study of word origins, or etymology, is a fascinating subject. The Greek and Latin roots in this list can form the basis for a number of vocabulary-building lessons. Roots are taught successfully in families such as *microscope, telescope, periscope*, to illustrate that *scope* means "see." In the following list, Greek roots are indicated with "G" and Latin roots with "L." Roots have been divided into two categories: more common and less common roots.

MORE COMMON ROOTS

Root	Meaning	Examples
act (L)	do	action, actor, react, transact, enact
aero (G)	air	aerobics, aerodynamics, aeronautics, aerate
agr (L)	field	agriculture, agrarian, agronomy, agribusiness
alter (L)	other	alter, alternate, alternative, altercation, alterego
anim (L)	life, spirit	animate, animosity, animal, inanimate
ann, enn (L)	year	annual, anniversary, annuity, biennial, millennium
aqua (L)	water	aquarium, aquatic, aqueous, aquamarine, aquifer
ast (G)	star	astronaut, astronomy, disaster, asterisk, asteroid
aud (L)	hear	audience, auditorium, audible, audition, audiovisual
biblio (G)	book	bibliography, Bible, bibliophile, bibliotherapy
bio (G)	life	biology, biography, biochemistry, biopsy, biosphere
card, cord (L)	heart	cardiac, cardiology, cardiogram, cardiovascular cordial, accord, concord, discord
chron (G)	time	chronological, synchronize, chronicle, chronic
claim, clam (L)	shout	proclaim, exclaim, acclaim, clamor, exclamation
cogn (L)	know	recognize, incognito, cognition, cognizant
corp (L)	body	corporation, corpse, corps, corpuscle, corpus
cosm (G)	universe	cosmonaut, cosmos, cosmopolitan, microcosm
cred (L)	believe	credit, discredit, incredible, credential, credulous
cycl (G)	circle, ring	bicycle, cyclone, cycle, encyclopedia, recycle
dic (L)	speak	dictate, predict, contradict, verdict, diction
doc (L)	teach	doctrine, document, doctor, indoctrinate, docile
don, donat (L)	give	donation, donor, pardon, donate
duc (L)	lead	duct, conduct, educate, induct, aquaduct
fac, fic (L)	make, do	factory, manufacture, benefactor, facsimile efficient, proficient, sufficient, beneficial
flect, flex (L)	bend	reflect, deflect, reflection, inflection, genuflect reflex, flexible
form (L)	shape	form, uniform, transform, reform, formal
gen (G)	birth, race	generation, generate, genocide, progeny, genealogy
geo (G)	earth	geography, geometry, geology, geophysics

The Reading Teacher's Book of Lists, Fourth Edition, © 2000 by John Wiley & Sons, Inc.

Root	Meaning	Examples
gram (G)	letter, written	telegram, diagram, grammar, epigram, monogram
graph (G)	write	photograph, phonograph, autograph, biography, graphite
homo, hom (L)	man	homicide, hombre, homage, Homo sapiens
junct (L)	join	juncture, conjunction, adjunct, injunction
jud, jur, jus (L)	law	judge, judicial, jury, jurisdiction, justice, justify
lab (L)	work	labor, laboratory, collaborate, elaborate
liber (L)	free	liberty, liberal, liberate, libertine
loc (L)	place	location, locate, dislocate, allocate, local
man (L)	hand	manual, manufacture, manuscript, manipulate
mar (L)	sea	marine, submarine, mariner, maritime
mater, matr (L)	mother	maternal, maternity, matricide, matrimony, matron
meter (G)	measure	thermometer, centimeter, diameter, barometer
migr (L)	change, move	migrate, immigrant, emigrate, migratory
miss, mit (L)	send	missile, dismiss, mission, remiss submit, remit, admit, transmit
mob, mot, mov (L)	move	mobile, automobile, mobilize, motion, motor, promote, demote, motile, remove, movement
morph (G)	shape	amorphous, metamorphoses, morphology, polymorphous, anthropomorphic
mort (L)	death	mortician, mortuary, mortal, immortal, mortify
nat (L)	born	natal, native, nation, nativity, innate
ordin ord (L)	row, rank	order, ordinary, ordinal, extraordinary, ordinance
ortho (G)	straight, right	orthodontist, orthodox, orthopedist, orthography
pater, patr (L)	father	paternity, paternal, patricide, patriarch
path (G)	disease, feeling	pathology, sympathy, empathy, antipathy, pathos
ped (G)	child	pedagogy, pediatrician, encyclopedia
ped (L)	foot	pedal, pedestrian, biped, pedestal
phil (G)	love	philosophy, philanthropist, philharmonic, Anglophile, philology
phon (G)	sound	phonograph, symphony, telephone, microphone, phonics
photo (G)	light	photograph, telephoto, photosynthesis, photogenic
pod (G)	foot	podiatrist, podium, tripod
poli (G)	city	metropolis, cosmopolitan, police, political
port (L)	carry	portable, transport, import, export, porter
psych (G)	mind, soul	psychology, psyche, psychopath, psychiatrist
ques, quer, quis (L)	ask, seek	question, inquest, request, query, inquisitive
rad (L)	ray, spoke	radius, radio, radiation, radium, radiator, radiology
rect (L)	straight	erect, rectangle, rectify, direction, correct
rupt (L)	break	rupture, erupt, interrupt, abrupt, bankrupt
san (L)	health	sanitary, sanitation, sane, insanity, sanitarium

Root	Meaning	Examples
saur (G)	lizard	dinosaur, brontosaurus, stegosaurus
sci (G)	know	science, conscience, conscious, omniscient
scop (G)	see	microscope, telescope, periscope, stethoscope
scribe, script (L)	write	scribe, inscribe, describe, prescribe, script, transcript, scripture
sign (L)	mark	signal, signature, significant, insignia
spec (L)	see	inspect, suspect, respect, spectator, spectacle
struct (L)	build	structure, construct, instruct, destruction
tact (L)	touch	tactile, intact, contact, tact
terr (L)	land	territory, terrain, terrestrial, terrace
therm (G)	heat	thermometer, thermal, thermostat, Thermos
tract (L)	pull, drag	tractor, attract, subtract, traction, extract, contract
trib (L)	give	contribute, tribute, tributary, attribute
urb (L)	city	urban, suburb, urbane, suburban
vac (L)	empty	vacant, vacation, vacuum, evacuate, vacate
var (L)	different	vary, invariable, variant, variety, various
vid, vis (L)	see	video, evidence, provide, providence, visible
voc (L)	voice	vocal, advocate, evocation, convocation
void (L)	empty	void, devoid, avoid, voided, unavoidable
vol (L)	wish, will	volition, volunteer, voluntary, benevolent
volv (L)	turn	revolve, involve, evolve, revolver, revolution

LESS COMMON ROOTS

Root	Meaning	Examples
aesthet, esthet (G)	sense, perception	aesthetic, aesthete, anesthesia, anesthetist
alt (L)	high	altitude, altimeter, alto, altocumulus
ambul, amb (L)	walk, go	ambulance, circumambulate, somnambulate, amble, preamble
amo, ami (L)	love	amiable, amorous, amateur, amity
ang (L)	bend	angle, triangle, rectangle, angular, quadrangle
anthr (G)	man	anthropology, philanthropist, misanthrope
arch (G)	ruler, leader	monarch, archbishop, matriarch, oligarchy
archi, arch (G)	primitive, original	archaeology, archaic, archetype, archive
belli (L)	war	bellicose, antebellum, belligerent, rebellion
brev (L)	short	abbreviation, brevity, breve
cad, cas (L)	fall	cadence, cadaver, decadence, cascade
cam (L)	field	camp, campus, encamp, campaign
cand (L)	shine, white	candle, incandescent, candid, candidate
cap (L)	head	cap, captain, capital, decapitate, caput
cede, ceed, cess (L)	go, yield	concede, secede, proceed, exceed, succeed, process, recess, access, concession, cessation
ceive, cept (L)	take, receive	receive, reception, accept, conception, intercept

The Reading Teacher's Book of Lists, Fourth Edition, © 2000 by John Wiley & Sons, Inc.

Root	Meaning	Examples
centr (L)	center	central, centrifugal, egocentric, eccentric, geocentric
cert (L)	sure	certain, certify, ascertain, certificate
cide, cise (L)	cut, kill	suicide, insecticide, genocide, scissors, incision
clar (L)	clear	clarity, declare, clarify, declaration
cline (L)	lean	incline, recline, decline, inclination
clud (L)	shut	include, conclude, exclude, preclude, seclude
commun (L)	common	community, communicate, communism, communion, communal
cum (L)	heap	cumulative, accumulate, cumulus
cur (L)	care	cure, manicure, pedicure, curator, curette
cur (L)	run	current, occur, excursion, concur, recur
dem (G)	people	democracy, demography, endemic, epidemic
dent (L)	tooth	dentist, trident, dentifrice, indent, denture
div (L)	divide	divide, divorce, division, dividend, indivisible
domin (L)	master	dominate, predominate, dominion, A.D. (*Anno Domini*)
dox (G)	belief, praise	orthodox, heterodox, paradox, doxology
fer (L)	bear, carry	ferry, transfer, infer, refer, conifer
fid (L)	faith	fidelity, confidence, infidel, bona fide
fig (L)	form	figure, figment, configuration, disfigure, effigy
firm (L)	securely fixed	firm, confirm, infirm, affirm, firmament
fract, frag (L)	break	fracture, fraction, infraction, fractious fragment, fragile, fragmentary
frater (L)	brother	fraternal, fraternity, fratricide, fraternize
fric (L)	rub	friction, dentifrice, fricative
funct (L)	perform	function, malfunction, dysfunctional, perfunctory
gam (G)	marriage	polygamy, monogamy, bigamy, gamete, exogamy
gnos (G)	know	diagnose, prognosis, agnostic
gon (G)	angle	pentagon, diagonal, trigonometry, orthogonal
grad, gress (L)	step, go	gradual, grade, gradation, centigrade, graduation progress, egress, regress, aggression, congress
grat (L)	pleasing	gratitude, gradify, congratulate, ungrateful, ingrate
greg (L)	gather	gregarious, congregation, segregation, aggregate
gyn (G)	woman	gynecologist, misogynist, monogyny, androgyny
hab, hib (L)	hold	habit, habitual, habitat, prohibit, inhibit, exhibit
hosp, host (L)	guest, host	hospitality, hospital, hospice, hostess, host
hydr (G)	water	hydroelectric, hydrogen, hydrant, dehydrate
iatr (G)	medical care	psychiatry, podiatry, pediatrician, geriatrics
imag (L)	likeness	image, imagine, imaginative, imagery
init (L)	beginning	initial, initiate, initiative

Root	Meaning	Examples
integ (L)	whole	integrate, integral, integrity, integer
ject (L)	throw	project, inject, reject, subject, eject, conjecture
kine, cine (G)	movement	kinetic, kinesiology, telekinesis, cinema, cinematic
laps (L)	slip	elapse, collapse, relapse, prolapse
lith (L)	stone	lithograph, monolith, neolithic, paleolithic, megalith
log (G)	word	prologue, apology, dialogue, eulogy, monologue
luc, lum (L)	light	lucid, elucidate, translucent, illuminate, luminous
luna (L)	moon	lunar, lunatic, lunette
lust (L)	shine	luster, illustrate, lackluster, illustrious
lys (G)	break down	analysis, paralysis, electrolysis, catalyst
mand (L)	order	command, demand, mandate, remand
mania (G)	madness	maniac, pyromania, cleptomania, megalomania
max (L)	greatest	maximum, maxim, maximize
mech (G)	machine	mechanic, mechanism, mechanize
mem, ment (L)	mind	memory, remember, memorial, commemorate mental, mention, demented
merge, mers (L)	dive	submerge, emerge, merge, merger submerse, immerse
mim (L)	same	mimic, pantomime, mimeograph, mime
min (L)	small, less	mini, minimum, minor, minus, minimize
minist (L)	serve	minister, administer, administration
mon (L)	advise	admonish, premonition, monitor, admonition
mut (L)	change	mutation, immutable, mutual, commute
nav (L)	ship	navy, naval, navigate, circumnavigate
neg (L)	no	negation, abnegation, negative, renege
neo (L)	new	neophyte, neoclassical, neonatal, neologism
not (L)	mark	notation, notable, denote, notice, notify
noun, nun (L)	declare	announce, pronounce, denounce, enunciate
nov (L)	new	novel, novelty, novice, innovate, nova
numer (L)	number	numeral, enumerate, numerous, enumerable
ocu (L)	eye	oculist, binocular, monocular
onym (G)	name	synonym, antonym, pseudonym, anonymous
opt (G)	eye	optician, optometrist, optic, optical
opt (L)	best	optimum, optimist, optimal, optimize
orig (L)	beginning	origin, original, originate, aborigine
pel (L)	drive	propel, compel, expel, repel, repellant
pend (L)	hang	pendulum, suspend, append, appendix
phob (G)	fear	claustrophobia, xenophobia (See List 29, -Phobia and -Cide Word Families)
plur (L)	more	plural, plurality, pluralism
pop (L)	people	population, popular, pop, populace
pug (L)	fight	pugnacious, pugilist, repugnant, impugn

The Reading Teacher's Book of Lists, Fourth Edition, © 2000 by John Wiley & Sons, Inc.

Root	Meaning	Examples
reg (L)	rule, guide	regal, regent, reign, regulate, regime
rid (L)	laugh	ridiculous, deride, derisive, ridicule
scend (L)	climb	ascend, descend, transcend, descent
sect (L)	cut	section, dissect, intersect, sect, bisect
sed (L)	settle	sedative, sediment, sedentary, sedate
sens, sent (L)	feel	sensation, sense, sensitive, sensible, sensory sentimental, assent, dissent, consent
serv (L)	watch over	conserve, preserve, reserve, reservoir
serv (L)	slave	serve, servant, service, servile
sim (L)	like	similar, simultaneous, simulate, simile
sist (L)	stand	consist, resist, subsist, assist
sol (L)	alone	solo, solitary, desolate, soliloquy
solv (L)	loosen	dissolve, solve, solvent, resolve
son (L)	sound	sonar, sonata, sonnet, unison, sonorous
soph (G)	wise	philosopher, sophomore, sophisticated, sophist
spir (L)	breathe	respiration, inspire, spirit, perspire, conspire
sta (L)	stand	station, status, stabile, stagnant, statue
strict (L)	draw tight	strict, restrict, constrict, stricture
sum (L)	highest	summit, summary, sum, summons
surg, surr (L)	rise	surge, insurgent, resurgent, resurrect, insurrection, resurrection
tain, ten (L)	hold	retain, contain, detain, attain, maintain, sustain tenacious, tenure, tenant, retentive, tenable
ten (L)	stretch	tendon, tendency, tension, tent, tense
term (L)	end	terminal, terminate, determine, exterminate
tex (L)	weave	textile, texture, text, context
tort (L)	twist	torture, contort, retort, tort, contortion
trud, trus (L)	push	intrude, protrude, intruder, intrusive, obtrusive
turb (L)	confusion	disturb, turbulent, perturb, turbid
ven (L)	come	convene, convention, advent, invent, venue
ver (L)	truth	verify, verity, verdict, aver, veracity
ver (L)	turn	convert, reverse, versatile, introvert, convertible
vict, vinc (L)	conquer	victory, conviction, convince, invincible, vincible
vor (L)	eat	voracious, carnivore, herbivore, omnivorous

See also List 23, Prefixes; List 28, -Ology Word Family; List 29, -Phobia and -Cide Word Families.

The Reading Teacher's Book of Lists, Fourth Edition, © 2000 by John Wiley & Sons, Inc.

List 28. -OLOGY WORD FAMILY

Many subjects studied in schools and colleges have *-ology* in their names. The suffix *-ology* comes from Greek and means "science of" or "the study of." For example, since *cardia* means "heart," cardiology means "science of the heart." Moreover, since the suffix *-ist* means "one who practices" (see List 24, Suffixes), a cardiologist is "one who practices science of the heart."

WORD	MEANING	WORD	MEANING
anthropology	people, culture	ideology	doctrine of a group
archaeology	antiquities	immunology	immunity to disease
astrology	stars (supposed influence of stars and planets on human affairs—study of stars is astronomy)	meteorology	weather
		microbiology	microbes
		mineralogy	minerals
		morphology	structure of animals and plants
audiology	hearing	musicology	music
bacteriology	bacteria	mythology	myths
biology	life	neurology	nerves
biotechnology	using living organisms to make or improve things	oncology	tumors
		ornithology	birds
		ophthalmology	eyes
cardiology	heart	paleontology	fossils
chronology	measuring time	pathology	diseases
climatology	climate	pharmacology	drugs
cosmetology	cosmetics	physiology	life processes
cosmology	universe	pomology	fruit
criminology	crime	psychology	mind
cryptology	codes and ciphers	radiology	radiation
cytology	cells	seismology	earthquakes
dermatology	skin	sociology	society
ecology	relationship of organisms to their environment	technology	applied science
		theology	God
		toxicology	poisons
embryology	embryo	typology	classification based on type
entomology	insects		
epidemiology	widespread disease among people	zoology	animals
epistemology	knowledge		
ethnology	historical development of cultures		
etymology	word origins		
genealogy	ancestors		
geology	earth		
gerontology	old age		
gynecology	women		
hematology	blood		
herpetology	reptiles		
histology	living tissue		
hydrology	water		

See also List 27, Greek and Latin Roots; List 29, -Phobia and -Cide Word Families.

The Reading Teacher's Book of Lists, Fourth Edition, © 2000 by John Wiley & Sons, Inc.

List 29. -PHOBIA AND -CIDE
WORD FAMILIES

The Greek word *phobos,* meaning "fear," is combined with a variety of roots to form an interesting group of phobias. Some of these, such as claustrophobia (fear of closed spaces) or acrophobia (fear of high places), are quite common; others may be new to you. Use the root words of List 27 to coin a few of your own. How about "bibliophobia"? The root *cide* comes from Latin and means "killing."

The Reading Teacher's Book of Lists, Fourth Edition, © 2000 by John Wiley & Sons, Inc.

PHOBIA WORD	MEANING
acrophobia	fear of heights (edges)
aerophobia	fear of flying
agoraphobia	fear of open spaces
ailurophobia	fear of cats
amaxophia	fear of vehicles, driving
androphobia	fear of men
anthophobia	fear of flowers
anthropophobia	fear of people
arachnophobia	fear of spiders
aquaphobia	fear of water
arachibutyrophobia	fear of peanut butter sticking to the roof of your mouth
astraphobia	fear of lightning
brontophobia	fear of thunder
claustrophobia	fear of closed spaces
chromophobia	fear of color
cynophobia	fear of dogs
dementophobia	fear of insanity
gephyrophobia	fear of bridges
gerontophobia	fear of old age
gynophobia	fear of women
hemophobia	fear of blood
herpetophobia	fear of reptiles
ideophobia	fear of ideas
mikrophobia	fear of germs
murophobia	fear of mice
nebulaphobia	fear of clouds
necrophobia	fear of death
numerophobia	fear of numbers
nyctophobia	fear of darkness
ochlophobia	fear of crowds

PHOBIA WORD	MEANING
ophidiophobia	fear of snakes
optophobia	fear of opening your eyes
ornithophobia	fear of birds
phonophobia	fear of speaking aloud
pyrophobia	fear of fire
thaasophobia	fear of being bored
trichophobia	fear of hair
triskaidekaphobia	fear of the number thirteen
xenophobia	fear of strangers

CIDE WORD	MEANING
bactericide	killing of bacteria
fratricide	killing of a brother
genocide	killing of people of one race
herbicide	killing of plants
homicide	killing of a person
infanticide	killing of a baby
insecticide	killing of insects
matricide	killing of one's mother
patricide	killing of one's father
regicide	killing of a king, ruler
rodenticide	killing of rodents
sororicide	killing of a sister
suicide	killing of self
uxoricide	killing of one's wife

See also List 27, Greek and Latin Roots;
List 28, -Ology Word Family.

List 30. FOREIGN WORDS

These lists contain a collection of words of foreign origin that have been adopted into the English language. Many are so common we forget where they came from. Words of Greek and Latin origin are not included here because many of them can be found in the example words in List 27, Greek and Latin Roots.

African Words
banana
cola
marimba
mumbo jumbo
raffia
safari
samba
yam
zombie

Arabic Words
admiral
alcohol
alfalfa
algebra
artichoke
carafe
coffee
cotton
kebab
magazine
monsoon
sofa
tariff
zero

Australian (Aboriginal) Words
boomerang
kangaroo
koala

Chinese Words
china (porcelain)
chow
gung ho
kowtow
mahjong
shantung
soy
tea
tofu
typhoon

Dutch Words
bush
cole slaw
cookie
drill
maelstrom
monsoon
pickle
Santa Claus
skate
sketch
skipper
sled
sleight
sloop
split
stoop
stove
wagon
yacht

East Indian Words
bungalow
cashmere
catamaran
cheetah
curry
dinghy
jungle
khaki
loot
pajamas
shampoo
shawl
teak
thug
veranda

French Words
ambiance
attorney
authority
bail

ballet
bizarre
blond
boulevard
bouquet
brochure
cadet
caprice
carousel
chagrin
charade
charity
chef
clergy
clientele
coroner
crime
debris
depot
detour
entourage
essay
expose
fiance
fiancee
gourmet
government
impromptu
judge
jury
justice
liberty
lingerie
malapropos
mayor
migraine
minister
morale
morgue
motif
naive
nee
noël

nocturne
nuance
pastor
penchant
pension
progress
protege
public
raconteur
rebel
religion
résumé
sabotage
suede
suite
ticket
traitor
treasurer
troop
trophy
vague
verdict
viola
vis-a-vis

German Words
angst
automat
delicatessen
diesel
ecology
Fahrenheit
flak
frankfurter
gestalt
Gestapo
Gesundheit
hamburger
kaput
liverwurst
loaf
polka
pumpernickel
sauerkraut
schema
spiel
strudel
torte
wanderlust

Italian Words
alfresco
attitude
balcony
bandit
banister
bologna
brigade
bronze
cannon
carnival
casino
cavalry
cello
colonel
confetti
duel
fiasco
finale
ghetto
gondola
incognito
infantry
influenza
jean
macaroni
malaria
mascara
pasta
pastel
piano
prima dona
relief
sentinel
spaghetti
stiletto
stucco
torso
trio
virtuoso
vista
volcano
wig

Japanese Words
banzai
bonsai
hibachi
honcho

judo
jujitsu
kamikaze
karate
origami
sayonara
tycoon

Lap Word
tundra

Philippine Word
boondocks

Polynesian Word
taboo

Portuguese Words
commando
pagoda
peon
samba

Russian Words
commissar
cosmonaut
czar
dacha
intelligentsia
Kremlin
mammoth
parka
politburo
sputnik

Sanskrit Words
karma
mantra
nirvana
yoga

Spanish Words
adios
adobe
albino
alfalfa
avocado
armada
bronco

burro
cafeteria
canoe
canyon
chocolate
corral
coyote
fiesta
flotilla
hurricane
junta
loco
manana
mesa
Montana
mosquito

palomino
patio
pinto
plaza
poncho
potato
ranch
rodeo
rumba
sierra
silo
tobacco
tomato
tornado
tortilla

Turkish Words
sherbet
shish kebab
yogurt

Yiddish Words
kibbutz
klutz
nosh
bagel
pastrami
schmaltz

See also List 27, Greek and Latin Roots; List 31, French and Latin Phrases; List 33, Words Borrowed From Names.

List 31. FRENCH AND LATIN PHRASES

French and Latin phrases are used in many novels, magazines, and newspapers; in academic and legal writing; and sometimes even in speech. Your students might enjoy learning some of the more common ones. They may well demonstrate a *penchant* for picking up foreign phrases *tout de suite* and using them to impress their friends. *N'est-ce pas?*

FRENCH PHRASES

à la carte—according to the menu, i.e., ordering individual items off the menu as opposed to complete dinners

à la mode—in fashion; frequently used to indicate desserts served with ice cream

à votre sante—to your health; a toast used in drinking

au contraire—on the contrary

au courant—well informed

au revoir—until we meet again

bon appetit—good appetite

bonjour—good day, hello

bon vivant—lover of good living

bon voyage—have a good trip

carte blanche—full discretionary authority

coup d'etat—sudden overthrow of a government

cul de sac—dead end

de rigeur—required

double entendre—double meaning

en masse—in a large group

en route—on the way

esprit de corps—group spirit

fait accompli—a thing accomplished; done with

faux pas—mistake

hors d'oeuvre—appetizer

je ne sais quoi—I don't know what

laissez faire—noninterference

n'est-ce pas?—isn't that so?

noblesse oblige—rank imposes obligations

nom de plume—pen name

objet d'art—article of artistic value

pardonnez moi—excuse me

piece de resistance—irresistible item or event

raison d'etre—reason or justification for existence

savoir faire—social know-how

tout de suite—immediately

vis-a-vis—in relation to

LATIN PHRASES

ad hoc—with respect to the particular case at hand

ad infinitum—to infinity

ad nauseam—to the point of disgust

bona fide—in good faith

caveat emptor—let the buyer beware

cogito ergo sum—I think, therefore I am

e pluribus unum—one from many

et cetera—and others

in memorium—in memory of

in toto—totally

mea culpa—my fault

modus operandi—manner of working

non sequitur—it does not follow

nota bene—note well

persona non grata—person not accepted

pro forma—done as a matter of formality

pro rata—according to rate or proportion

quid pro quo—one thing for another

sine qua non—indispensable

status quo—the way things are

sub rosa—secret or confidential

tempus fugit—time flies

vice versa—conversely

List 32. BRITISH AND AMERICAN WORDS

Even though our languages are more alike than different, there are certain British words that are very foreign to Americans and vice versa. You and your students can have some fun with the following.

British Words	American Words
anorak	parka
aubergine	eggplant
autumn	fall
bank holiday	legal holiday
bathing costume	bathing suit
bill	check (restaurant)
billion (one million million)	billion (thousand million)
biscuit (sweet)	cookie
biscuit (unsweetened)	cracker
block of flats	apartment house/building
bonnet	automobile hood
book (v.)	make reservation
boot	automobile trunk
braces	suspenders
break (school)	recess
caravan	trailer
caretaker/porter	janitor
catapult	slingshot
centre (city/business)	downtown
centre reservation	median strip/divider
chemist	druggist
chemist's shop	pharmacy/drugstore
chips	fried pieces of potato, French fries
chocolate/sweets	candy
class/form (school)	grade
cooker	stove
corporation	city/municipal government
crisps	chips (potato)
dale	river valley
diversion	detour
dress circle	mezzanine/loge
dressing-gown	bathrobe
dustbin/bin	garbage can, ash can, trash can
estate agent	realtor
face flannel	wash cloth
Father Christmas	Santa Claus
fen	low marshy land
first floor	second floor
flat	apartment

The Reading Teacher's Book of Lists, Fourth Edition, © 2000 by John Wiley & Sons, Inc.

British Words	American Words
frock	dress
full stop (punc.)	period
gallery (theatre)	balcony
geyser (gas)	water heater
grill (v.)	to broil
headmaster/mistress	principal
hire purchase	time payment/installment
holiday	vacation
hoover (n.)	vacuum cleaner
housing estate	subdivision
ironmonger	hardware store
jab (injection)	shot
joint (meat)	roast
lavatory/toilet/w.c.	toilet/john/bathroom
left luggage office	baggage room
let/lettings	lease, rent/rentals
lift	elevator
lorry	truck
lounge suit	business suit
mackintosh	raincoat
marks	grades
mince	hamburger meat
moor	tract of rough wilderness
motorway	freeway/throughway/super highway
nappy	diaper
nought	zero
off license/wine merchant	liquor store
oven cloth	pot holders
overtake (vehicle)	pass
pack (of cards)	deck
pants	shorts (underwear)
paraffin	kerosene
pavement/footpath	sidewalk
pence	penny
personal call	person-to-person
petrol	gasoline
pillar box	mail box/mail drop
post	mail
pram	baby carriage/baby buggy
public school	fee-charging school
put through (telephone)	connect

British Words	American Words
queue	line (to form a line)
rates/ratings	taxes
read	studied
reception (hotel)	front desk
return ticket	round-trip ticket
revising	reviewing
roundabout (road)	traffic circle
saloon (car)	sedan
scent	perfume
school leavers	graduates
shire	a county
shop assistant	sales clerk/sales girl
single ticket	one-way ticket
sister	nurse
sitting room/living room/lounge	living room
smalls	underclothing
solicitor	lawyer/attorney
spanner	monkey wrench
spirits (drink)	liquor
staff (academic)	faculty
stalls (theatre)	orchestra seats
stand (for public office)	run
sweet shop/confectioner	candy store
sweets/chocolate	candy
tap	faucet
term (academics—three in a year)	semester (two in a year)
torch	flashlight
trunk call	long distance
tube/underground	subway
turn-ups (trousers)	cuffs (pants)
unit trust	mutual fund
vest	undershirt
wash up	do the dishes
windscreen	windshield
wind/mudguard	fender
zed	zee (last letter)

The Reading Teacher's Book of Lists, Fourth Edition, © 2000 by John Wiley & Sons, Inc.

List 33. WORDS BORROWED FROM NAMES

Did you know that the popular *cardigan* sweater was named after the Earl of Cardigan? Or that the word *maverick* came into use after Samuel Maverick, a Texan, refused to brand his cattle? These and other eponyms, words borrowed from names, can be used to stimulate an interest in word origins.

WORDS COINED FROM PEOPLE'S NAMES

Adam's apple	Adam, the first man, who tradition says ate the forbidden fruit, an apple, in the Garden of Eden
America	Amerigo Vespucci, an Italian merchant–explorer who came to the New World shortly after Columbus
baud	Jean Baudot, a French inventor who worked on telegraphic communications
Beaufort scale	Sir Francis Beaufort, an English naval officer, who developed it to describe wind speed
bloomers	Amelia Bloomer, a pioneer feminist who made them popular
bowie knife	James Bowie, an American frontiersman who made this type of knife famous
boycott	Charles Boycott, a British army officer and first victim
braille	Louis Braille, a French teacher of the blind
bunsen burner	Robert Bunsen in 1855, as a heat source for his laboratory experiments
cardigan	Earl of Cardigan, a British officer whose soldiers wore the knitted sweaters during the Crimean War
chauvinist	Nicholas Chauvin, a soldier who worshipped France and Napoleon uncritically
Colt revolver	One of the best-known handguns, named for Samuel Colt, an American firearms designer in the 1800s
diesel	Rudolf Diesel, a German automotive engineer
dunce	Johannes Duns Scotus, a theologian whose followers were called Dunsmen
Ferris wheel	G. M. Ferris, an American engineer
Frisbee	William Frisbie, a pie company owner in Connecticut in 1871; Yale students played catch with the pie tins
fudge	Supposedly named after Captain Fudge, a seventeenth-century seaman who had a reputation for not telling the truth
gerrymander	Elbridge Gerry, a Massachusetts governor in 1810
graham crackers	Sylvester Graham, an American reformer in dietetics and a vegetarian
guillotine	Joseph Guillotin, a French physician who urged its use
Leninism	Nikolai Lenin, Russian communist revolutionary
leotard	Jules Leotard, a French acrobat who designed it as a costume for his trapeze act
loganberry	J.H. Logan, a judge and a gardener
lynch	William Lynch, an American vigilante
macadam	John Loudon McAdam, a Scottish engineer who invented this road-building material

The Reading Teacher's Book of Lists, Fourth Edition, © 2000 by John Wiley & Sons, Inc.

121

mackintosh	Charles MacIntosh, inventor of rainproof material
malapropism	Mrs. Malaprop, a character in Sheridan's *The Rivals*
martinet	Jean Martinet, a seventeenth-century French army drill master
Marxism	Karl Marx, a German communist philosopher
maverick	Samuel Maverick, a Texan who didn't brand his cattle
mesmerize	Frederich Mesmer, an Austrian physician who practiced hypnotism
Morse code	Communication code using dots and dashes invented by Samuel Morse
nicotine	Jean Nicot, a French diplomat who introduced the tobacco plant to France about 1561
pasteurize	Louis Pasteur, a French bacteriologist
platonic	Plato, the Greek philosopher
praline	A nut and sugar candy named for Marshal Duplessis-Praslin, whose cook invented it
pullman	George M. Pullman, railroad designer
sandwich	John Montagu, fourth Earl of Sandwich, who invented it so he could gamble without stopping for a regular meal
saxophone	Anton Sax, Belgian instrument maker who combined a clarinet's reed with oboe fingering
sequoia	A Cherokee Indian chief who invented an alphabet; the trees were named for him by a Hungarian botanist
shrapnel	Henry Shrapnel, an English artillery officer
sideburns	Ambrose Burnside, a Civil War general and governor of Rhode Island who had thick side whiskers
silhouette	Etienne de Silhouette, a French finance minister of Louis XV whose fiscal policies and amateurish portraits (by him) were regarded as inept
Stalinism	The political beliefs of Joseph Stalin, Russian political leader
stetson	John Stetson, an American who owned a hat factory in Philadelphia that featured western styles
tawdry	St. Audrey, queen of Northumbria; used to describe lace sold at her fair
teddy bear	Teddy Roosevelt, president of the United States, who spared the life of a bear cub on a hunting trip in Mississippi
valentine	St. Valentine, a Christian martyr whose feast day is February 14—the same date, according to Roman tradition, that birds pair off to nest
vandal	Vandals, the Germanic tribe that sacked Rome
Winchester rifle	Oliver F. Winchester, American manufacturer
zeppelin	German Count von Zeppelin

SCIENCE WORDS COINED FROM PEOPLE'S NAMES

ampere	Andre Ampere, a French physicist
celsius	Anders Celsius, a Swedish astronomer and inventor
decibel	Alexander Bell, a Scottish–American inventor of the telephone
fahrenheit	Gabriel Fahrenheit, a German physicist
mach number	Ernst Mach, an Austrian philosopher and physicist
ohm	Georg Simon Ohm, a German physicist

The Reading Teacher's Book of Lists, Fourth Edition, © 2000 by John Wiley & Sons, Inc.

Richter scale	Charles Richter, an American seismologist
volt	Alessandro Volata, an Italian physicist
watt	James Watt, a Scottish engineer and inventor

FLOWER NAMES COINED FROM PEOPLE'S NAMES

begonia	Michel Begon, French governor of Santo Domingo and a patron of science
camellia	George Kamel, European Jesuit missionary to the Far East
dahlia	Andreas Dahl, a Swedish botanist
gardenia	Alexander Garden, a Scottish–American botanist
magnolia	Pierre Magnol, a French botanist
poinsettia	Joel Poinsettia, U.S. ambassador to Mexico
wisteria	Caspar Wistar, an American anatomist
zinnia	J. G. Zinn, a German botanist

WORDS COINED FROM PLACE NAMES (TOPONYMS)

academy	Academeia, a garden where Plato taught his students
calico	Calicut, India
cashmere	Kashmir, India
cologne	Cologne, Germany
damask	Damascus, Syria
denim	Nimes, France—serge de Nimes (fabric of Nimes)
frankfurter	Frankfurt, Germany
gauze	Gaza, Palestine
hamburger	Hamburg, Germany
laconic	Laconia (Sparta, Greece)
Leyden jar	Leyden, Holland
limousine	Limousin, an old French province
mackinaw	Mackinac City, Michigan
manila paper	Manila, the Philippines
muslin	Mosul, Iraq
panama hat	Panama, Central America
rhinestone	Rhine, river that flows from Switzerland through Germany and the Netherlands
Roquefort cheese	Roquefort, a French town
Tabasco sauce	Tabasco, Mexico
tangerine	Tangier, Morocco
worsted wool	Worsted, England

BORROWED CALENDAR WORDS

Sunday	The sun's day
Monday	The moon's day
Tuesday	Tiw's day; Tiw was the Teutonic god of war
Wednesday	Woden's day; Woden was the Norse god of the hunt
Thursday	Thor's day; Thor was the Norse god of the sky
Friday	Fria's day; Fria, the wife of Thor, was the Norse goddess of love and beauty
Saturday	Saturn's day; Saturn was the Roman god of agriculture

January	In honor of Janus, the Roman god with two faces, one looking forward and one looking backward
February	In honor of *februa*, the Roman feast of purification
March	In honor of Mars, the Roman god of war
April	A reference to spring, *aprilis*, the Latin word for opening
May	In honor of Maia, a Roman goddess and mother of Mercury
June	In honor of Juno, the Roman goddess of marriage
July	In honor of the Roman general and statesman Julius Caesar
August	In honor of the Roman emperor Augustus Caesar
September	In reference to *septem*, the Latin word for seven; September was the seventh month of the Roman calendar
October	In reference to *octo*, the Latin word for eight; October was the eighth Roman month
November	In reference to *novem*, the Latin word for nine; November was the ninth Roman month
December	In reference to *decem*, the Latin word for ten; December was the tenth Roman month

WORDS FROM ROMAN AND GREEK MYTHOLOGY

Achilles heel	Greek warrior and leader in the Trojan War whose only vulnerable spot was his heel
amazon	Amazons, in Greek mythology, were a tribe of female warriors
aphrodisiac	Aphrodite, Greek goddess of love and beauty
atlas	Atlas, in Greek mythology, was forced to hold the heavens on his shoulders
cereal	Ceres, a Roman goddess of agriculture
echo	Echo, in Greek mythology, was a wood nymph cursed with repeating the last words anyone said to her
electricity	Electra, daughter of Agamemnon
erotic	Eros, Greek god of love and son of Aphrodite
hygiene	Hygeia, the Greek goddess of health
mentor	Mentor, in Greek mythology, was a loyal friend and advisor to Odysseus and teacher to his son, Telemachus
morphine	Morpheus, the Greek god of dreams
oedipus complex	King Oedipus, in Greek mythology, unwittingly murdered his father and married his mother
ogre	Orcus, the Roman god of the underworld
panacea	Panacea, the Roman goddess of health
volcano	Volcan, Roman god of fire

See also List 27, Greek and Latin Roots.

The Reading Teacher's Book of Lists, Fourth Edition, © 2000 by John Wiley & Sons, Inc.

List 34. OXYMORONS

An oxymoron is the use of words with contradictory or clashing ideas next to one another. Oxymorons are fun to collect and appear frequently in newspapers and advertising. These are some of our favorites.

accidentally on purpose	freezer burn	organized mess
accurate estimate	fresh frozen	original copy
act naturally	genuine imitation	passive aggressive
adult child	global village	plastic glasses
advanced beginner	graduate student	plastic silverware
alone together	honest crook	plastic straw
approximately equal	hopelessly optimistic	poor little rich girl
awfully good	increasing declines	pretty ugly
bankrupt millionaire	inside out	random order
bittersweet	jumbo shrimp	real-life fairy tale
black gold	larger half	resident alien
clearly confused	liquid crystal	same difference
clearly misunderstood	literal interpretation	science fiction
clever fool	little giant	serious fun
completely unfinished	live recording	sleepwalk
constant change	living dead	steel wool
constant variable	living death	student teacher
curved line	loud whisper	sun shade
deafening silence	love–hate relationship	sweet sorrow
definite maybe	make haste slowly	sweet tart
deliberate mistake	minor disaster	synthetic natural gas
even odds	musical comedy	wordless book
exact estimate	never again	work party
expert amateur	new antiques	working vacation
first annual	new routine	young old person
found missing	now then	
free slave	old news	

The Reading Teacher's Book of Lists, Fourth Edition, © 2000 by John Wiley & Sons, Inc.

4

SUBJECT WORDS

List 35. MATH VOCABULARY—PRIMARY

Beginning math is challenging for many primary-grade students. Students must learn concepts like equal, number and zero, number names, and what they represent. They also need to learn the specialized vocabulary of math, rules of computation, and how to write the numeral and name of numbers. This is no small feat for students just learning basic word recognition and comprehension skills! Use the words in this list to review meaning and develop word problem skills. Post them on newsprint to help remember the terms and their spelling.

Common Words

add
addition
alike
all
amount
Arabic numeral

between
billion
both

center
change
column
compare
connect
contain
count
counting numbers
curve

degree
difference
digit
distance
double
dozen

equal
even number

fewer
figure
fraction

graph
greater than (>)
group
grouping

half
horizontal
inside
join
least
less
less than (<)

many
match
mathematics
measure
member
middle
million
minus

missing
more
most

negative
number
number fact
number line

odd number
opposite
order

pair
pattern
plus
positive
problem

rounded number
row

same
score
sequence
set
shaded
sharing
similar

single
size
solution
solve
some
space
straight
subset
subtract
sum
symbol

table
temperature
thermometer
thousand
times
total

unequal
unit
unknown
value
vertical
weight
zero

Money Words

cent
cents
change
coin

cost
dime
dollar
dollar bill

dollar sign ($)
half-dollar
nickel
penny

quarter
silver dollar

Time Words

A.M.	fall	night	spring
afternoon	hour	noon	summer
autumn	midnight	P.M.	week
calendar	minute	Roman numerals	winter
clock	month	season	wristwatch
day	morning	second	year

Measurement Words

centimeter	inches	metric ton	quart
cup	kilogram	mile	ruler
customary system	kiloliter	milligram	ton
foot	kilometer	milliliter	yard
gallon	length	millimeter	yardstick
gram	liter	ounce	
half-gallon	meter	pint	
inch	metric system	pound	

Counting Words

one	nine	seventeen	sixty
two	ten	eighteen	seventy
three	eleven	nineteen	eighty
four	twelve	twenty	ninety
five	thirteen	twenty-one	hundred
six	fourteen	thirty	thousand
seven	fifteen	forty	million
eight	sixteen	fifty	billion

Ordinal Numbers

first	sixth	twentieth
second	seventh	thirtieth
third	eighth	fortieth
fourth	ninth	fiftieth
fifth	tenth	hundredth

See also List 38, Reading Math;
List 177, Measurement System Abbreviations.

List 36. MATH VOCABULARY—ELEMENTARY

Math knowledge and understanding are essential. To help develop understanding, greater emphasis is being placed on how students learn math concepts. These math words should be in every elementary student's word bank. Share the list with your math colleagues and encourage them to post key words for better word recognition, spelling, and review.

Common Words

addend
array
associative property
average
bar graph
base

Celsius
circle graph
combine
common denominator
common factor
common multiple
commutative property
compass
compatible number
composite number
coordinates

data
decimal
decimal point
degree Celsius
degree Fahrenheit
denominator
distributive property
divide
dividend
divisible
divisor

element
empty set
equally likely
equation
equivalent
estimate
expanded numeral

factor
factor tree
Fahrenheit
flow chart

fluid ounce
frequency

gram
greatest
grid
grouping property
hundredth

identify
improper fraction
inequality
infinite
integers

label
least
lowest terms

mass
mean
median
minuend
mixed number
mode
model
multiple
multiplication
multiply

natural order
net
number pair
number sentence
numerator

one hundredth
one tenth
one-to-one
operation
order property
ordered pair
ordinal

ordinal number
outcome

parentheses
parenthesis
percent
perimeter
pint
place holder
place value
prediction
prime factor
prime number
principle
probability
procedure
product
proper fraction

quotient
range
ratio
reciprocal
regroup
related facts
remainder
rename

sign
simplest form
square number
square products
statistics
subtrahend
survey

tally chart
tenth
union
unit price
unnamed
whole number

Geometry Words

acute angle
angle
area
center
circle
circumference
closed figure
cone
congruent
congruent figures
cube
cylinder
degree
diagonal
diameter
edge
endpoint
geometric

geometry
height
hexagon
intersect
length
obtuse angle
octagon
parallel
parallelogram
pentagon
perpendicular
plane
plot
polygon
polyhedron
prism
pyramid
quadrilateral

radius
ray
rectangle
rectangular
rhombus
segment
solid
sphere
square
surface
symmetric
symmetrical
symmetry
triangle
vertex
vertices
volume
width

Measurement Words

acre (A.)
area
capacity
centigram (cg)
centiliter (cl)
centimeter (cm)
cubic centimeter (cc^3)
cubic decimeter (dm^3)
cubic foot (cu. ft.)
cubic inch (cu. in.)
cubic meter (m^3)
cubic millimeter (mm^3)
cubic yard (cu. yd.)
cup (c.)
customary system
decimeter (dm)
fluid ounce (fl. oz.)

foot (ft.)
furlong (fur.)
gallon (gal.)
gram (gm)
hectare (ha)
height (h)
inch (in.)
kilogram (kg)
kilometer (km)
length (l)
liter (L)
mass
measurement
meter (m)
metric system
metric ton (t)
mile (mi.)

milligram (mg)
millimeter (mm)
ounce (oz.)
pint (pt.)
pound (lb.)
quart (qt.)
square centimeter (cm^2)
square foot (sq. ft.)
square inch (sq. in.)
square meter (m^2)
square millimeter (mm^2)
square yard (sq. yd.)
ton (T.)
volume (vol.)
weight (wt.)
width (w)
yard (yd.)

The Reading Teacher's Book of Lists, Fourth Edition, © 2000 by John Wiley & Sons, Inc.

See also List 38, Reading Math; List 177, Measurement System Abbreviations.

List 37. MATH VOCABULARY— INTERMEDIATE

The concepts behind these words build on those learned in elementary math. This list is based on words found in math texts for grades 4 through 8. Many will also be repeated in secondary school texts. Consider a lesson on "math verbs"—knowing **what to do** is key to carrying out mathematical operations. Here are a few examples of "math verbs": **decrease, subtract, convert, determine, reduce**.

The Reading Teacher's Book of Lists, Fourth Edition, © 2000 by John Wiley & Sons, Inc.

abscissa
absolute value
actual
additive
additive inverse
alternate
approximately
arithmetic mean
associative property
avoirdupois

baker's dozen
base (of an exponent)
binary operation
binary system
box plot

calculate
cardinal
caret
cast out
centigram (cg)
centiliter (cl)
closure property
combination
commutative property
comparison
complex
computation
consecutive
constant
convert
cosine
cross-product
cross-section
cubed
cubic
currency

decade
decrease
depth

derive
determine
deviation
diagram
discount
disprove
distributive property
division
dot graph
duplicate

equal ratios
equality
equivalent ratios
error of measurement
evaluate
exact
experiment
exponent
exponential notation
expression
extend

face value
factorial
family of facts
Fibonacci sequence
finite
fixed
foci
formula
frequency
function

generalization
given
graduated scale
graph
graph of the equation
greatest possible error
greatest possible multiple
gross

gross weight
histogram

identity property
imply
include
increase
inequality
inference
input
interest rate
interpret
interval
inverse
irrational number

like terms
line plot
linear
linear equation
magic square
markup
maximum
metric system
micron
midpoint
midway
minimum
mixed numeral
multiplicand
multiplication principle
multiplier

natural number
negative correlation
negative number
negative slope
notation
numeral

odds
open equation
open sentence

opposites
order of operations
ordered pair
output
overestimate

partial
pattern
per
percent
percentage
percentiles
perfect number
perfect square
period
permutation
pi
plot
population
positive correlation
positive numbers
positive slope
power
precision
probability
profit
progression
proportion
proportional

quadrant
quantity
quartile

quartiles
random
random sample
ranking
rate
ratio
rational number
real numbers
reduce
reflexive property
relation
relative error
reverse

sample
satisfies
scatter plot
scientific notation
sequence
short division
signed number
significant digits
simplest terms
simplify
sine
sine ratio
skip counting
slope
solution
square root
squared
statistics

stem-and-leaf plot
story problem
string
subscript
substitute
successive
super set
system

tally
term
terminate
theorem
topology
transformation
transitive property
tree diagram
trigonometry
triple
truncate

underestimate
undivided
union of sets
universal set
unlimited
unmatched
upper limit
variable
variable expression
Venn diagram
word problem

The Reading Teacher's Book of Lists, Fourth Edition, © 2000 by John Wiley & Sons, Inc.

Geometry Words

30–60–90 triangle
45–45–90 triangle

acute triangle
adjacent
alternate
altitude
angle
arc
axis

bisect
circumscribe
closed curve
complimentary
concave polygon
concentric

construct
convex polygon
coordinate axis
coordinate plane
corresponding

dimension
equiangular triangle
equilateral triangle
exterior
hemisphere
hexagonal
hypotenuse

inscribed angle
interior
intersection

irregular polygon
isosceles triangle
lateral
line of best fit
line of symmetry

median
mirror image
obtuse triangle
open figure
perpendicular bisector
plane figure
Pythagorean theorem

quadrilateral
radii
reflection (flip)

regular polyhedron
rotation (turn)
scale
scale drawing
scalene triangle
sector
segment
semicircle

skew lines
straight angle
supplementary angles
surface area
symmetry
tangent
tangent ratio
tessellation

trapezoid
triangular pyramid
two-dimensional
vertical axis
x-axis
x-coordinate
y-axis
y-coordinate

Prefixes for Super-Small Numbers

Prefix	Meaning	Example
deci-	tenth, 10^{-1}	decimeter
centi-	hundredth, 10^{-2}	centimeter
milli-	thousandth, 10^{-3}	millimeter
micro-	millionth, 10^{-6}	micrometer (micron)
nano-	billionth, 10^{-9}	nanometer (10^{-10} = angstrom)
pico-	trillionth, 10^{-12}	picometer
femto-	quadrillionth, 10^{-15}	femtometer (fermi)
atto-	quintillionth, 10^{-18}	attometer

Prefixes for Super-Large Numbers

Prefix	Meaning	Example
kilo-	thousand, 10^{3}	kilometer
mega-	million, 10^{6}	megameter
giga-	billion, 10^{9}	gigameter
tera-	trillion, 10^{12}	terameter
peta-	quadrillion, 10^{15}	petameter
exa-	quintillion, 10^{18}	exameter

See also List 38, Reading Math; List 177, Measurement System Abbreviations; List 178, Other Measurement Abbreviations.

List 38. READING MATH

In addition to needing to understand the special meanings and usage of math vocabulary (see Lists 35, 36, and 37), students need to master the art of "reading" math symbols. Without this skill, direct instruction is difficult and students' ability to restate, explain, question, and apply functions is limited. Share this list with your math colleagues.

PRIMARY

See	Say	See	Say
+	and or plus	−	take away or minus
×	times	÷	is divided by
=	is equal to or equals	≠	is not equal to
<	is less than	>	is more than or is greater than
¢	cent or cents	$	dollar or dollars
$\frac{1}{2}$	one half	$\frac{1}{4}$	one quarter
$\frac{3}{4}$	three quarters	$\frac{1}{3}$	one third
%	percent	#	number or pound

ELEMENTARY

See	Say	See	Say
+	plus or positive	−	minus or negative
×	is multiplied by	÷	is divided by
=	is equal to or equals	≠	is not equal to
<	is less than	>	is more than or is greater than
∗	is multiplied by	/	is divided by
?	a missing number	∠	angle
≥	is greater than or equal to	≤	is less than or equal to
(	open parenthesis	)	closed parenthesis
[	open bracket	]	closed bracket
@	at	ø	null set or zero
:	is to	::	as
∴	therefore	≈	is approximately
∪	in union with or union	∩	intersects or intersection
⊂	contained in or is a subset of	⊄	is not a subset of

See List 177, Measurement System Abbreviations; List 178, Other Measurement Abbreviations.

The Reading Teacher's Book of Lists, Fourth Edition, © 2000 by John Wiley & Sons, Inc.

INTERMEDIATE

See	**Say**
$a + b = c$	a plus b equals c
$a - b = c$	a minus b equals c
$-a - b$	minus a minus b
$a - (b + c) = d$	a minus the sum of b plus c is equal to d
$a - (b - c) = d$	a minus the difference b minus c is equal to d
$a - (b - c) = d$	a minus the quantity b minus c is equal to d
$a \times b$	a times b or the product of a and b
$a * b$	a times b or the product of a and b
$a \cdot b$	a times b or the product of a and b
ab	a times b or the product of a and b
ab	a multiplied by b
$ab + c$	a b plus c
$ab - c$	a b minus c
$a (b - c)$	a times the quantity b minus c
$a + (bc)$	a plus the quantity b times c
$a - (b + c)$	a minus the quantity b plus c
$(a + b) + (c + d)$	the quantity a plus b plus the quantity c plus d

List 39. SOCIAL STUDIES VOCABULARY— ELEMENTARY

Students in grades 3 through 5 will encounter these words. Younger students will benefit from frequent pronunciation and spelling review of the more "difficult" words. Teach the related words as part of Language Arts to introduce and reinforce the meaning and use of suffixes.

adobe
age
American Revolution
ancestors
ancient
appointed
archaeology
armada
artifact
astronaut
authority

barbarian
barter
bill
Bill of Rights
boundary

cabinet
campaign
candidate
capital
capitol
census
century
charter
checks and balances
chronological order
citizen
city
civil
civil rights
civil war
civilization
colony
commerce
communities

compromise
Congress
conquer
Constitution
contiguous states
continents
convention
convert
country

Declaration of Independence
democracy
discover
document
election
expedition
explore
fleet
foreign
founded
freedom
frontier

goods
government
governor
heritage
history
illegal
immigrant
invention
labor
law
legal
majority
manufacture
mayor

militia
millennium
minimum
minority
minutemen
missionary
museum
Native American
New World
nobles
northwest passage

official
opinion
opposed
oral history
Oregon Trail
organization
Parliament
passage
patriot
peasant
peon
pilgrim
pioneer
plantation
political party
population
poverty
president
property
Puritans

religion
represent
Revolutionary War
rule
rural

Senate
settlements
shortage
slave state
slavery
society
space travel
Sputnik
strike
suburbs

term
territory
timeline
town meeting
trade
traditional
trails
treaty
trial
tribes
troops
truce

union
unite
United Nations
urban
veteran
violence
volunteer
voyage
wages
warfare
wilderness
worship

The Reading Teacher's Book of Lists, Fourth Edition, © 2000 by John Wiley & Sons, Inc.

See also List 40, Social Studies Vocabulary—Intermediate; List 41, Geography Vocabulary.

List 40. SOCIAL STUDIES VOCABULARY—INTERMEDIATE

Social Studies—the story of the relationships between people and nations—can come alive through class or independent reading of historical fiction, biography, travel books, and histories told through memoirs and other artifacts. Events take on greater meaning when students are able to imagine and identify with people. Details will be remembered more easily if the storytelling is superb. This list is based on words in social studies texts for grades 4 through 8. Many are also basic in secondary school texts.

abolish
abolitionist
absolute monarchy
aggressor
agribusiness
alien
alliance
Allied Powers
ally
amendment
amnesty
annex
apartheid
aristocracy
armistice
assassinate
assembly
autocracy
automation
Axis Powers

balance of power
bloc
blockade
boom
boycott
bureaucracy

capitalism
captains of industry
carpetbaggers
caucus
Central Powers
cold war
collective bargaining
collective farm
colonization
colony
commonwealth
communism
concentration camps

Confederacy
confederation
conflicts
conservative
contraband
cooperative
credit
crisis
crude oil
currency
customs
czar

death rate
debate
debt
declaration
defense
delegates
demarcation
democrat
desegregation
dictatorship
diplomat
disarmament
discrimination
dissent
divine right
draft
duty
dynasty

economy
elastic clause
electoral vote
emancipation
embargo
emigration
emperor
empire

enforce
equality
ethnic
excise
executive
exile
exploration
export
fascism
federal
Federal Reserve
Federalist
filibuster
foreign policy
fossil fuels
free enterprise
Free World

graduated tax
granges
Great Depression
habeas corpus
homestead
hostage
humanitarian
illiteracy
immigration
impeach
imperialism
import
inaugurate
indenture
independence
inflation
initiative
integration
invasion
investment
Iron Curtain
isolationism

judicial
jury
justice
labor union
laissez faire
Latin America
legislature
liberal
literacy
loyalist

mandate
Manifest Destiny
manufacturing
martial law
mass production
megalopolis
mercantilism
merchant
metropolitan area
middle class
Middle East
migrant
migratory farming
minority groups
missile
moderates
monarchy
monopoly
monotheism
Monroe Doctrine
mother country
movement
muckrakers

nationalism
NATO
natural resources
Nazism
negotiate
neutral

139

New Deal
nobility
nominate
nonviolence
nuclear weapons
null and void
occupied
oppression
Orient

pacifists
patriotism
per capita
persecute
petition
platform
pocket veto
policy
political process
politics
poll tax
polytheism
postwar
preamble
precedent
prehistoric
prejudice
primary
primary source
prime minister
proclamation
profit

progressive
prohibit
prohibition
propaganda
prospector
protectorate
protest
Protestant
province
provision
public domain
public opinion
public works

radicals
ratify
ration
raw materials
reapportionment
rebellion
rebels
recall
recession
reconstruction
referendum
reform
Reformation
refugee
regulation
repeal
representative
republic

republican
reservations
reserves
resign
resolution
resources
retreat
revenue
revolt
revolution
riots
royalist

sabotage
sanction
scandal
secede
secession
secondary source
sectionalism
segregation
Selective Service
senator
seniority
sharecropper
siege
smuggling
social security
socialist
sociology
sovereignty
Soviet

spoils system
standard of living
stock market
strategy
surplus
surrender
survive
sweatshops
system

tariff
taxation
technology
terrorism
textile
theory
tolerance
totalitarian
traitor
transcontinental
treason
trend
triangular trade
tyranny
tyrant

unanimous
unconstitutional
underdeveloped
unskilled worker
veto
war hawks
welfare

The Reading Teacher's Book of Lists, Fourth Edition, © 2000 by John Wiley & Sons, Inc.

See also List 39, Social Studies Vocabulary—Elementary; List 41, Geography Vocabulary.

List 41. GEOGRAPHY VOCA

The world in which we live is a fascinating place. Compute
changing boundaries have moved us into a global village.
and political ties to countries around the world increase
knowledge of geography. Encourage students to become
links, with others across the globe. International student e
for penpal information. The words listed here are from re
geography texts. How worldwise and wordwise are your s
locate the major cities and other key geographic sites? Th
world literacy.

Primary

The Reading Teacher's Book of Lists, Fourth Edition, © 2000 by John Wiley & Sons, Inc.

arid	drought	legend	
atmosphere	earth	longitude	scale of miles
axis	east	map	sea
barren	eastern	marsh	season
bay	ecology	mass	south
boundary	economy	meadow	South Pole
branch	environment	meridian	southern
canyons	equator	mesa	sphere
capital	ethnic	moderate	state
cartographer	evaporation	mountain	suburb
census	farming	nation	swamp
central	fertile	native	temperature
city	fossil	neighborhood	tide
climate	glacier	nomad	timeline
coast	globe	north	trade
community	grain	North Pole	tropical
compass	grasslands	northern	tundra
Compass Rose	gulf	oasis	urban
continent	harbor	ocean	valley
contour	harvest	peak	vast
country	hemisphere	plain	vegetation
county	highlands	planet	volcano
crops	horizon	plateau	weather
crust	ice cap	prairie	west
cultivation	iceberg	precipitation	western
culture	island	rainfall	wilderness
customs	jungle	range	zone
data	lake	region	
desert	latitude	religion	
diversity	lava	river	

Intermediate

agriculture
alluvial
altitude
Antarctic Circle
arable
archipelago
Arctic Circle
autonomy
axis
barren
basin
belt

canal
canyons
cape
capital
cartographer
cash crop
census
cliff
climate
coast
commercial
community
condensation
coniferous
continental divide
contour
cottage industry
country
crater
crop rotation
cultivation
cultural region
culture
current

dam
data
death rate
deciduous
degree
delta
density
desert
developing nation
dew point
diversity
domestic
drought

dust storm
earthquake
eclipse
ecology
economy
elevation
environment
equal area map
equator
equinox
erosion
ethnic
evaporation
evergreen
export

fault
fertile
flash flood
flood plain
foliage
fossil
fuel
geologist
geyser
glacier
goods
grasslands
gravity
greenhouse effect
grid
gross national
  product
growing season
gulf
Gulf Stream

harbor
harvest
hemisphere
highlands
hinterlands
horizon
humidity
hurricane
hydroelectric
import
income
industry
inland

International Date
  Line
international waters
irrigation
island
isolated

jet stream
landlocked
latitude
lava
levee
life expectancy
literacy
longitude
lowlands
mainland
manufacture
marine climate
marsh
meadow
megalopolis
Mercator map
meridian
mesa
metropolitan area
monsoon
mountain
nationalism
nationality
natural resources
navigable
navigation
neighborhood
neutral
nomad

oasis
ocean current
oceanography
orbit
parallel
pasture
peninsula
petroleum
physical map
plain
plateau
polar
pollution
population density

port
prairie
precipice
precipitation
Prime Meridian
rain forest
rainfall
range
raw materials
reef
refinery
region
relief map
religion
renewable resource
reservoir
resources
rotation

scale
scale of miles
sea level
sediment
seismograph
semiarid
silt
smog
standard of living
steppe
strait
subtropical
supply
surplus
survey
swamp

temperate
temperature
tidal wave
timberline
timeline
topography
topsoil
trade
tributary
tropic
tundra
typhoon
universal
vegetation
vital statistics
water power

The Reading Teacher's Book of Lists, Fourth Edition, © 2000 by John Wiley & Sons, Inc.

CONTINENTS (in size order)

	Square Miles	% Land	Population*	% Population
Asia	17,200,000	30.0	3,641,000,000	60.7
Africa	11,700,000	20.4	778,000,000	13.0
North America	9,400,000	16.3	476,000,000	7.9
South America	6,900,000	11.9	343,000,000	5.7
Antarctica	5,400,000	9.3	0	0.0
Europe	3,800,000	6.6	727,000,000	12.6
Australia	330,000	5.2	30,000,000	0.5

*As of 1999, Bureau of the Census, U.S. Dept. of Commerce

WORLD OCEANS

Ocean		Square Miles
Pacific Ocean		**63,800,000**

- South China Sea
- Bering Sea
- East China Sea
- Sea of Okhotsk
- Sea of Japan
- Yellow Sea

Atlantic Ocean   **31,800,000**

- Caribbean Sea
- Norwegian Sea
- Hudson Bay
- North Sea
- Baltic Sea
- Mediterranean Sea
- Gulf of Mexico
- Greenland Sea
- Black Sea
- Arctic Ocean

Indian Ocean   **28,300,000**

- Arabian Sea
- Red Sea
- Bay of Bengal

MAJOR RIVERS OF THE WORLD

Name	Length (mi.)	Continent	Name	Length (mi.)	Continent
Nile	4,180	Africa	Zaire (Congo)	2,716	Africa
Amazon	3,912	So. America	Amur (Heilong)	2,704	Asia
Yangtze	3,602	Asia	Lena	2,652	Asia
Ob	3,459	Asia	MacKenzie	2,635	No. America
Huang Ho (Yellow)	2,900	Asia	Niger	2,600	Africa
			Mekong	2,500	Asia
Yenisei	2,800	Asia	Mississippi	2,348	No. America
Parana	2,795	So. America	Missouri	2,313	No. America
Irtish	2,758	Asia			

The Reading Teacher's Book of Lists, Fourth Edition, © 2000 by John Wiley & Sons, Inc.

WORLD'S POPULATION CENTERS

Rank	City, Country	Population in Millions	Rank	City, Country	Population in Millions
1	Seoul, South Korea	10.2	9	Tokyo, Japan	8.0
2	Sao Paulo, Brazil	10.0	10	New York City, U.S.	7.4
3	Bombay, India	9.9	11	Beijing, China	7.4
4	Jakarta, Indonesia	9.1	12	Delhi, India	7.2
5	Moscow, Russia	8.4	13	London, England	7.1
6	Istanbul, Turkey	8.3	14	Cairo, Egypt	6.8
7	Mexico City, Mexico	8.2	15	Teheran, Iran	6.8
8	Shanghai, China	8.2	16	Hong Kong, China	6.5

LARGEST U.S. CITIES (1998 Census Bureau Estimate)

Rank	City, State	Rank	City, State	Rank	City, State
1	New York, NY	11	San Jose, CA	21	Austin, TX
2	Los Angeles, CA	12	San Francisco, CA	22	Seattle, WA
3	Chicago, IL	13	Indianapolis, IN	23	Washington, D.C.
4	Houston, TX	14	Jacksonville, FL	24	Nashville, TN
5	Philadelphia, PA	15	Columbus, OH	25	Charlotte, NC
6	San Diego, CA	16	Baltimore, MD	26	Portland, OR
7	Phoenix, AZ	17	El Paso, TX	27	Denver, CO
8	San Antonio, TX	18	Memphis, TN	28	Cleveland, OH
9	Dallas, TX	19	Milwaukee, WI	29	Fort Worth, TX
10	Detroit, MI	20	Boston, MA	30	Oklahoma City, OK

RELIGIONS OF THE WORLD

Religion	# Members	% Worshipers
Christianity	1,955,229,000	40.3
Islam	1,126,325,000	23.2
Hinduism	793,076,000	16.3
Regional/Tribal	416,066,000	8.6
Buddhism	325,275,000	6.7
Non-religious/Atheist	222,195,000	4.6
Judaism	13,866,000	0.3

The Reading Teacher's Book of Lists, Fourth Edition, © 2000 by John Wiley & Sons, Inc.

List 42. SCIENCE VOCABULARY— ELEMENTARY

Harness a student's natural curiosity with books about dinosaurs, volcanoes, and optical illusions and you'll create a life-long interest in science. These terms are from elementary-grade science texts. Science words pose pronunciation and spelling challenges to many students. Reviewing key words before independent reading assignments and posting them on a science word wall will help students learn their spellings as well as their meanings.

abdomen
absorb
accurate
adaptation
air current
air pressure
algae
amoeba
amphibian
ancestor
astronaut
astronomer
atmosphere
atom

backbone
bacteria
balance
barometer
battery
behavior
biologist
biology
blood vessels
boil
breathe

calcium
capillary
carbohydrate
carbon dioxide
cartilage
cell
Celsius
centimeter
chemical
chemical symbol
chemistry
chlorine
chlorophyll
circuit

circulation
classify
climate
cloud
community
compass
compound
concave
condense
conductor
constant
constellation
continent
contract
control
convection
convex
core crust
current

decay
decompose
degree
density
desert
dew
diaphragm
digestion
dinosaur
disease
dissolve

earth
earthworm
eclipse
egg
electricity
embryo
energy
environment
equator

erosion
esophagus
evaporate
evidence
expand
extinct
Fahrenheit
fern
fertile
fertilizer
filament
flow
focus
fog
food chain
force
fossil
friction
frost
fuel
funnel
gas
geyser
gills
glacier
grain
gravity

habitat
hail
hatch
heat
hemisphere
hibernate
horizon
human
hurricane
iceberg
image
incisor

infection
insect
instinct
insulate
joint
larva
lava
lens
liquid
lungs

magnet
mammal
mantle
marine life
mass
matter
melting point
membrane
mercury
meteor
microscope
mineral
model
moisture
molar
mold
molecule
moon
motion
muscle

natural resource
nerves
nucleus
optical
orbit
organ
organism
outlet
ovary
oxygen

paramecium
parasite

pendulum
periodic
pesticide
phase
physical
planet
plankton
pollen
pollute
population
power
predator
predict
prescribe
preserve
prey
produce
property
protein
protozoan
prove
pulse
pupa
pupil
pure

radiant
rainfall
range
rate
recycle
red blood cell
reflection
reproduction
reptile
response
retina
revolve
rib
ridge
root

saliva
satellite

scale
season
sediment
sedimentary
seed
senses
series
skeleton
skin
smog
solid
solution
sound
space
sperm
spinal
spore
starch
stem
stimulus
stomach
surface
survive
switch
system

taste
temperature
tendon
terrarium
thermometer
thunder
tides
transparent
treatment

variable
vein
vibration
vitamin
volcano
water vapor
wave
weight

See also List 177, Measurement System Abbreviations; List 178, Other Measurement Abbreviations.

List 43. SCIENCE VOCABULARY—INTERMEDIATE

Understanding ourselves and the world around us requires a solid foundation of basic concepts in science. As the frontiers of science expand and impact our daily lives, every citizen will need to be familiar with concepts in biology, ecology, chemistry, and physics. The list below was drawn from vocabulary in science texts grades 4 through 9. Consider a lesson or two on science-related prefixes, suffixes, and root words. They will help science word recognition and comprehension. Teach word variants when vocabulary is introduced. For example, when introducing **immune**, also teach **immunity, immunize, immunology**.

The Reading Teacher's Book of Lists, Fourth Edition, © 2000 by John Wiley & Sons, Inc.

absolute zero
acceleration
acid rain
acoustics
adrenal
air pressure
algae
allergy
alloy
amino acid
ampere
amplify
amplitude
anaphase
anatomy
antibiotic
antigen
aorta
Archimedes
artery
asexual
astronomy
atomic mass
atomic number
atrium
aurora
autonomic nervous
  system

bacillus
bacterium
benign
Bernoulli
binary fission
biome
biotechnology
boiling point
buoyancy

calorie
calorimeter
canine
carcinogen
cardiac
cardiovascular
carnivore
cartilage
catalyst
cell membrane
cellulose
cerebellum
cerebrum
chemical bonding
chemical equation
chemical reaction
chloroplast
cholesterol
chromosome
cilium
circuit breaker
circulatory system
classification
cleavage
coefficient
cold-blooded
collision theory
colorblindness
combustion
communicable
competition
compound
compression
concave
concentrated
condensation
conduction

coniferous
connective tissue
conservation
consumer
conversion factor
convex
corrosion
covalent bonding
crest
cross-pollination
crystal lattice
cytoplasm

deceleration
deciduous
decomposition
dendrite
density
dependence
depletion
depressant
dermas
desert
diatom
diffraction
diffusion
digestive system
dilute solution
diode
distillation
DNA
dominant
Doppler effect
drag
drug
drug abuse
dry cell

ecology
ecosystem
efficiency
effort
electrochemical cell
electrode
electrolyte
electromagnetic
electron
element
embryology
endangered species
endocrine system
endothermic
enzyme
epidermis
erosion
estrogen
evaporation
evolution
excretion
exothermic
extinction

Fallopian
fermentation
fertilization
fetus
fiber optics
flammable
fluorescent
focus
food web
formula
fossil
fracture
freezing point
frequency

147

fulcrum
fungus
fuse

galvanometer
gamma ray
Geiger counter
gene
generator
genetic engineering
genetics
genotype
genus
geothermal energy
germination
glacier
glucose
grassland
gravity
grounding

half-life
hallucinogen
halogen
hazardous waste
heat transfer
hemoglobin
herbivore
hertz
heterogeneous
hologram
homeostasis
homogeneous
homologous
hormone
horsepower
host
hybrid
hydrocarbon
hydroelectric
hypertension
hypothalamus
hypothesis

igneous
illuminate
immune
immunity
incandescent
inclined plane
incubate
induction
inert

inertia
infectious
inflammation
infrared ray
ingestion
inhale
inorganic
insoluble
intensity
interference
interferon
interphase
intrusive
invertebrate
invisible spectrum
ion
ionic bonding
ionization
isomer
isotope

jet stream
joule
Kelvin scale
kidney
kinetic
kingdom
large intestine
larva
larynx
laser
leaching
lever
lichen
life span
lift
ligament
liver
lubricant
luster
lymph

machine
magma
magnetic field
magnetism
malignant
malleable
marrow
marsupial
mechanical
medulla
meiosis

meniscus
metabolism
metallic bond
metamorphosis
metaphase
microbiology
microorganism
migrate
mitosis
modulation
molecule
momentum
monoclonal
multicellular
mutation
neon
nerve tissue
nervous system
neutralization
neutron
niche
noble gas
node
nomenclature
nonmetal
nonrenewable
nuclear energy
nuclear fission
nuclear fusion
nuclear waste
nucleic acid
nucleolus
nutrient

ohm
omnivore
opaque
opiate
orbital motion
ore
organic
organic rock
osmosis
ossification
ovary
over-the-counter
ovulation
oxidation number
ozone

pancreas
parallel circuit
parathyroid

particle accelerator
pasteurization
periodic law
peripheral
peristalsis
permafrost
permanent magnet
petroleum
phase
pheromone
photoelectric effect
photon
photosynthesis
phylum
physics
pistil
piston
pituitary
plasma
plateau
platelet
polarity
polarized light
pollen
pollution
polymer
precipitation
prescription drug
primary coil
primate
probability
projectile
property
prophase
proton
protoplasm
pseudopod
psychological
puberty
pulley

quark
radar
radiation
radioactive dating
radioactive material
radioactivity
rarefaction
reactant
receptor
recessive
recombinant DNA

reflection
reflex
refraction
regeneration
renewable resource
replication
reproduction
resistance
resonance
respiration
respiratory system
retina
reverberation
rhizoid
rhizome
ribosome
RNA

saturated
savanna
scavenger
scientific method
sedimentary rock
seismic
seismograph
self-pollination
semiconductor
sensory neuron
series circuit
sex chromosome

sex-linked trait
sexual reproduction
slope
small intestine
smog
smooth muscle
solar energy
solubility
soluble
solvent
sonar
species
specific gravity
sperm
sphygmomanometer
spinal cord
stamen
static electricity
stimulant
stoma
stratosphere
structural formula
subatomic particle
sublimation
subscript
supersaturated
suspension
symbiosis
symptom
synapse

synthesis reaction
synthetic element

taiga
taxonomy
telophase
temperature
  inversion
terminal velocity
testosterone
theory
thermal expansion
thermocouple
thermostat
thrust
thyroid
tolerance
toxin
trachea
trait
transfusion
transistor
translucent
transmutation
transpiration
transverse wave
tropical rain forest
trough
tumor
tundra

ultrasonic
ultraviolet ray
unicellular
universal gravitation
uterus
vaccine
valence electron
valley glacier
valve
vaporization
variable
variation
velocity
ventricle
vertebrate
virus
viscosity
visible spectrum
vocal cord
voltage
volume

warm-blooded
water table
watt
wavelength
wheel and axle
white blood cell
zoology
zygote

The Reading Teacher's Book of Lists, Fourth Edition, © 2000 by John Wiley & Sons, Inc.

See also List 177, Measurement System Abbreviations; List 178, Other Measurement Abbreviations.

5

LITERATURE

List 44. BOOK WORDS

Good readers know how to talk about parts of a book. Here are some terms that can help you in discussing a book, its parts, and some book types. For book contents, see the Library Classifications, List 188 (Library of Congress and Dewey Decimal classifications systems). Your school or neighborhood librarian can also help you with book parts and book classification lessons.

BOOK PARTS

Jacket
Cover—soft
       hard
Spine
Endpapers
Binding—sewn
      perfect
      spiral
Title page—title
      author
      publisher
      (date)
Copyright—date
      L.C. Number
      Dewey Number
      ISBN
      Copying Limits
Dedication
Acknowledgments
Preface
Introduction
Table of Contents
List of Figures
List of Tables
Chapters
Subheadings
Divisions
Index—subject
      author
      (mixed together)
Glossary
Bibliography
References
Appendices
Series
Volume

BOOK TYPES

Reference
Trade
Text
Picture
Coffee table
Juveniles
Fiction

REFERENCE BOOKS

Dictionary
Encyclopedia
Thesaurus
Atlas
Reader's Guide
Almanac
Reading Teacher's Book
  of Lists

TYPE FONTS (examples)

Bookman
Contemporary Brush
Baskerville (a serif typeface)
Helvetica (a sans serif
  typeface)

TYPE SIZES (examples)

8 point
9 point
10 point
12 point
14 point

THE PAGE

Footnotes
Running head
Subtitles
Paragraph
Indentation
Single space
Double space
Leading
Margins (left and right)

PAPER

Newsprint
Bond
Coated
Rag
Weight (thickness)
Tint (color)
Special purpose (photocopy,
  ditto)

List 45. GENRE

There are many different kinds of writing to read. Genre (pronounced "zhan rah") refers to the categories of written material. Some categories are very broad with many subcategories, like prose and poetry or fiction and nonfiction. Others are very specific, like historic speeches. This is a partial list of the ways written materials can be grouped.

action
adventure
animals
autobiography
ballad
biography
book review
character sketch
comedy
coming of age
contemporary realistic fiction
diary
drama
editorial
e-mail
epic
essay
ethnic
expository
fable
fairy tale
fantasy
fiction
folk tale
futuristic

ghost/angels
gothic romance
historical fiction
horror
how-to
humor
inspirational
interview
joke
journal
juvenile
letter
literary criticism
man against man
man against nature
man against society
multicultural
mystery
news article
nonfiction
novel
novella
occult
ode
picture book

play
poetry
political satire
prose
reference
religious
report
research report
romance
saga
satire
self improvement
serial
sermon
short story
song
speech
sports
suspense
technical
textbook
tragedy
verse
western
young adult

The Reading Teacher's Book of Lists, Fourth Edition, © 2000 by John Wiley & Sons, Inc.

See also List 79, Characteristics of Narrative and Expository Text.

List 46. LITERARY TERMS

Every area of knowledge has its own specialized vocabulary—literature included. Knowing these terms and their meanings will help students recognize the use of these elements in literature. These terms are basic to discussions about an author's skilled use of language. Many of them can also be used to help beginning writers improve or add interest to their writing.

Accented. A part of a word, phrase, or sentence spoken with greater force or a stronger tone.

Act. Part or section of a play, similar to a book chapter. Acts are usually made up of groups of scenes.

Allegory. Links the objects, characters, and events of a story with meanings beyond the literal meaning of the story.

Alliteration. Occurs when two or more words have the same beginning sound. Example: *Mike mixed some malt in his milk.*

Anadiplosis. The use of the ending word of a phrase or clause as the beginning or base word for the next one. Example: *Pleasure might cause her to read, reading might cause her to know, knowledge might win piety, and piety might grace obtain.*

Analysis. Occurs when we look at and try to understand the parts of something so that we can better understand the whole thing.

Antithesis. Contrasting words or ideas by asserting something and then denying by parallel or balanced phrases. Example: *This soup should be eaten cold, not hot.*

Assonance. Occurs when an internal vowel sound is repeated in two or more words. Example: *He feeds the deer.*

Author's purpose. Authors write for four main purposes: to entertain, to inform, to express their opinions, and to persuade.

Ballad. A long poem that tells a story. Ballads usually have strong rhythm and rhyme.

Biography. Gives a factual account of someone's life. If the writer tells of his or her own life, it is called an *autobiography*.

Cast of characters. List of names of all the characters in a play.

Cause and effect. Sometimes an event or circumstance makes another event or circumstance happen. The first one is called the cause or reason for the second one. The second one is called the effect or result.

Characters. People or animals in a story or other writing.

Chiasmus. Change or word order to get the reader's attention and to highlight something. Example: *Down he fell.*

Chronological order. The telling of a group of events in the time order in which they happened.

Cliché. An overused phrase. Examples: *busy as a bee; gala occasion.*

Comparison. Points out the ways in which two or more things are alike or similar.

Conclusions. A decision made after considering several pieces of information. The information may include facts from the reading and ideas that the reader already had.

Conflict. The problem the characters face in the plot. The conflict can be a problem between two characters or between a character and something in nature or society. Sometimes the conflict makes a character choose between two important ideas.

Contrast. Points out the ways in which two or more things are different.

Description. A group of details the writer gives that help the reader imagine a person, place, object, or event. The details help create a picture in the reader's mind.

Dialogue. A conversation between characters in a story or play.

Drama. A story written to be acted out in front of an audience. Another word for drama is play.

Epic. A long narrative poem about the deeds of a hero.

Fact. A statement that can be proven.

Fairy tale. An imaginary story about fairies, elves, magical deeds, giants, etc.

Fantasy. A story that has imagined characters, settings, or other elements that could never really exist.

Fiction. A form of literature that tells stories about characters, settings, and events that the writer invents. Fiction may be based on some real places, people, or events, but it is not a true, factual story about them.

Figure of speech. Words or phrases that have meaning different from the literal meaning, such as idioms, metaphors, and similes. Example: *It's raining cats and dogs.*

Folk tale. A story about people or animals that has been handed down from one generation to the next. Folk tales often explain something that exists in nature or they tell about a hero.

Form. The structure or arrangement of elements in literature. Example: *The form of traditional poetry is lines of poetry in groups called stanzas.*

Generalization. A statement about a whole group that is made based on information about part of the group.

Genre. A category or type of writing, such as fiction and nonfiction, biography, adventure, and science fiction.

Historical fiction. Uses details about real places, events, and times from history as the setting for an imagined story.

Hyperbole. An exaggeration. Example: *He must have been nine feet tall.*

Idiom. An expression that cannot be understood from the literal meaning of its words. Example: *Tom is barking up the wrong tree.*

Imagery. The author's use of description and words to create vivid pictures or images in the reader's mind. Example: *A blanket of soft snow covered the sleeping tractors.*

Inference. A guess or conclusion based on known facts and hints or evidence. Sometimes readers use information from experience to help make inferences about what they are reading.

Irony. The use of tone, exaggeration, or understatement to suggest the opposite of the literal meaning of the words used. Example: *I didn't mind waiting two hours; it was restful.*

Kenning. A short metaphor for a thing that is not actually named. Example: *Sky candle is a kenning for the word sun.*

Litote. An understatement or assertion made by denying or negating its opposite. Example: *He wasn't unhappy about winning the bet.*

The Reading Teacher's Book of Lists, Fourth Edition, © 2000 by John Wiley & Sons, Inc.

Main idea. The one idea that all the sentences in a paragraph tell about. Sometimes the main idea is stated in a topic sentence; sometimes it is not stated but is implied.

Metaphor. The comparison of two things without using the words "like" or "as." Example: *Habits are first cobwebs, then cables.*

    Sense metaphor. Relates one of the five senses to an object or situation. Example: *a cool reception.*

    Frozen metaphor. A metaphor so frequently used that it has become an idiom or an expression with understood but not literal meaning. Example: *head of the class.*

    Humanistic metaphor. Gives inanimate objects human qualities or humans inanimate qualities. Example: *a user-friendly computer; her porcelain skin.*

    Inanimate metaphor. Pairs the quality of an inanimate object with another inanimate object. Example: *The walls were paper.*

    Abstract metaphor. Links an abstract concept with an object. Example: *Death is the pits.*

    Animal metaphor. Associates the characteristics of an animal with a human or object. Example: *What a teddy bear he is!*

    Incarnation metaphor. Links the attributes of a deceased person to another person or entity. Example: *He is a modern George Washington.*

Metonymy. The use of a related word in place of what is really being talked about. Example: *"pen"* instead of *"writing."*

Moral. The lesson that a story or fable teaches. Sometimes the moral of a fable is stated at the end of the story.

Motive. A reason a character does something.

Narrative poetry. Poetry that tells a story.

Narrator. The teller of a story.

Nonfiction. Writing that tells about real people, places, and events.

Novel. A long work of fiction.

Ode. A poem written in praise of someone or something.

Onomatopoeia. Words in which the sounds suggest the meaning of the words. Example: *Ouch.*

Opinion. A statement of someone's idea or feelings. An opinion cannot be proven. An opinion can be based on facts.

Oxymoron. The use of words with contradictory or clashing ideas next to one another. Example: *free slaves.*

Personification. The linking of a human quality or ability to an animal, object, or idea. Example: *The wind whispered through the night.*

Plot. Or storyline. The group of events that happen in order to solve the problem or conflict in the story.

Poetry. An expression of ideas or feeling in words. Poetry usually has form, rhythm, and rhyme.

Point of view. Refers to how a story is narrated. If a story is narrated from the first-person point of view, the narrator is a character in the story and uses the first-person pronouns *I, me, mine, we,* and *our.* If the story is narrated from the third-person point of view, the narrator is not part of the story and uses the third-person pronouns *he, him, she, her,* and *them.*

Predictions. The use of facts in the story and other information you know about the world to guess what will happen.

Rhyme. Two or more words that have the same ending sound.

Rhythm. A pattern of accented and unaccented syllables.

Science fiction. A type of story that is based on science-related ideas. Some of the scientific "facts" and developments in science fiction are not real and may never be possible.

Sequence. The order in which events occur or ideas are presented.

Setting. The time and place in which the story happens.

Simile. A comparison of two things using the words "like" or "as." Example: *She felt as limp as a rag doll.*

Solution. The turning point in a storyline or plot. It is the part in which a decision or important discovery is made or an important event happens that will solve the story's problem or end the conflict. The solution is also called the resolution or the climax of the plot.

Stage directions. What tells actors how to perform their parts of a play. They describe movements, tone, use of props, lighting, and other details.

Stanza. A group of related lines in a poem.

Theme. The message about life or nature that the author wants the reader to get from the story, play, or poem.

Topic sentence. A sentence, often at the beginning of a paragraph, that presents the main idea, theme, mood, or summary.

The Reading Teacher's Book of Lists, Fourth Edition, © 2000 by John Wiley & Sons, Inc.

See also List 44, Book Words.

List 47. OLD AND NEW FAVORITE BOOKS TO READ ALOUD

The benefits of reading aloud to children of all ages are well documented. It instills a love of books and reading, models fluent reading and inflection, aids comprehension and understanding story patterns, develops vocabulary, and is a very enjoyable experience. Because listening levels exceed children's reading levels, particularly in the primary grades, books for reading aloud may be at students' developmental reading level or two to three years above it. It has been determined that beginning picture books are written at a third-grade reading level.

Kindergarten

Allison's Zinnia, Anita Lobel

Animals Should Definitely Not Wear Clothing, Judi and Ron Barrett

Anno's Counting House, Mitsumasa Anno

Brown Bear, Brown Bear, What Do You See?, Bill Martin, Jr., illustrated by Eric Carle

Bunny Cakes, Rosemary Wells

Dinorella: A Prehistoric Fairy Tale, Pamela Duncan Edwards

Elmer, David McKee

The Enormous Crocodile, Roald Dahl

Flossie and the Fox, Patricia McKissack

Gathering the Sun: An Alphabet in Spanish and English, Alma Flor Ada

Give Me a Sign! What Pictograms Tell Us Without Words, Tiphaine Samoyault

The Great Kapok Tree, Lynne Cherry

The Grey Lady and the Strawberry Snatcher, Molly Bang

Growing Vegetable Soup, Lois Ehlert

Hattie and the Fox, Mem Fox

Horace, Holly Keller

I Do Not Want to Get Up Today, Dr. Seuss

If You Give a Moose a Muffin, Laura Numeroff

In a Cabin in a Wood, Darcy McNally

Last Tales of Uncle Remus, Julius Lester, illustrated by Jerry Pinkney

Lon Po Po, Ed Young

Madeline, Ludwig Bemelmans

The Mitten, Jan Brett

My Very First Mother Goose, Iona Opie, illustrated by Rosemary Wiles

Nana Upstairs, Nana Downstairs, Tomie dePaola

The Napping House, Don and Audrey Wood

The New Adventures of Mother Goose, Bruce Lansky

The Snowy Day, Ezra Jack Keats

The Three Little Javelinas, Susan Lowell

26 Letters and 99 Cents, Tana Hoban

Grade One

Abuela, A. Dorros

The Adventures of Taxi Dog, Debra and Sal Barracca, illustrated by Mark Buehner

Araminta's Paint Box, Karen Ackerman

Bearsie Bear and the Surprise Sleepover Party, Bernard Waber

Bunny Money, Rosemary Wells

Buz, Richard Egielski

The Chanukkah Guest, Eric Kimmel

Charlotte's Web, E. B. White

Chester's Way, Kevin Henkes

Chicken Sunday, Patricia Polacco

Elizabeth and Larry, Marilyn Sadler

Emily and the Enchanted Frog, Helen V. Griffith

Eppie M. Says, Olivier Dunrea

Everybody Needs a Rock, Byrd Baylor

Feathers for Lunch, Lois Ehlert

Good Driving, Amelia Bedelia, Peggy Parish

The Handmade Alphabet, Laura Rankin

James and the Giant Peach, Roald Dahl

Julius, the Baby of the World, Kevin Henkes

Lester's Dog, Karen Hesse

Little Red Riding Hood—A Newfangle Prairie Tale, Lisa C. Ernst

Ma Dear's Apron, Patricia McKissack, illustrated by Floyd Cooper

Millions of Cats, Wanda Gag

The Mixed-Up Chameleon, Eric Carle

The Mud Flat Olympics, James Stevenson

My Painted House, My Friendly Chicken and Me, Maya Angelou

Once Upon a Springtime, Jean Marzollo

The Polar Express, Chris Van Allsburg

Squirrels, Brian Wildsmith

Town Mouse, Country Mouse, Jan Brett

Two of Everything, L. Hong

Unanana and the Elephant, retold by Kathleen Arnott

Why Mosquitoes Buzz in People's Ears, Verna Aardema

The World That Jack Built, Ruth Brown

Grade Two

A House Is a House for Me, Maryann Hoberman, illustrated by Betty Fraser

A River Ran Wild, Lynne Cherry

Alexander and the Terrible, Horrible, No Good, Very Bad Day, Judith Viorst

Amazing Grace, Mary Hoffman

Amelia's Road, Linda Altman

Anno's Mysterious Multiplying Jar, Mitsumasa Anno

Arthur's TV Trouble, Marc Brown

Cecil's Story, George Ella Lyon

Chickens Aren't the Only Ones, Ruth Heller

Cricket in Times Square, George Selden

Dandelions, Eve and Greg Shed Bunting

The Disappearing Alphabet, Richard Wilbur

Ella Enchanted, Gail Carson Levine

Emma, Wendy Kesselman

Fanny's Dream, Mark and Caralyn Buehner

Freckle Juice, Beverly Cleary

Hailstones and Halibut Bones, Mary O'Neill, illustrated by John Wallner

Henry Huggins, Beverly Cleary

In a Messy, Messy Room, J. Gorog

Jumanji, Chris Van Allsburg

Lily's Purple Plastic Purse, Kevin Henkes

Many Nations, An Alphabet of Native America, Joseph Bruchac, illustrated by Robert G. Goetzl

Miss Rumphius, Barbara Cooney

My Father's Dragon, R. Gannet

One Duck Stuck, Phyllis Root

Owl Moon, Jane Yolen

Ramona the Pest, Beverly Cleary

Song and Dance Man, Karen Ackerman, illustrated by Stephen Gammell

Stuart Little, E. B. White

Summer of the Monkeys, Wilson Rawls

The Table Where Rich People Sit, Byrd Baylor

There Was an Old Lady Who Swallowed a Fly, Simms Taback

Tops and Bottoms, Janet Stevens

What Do Authors Do?, Eileen Christelow

The Widow's Broom, Chris Van Allsburg

Grade Three

Babe the Gallant Pig, Dick King-Smith

Castle in the Attic, Elizabeth Winthrop

Charlie and the Chocolate Factory, Roald Dahl

The Drop in My Drink: The Story of Water on Our Planet, Meredith Hooper

Fly Away Home, Eve Bunting

Frindle, Andrew Clements

Gabriella's Song, Candace Fleming

The Ghost Belonged to Me, Richard Peck

Grasshopper Summer, Ann Turner

The Great Frog Race and Other Poems, Kristine O'Connell George

The Lion, the Witch and the Wardrobe, C. S. Lewis

The Little House on the Prairie, Laura Ingalls Wilder

Maniac Magee, Jerry Spinelli

My Great-Aunt Arizona, Gloria Houston

Old Henry, Joan W. Blos

Passage to Freedom: The Sugihara Story, Ken Mochizuki
Rebel, Allan Baillie
Sami and the Time of the Troubles, Florence Parry Heide
Sarah, Plain and Tall, Patricia MacLachlan
Twenty-one Mile Swim, Matt Christopher
Wan Hu Is in the Stars, Jennifer Armstrong
Water Dance, Thomas Locker
Where the Red Fern Grows, Wilson Rawls
Witch Week, Dianna Wynne Jones

Grade Four

A Light in the Attic, Shel Silverstein
A Long Way from Chicago, Richard Peck
Afternoon of the Elves, Janet Taylor Lisle
Autumn Street, Lois Lowry
The Bones in the Cliff, James Stevenson
BoshBlobBerBosh:Runcible Poems for Edward Lear, J. Patrick Lewis
Coyote Dreams, Susan Nunes
Dear Mom, You're Ruining My Life, Jean Van Leeuwen
Gifted Hands: The Ben Carson Story, Ben Carson
Harry Potter and the Sorcerer's Stone, J. K. Rowling
Homecoming, Cynthia Voigt
How to Eat Fried Worms, Thomas Rockwell
Kokopelli's Flute, Will Hobbs
Lassie, Come-Home, Eric Knight
Meanwhile, Jules Feiffer
The Night Journey, Kathryn Lasky
No Mirrors in My Nana's House, Ysaye M. Barnwell
Nothing Ever Happens on 90th Street, Roni Schotter
On the Far Side of the Mountain, Jean C. George
Poems Have Roots, Lilian Moore
Redwall, Brian Jacques
Roll of Thunder, Hear My Cry, Mildred Taylor
Shades of Gray, Carolyn Reeder
Tom's Midnight Garden, Philippa Pearce

Grade Five

A Crack in the Clouds and Other Poems, Constance Levy
A Dog Called Kitty, Bill Wallace
A Taste of Salt, Frances Temple
A Wrinkle in Time, Madeline L'Engle
Cousins in the Attic, Gary Paulsen
I Am Regina, Sally M. Keehn
The Indian in the Cupboard, Lynn Reid Banks
Insectlopedia, Douglas Florian

Lyddie, Katherine Paterson
Mary on Horseback: Three Mountain Stories, Rosemary Wells
The Midwife's Apprentice, Karen Cushman
Mississippi Mud: Three Prairie Journals, Ann Turner
The Night the Bells Rang, Natalie Kinsey-Warnock
Nothing But the Truth, Avi
Once Upon a Dark November, Carol Beach York
The Pinballs, Betsy Byars
Seedfolks, Paul Fleschman
Shadow Spinner, Susan Fletcher
The Secret Garden, Frances Hodgson Burnett
The Spell of the Sorcerer's Skull, John Bellairs
What Jamie Saw, Carolyn Coman
Where the Sidewalk Ends, Shel Silverstein
White Wash, Ntozake Shange
The Wreckers, Iain Lawrence

Grade Six

Balyet, Patricia Wrightson
Beauty, Robin McKinley
Call of the Wild, Jack London
Cool Melons—Turn to Frogs! The Life and Poems of Issa, Matthew Gollub
Crossing the Delaware: A History in Many Voices, Louise Peacock
Everywhere, Bruce Brooks
The Foxman, Gary Paulsen
The Hatmaker's Sign: A Story by Benjamin Franklin, retold by Candace Fleming
Holes, Louis Sachar
The House of Dies Drear, Virginia Hamilton
I Know What You Did Last Summer, Lois Duncan
The Islander, Cynthia Rylant
Moaning Bones: African American Ghost Stories, retold by Jim Haskins
Out of the Dust, Karen Hesse
Prairie Songs, Pam Conrad
Radiance Descending, Paula Fox
Shiloh, Phyllis Reynolds Naylor
The Shakespeare Stealer, Gary Blackwood
The Slave Dancer, Paula Fox
Treasures in the Dust, Tracey Porter
Truth to Tell, Nancy Bond
Tuck Everlasting, Natalie Babbitt
Twin in the Tavern, Gary Paulsen
The Upstairs Room, Johanna Reiss

See also List 82, Oral Reading Activities.

The Reading Teacher's Book of Lists, Fourth Edition, © 2000 by John Wiley & Sons, Inc.

List 48. AWARD-WINNING CHILDREN'S BOOKS

Each year many distinguished panels recognize the best in new children's books. Three prestigious awards given the same day are the Caldecott Medal, the Newbery Medal, and the Coretta Scott King Award. The Caldecott Medal, in honor of Randolph Caldecott, an English illustrator of children's books, has been awarded since 1938 to the artist of the most distinguished American picture book published in the preceding year. Since 1922, the Newbery Medal, honoring John Newbery, an eighteenth-century publisher of quality children's books, has been awarded to the author of the most distinguished contribution to American literature for children. The Coretta Scott King Award recognizes African-American authors and illustrators for outstanding contributions to children's and young adult literature that promotes multicultural understanding and appreciation.

Caldecott Medal Winners

1938 *Animals of the Bible* by Helen Dean Fish, illustrated by Dorothy P. Lathrop. Philadelphia: Lippincott.

1939 *Mei Li* by Thomas Handforth. New York: Doubleday.

1940 *Abraham Lincoln* by Ingri and Edgar Parin d'Aulaire. New York: Doubleday.

1941 *They Were Strong and Good* by Robert Lawson. New York: Viking.

1942 *Make Way for Ducklings* by Robert McCloskey. New York: Viking.

1943 *The Little House* by Virginia Lee Burton. Boston: Houghton Mifflin.

1944 *Many Moons* by James Thurber, illustrated by Louis Slobodkin. New York: Harcourt Brace Jovanovich.

1945 *Prayer for a Child* by Rachel Field, illustrated by Elizabeth Orton Jones. New York: Macmillan.

1946 *The Rooster Crows . . .* (traditional Mother Goose), illustrated by Maud and Miska Petersham. New York: Macmillan.

1947 *The Little Island* by Golden MacDonald, illustrated by Leonard Weisgard. New York: Doubleday.

1948 *White Snow, Bright Snow* by Alvin Tresselt, illustrated by Roger Duvoisin. New York: Lothrop.

1949 *The Big Snow* by Berta and Elmer Hader. New York: Macmillan.

1950 *Song of the Swallows* by Leo Politi. New York: Scribner's.

1951 *The Egg Tree* by Katherine Milhous. New York: Scribner's.

1952 *Finders Keepers* by William Lipkind, illustrated by Nicolas Mordvinoff. New York: Harcourt Brace Jovanovich.

1953 *The Biggest Bear* by Lynd Ward. Boston: Houghton Mifflin.

1954 *Madeline's Rescue* by Ludwig Bemelmans. New York: Viking.

1955 *Cinderella, or the Little Glass Slipper* by Charles Perault, translated and illustrated by Marcia Brown. New York: Scribner's.

1956 *Frog Went A-Courtin'* edited by John Langstaff, illustrated by Feodor Rojankovsky. New York: Harcourt Brace Jovanovich.

1957 *A Tree Is Nice* by Janice May Udry, illustrated by Marc Simont. New York: Harper.

1958 *Time of Wonder* by Robert McCloskey. New York: Viking.

The Reading Teacher's Book of Lists, Fourth Edition, © 2000 by John Wiley & Sons, Inc.

1959 *Chanticleer and the Fox* adapted from Chaucer and illustrated by Barbara Cooney. New York: Thomas Y. Crowell.

1960 *Nine Days to Christmas* by Marie Hall Ets and Aurora Labastida, illustrated by Marie Halls Ets. New York: Viking.

1961 *Baboushka and the Three Kings* by Ruth Robbins, illustrated by Nicolas Sidjakov. New York: Viking.

1962 *Once a Mouse. . .* by Marcia Brown. New York: Scribner's.

1963 *The Snowy Day* by Ezra Jack Keats. New York: Viking.

1964 *Where the Wild Things Are* by Maurice Sendak. New York: Harper.

1965 *May I Bring a Friend?* by Beatrice Schenk de Regniers, illustrated by Beni Montresor. New York: Atheneum.

1966 *Always Room for One More* by Sorche Nic Leodhas, illustrated by Nonny Hogrogian. New York: Holt, Rinehart & Winston.

1967 *Sam, Bangs & Moonshine* by Evaline Ness. New York: Holt, Rinehart & Winston.

1968 *Drummer Hoff* by Barbara Emberley, illustrated by Ed Emberley. Englewood Cliffs, NJ: Prentice-Hall.

1969 *The Fool of the World and the Flying Ship* by Arthur Ransome, illustrated by Uri Shulevitz. New York: Farrar, Straus & Giroux.

1970 *Sylvestor and the Magic Pebble* by William Steig. New York: Windmill.

1971 *A Story—A Story* by Gail E. Haley. New York: Atheneum.

1972 *One Fine Day* by Nonny Hogrogian. New York: Macmillan.

1973 *The Funny Little Woman* retold by Arlene Mosel, illustrated by Blair Lent. New York: Dutton.

1974 *Duffy and the Devil* by Harve Zemach, illustrated by Margot Zemach. New York: Farrar, Straus & Giroux.

1975 *Arrow to the Sun* adapted and illustrated by Gerald McDermott. New York: Viking.

1976 *Why Mosquitoes Buzz in People's Ears* retold by Verna Aardema, illustrated by Leo and Diane Dillon. New York: Dial Press.

1977 *Ashanti to Zulu; African Traditions* by Margaret Musgrove, illustrated by Leo and Diane Dillon. New York: Dial Press.

1978 *Noah's Ark* by Peter Spier. New York: Doubleday.

1979 *The Girl Who Loved Wild Horses* by Paul Goble. Scarsdale, NY: Bradbury.

1980 *Ox-Cart Man* by Donald Hall. New York: Viking.

1981 *Fables* by Arnold Lobel. New York: Harper.

1982 *Jumanji* by Chris van Allsburg. Boston: Houghton Mifflin.

1983 *Shadow* translated by Blaise Cendrars, illustrated by Marcia Brown. New York: Scribner's.

1984 *The Glorious Flight Across the Channel with Louis Bleriot* by Alice and Martin Provensen. New York: Viking.

1985 *Saint George and the Dragon* as retold by Margaret Hodges, illustrated by Trina Schart Hyman. Boston: Little, Brown.

1986 *The Polar Express* by Chris van Allsburg. Boston: Houghton Mifflin.

1987 *Hey, Al* by Arthur Yorinks, illustrated by Richard Egielski. New York: Farrar, Straus & Giroux.

1988 *Owl Moon* by Jane Yolen, illustrated by John Schoenherr. New York: Philomel.

1989 *Song and Dance Man* by Karen Ackerman, illustrated by Stephen Gammell. New York: Alfred A. Knopf.

1990 *Lon Po Po: A Red-Riding Hood Story from China* by Ed Young. New York: Philomel.

1991 *Black and White* by David Macaulay. Boston: Houghton Mifflin.

1992 *Tuesday* by David Weisner. New York: Clarion Books.

1993 *Mirette on the High Wire* by Emily Arnold McCully. New York: Putnam.

1994 *Grandfather's Journey* by Allen Say; Walter Lorraine, text editor. Boston: Houghton Mifflin.

1995 *Smoky Night* by Eve Bunting, illustrated by David Diaz. San Diego: Harcourt Brace Jovanovich.

1996 *Officer Buckle and Gloria* by Peggy Rathmann. New York: Putnam.

1997 *Golem* by David Wisneiwski. New York: Clarion.

1998 *Rapunzel* by Paul O. Zelinsky. New York: Dutton.

1999 *Snowflake Bentley* by Mary Azarian and Jacqueline B. Martin. Boston: Houghton Mifflin.

Web site: www.ala.org/alsc/caldecott.html

Newbery Medal Winners

1922 *The Story of Mankind* by Hendrik Willem van Loon. New York: Liveright.

1923 *The Voyages of Doctor Dolittle* by Hugh Lofting. Philadelphia: J. B. Lippincott.

1924 *The Dark Frigate* by Charles Hawes. Boston: Atlantic/Little.

1925 *Tales from Silver Lands* by Charles Finger. New York: Doubleday.

1926 *Shen of the Sea* by Arthur Bowie Chrisman. New York: Dutton.

1927 *Smoky, the Cowhorse* by Will James. New York: Scribner's.

1928 *Gayneck, The Story of a Pigeon* by Dhan Gopal Mukerji. New York: Dutton.

1929 *The Trumpeter of Krakow* by Eric P. Kelly. New York: Macmillan.

1930 *Hitty, Her First Hundred Years* by Rachel Field. New York: Macmillan.

1931 *The Cat Who Went to Heaven* by Elizabeth Coatsworth. New York: Macmillan.

1932 *Waterless Mountain* by Laura Adams Armer. New York: Longman.

1933 *Young Fu of the Upper Yangtze* by Elizabeth Forman Lewis. New York: Winston.

1934 *Invincible Louisa* by Cornelia Meigs. Boston: Little, Brown.

1935 *Dobry* by Monica Shannon. New York: Viking.

1936 *Caddie Woodlawn* by Carol Brink. New York: Macmillan.

1937 *Roller Skates* by Ruth Sawyer. New York: Viking.

1938 *The White Stag* by Kate Seredy. New York: Viking.

1939 *Thimble Summer* by Elizabeth Enright. New York: Rinehart.

1940 *Daniel Boone* by James Daugherty. New York: Viking.

1941 *Call It Courage* by Armstrong Sperry. New York: Macmillan.

1942 *The Matchlock Gun* by Walter D. Edmonds. New York: Dodd.

1943 *Adam of the Road* by Elizabeth Janet Gray. New York: Viking.

1944 *Johnny Tremain* by Esther Forbes. Boston: Houghton Mifflin.

1945 *Rabbit Hill* by Robert Lawson. New York: Viking.

1946 *Strawberry Girl* by Lois Lenski. Philadelphia: J. B. Lippincott.

1947 *Miss Hickory* by Carolyn Sherwin Bailey. New York: Viking.

1948 *The Twenty-one Balloons* by William Pene du Bois. New York: Viking.

1949 *King of the Wind* by Marguerite Henry. Chicago: Rand McNally.

1950 *The Door in the Wall* by Marguerite de Angeli. New York: Doubleday.

1951 *Amos Fortune, Free Man* by Elizabeth Yates. New York: Aladdin.

1952 *Ginger Pye* by Eleanor Estes. New York: Harcourt Brace Jovanovich.

1953 *Secret of the Andes* by Ann Nolan Clark. New York: Viking.

1954 *. . . and now Miguel* by Joseph Krumgold. New York: Thomas Y. Crowell.

1955 *The Wheel on the School* by Meindert DeJong. New York: Harper.

1956 *Carry on, Mr. Bowditch* by Jean Lee Latham. Boston: Houghton Mifflin.

1957 *Miracles on Maple Hill* by Virginia Sorensen. New York: Harcourt Brace Jovanovich.

1958 *Rifles for Watie* by Harold Keith. New York: Thomas Y. Crowell.

1959 *The Witch of Blackbird Pond* by Elizabeth George Speare. Boston: Houghton Mifflin.

1960 *Onion John* by Joseph Krumgold. New York: Thomas Y. Crowell.

1961 *Island of the Blue Dolphins* by Scott O'Dell. Boston: Houghton Mifflin.

1962 *The Bronze Bow* by Elizabeth George Speare. Boston: Houghton Mifflin.

1963 *A Wrinkle in Time* by Madeleine L'Engle. New York: Farrar, Straus & Giroux.

1964 *It's Like This, Cat* by Emily Cheney Neville. New York: Harper.

1965 *Shadow of a Bull* by Maia Wojciechowska. New York: Atheneum.

1966 *I, Juan de Pareja* by Elizabeth Borton de Trevino. New York: Farrar, Straus & Giroux.

1967 *Up a Road Slowly* by Irene Hunt. New York: Follett.

1968 *From the Mixed-Up Files of Mrs. Basil E. Frankweiler* by E. L. Konigsburg. New York: Atheneum.

1969 *The High King* by Lloyd Alexander. New York: Holt.

1970 *Sounder* by William H. Armstrong. New York: Harper.

1971 *Summer of the Swans* by Betsy Byars. New York: Viking.

1972 *Mrs. Fisby and the Rats of NIMH* by Robert C. O'Brien. New York: Atheneum.

1973 *Julie of the Wolves* by Jean C. George. New York: Harper.

1974 *The Slave Dancer* by Paula Fox. New York: Bradbury.

1975 *M. C. Higgins, The Great* by Virginia Hamilton. New York: Macmillan.

1976 *The Grey King* by Susan Cooper. New York: Atheneum.

1977 *Roll of Thunder, Hear My Cry* by Mildred D. Taylor. New York: Dial Press.

1978 *Bridge to Terabithia* by Katherine Paterson. New York: Thomas Y. Cromwell.

1979 *The Westing Game* by Ellen Raskin. New York: Dutton.

1980 *A Gathering of Days: A New England Girl's Journal, 1830–32* by Joan Blos. New York: Greenwillow.

1981 *Jacob Have I Loved* by Katherine Paterson. New York: Thomas Y. Crowell.

1982 *A Visit to William Blake's Inn: Poems for Innocent and Experienced Travelers* by Nancy Willard. New York: Harcourt Brace Jovanovich.

1983 *Dicey's Song* by Cynthia Voigt. New York: Atheneum.

1984 *Dear Mr. Henshaw* by Beverly Cleary. New York: Morrow.

1985 *The Hero and the Crown* by Robin McKinley. New York: Greenwillow.

1986 *Sarah, Plain and Tall* by Patricia MacLachlan. New York: Harper.

1987 *The Whipping Boy* by Sid Fleischman. New York: Greenwillow.

1988 *Lincoln: A Photobiography* by Russell Freedman. Boston: Houghton Mifflin.

1989 *Joyful Noise: Poems for Two Voices* by Paul Fleischman. New York: Harper.

1990 *Number the Stars* by Lois Lowry. Boston: Houghton Mifflin.

1991 *Maniac Magee* by Jerry Spinelli. Boston: Little, Brown.

1992 *Shiloh* by Phyllis Reynolds Naylor. New York: Atheneum.

1993 *Missing May* by Cynthia Rylant. New York: Orchard Books.

1994 *The Giver* by Lois Lowry. Boston: Houghton Mifflin.

1995 *Walk Two Moons* by Sharon Creech. New York: HarperCollins.

1996 *The Midwife's Apprentice* by Karen Cushman. New York: Clarion.

1997 *The View from Saturday* by E. L. Koningsburg. New York: Jean Karl/Atheneum.

1998 *Out of the Dust* by Karen Hesse. New York: Scholastic.

1999 *Holes* by Louis Sachar. New York: Farrar, Straus & Giroux.

Web site: www.ala.org/alsc/newbery.html

The Reading Teacher's Book of Lists, Fourth Edition, © 2000 by John Wiley & Sons, Inc.

Coretta Scott King Awards

The Coretta Scott King Award was founded by the late Glyndon Flynt Greer, a school librarian in Englewood, New Jersey, who envisioned an award that would recognize the talents of outstanding African-American authors and encourage them to continue writing books for children and young adults. In 1969, Green—along with school librarian Mable McKissack, book publisher John Carroll, and New York state librarian Roger McDonough—established the Coretta Scott King Award to commemorate the life and work of the late Dr. Martin Luther King, Jr., and honor his widow, Coretta Scott King, for continuing to work for peace and world brotherhood. Titles honored are selected by a panel of librarians on the basis of appeal to children and young adults and sensitivity to "the true worth and value of all beings." This award is presented at the American Library Association Annual Conference to an African-American author and an African-American illustrator; the separate award for illustrator was added in 1979.

1970 AUTHOR
Dr. Martin Luther King, Jr.: Man of Peace by Lillie Patterson, illustrations by Victor Mays.

1971 AUTHOR
Black Troubadour: Langston Hughes by Charlemae Rollins.

1972 AUTHOR
Seventeen Black Artists by Elton C. Fax.

1973 AUTHOR
I Never Had It Made: The Autobiography of Jackie Robinson by Jackie Robinson as told to Alfred Duckett.

1974 AUTHOR
Ray Charles by Sharon Bell Mathis, illustrations by George Ford.

1975 AUTHOR
The Legend of Africania by Dorothy Robinson, illustrations by Herbert Temple.

1976 AUTHOR
Duey's Tale by Pearl Bailey, illustrations by Arnold Skolnick and Gary Azon.

1977 AUTHOR
The Story of Stevie Wonder by James Haskins.

1978 AUTHOR
Africa Dream by Eloise Greenfield, illustrations by Carole Byard.

1979 AUTHOR
Escape to Freedom: A Play about Young Frederick Douglass by Ossie Davis.

ILLUSTRATOR
Something on My Mind by Nikki Grimes, illustrations by Tom Feelings.

1980 AUTHOR
The Young Landlords by Walter Dean Myers.

ILLUSTRATOR
Cornrows by Camille Yarbrough, illustrations by Carole Byard.

1981 AUTHOR
This Life by Sidney Poitier.

ILLUSTRATOR
Beat the Story-Drum, Pum-Pum illustrated by Ashley Bryan.

1982 AUTHOR
Let the Circle Be Unbroken by Mildred D. Taylor.

ILLUSTRATOR
Mother Crocodile: An Uncle Amadou Tale from Senegal translated by Rosa Guy, illustrations by John Steptoe.

1983 AUTHOR
Sweet Whispers, Brother Rush by Virginia Hamilton.

ILLUSTRATOR
Black Child illustrated by Peter Magubane.

1984 AUTHOR
Everett Anderson's Goodbye by Lucille Clifton, illustrations by Ann Grifalconi.

ILLUSTRATOR
My Mamma Needs Me by Mildred Pitts Walter, illustrations by Pat Cummings.

1985 AUTHOR
Motown and Didi: A Love Story by Walter Dean Myers.

ILLUSTRATOR—NO AWARD

1986 AUTHOR
The People Could Fly: American Black Folktoles by Virginia Hamilton, illustrations by Leo Dillon and Diane Dillon.

ILLUSTRATOR
The Patchwork Quilt by Valerie Flourney, illustrations by Jerry Pinkney.

1987 AUTHOR
Justin and the Best Biscuits in the World by Mildred Pitts Walter, illustrations by Catherine Stock.

ILLUSTRATOR
Half a Moon and One Whole Star by Crescent Dragonwagon, illustrations by Jerry Pinkney.

1988 AUTHOR
The Friendship by Mildred D. Taylor, illustrations by Max Ginsburg.

ILLUSTRATOR
Mufaro's Beautiful Daughters: An African Tale by John Steptoe.

1989 AUTHOR
Fallen Angels by Walter Dean Myers.

ILLUSTRATOR
Mirandy and Brother Wind by Patricia C. McKissack, illustrations by Jerry Pinkney.

1990 AUTHOR
A Long Hard Journey: The Story of the Pullman Porter by Patricia C. McKissack and Frederick McKissack.

ILLUSTRATOR
Nathanial Talking by Eloise Greenfield, illustrations by Jan Spivey Gilchrist.

1991 AUTHOR
The Road to Memphis by Mildred D. Taylor.

ILLUSTRATOR
Aida by Leontyne Price, illustrations by Leo Dillon and Diane Dillon.

1992 AUTHOR
Now Is Your Time! The African American Struggle for Freedom by Walter Dean Myers.

ILLUSTRATOR
Tar Beach illustrated by Faith Ringgold.

1993 AUTHOR
The Dark-Thirty: Southern Tales of the Supernatural by Patricia C. McKissack.

ILLUSTRATOR
The Origin of Life on Earth: An African Creation Myth retold by David A. Anderson, illustrations by Kathleen Atkins Wilson.

1994 AUTHOR
Toning the Sweep by Angela Johnson.

ILLUSTRATOR
Soul Looks Back in Wonder: Collection of African-American Poets edited by Phyllis Fogelman, illustrations by Tom Feelings.

1995 AUTHOR
Christmas in the Big House, Christmas in the Quarters by Patricia C. McKissack and Frederick McKissack, illustrations by John Thompson.

ILLUSTRATOR
The Creation by James Weldon Johnson, illustrations by James Ransome.

1996 AUTHOR
Her Stories: African American Folktales, Fairy Tales and True Tales by Virginia Hamilton, illustrations by Leo Dillon and Diane Dillon.

ILLUSTRATOR
The Middle Passage: White Ships/Black Cargo, illustrated by Tom Feelings, introduction by John Henrik Clarke.

1997 AUTHOR
Slam! by Walter Dean Myers.

ILLUSTRATOR
Minty: A Story of Young Harriet Tubman by Alan Schroeder, illustrations by Jerry Pinkney.

1998 AUTHOR
Forged by Fire by Sharon M. Draper.

ILLUSTRATOR
In Daddy's Arms I Am Tall illustrated by Javaka Steptoe.

1999 AUTHOR
Heaven by Angela Johnson.

ILLUSTRATOR
I See the Rhythm by Toyomi Igus, illustrated by Michelle Wood.

Web site: www.ala.org/srrt/csking/

List 49. OTHER CHILDREN'S BOOK AWARDS

In addition to the well-known Caldecott, Newbery, and King awards, there are many other prestigious awards for excellence in children's literature. This list will help you identify sources for award winners in many categories. For a list of the winners for this and previous years, visit the web site of the organization presenting the award. Most can be reached through links found in children's literature web addresses such as the Children's Literature Web Guide (see List 140) or from the organization's online home page (e.g., www.ala.org).

American Book Award was established in 1979, replacing The National Book Award, and is awarded annually for a juvenile title. The award-winning book must be written by an American citizen and published the preceding year in the United States.

Americas Award for Children's and Young Adult Literature was launched in 1993 by the Consortium of Latin American Studies Programs to recognize annually excellence in an English or Spanish language picture book, poetry, fiction, or folklore published in the United States. The award-winning books focus on the experience and cultural heritage of Latinos in the U.S., Latin America, or the Caribbean.

Award for Excellence in Poetry for Children is given every three years by the National Council of Teachers of English to a living American poet in recognition of a body of work. It was first given in 1977.

Boston Globe–Horn Book Awards are jointly awarded annually (since 1967) to a children's author of fiction or poetry, an author of nonfiction, and to an illustrator by *The Boston Globe* and *The Horn Book Magazine.*

Carnegie Medal was established in 1937 by the British Library Association's Youth Libraries Group and is awarded annually for an outstanding book published in the United Kingdom.

Christopher Awards, Books for Young People category, began in 1970 by The Christophers, a nondoctrinal organization with Catholic roots, to recognize books that "affirm the highest values of the human spirit."

Edgar Allen Poe Awards given each year since 1945 by the Mystery Writers of America to recognize excellence in the field of mystery writing. It was named for Edgar Allan Poe, the "Father of the Detective Story." Of the 13 categories, there is one for the best mystery book for children and one for the best mystery for young adults.

Golden Kite Award is made by the members of the Society of Children's Book Writers and Illustrators to fellow members for excellence in the field of children's fiction, nonfiction, picture book, and picture illustration. It began in 1974.

Hans Christian Andersen Medals have been awarded since 1956 by the International Board on Books for Young People to an author and an illustrator to recognize their significant contribution of their entire body of work to children's literature.

International Reading Association Children's Book Awards were established in 1975 to encourage new talent in children's literature. They are presented for an author's first or second published fiction or nonfiction book for young (4–10) and older (10–17) readers.

Jane Addams Children's Book Award, a presentation by the Women's International League for Peace and Freedom and the Jane Addams Peace Association since 1953, recognizes a recently published children's book that promotes peace, social justice, and world community. It is awarded on September 6 each year commemorating the birthday of Jane Addams, the first American woman to win the Nobel Peace Prize.

Kate Greenaway Medal is given each year by the British Library Association. It was established in 1956 to honor the most distinguished UK children's book illustrator.

Laura Ingalls Wilder Medal, named after its first honoree, is a tribute to a U.S. author or illustrator whose books have made a lasting contribution to children's literature. The award, established in 1954 by the Association for Library Service to Children (a part of the American Library Association), was given every five years from 1960 to 1980; it is now given every three years.

Lee Bennett Hopkins Promising Poet Award, made by the International Reading Association, is a monetary award given each three years to a promising new author of children's poetry.

Margaret A. Edwards Award for Outstanding Literature for Young Adults is awarded to an author for lifetime achievement writing for teens by the Young Adult Library Services Association, a part of the American Library Association. The award was established in 1988 to honor authors who help teens better understand themselves and the world.

Mildred L. Batchelder Award has been presented annually since 1968 by the American Library Association for an outstanding book for children translated into English. The award goes to the U.S. publisher responsible for the English edition.

National Book Award for Young People's Literature was added to the National Book Awards in 1996. Before that, a Children's Book category was used by the National Book Award/American Book Award Program from 1969 to 1983. It recognizes an outstanding contribution by a U.S. author to children's literature and is based on literary merit.

Orbis Pictus Award for Outstanding Nonfiction for Children has been given by the National Council of Teachers of English since 1990 to recognize and encourage excellence in nonfiction writing for children. It takes its name from the first nonfiction book written for children, *Orbis Pictus* (The World in Pictures) by Johann Comenius, which was published in 1657.

Regina Medal was established in 1959 by the Catholic Library Association and honors a writer whose work is a distinguished contribution to children's literature. It is not a religiously-based award, but recognizes literature of lasting quality.

Scott O'Dell Award for Historical Fiction, established in 1981, is awarded for the best U.S. book of historical fiction written for children and set in the New World.

Sydney Taylor Awards are given annually to two authors of books (one for young children, one for older children) selected as the most significant contributions to Jewish children's literature published during the preceding year. The books present "positive Jewish content for children." The awards have been made since 1968.

Young Reader's Choice Award, though made by the regional Pacific Northwest Library Association, has been respected and widely-known since 1940 for its recognition of books that children and young adults find enjoyable and therefore promote leisure reading. Books are nominated primarily by students, parents, teachers, and librarians.

See also List 48, Award-Winning Children's Books.

The Reading Teacher's Book of Lists, Fourth Edition, © 2000 by John Wiley & Sons, Inc.

List 50. BOOKS WITHOUT WORDS

It's never too early to enjoy reading a good book and the books listed below are just the thing for very young children. Wordless books allow preschoolers to "read" the stories through pictures. Early positive reading experiences through picture books can be a real boost to learning to read.

Anno Mitsumasa. *Anno's Counting Book.*

———. *Anno's Flea Market.*

———. *Anno's Journey.*

———. *Topsy-Turvies: Pictures to Stretch the Imagination.*

Baker, Jeannie. *Window.*

Bang, Molly. *The Grey Lady and the Strawberry Snatcher.*

Banyai, Istavan. *R.E.M.*

———. *Zoom.*

Briggs, Raymond. *The Snowman.*

Bruna, Dick. *Another Story to Tell.*

Burlson, Joe. *Space Colony.*

Carle, Eric. *Do You Want to Be My Friend?*

Collington, Peter. *The Angel and the Soldier Boy.*

———. *On Christmas Eve.*

Day, Alexandra. *Carl Goes Shopping.*

———. *Carl's Birthday.*

———. *Carl's Christmas.*

———. *Good Dog, Carl.*

De Groat, Diane. *Alligator's Toothache.*

dePaola, Tomie. *Pancakes for Breakfast.*

Drescher, Henrik. *The Yellow Umbrella.*

Goodall, John. *Creepy Castle.*

———. *The Midnight Adventures of Kelly, Dot and Esmeralda.*

———. *Paddy Pork's Holiday.*

———. *The Surprise Picnic.*

Gorey, Edward. *The Tunnel Calamity.*

Hanford, Martin. *Find Waldo Now.*

———. *Where's Waldo.*

Hoban, Tana. *Big Ones, Little Ones.*

———. *I Read Signs.*

———. *I Read Symbols.*

———. *Is It Red? Is It Yellow? Is It Blue?*

———. *Look Book.*

———. *Over, Under, Through, and Other Spacial Concepts.*

Hutchins, Pat. *1 Hunter.*

———. *Changes, Changes.*

———. *Rosie's Walk.*

Jenkins, Steve. *Looking Down.*

The Reading Teacher's Book of Lists, Fourth Edition, © 2000 by John Wiley & Sons, Inc.

Keats, Ezra Jack. *Skates!*
Kitchen, Bert. *Animal Alphabet.*
Krahn, Fernando. *April Fools.*
———. *The Creepy Thing.*
———. *The Secret in the Dungeon.*
Martin, Rafe. *Will's Mammoth.*
Mayer, Mercer. *A Boy, a Dog, a Frog and a Friend.*
———. *Frog Goes to Dinner.*
———. *Frog, Where Are You?*
———. *The Great Cat Chase.*
———. *Hiccup.*
McCully, Emily Arnold. *Picnic.*
Ormerod, Jan. *Moonlight.*
Pilkey, Dav. *The Paperboy.*
Rohmann, Eric. *Time Flies.*
Sasaki, Isao. *Snow.*
Sesame Street. *Can You Find What's Missing?*
Spier, Peter. *Noah's Ark.*
———. *People.*
———. *Peter Spier's Rain.*
Tafuri, Nancy. *Follow Me!*
———. *Junglewalk.*
Turk, Hanne. *Happy Birthday Max.*
———. *Max Packs.*
———. *Snapshot Max.*
Turkle, Brinton. *Deep in the Forest.*
Ward, Lynd. *The Silver Pony.*
Weisner, David. *Free Fall.*
———. *Tuesday.*
Winter, Paula. *The Bear and the Fly.*

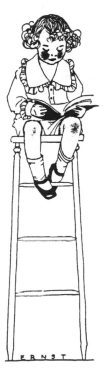

List 51. PREDICTABLE BOOKS

These books contain a lot of repetition and still maintain high interest. Some teachers use them regularly as part of beginning reading instruction.

Becker, John. *Seven Little Rabbits.*

Bonne, Rose and Mills, Alan. *I Know an Old Lady.*

Brown, Marcia. *The Three Billy Goats Gruff.*

Burningham, John. *Hey! Get Off Our Train.*

———. *Mr. Gumpy's Outing.*

Carle, Eric. *The Very Busy Spider.*

———. *The Very Hungry Caterpillar.*

Charlip, Remy. *Fortunately.*

Domanska, Janina. *Busy Monday Morning.*

Elting, Mary and Folsom, Michael. *Q Is for Duck, An Alphabet Guessing Game.*

Galdone, Paul. *The Gingerbread Boy.*

———. *Henny Penny.*

———. *The Little Red Hen.*

———. *The Three Little Bears.*

———. *The Three Little Pigs.*

Gelman, Rita. *More Spaghetti I Say!*

Ginsburg, Mirra. *The Chick and the Duckling.*

Hutchins, Pat. *Good Night, Owl.*

———. *Happy Birthday Sam.*

———. *Rosie's Walk.*

Kellogg, Steven. *Can I Keep Him?*

Kraus, Robert. *Where Are You Going, Little Mouse?*

Langstaff, John. *Oh, A-Hunting We Will Go.*

Lobel, Arnold. *A Treeful of Pigs.*

Mars, W. *The Old Woman and Her Pig.*

Martin, Bill. *Brown Bear, Brown Bear, What Do You See?*

———. *Polar Bear, Polar Bear, What Do You Hear?*

McGovern, Ann. *Too Much Noise.*

Peppe, Rodney. *The House that Jack Built.*

Sendak, Maurice. *Chicken Soup with Rice.*

———. *Where the Wild Things Are.*

Williams, Sue. *I Went Walking.*

Wylie, Joanne and David. *A Funny Fish Story.*

The Reading Teacher's Book of Lists, Fourth Edition, © 2000 by John Wiley & Sons, Inc.

The following sets of predictable books provide many enjoyable reading experiences for students.

City Kids. Cypress; Rigby. Short comic paperbacks that include no text versions to encourage writing.

Predictable Books. Scholastic. Two sets containing 15 books each that are designed for grades K–1 and grades 1–2.

Ready to Read. Richard C. Owens. 45 paperback books from New Zealand that contain different formats and natural language. Big books available.

The Story Box. Wright Group. 117 books from New Zealand that are color coded for different levels. Big books and cassettes available.

Sunshine Books. Wright Group. Easy reading books that are short and small.

Theme Packs. Rigby. One big book and several matching small books that cover such themes as space, dinosaurs, and family.

Willie MacGurkle and Friends; Finnigan and Friends. Curriculum Associates. Ten books in each set that develop language skills through the use of rhymes, rhythm, and amusing characters.

The Reading Teacher's Book of Lists, Fourth Edition, © 2000 by John Wiley & Sons, Inc.

List 52. SOUND-AWARENESS BOOKS

Here are some books that are particularly useful for encouraging sound recognition and production. They have lots of repetition and are a natural setting for exploring sounds, developing auditory discrimination, and rhyming.

Allen, P. *Bertie and the Bear.*

Antle, Nancy. *The Good Bad Cat.*

Arnold, Marsha. *Quick, Quack, Quick!*

Barrett, Jan. *Animals Should Definitely Not Act Like People.*

———. *Animals Should Definitely Not Wear Clothing.*

Blocksma, Mary. *Yoo, Hoo, Moon!*

Boegehold, B. *You Are Much Too Small.*

Cameron, Alyssa. *The Cat Sat on the Mat.*

Capucilli, A. *Biscuit.*

Carle, Eric. *Have You Seen My Cat?*

Child, Lydia Maria. *Over the River and Through the Wood.* Pictures by Brinton Turkle.

Cleary, Beverly. *The Hullabaloo ABC.* Illustrated by Ted Rand.

Coxe, Molly. *Big Egg.*

Degen, Bruce. *Jamberry.*

Goode, Diane. *Diane Goode's Book of Scary Stories and Songs.*

Grimes, Nikki. *C Is for City.* Pictures by Pat Cummings.

Hoberman, Maryann. *A House Is a House for Me.*

Hoff, Sid. *Mrs. Brice's Mice.*

Hutchins, Pat. *Don't Forget the Bacon!*

———. *Follow That Bus!*

Kovalski, Maryann. *The Wheels on the Bus.*

Leedy, Loreen. *Pingo the Plaid Panda.*

Maccarone, Grace. *What Is THAT? Said the Cat.*

Marshall, James. *Fox Be Nimble.*

Martin, Bill, Jr. and Archambault, John. *Chicka Chicka Boom Boom!* Illustrated by Lois Ehlert.

Modesitt, Jeanne and Johnson, Lonni Sue. *The Story of Z.*

Oppenheim, Joanne. *Uh, Oh, Said the Crow.*

———. *Wake Up, Baby!*

Peet, Bill. *No Such Things.*

———. *Zella, Zack, and Zodiac.*

Petrie, Catherine. *Joshua James Likes Trucks.*

Provensen, Alice and Provensen, Martin. *A Peaceable Kingdom: The Shaker ABCEDARIUS.*

Pomerantz, Charlotte. *How Many Trucks Can a Tow Truck Tow?*

Raffi. *Shake My Sillies Out.*

Rosen, Michael. *We're Going on a Bear Hunt.* Illustrated by Helen Oxenbury.

Schade, Susan and Buller, Jon. *Toad on the Road.*

Seuss, Dr. *Hop on Pop.*

————. *I Am Not Going to Get Up Today!*

————. *Marvin K. Mooney, Will You Please Go Now!*

Shannon, George. *Tomorrow's Alphabet.* Illustrated by Donald Crews.

Shaw, Nancy. *Sheep in a Jeep.*

————. *Sheep on a Ship.*

Showers, Paul. *The Listening Walk.* Illustrated by Aliki.

Siracusa, Catherine. *Bingo, the Best Dog in the World.*

Snow, Pegeen. *A Pet for Pat.*

Taback, Simms. *There Was an Old Lady Who Swallowed a Fly.*

Terban, M. *I Think I Thought.*

Wadsworth, Olive. *Over in the Meadow.*

Williams, Linda. *The Little Old Lady Who Was Not Afraid of Anything.* Illustrated by Megan Lloyd.

Zieffert, H. *Oh, What a Noisy Farm!*

List 53. ALL-TIME FAVORITES

What does it take to be an all-time favorite? A great story. Fascinating characters. Superb writing. The following selections have all three characteristics and have been enjoyed by millions of readers since they were first published. Some have been favorites of our parents, grandparents, and even our great-grandparents. Read these and see which ones will be on *your* list of all-time favorites.

Aesop's Fables.

Alcott, Louisa May. *Little Women.*

Andersen, Hans Christian. *The Complete Fairy Tales and Stories.*

Armstrong, William. *Sounder.*

Barrie, Sir James. *Peter Pan.*

Baum, L. Frank. *The Wizard of Oz.*

Bemelmans, Ludwig. *Madeline.*

Blume, Judy. *Are You There, God? It's Me, Margaret.*

Brown, Margaret Wise. *Goodnight Moon.*

Brunhoff, Jean de. *The Story of Babar.*

Burnett, Frances Hodgson. *The Secret Garden.*

Carle, Eric. *The Very Hungry Caterpillar.*

Carroll, Lewis. *Alice in Wonderland and Through the Looking Glass.*

Chaucer, Geoffrey. *Chanticleer and the Fox.*

Cinderella.

Dahl, Roald. *Charlie and the Chocolate Factory.*

Dickens, Charles. *A Christmas Carol.*

Farley, Walter. *The Black Stallion.*

Frank, Anne. *Diary of a Young Girl.*

Freeman, Don. *Corduroy.*

Goble, Paul. *The Girl Who Loved Wild Horses.*

Grahame, Kenneth. *The Wind in the Willows.*

Grimm, Jakob and Grimm, Wilhelm. *The Complete Fairy Tales.*

Henry, Marguerite. *Album of Horses.*

Hutchins, Pat. *Pat the Bunny.*

Keats, Ezra Jack. *The Snowy Day.*

Kotzwinkle, William. *ET the Extra-Terrestrial Story Book.*

L'Engle, Madeline. *A Wrinkle in Time.*

Lang, Andrew (ed.). *The Blue Fairy Book.*

McCloskey, Robert. *Make Way for Ducklings.*

Milne, A. A. *Winnie-the-Pooh.*

Moore, Clement. *The Night Before Christmas.*

Potter, Beatrix. *The Tale of Peter Rabbit.*

The Reading Teacher's Book of Lists, Fourth Edition, © 2000 by John Wiley & Sons, Inc.

Red Riding Hood.

Saint-Exupery, Antonie de. *The Little Prince.*

Sendak, Maurice. *Where the Wild Things Are.*

Seuss, Dr. *The Cat in the Hat.*

Silverstein, Shel. *A Light in the Attic.*

————. *Where the Sidewalk Ends.*

Stevenson, Robert Louis. *A Children' Garden of Verses.*

————. *Treasure Island.*

Swift, Jonathan. *Gulliver's Travels.*

The Three Bears.

Tolkien, J.R.R. *The Hobbit.*

Travers, P. L. *Mary Poppins.*

Twain, Mark. *The Adventures of Tom Sawyer.*

White, E.B. *Charlotte's Web.*

————. *The Trumpet of the Swan.*

Wilder, Laura Ingalls. *Little House on the Prairie.*

————. *Little House in the Big Woods.*

Williams, Margery. *The Velveteen Rabbit.*

Wright, Blanche F. (illus.). *The Real Mother Goose.*

See also List 48, Award-Winning Children's Books.

List 54. BOOKS FOR RELUCTANT AND DEVELOPING READERS

The best motivation for reading is a great book. The ones on these lists were selected to appeal to even the most reluctant readers. The books on the elementary level (for ages 8–11) are high-interest "easy readers." Many have a great deal of illustration (a few are advanced picture books) and strong story lines that help struggling readers. The books on the intermediate and older reader list will hold the attention of students in the middle grades and above but are written to be less challenging for the developmental/remedial reader aged 12 to 16. The lists contain a wide range of poetry, sports, mysteries, biography, historical fiction, adventure, and fiction.

Elementary Level

Abbott, Tony. *Danger Guys.* HarperCollins, 1994.

Adler, David. *Cam Jansen and the Mystery of the Stolen Diamonds.* Viking, 1997.

———. *Cam Jansen and the Scary Snake Mystery.* Penguin-Putnam, 1999.

Ballard, Robert D. and Froman, Nan. *Finding the Titanic.* Scholastic, 1993.

Benchley, Nathaniel. *George the Drummer Boy.* HarperCollins, 1987.

Blachford, Claire H. *Going with the Flow.* Carolrhoda, 1998.

Boyd, Candy Dawson. *Chevrolet Saturdays.* Penguin, 1995.

Bulla, Clyde R. *The Chalk Box Kid.* Random House, 1987.

———. *Shoeshine Girl.* HarperCollins, 1989.

Bunting, Eve. *December.* Harcourt, 1997.

———. *Fly Away Home.* Houghton Mifflin, 1993.

Byars, Betsy. *The Golly Sisters Go West.* HarperCollins, 1989.

Cole, Joanna and Calmeson, Stephanie. *Yours Till Banana Splits.* Morrow, 1995.

Collins, Beverly. *Monster Manners.* Scholastic, 1995.

Coville, Bruce. *I Left My Sneakers in Dimension X.* Pocket Books, 1994.

Del Prado, Dana. *Terror Below! True Shark Stories.* Putnam, 1997.

dePaola, Tomie. *The Clown of God.* Weston Woods, 1985.

Demi. *Budda.* Henry Holt, 1996.

Demuth, Patricia. *Way Down Deep: Strange Ocean Creatures.* Putnam, 1995.

Donnelly, Judy. *Moonwalk: The First Trip to the Moon.* Random House, 1989.

Dorros, Arthur. *Ant Cities.* HarperCollins, 1987.

Feiffer, Jules. *Meanwhile.* HarperCollins, 1999.

Fritz, Jean. *George Washington's Mother.* Putnam, 1992.

Giff, Patricia Reilly. *Shark in School.* Delacorte, 1994.

Gorog, Judith. *In a Creepy, Creepy Place & Other Scary Stories.* HarperCollins, 1997.

Greenburg, Dan. *The Zack Files, My Son the Time Traveler.* Grossett & Dunlap, 1997.

Greenfield, Eloise. *Nathaniel Talking.* Writers and Readers Publishing, 1990.

Gutelle, Andrew. *Baseball's Best: Five True Stories.* Random House, 1990.

Haas, Jessie. *Beware the Mare.* Morrow, Williams, 1996.

Hopkins. L. B. (ed.). *Questions, Poems of Wonder.* HarperCollins, 1992.

The Reading Teacher's Book of Lists, Fourth Edition, © 2000 by John Wiley & Sons, Inc.

Hudson, Wade. *Great Black Heroes: Five Notable Inventors*. Scholastic, 1995.

———. *Pass It On: African American Poetry for Children*. Scholastic, 1993.

Jones, Charlotte F. *Mistakes That Worked*. Doubleday, 1994.

Kramer, Sydelle A. *Hoop Stars*. Putnam, 1995.

Levy, Elizabeth. *My Life as a Fifth-Grade Comedian*. HarperCollins, 1997.

Lundell, Margo. *A Girl Named Helen Keller*. Scholastic, 1995.

———. *Lad, a Dog*. Scholastic, 1997.

MacLachlan, Patricia. *Skylark*. HarperCollins, 1994.

Marschall, Ken. *Inside the Titanic*. Little, Brown, 1997.

Mills, Claudia. *Losers, Inc*. HarperCollins, 1997.

Milton, Joyce. *Big Cats*. Putnam, 1994.

Moore, Eva. *Buddy: The First Seeing Eye Dog*. Scholastic, 1996.

Nirgiotis, Nicholas. *Volcanoes: Mountains That Blow Their Tops*. Putnam, 1996.

O'Connor, Jim. *Comeback! Four True Stories*. Random House, 1992.

Osborne, Mary Pope. *Afternoon on the Amazon*. Random House, 1995.

Paulsen, Gary. *My Life in Dog Years*. Delacourte Press, 1998.

Peason, Kit. *Awake and Dreaming*. Viking, 1996.

Peet, Bill E. *Bill Peet: An Autobiography*. Houghton Mifflin, 1989.

Penner, Lucille Recht. *Sitting Bull*. Grossett & Dunlap, 1995.

———. *Twisters*. Random House, 1996.

Pinkwater, Daniel. *Mush, a Dog from Space*. Atheneum, 1995.

Prelutsky, Jack. *The Beauty of the Beast*. Knopf, 1997.

———. *A Pizza the Size of the Sun. Poems by Jack Prelutsky*. Greenwillow, 1996.

Provensen, Alice. *The Buck Stops Here: Presidents of the United States*. Harcourt Brace, 1997.

Rylant, Cynthia. *Every Living Thing*. Simon & Schuster, 1988.

Sachar, Louis. *Wayside School Gets a Little Stranger*. Avon, 1995.

Scieszka, Jon. *The Good, the Bad, and the Goofy*. Penguin/Putnam, 1993.

———. *Math Curse*. Viking, 1995.

Shannon, George. *True Lies: 18 Tales for You to Judge*. Morrow, Williams, 1998.

Shea, George. *Amazing Rescues*. Random House, 1992.

Simms, Laura. *The Bone Man: A Native American Modoc Tale*. Hyperion, 1997.

Spinelli, Jerry. *Crash*. Knopf, 1996.

———. *Wringer*. HarperCollins, 1997.

Strasser, Todd. *Kidnap Kids*. Putnam, 1998.

Talbott, Hudson and Greenberg, Mark. *Amazon Diary: The Jungle Adventures of Alex Winters*. Putnam, 1998.

Tamar, Erika. *The Junkyard Dog*. Knopf, 1995.

Tunnel, Michael O. *Mailing May*. Greenwillow, 1998.

Vozar, David. *M.C. Turtle and the Hip Hop Hare: A Happenin' Rap*. Dell, 1997.

———. *Rapunzel: A Happenin' Rap*. Bantam Doubleday Dell, 1999.

Wells, Robert E. *What's Faster Than a Speeding Cheetah?* Whitman, 1997.

Wick, Walter. *A Drop of Water*. Scholastic, 1997.

Willis, Meredith Sue. *Marco's Monster*. HarperCollins, 1996.

Willner-Pardo, Gina. *Jason and the Losers*. Morrow, Williams, 1997.

The Reading Teacher's Book of Lists, Fourth Edition, © 2000 by John Wiley & Sons, Inc.

Middle Grades and Above

Aebi, Tania. *Maiden Voyage.* Ballantine Books, 1998.

Agee, Jon. *So Many Dynamos! And Other Palindromes.* Farrar, 1995.

Alabisco, Vincent (ed.). *Flash! The Associated Press Covers the World.* Harry N. Abrams. 1998.

Aldrich, Bess Streeter. *A Lantern in Her Hand.* Viking Penguin, 1998.

Armstrong, Jennifer. *Steal Away.* Scholastic, 1998.

Ash, Russell. *The Top 10 of Everything.* Dorling Kindersley, 1995.

Atkin, S. Beth. *Voices from the Streets: Young Former Gang Members Tell Their Stories.* Little, Brown, 1997.

Balmes, Pat. *Danger at the Flying Y.* High Noon Books, 1982.

Barr, Nevada. *Firestorm.* Avon Books, 1998.

Barrie, Barbara. *Adam Zigzag.* Bantam Doubleday Dell, 1998.

Barron, T. A. *Lost Years of Merlin.* Philomel, 1997.

Bartoletti, Susan Campbell. *Growing Up in Coal Country.* Houghton, 1998.

Begay, Shonto. *Navajo: Voices and Vision across the Mesa.* Scholastic, 1996.

Bennett, James. *Dakota Dream.* Scholastic, 1995.

Berry, Liz. *The China Garden.* Farrar, Straus & Giroux, 1997.

Blackwood, Gary. *The Shakespeare Stealer.* Dutton, 1998.

Bosse, Malcolm. *Examination.* Farrar, Straus & Giroux, 1998.

Brandenburg, Jim. *To the Top of the World: Adventures With Arctic Wolves on Ellesmere Island.* Walker and Company, 1998.

Brimner, Larry D. *Snowboarding.* Franklin Watts, 1997.

Busenberg, Bonnie. *Vanilla, Chocolate & Strawberry: The Story of Your Favorite Flavors.* Lerner, 1995.

Callahan, Steven. *Adrift: Seventy-six Days Lost at Sea.* Ballantine Books, 1998.

Canfield, Jack. *Chicken Soup for the Teenage Soul.* Health Communications, 1998.

Carlson, Lori M. (ed.). *American Eyes: New Asian-American Short Stories for Young Adults.* Holt, 1996.

————. *Cool Salsa: Bilingual Poems on Growing Up Latino in the United States.* Holt, 1995.

Carol, Joyce A. and Wilson, Edward E. (eds.). *Poetry after Lunch: Poems to Read Aloud.* Absey, 1998.

Carter, Alden R. *Bull Catcher.* Scholastic, 1998.

Chadwick, Douglas and Sartore, Joel. *The Company We Keep: America's Endangered Species.* National Geographic Society, 1998.

Chambers, Veronica. *Mama's Girl.* Riverhead Books, 1997.

Chang, Pang-Mei Natasha. *Bound Feet & Western Dress.* Doubleday, 1998.

Christiansen, C. B. *I See the Moon.* Simon & Schuster/Atheneum, 1996.

Clinton, Catherine. *I, Too, Sing America: African American Poetry.* Houghton Mifflin, 1998.

Colman, Penny. *Corpses, Coffins, and Crypts: A History.* Holt, 1997.

Cooney, Caroline B. *The Voice on the Radio.* Delacorte, 1997.

————. *What Child Is This? A Christmas Story.* Delacorte, 1998.

Corbett, Sara. *Venus to the Hoop.* Doubleday, 1998.

Dereske, Jo. *Miss Zukas and the Library Murders.* Avon Books, 1998.

Drotar, David Lee. *The Fire Curse and Other True Medical Mysteries.* Walker, 1995.

Duffey, Betsy. *Coaster.* Viking, 1995.

Dyer, Daniel. *Jack London: A Biography.* Scholastic, 1998.

Elders, Joycelyn and Chanoff, David. *Joycelyn Elders, M.D.: From Sharecropper's Daughter to Surgeon General of the United States of America.* Morrow, 1998.

Farrell, Jeanette. *Invisible Enemies: Stories of Infectious Diseases.* Farrar, Straus & Giroux, 1998.

Feelings, Tom. *The Middle Passage: White Ships/Black Cargo.* Dial, 1996.

Filipovic, Zlata. *Zlata's Diary: A Child's Life in Sarajevo.* Viking, 1995.

Fleischman, Paul. *Bull Run.* HarperCollins Children's Books, 1998.

Fleischman, Sid. *The Abracadabra Kid: A Writer's Life.* Greenwillow Books, 1997.

Fleming, Robert and Boyd, Robert. *The Big Book of Urban Legends: Adapted from the Works of Jan Harold Brunvand.* DC Comics/Paradox Press, 1995.

Fradin, Dennis B. *Planet Hunters: The Search for Other Worlds.* Simon & Schuster, 1998.

Freedman, Russell. *The Life and Death of Crazy Horse.* Holiday House, 1997.

———. *Martha Graham: A Dancer's Life.* Clarion, 1998.

Fremon, Celeste. *Father Greg & the Homeboys.* Hyperion, 1996.

Frey, Darcy. *The Last Shot: City Streets, Basketball Dreams.* Houghton, 1996.

George, Jean Craighead. *The Talking Earth.* HarperCollins Children's Books, 1998.

Getz, David. *Frozen Man.* Holt, 1995.

Glenn, Mel. *Jump Ball: A Basketball Season in Poems.* Dutton/Lodestar, 1998.

———. *Who Killed Mr. Chippendale? A Mystery in Poems.* Lodestar Books, 1997.

Godfrey, Martyn. *Please Remove Your Elbow from My Ear.* Avon Books, 1998.

Goldman, E. M. *Getting Lincoln's Goat.* Delacorte, 1996.

Greenberg, Jan and Jordan, Sandra. *American Eye: Eleven Artists of the Twentieth Century.* Delacorte, 1996.

Greene, Bette. *Summer of My German Soldier.* Dell, 1998.

Greenfield, Susan (ed.). *The Human Mind Explained: An Owner's Guide to the Mysteries of the Mind.* Holt, 1998.

Gregory, Kristiana. *Earthquake at Dawn.* Harcourt Brace and Co., 1998.

Griffin, Adele. *The Other Shepards.* Hyperion, 1998.

Haddix, Margaret Peterson. *Don't You Dare Read This, Mrs. Dunphrey.* Simon & Schuster Books for Young Readers, 1997.

Hamilton, Virginia. *Her Stories: African American Folktales, Fairy Tales, and True Tales.* Scholastic/Blue Sky, 1996.

Hardman, Ric Lynden. *Sunshine Rider: The First Vegetarian.* Western Delacorte, 1998.

Haugaard, Erik. *The Samurai's Tale.* Houghton Mifflin, 1998.

Hesse, Karen. *The Music of Dolphins.* Scholastic Press, 1997.

Hewetson, Sarah. *Eye Magic: Fantastical Optical Illusions.* Golden, 1995.

Hill, Ernest. *A Life for a Life.* Simon & Schuster, 1998.

Hillerman, Tony. *Thief of Time.* HarperCollins, 1998.

Hockenberry, John. *Moving Violations.* Hyperion, 1996.

Holyoke, Nancy. *Oops! The Manners Guide for Girls.* Pleasant Co. Pub., 1996.

Hopkins, Lee Bennett. *Been to Yesterdays: Poems of Life.* Boyd Mills/Wordsong, 1996.

Hotze, Sollace. *A Circle Unbroken.* Houghton Mifflin, 1998.

Hudgins, Andrew. *The Glass Hammer: A Southern Childhood.* Houghton Mifflin, 1995.

Hughes, Langston. *The Block.* Viking, 1996.

Hurwin, Davida Wills. *A Time for Dancing.* Little, Brown, 1996.

Huth, Angela. *Land Girls.* St. Martin's, 1997.

Ingold, Jeanette. *The Window.* Harcourt Brace, 1997.

Jiang, Ji-li. *Red Scarf Girl: A Memoir of the Cultural Revolution.* HarperCollins, 1998.

Jimenez, Francisco. *The Circuit: Stories from the Life-Migrant Child.* University of New Mexico Press, 1997.

Johnson, Angela. *Heaven.* Simon & Schuster, 1998.

Johnson, LouAnne. *Dangerous Minds.* St. Martin's Press, 1998.

Jordan, Michael. *I Can't Accept Not Trying: Michael Jordan on the Pursuit of Excellence.* Harper San Francisco, 1995.

Juster, Norton. *Otter Nonsense.* Morrow, 1995.

Keillor, Garrison and Nilson, Jenny Lind. *The Sandy Bottom Orchestra.* Hyperion, 1997.

Kerr, M. E. *Deliver Us from Evie.* HarperCollins, 1995.

King, Laurie. *Beekeeper's Apprentice.* Bantam Books, 1998.

Klass, David. *California Blue.* Scholastic, 1995.

Konigsburg, E. L. *The Second Mrs. Giaconda.* Simon & Schuster Children's, 1998.

Kozol, Jonathan. *Amazing Grace.* Crown, 1997.

Laird, Crista. *But Can the Phoenix Sing?* Greenwillow, 1996.

Laksy, Kathryn. *Beyond the Burning Time.* Scholastic, 1998.

Lester, Julius. *Othello.* Scholastic, 1996.

Levy, Marilyn. *Run for Your Life.* Houghton Mifflin, 1997.

Lobel, Anita. *No Pretty Pictures: A Child of War.* Greenwillow, 1998.

Lopez, Steve. *Third and Indiana.* Viking, 1996.

Lynch, Chris. *Iceman.* HarperCollins, 1995.

Macy, Sue. *Winning Ways: A Photohistory of American Women in Sports.* Henry Holt, 1997.

Marrin, Albert. *Virginia's General: Robert E. Lee and the Civil War.* Simon & Schuster/Atheneum, 1996.

Marsden, John. *Letters from the Inside.* Houghton Mifflin, 1995.

Mastoon, Adam. *The Shared Heart.* Morrow, 1997.

Maxwell, Robin. *Secret Diary of Anne Boleyn.* Arcade, 1998.

McCaughrean, Geraldine. *The Pirate's Son.* Scholastic, 1998.

McKissack, Patricia and McKissack, Frederick. *Red-Tail Angels: The Story of the Tuskegee Airmen of World War II.* Walker, 1996.

McLaren, Clemence. *Inside the Walls of Troy.* Simon & Schuster/Atheneum, 1998.

Meyer, Carolyn. *Drummers of Jericho.* Harcourt, 1996.

Miller, E. E. (ed.). *In Search of Color Everywhere: A Collection of African-American Poetry.* Stewart, Tabori & Chang, 1996.

Monceaux, Morgan. *Jazz: My Music, My People.* Knopf, 1995.

Mori, Kyoko. *One Bird.* Holt, 1996.

Morpurgo, Michael. *War of Jenkins' Ear.* Putnam/Philomel, 1996.

Murphy, Jim. *The Great Fire.* Scholastic, 1996.

Myers, Walter Dean. *Harlem.* Scholastic, 1998.

———. *One More River to Cross: An African American Photograph Album.* Harcourt Brace, 1997.

———. *Slam!* Scholastic Press, 1997.

The Reading Teacher's Book of Lists, Fourth Edition, © 2000 by John Wiley & Sons, Inc.

Nelson, Theresa. *Earthshine.* Orchard, 1995.

Newth, Mette. *The Dark Light.* Farrar, Straus & Giroux, 1998.

Nix, Garth. *Shade's Children.* HarperCollins, 1998.

Nolan, Han. *Dancing on the Edge.* Harcourt, 1998.

O'Brien, Robert C. *Z for Zachariah.* Macmillan Publishing, 1998.

O'Dell, Scott. *Black Star, Bright Dawn.* Fawcett Book Group, 1998.

Paschen, Elise, et al. (eds.). *Poetry in Motion: One Hundred Poems from the Subways and Buses.* W. W. Norton, 1997.

Paulsen, Gary. *Father Water, Mother Woods: Essays on Fishing and Hunting in the North Woods.* Delacorte, 1995.

Philip, Neil (ed.). *In a Sacred Manner I Live: Native American Wisdom.* Clarion, 1998.

Poe, Edgar Allan, et al. *Tales of Horror.* Random House Step-Up Classic Chillers, 1994.

Quarles, Heather. *A Door Near Here.* Delacorte, 1998.

Randle, Kristen. *Only Alien on the Planet.* Scholastic, 1996.

Rinaldi, Ann. *Hang a Thousand Trees with Ribbons: The Story of Phillis Wheatley.* Harcourt Brace, 1997.

Ritter, John H. *Choosing Up Sides.* Philomel, 1998.

Richman, Hazel and McCamp-Bell, Darlene Z. (eds.) *Bearing Witness: Stories of the Holocaust.* Orchard/Melanie Kroupa, 1996.

Rostkowski, Margaret I. *Moon Dancer.* Harcourt Brace and Co., 1998.

Ryan, Joan. *Little Girls in Pretty Boxes: The Making and Breaking of Elite Gymnasts and Figure Skaters.* Doubleday, 1996.

Salzman, Mark. *Lost in Place.* Random House, 1997.

Savage, Candace. *Cowgirls.* Ten Speed Press, 1997.

Shihab Nye, Naomi (ed.). *Tree Is Older Than You Are: A Bilingual Gathering of Poems and Stories from Mexico with Paintings by Mexican Artists.* Simon & Schuster, 1996.

Southgate, Martha. *Another Way to Dance.* Delacorte Press, 1997.

Staples, Suzanne Fisher. *Dangerous Skies.* Farrar, Straus & Giroux, 1997.

Sullivan, George. *Pitchers: Twenty-Seven of Baseball's Greatest.* Atheneum, 1995.

Swanson, Diane. *Safari Beneath the Sea.* Sierra Club, 1995.

Tanaka, Shelley. *Discovering the Iceman.* Hyperion Books for Children, 1996.

Vande Velde, Vivian. *Companions of the Night.* Harcourt/Jane Yolen, 1996.

Ward, Geoffrey. *25 Great Moments.* Knopf, 1995.

Weaver, Will. *Farm Team.* HarperCollins, 1996.

Wells, H. G., et al. *The War of the Worlds.* Random House Step-Up Classic Chillers, 1991.

Welter, John. *I Want to Buy a Vowel.* Algonquin, 1997.

Williams, Renault. *Formula 1 Motor Racing Book.* Dorling Kindersley, 1995.

Wormser, Richard. *Hoboes: Wandering in America, 1870–1940.* Walker, 1995.

List 55. KIDS' MAGAZINES

Magazines for children and their online counterparts (See Kids' Zines, List 141) are very important for helping students establish lifelong reading habits. Few can ignore the pull of the new weekly or monthly edition of a favorite source of up-to-date information on a hobby, sport, or other interest. Magazines are great sources of high-interest material for reluctant and/or developing readers.

The Acorn	1530 7th Street, Rock Island, IL 61201
American Girl Magazine	8400 Fairway Place, Middleton, WI 53562
Boodle: By Kids, For Kids	P.O. Box 1049, Portland, IN 47371
Boys' Life Magazine	1325 W. Walnut Hill Lane, P.O. Box 152350, Irving, TX 75015-2350
Calliope: World History for Young People	7 School Street, Peterborough, NH 03458
Child Life	1100 Waterway Blvd., P.O. Box 567, Indianapolis, IN 46202
Children's Digest	1100 Waterway Blvd., P.O. Box 567, Indianapolis, IN 46202
Cobblestone	20 Grove Street, Peterborough, NH 03458
Cricket	Box 2670, Boulder, CO 80321
Dragonfly	NSTA, 1480 Wilson Blvd., Arlington, VA 22201
Flying Pencil Press	P.O. Box 7667, Elgin, IL 60121
Highlights for Children	803 Church Street, Honesdale, PA 18431
Humpty Dumpty's Magazine	1100 Waterway Blvd., P.O. Box 567, Indianapolis, IN 46202
Ink Blot	7200 Burmeister, Saginaw, MI 48609
The McGuffey Writer	5128 Westgate Drive, Oxford, OH 45056
Ranger Rick	1412 16th Street NW, Washington, DC 20036
Skipping Stones	P.O. Box 3939, Eugene, OR 97403
Stone Soup, The Magazine by Children	Children's Art Foundation, P.O. Box 83, Santa Cruz, CA 95063
Young Authors Magazine	P.O. Box 81847, Lincoln, NE 68501-1847
Young Voices	P.O. Box 2321, Olympia, WA 98507
Your Big Backyard	1412 16th Street NW, Washington, DC 20036

See also List 141, Kids' Zines.

The Reading Teacher's Book of Lists, Fourth Edition, © 2000 by John Wiley & Sons, Inc.

List 56. BOOK-LIST COLLECTIONS

Use this list of indexes, anthologies, collections, and recommendations to identify and locate books for the classroom, school library, or personal library. Many of these reference or resource titles can be found in your public libraries.

FICTION AND NONFICTION COLLECTIONS

American Library Association. (1999) *ALA's Guide to Best Reading in 2000.* Chicago: ALA. These annotated book lists were compiled by librarians and book reviewers and include ALA's excellent long-time resources "Notable Children's Books," "Editors' Choice," "Quick Picks for Young Adults," and "Popular Paperbacks for Young Adults."

————. *Outstanding Books for the College Bound.* (annual) Chicago: ALA. A series of bibliographic lists highlighting the best in fiction, nonfiction, biographies, fine arts, and theater reading for pre-college students.

Barr, Catherine. (1998) *From Biography to History: Best Books for Children's Entertainment and Education.* New York: R. R. Bowker. Annotated list of 600 biographies of notable men and women for children in grades 3 through 9. Especially helpful for social studies enrichment.

Barstow, Barbara and Riggle, Judith. (1995) *Beyond Picture Books: A Guide to First Readers,* 2nd Ed. Help for selecting independent and developmental reading materials for students in primary grades.

Bernstein, Joanne and Rudman, Marsha. (1988) *Books to Help Children Cope with Separation and Loss.* Volume 3. New York: R. R. Bowker. A good reference guide to more than 600 titles dealing with separation themes and appropriate for children from kindergarten to junior high.

Bingham, Jane and Scholt, Grayce. (1980) *Fifteen Centuries of Children's Literature: An Annotated Chronology of British and American Works in Historical Context.* Westport, CT: Greenwood Press. A good resource for a history of children's literature.

Bishop, R. S. (Ed.). (1994). *A Multicultural Booklist for Grades K–8.* National Council of Teachers of English.

Breen, Karen. (1988) *Index to Collective Biographies for Young Readers.* New York: R. R. Bowker. Indexes over 1,000 collective biographies covering more than 10,000 famous people; easy-to-use indexes by name, field, and book title.

Calvert, Stephen J. (1997) *Best Books for Young Adult Readers Grades 7–12.* New York: R. R. Bowker. A guide to more than 6,500 books for teens for leisure and school reading.

Cavanaugh, Michael (Ed.). (1999) *The Barnes and Noble Guide to Children's Books.* An annotated guide to baby books, preschool books, picture books, early readers, and children's fiction and poetry. Also includes list of books for special needs (divorce, disability, adoption, death, etc.)

Children's Literature Center. (1990) *Children and Reading: A Reading List for Parents.* Washington, DC: Library of Congress. Recommended reading lists for use by parents.

————. (annual) *Books for Children.* Washington, DC: Library of Congress. Recommendations for good reading selected from recently published fiction and nonfiction. Books are listed by age group and entries include bibliographies and thematic information.

Children's Literature. (annual) *Children's Literature Choices for 1999.* Annual choices of the 150 best new children's books including books for children 3 and under, picture books for children ages 4 to 8, short books or picture books for young readers ages 5 to 10, longer books for middle readers ages 8–12. Selected from new children's, books for young adults aged 12 and up, and poetry.

Children's Magazine Guide: Subject Index to Children's Magazines. (Periodical) New York: R. R. Bowker. A unique source that lets children ages 8 to 12 find articles on subjects of interest in over fifty children's magazines.

Cole, Joanna. (1993) *Best-loved Folktales of the World.* New York: EconoClad Books. Anthology of 200 folktales from around the world.

Fakih, Kimberly Olson. (1993) *The Literature of Delight: A Critical Guide to Humorous Books for Children.* New York: R. R. Bowker. A guide to over 800 fiction and nonfiction titles sure to please students from preschool through junior high.

Faurot, Jeannette L. (1995) *Asian-Pacific Folktales and Legends.* New York: Touchstone Press. A diverse collection of folktales and legends designed to entertain and teach elementary children.

Freeman, Judy. (1995) *More Books Kids Will Sit Still For: A Read-Aloud Guide.* New York: R. R. Bowker. A guide to more than 1,400 of the best new fiction, poetry, folktales, and nonfiction to read aloud to students from grades preschool through six. Includes summary, suggested activities, and additional related classroom resources.

Friedberg, Joan; Mullins, June; and Sukiennik, Adelaide. (1991) *Portraying the Disabled: A Guide to Juvenile Non-Fiction.* New York: R. R. Bowker. Annotated bibliography of more than 350 nonfiction books covering physical, sensory, cognitive, and behavorial disabilities.

Gillespie, John T. (1998) *Best Books for Children: Preschool Through Grade 6,* 6th Ed. New York: R. R. Bowker. Annotated bibliography of more than 18,000 titles in 500 categories each with recommendations from two or more notable children's book journals.

Hearne, Betsy. (1999) *Choosing Books for Children: A Commonsense Guide.* University of Illinois Press. Helpful information about children's books including recommendations.

International Reading Association and Children's Book Council. (annual) *Children's Choices.* Newark, DE: IRA. Results of an annual survey of 10,000 students' preferences for recently published trade books. Winning books are annotated and divided by reader's age.

———. (annual) *Young Adults' Choices.* Newark, DE: IRA. Results of an annual survey of 4,500 middle school through high school students' preferences for recently published trade books. Bibliographic information and plot summaries are included for the winners.

Jensen, J. M. and Roser, N. L. (1993). *Adventuring with Books: A Booklist for Pre-K to Grade 6,* 10th edition. National Council of Teachers of English. A general collection of good books for elementary grade readers.

Kennedy, DayAnn; Spangler, Stella; and Vanderwerf, Mary Ann. (1990) *Science & Technology in Fact and Fiction.* A valuable source for good books on science topics for elementary school children. Readability levels are included.

Kimmel, Margaret and Segel, Elizabeth. (1991) *For Reading Out Loud!: A Guide to Sharing Books with Children.* Revised. New York: Dell. Annotated list of books recommended for reading aloud to children, preschool through grade 8.

The Reading Teacher's Book of Lists, Fourth Edition, © 2000 by John Wiley & Sons, Inc.

Lewis, Valerie and Mayes, Walter. (1998). *Valerie and Walter's Best Books for Children*. New York: Avon. A book-by-book guide for children, birth to age 14. Books are identified by listening, interest, and reading levels. Themes are identified and cross-referenced.

LiBretto, Ellen. (1990) *High/Lo Handbook: Encouraging Literacy in the 1990's*, 3rd Ed. New York: R. R. Bowker. A guide to books, magazines, and software for reluctant and remedial readers, grades 7 through high school.

Lima, Carolyn W. and Lima, John A. (1998) *A to Zoo*, 5th Ed. New York: R. R. Bowker. Annotated bibliography of 11,500 books indexed by subject, author, title, illustrator, and with bibliographic information.

Lipson, Eden Ross. (1991). *The New York Times Parent's Guide to the Best Books for Children*. New York: Random House. Hundreds of wordless books, picture books, story books, and fiction and nonfiction for readers in the primary, elementary, and middle grades.

Miller-Lachmann, Lyn. (1991) *Our Family, Our Friends, Our World: An Annotated Guide to Significant Multicultural Books for Children and Teenagers*. New York: R. R. Bowker. A bibliographic guide to fine fiction and nonfiction focusing on the life and culture of minority people in the U.S. and Canada as well as in their native lands.

Nadelman, Ruth. (1995) *Fantasy Literature for Children: An Annotated Bibliography*, 4th Ed. New York: R. R. Bowker. A guide to nearly 5,000 journal-recommended fantasy novels and story collections.

New York Public Library. (1999) *100 Favorite Children's Books for Today's Kids*. An annotated list of new and old favorites.

———. (1999) *Books for the Teen Age*. Annual lists of collections and books for women's history month, Black history month, science fiction, national poetry month, summer reading, and other themes.

———. (1999) *Looking Back, Looking Forward*. Annotated list of young adult books for Black history month.

Reading Is Fundamental. (1987) *When We Were Young*. Washington, DC: Reading Is Fundamental. Favorite book recommendations from RIF kids and volunteers. Also special section listing the favorite books of famous people including Stephen King, Michael Learned, and Billy Joel.

Schulman, L. (1990) *The Random House Book of Sports Stories*. New York: Random House. A collection of sports-related stories by some of the best modern authors.

Schwartz, Alvin (Ed.). (1983) *Scary Stories to Tell in the Dark*. New York: Harper. A list of the best thrillers for children.

Sinclair, Patti. (1992) *E for Environment: An Annotated Bibliography of Children's Books with Environmental Themes*. New York: R. R. Bowker. More than 500 children's books on environmental topics are profiled and indexed. Reading levels are included.

Stott, Jon. (1984) *Children's Literature from A to Z: A Guide for Parents and Teachers*. New York: McGraw-Hill. An annotated list of recommended books and other helpful information about selecting books for children.

Thomas, Rebecca L. (1996) *Connecting Cultures: A Guide to Multicultural Literature for Children*. New York: R. R. Bowker. Annotated guide to more than 1,600 preschool- to sixth-grade level books of fiction, folktales, poetry, and song books dealing with diverse cultural groups.

The Young Adult Reader's Adviser. (1992). New York: R. R. Bowker. A substantial reference for students, grades six through twelve. The two-volume work presents introductions to and recommendations for reading about key authors and about topics from the curriculum. Over 17,000 entries and 850 biographical profiles.

POETRY COLLECTIONS

Adoff, Arnold (ed.). (1970) *I Am the Darker Brother: An Anthology of Modern Poems by Black Americans.* New York: Macmillan.

———. (1995) *Street Music: City Poems.* New York: HarperCollins.

Bodecker, Nils. (1974) *"Let's Marry," Said the Cherry, and Other Nonsense Poems.* New York: Atheneum.

———. (1983) *Snowman Sniffles and Other Verse.* New York: Atheneum.

deRegniers, Beatrice Schenk. (1996) *Sing a Song of Popcorn.* New York: Harcourt Brace.

Elledge, Scott (ed.). (1990) *Wider Than the Sky: Poems to Grow Up With.* New York: HarperCollins.

Fishback, Margaret. (1942) *I Feel Better Now and Out of My Head.* New York: World.

Ferris, Helen (ed.). (1983) *Favorite Poems Old and New.* New York: Doubleday.

Greenfield, Eloise. (1978) *Honey I Love and Other Poems.* Pictures by Diane and Leo Dillon. New York: HarperCollins.

Hopkins, Lee Bennett (ed.). (1988) *Side by Side: Poems to Read Together.* Illustrated by Hilary Knight. New York: Simon & Schuster.

Jones, J. (ed.). (1993) *The Trees Stand Shining: Poetry of the North American Indians.* New York: Dial.

Kennedy, X. J. and D. M. Kennedy. (1982) *Knock at a Star: A Child's Introduction to Poetry.* Boston: Little, Brown.

Livingston, Myra Cohn (ed.). (1987) *Cat Poems.* Illustrated by Trina Schart Myman. New York: Holiday.

———. (1987) *I Like You, If You Like Me, Poems of Friendship.* New York: McElderry.

McCord, David. (1977) *One at a Time.* New York: Little, Brown.

Merriam, Eve. (1964) *It Doesn't Always Have to Rhyme.* Illustrated by Malcom Spooner. New York: Atheneum.

Obligato, Lillian. (1983) *Faint Frogs Feeling Feverish and Other Terrifically Tantalizing Tongue Twisters.* New York: Viking.

Pomerantz, Charlotte. (1982) *If I Had a Paka: Poems in Eleven Languages.* Illustrated by Nancy Tafuri. New York: Greenwillow.

Prelutsky, Jack and Arnold Lobel (anthology). (1983) *The Random House Book of Poetry for Children.* New York: Random House.

Silverstein, Shel. (1981) *A Light in the Attic.* New York: Harper & Row.

———. (1996) *Falling Up.* New York: HarperCollins.

———. (1974) *Where the Sidewalk Ends.* New York: Harper & Row.

Strickland, D. S. and M. R. Strickland (eds.). (1994) *Families: Poems Celebrating the African American Experience.* Honesdale, PA: Boyds Mills.

Wallace, Daisy. (1976) *Monster Poems.* New York: Holiday House.

Yolen, Jane (selected). (1996) *Sky Scrape/City Scrape, Poems of City Life.* Illustrated by Ken Condon. Honesdale, PA: Boyds Mills.

List 57. BOOK INTEREST AROUSERS

1. **Library corner in your classroom.** Change frequently. Add a bulletin board with rotating themes, such as horses, history, science, favorite authors, mysteries, and so forth.

2. **New-book advertisements.** Have a teacher or student make brief reviews, oral reports, posters, or a contest with a competing book.

3. **Book fair.** Exchange an exhibit of books with another class. Show off award winners. Specialize in some types of new books, old books, picture books, Native American books, joke books, novels, and so forth.

4. **Oral reading** by the teacher or a child. Read a whole book, read interesting parts, read just the first chapter, read about a specific character. Especially read to upper-grade children. They love it.

5. **Poetry reading** by a teacher or a student. Have students memorize classic poems. Read new poems by published authors or read students' poems. Read winners from a schoolwide poetry contest.

6. **Hold individual reading conferences** regularly with every student. Discuss books being read. Suggest similar books. Suggest other types of books.

7. **Visit libraries** both in school and in other classes, as well as your public library. Make sure every parent gets every student a public library card.

8. **Keep a books-read chart** for your class and for each student. Encourage progress and sometimes competition.

9. **Have book-related activities.** In art, design new book jackets or illustrations of book scenes. In drama, act out parts of a book. Discuss different endings.

10. **Tie in book with other subjects.** What was happening in history at the same time? Was the radio invented then? What causes volcanos? Are sports upsets really happening today?

The Reading Teacher's Book of Lists, Fourth Edition, © 2000 by John Wiley & Sons, Inc.

List 58. BOOK REPORT FORM

This form can be duplicated and distributed for reports on short stories, plays, and books.

TITLE _____

AUTHOR _____

ILLUSTRATOR _____

PUBLISHER _____

COPYRIGHT DATE _____

THEME:

MAIN CHARACTERS:

SETTING:

SUMMARY:

REACTION:

See also List 59, Book Report Alternatives; List 101, Story Guide.

The Reading Teacher's Book of Lists, Fourth Edition, © 2000 by John Wiley & Sons, Inc.

List 59. BOOK REPORT ALTERNATIVES

Once you have enticed your students to read, consult this list of alternatives for fifty exciting things to do in place of writing a book report.

1. Draw a timeline to illustrate the events in the story.
2. Construct a story map to show the plot and setting.
3. Create a jacket for the book, complete with illustrations and blurbs.
4. Prepare a chart showing the characters, their relationships, and a few biographical facts about each.
5. Create a poster-sized ad for the book.
6. Have a panel discussion if several students read the same book.
7. Dramatize an incident or an important character alone or with others.
8. Do a radio announcement to publicize the book.
9. Have individual conferences with students to get their personal reactions.
10. Appoint a committee to conduct peer discussion and seminars on books.
11. Illustrate the story, take slides, coordinate music and narration, and give a multi-media presentation.
12. Write a play based on the continuation of the story or a new adventure for the characters.
13. Give a demonstration of what was learned from a how-to book.
14. Compose a telegram about the book, limited to twenty words.
15. Dramatically read a part of the book to the class to get them hooked.
16. Keep a diary of one of the characters in the story, using first person.
17. Write a letter to the author telling why you liked the book, your favorite parts, what you would have done with the plot.
18. Be a newspaper columnist; write a review for the book section.
19. Explain how the story might have ended if a key character or incident were changed.
20. Write a letter to the key character to tell him or her how to solve the problem.
21. Write a newspaper article based on an incident from the book.
22. Write a biography of the leading character, using information from the book.
23. Write an obituary article about a key character, giving an account of what he or she was best known for.
24. Give a testimonial speech citing the character for special distinctions noted in the book.
25. Compare the movie and book versions of the same story.
26. Make a diorama to show the time and setting of the story.
27. Have a character day. Dress up as your favorite character in the story and relive some of the story.
28. Rewrite the story as a TV movie, including staging directions.
29. Examine the story for the author's craft and try to write a story of your own, imitating the use of tone, setting, style, and so on.
30. Memorize your favorite lines, or write them down for future quoting.

The Reading Teacher's Book of Lists, Fourth Edition, © 2000 by John Wiley & Sons, Inc.

31. Make sketches of some of the action sequences.

32. Read the story into a tape recorder so that others may listen to it.

33. Research the period of history in which the story is set.

34. Make a list of similes, metaphors, or succinct descriptions used in the book.

35. Make puppets and present a show based on the book.

36. Build a clay or papier-mâché bust of a key character.

37. Give a "chalk talk" about the book.

38. Paint a mural that shows the key incidents in the story.

39. Rewrite the story for students in a lower grade. Keep it interesting.

40. File information about the book in a classroom cross-reference. Include author, story type, list of books it is similar to, and so on.

41. Image a *Life* magazine story on the book you've just read. What are several scenes you think ought to be photographed? Describe the photographs and write captions for them.

42. Tell the general effect of the book on you. What made you feel the way you did?

43. Report on any new, interesting, or challenging ideas you gained through reading the book.

44. Letter the title of the book vertically; then write a brief phrase applicable to the book for each letter.

45. Tell what kind of people should read this book. Who shouldn't?

46. Explain why you would or would not recommend this book to your parents for their reading. Be specific in your references to characters, plot, and setting.

47. Explain why you think this book will/will not be read a hundred years from now. Support your viewpoint by making specific references to plot, setting, characters, and author's style.

48. Make a list of five to ten significant questions about this book that you think anyone who reads this book should be able to answer.

49. Write an original poem after you have read a book of poetry.

50. If it is a geographical book, make a map and locate places found in the book.

6
WRITING

List 60. DESCRIPTIVE WORDS

What do telling tales and writing poetry or reports have in common? They depend on descriptive words to create vivid and accurate images in the reader's mind. A good stock of descriptive words will bolster the quality of your students' writing exercises. Use these lists of adjectives and adverbs to nudge reluctant writers into developing characters and setting, or to help students "retire" overused words.

The Reading Teacher's Book of Lists, Fourth Edition, © 2000 by John Wiley & Sons, Inc.

Ability—Condition

able	confident	gentle	lucky	smooth
adequate	courageous	hardy	manly	spirited
alive	curious	healthy	mighty	stable
assured	daring	heavy	modern	steady
authoritative	determined	heroic	open	stouthearted
bold	durable	important	outstanding	strong
brainy	dynamic	influential	powerful	super
brave	eager	innocent	real	sure
busy	easy	intense	relaxed	tame
careful	effective	inquisitive	rich	tough
cautious	energetic	jerky	robust	victorious
clever	firm	light	sharp	zealous
competent	forceful	lively	shy	
concerned	gallant	loose	skillful	

Anger—Hostility

agitated	combative	evil	irritated	rude
aggravated	contrary	fierce	mad	savage
aggressive	cool	furious	mean	severe
angry	cranky	hard	nasty	spiteful
annoyed	creepy	harsh	obnoxious	tense
arrogant	cross	hateful	obstinate	terse
belligerent	cruel	hostile	outraged	vicious
biting	defiant	impatient	perturbed	vindictive
blunt	disagreeable	inconsiderate	repulsive	violent
bullying	enraged	insensitive	resentful	wicked
callous	envious	intolerant	rough	wrathful

See also List 25, Synonyms.

199

Depression—Sadness—Gloom

abandoned
alien
alienated
alone
awful
battered
blue
bored
burned
cheapened
crushed
debased
defeated
degraded
dejected
demolished

depressed
desolate
despairing
despised
despondent
destroyed
discarded
discouraged
dismal
downcast
downhearted
downtrodden
dreadful
estranged
excluded
forlorn

forsaken
gloomy
glum
grim
hated
homeless
hopeless
horrible
humiliated
hurt
jilted
kaput
loathed
lonely
lonesome
lousy

low
miserable
mishandled
mistreated
moody
mournful
obsolete
ostracized
overlooked
pathetic
pitiful
rebuked
regretful
rejected
reprimanded
rotten

ruined
rundown
sad
scornful
sore
stranded
tearful
terrible
tired
unhappy
unloved
whipped
worthless
wrecked

Distress

afflicted
anguished
awkward
baffled
bewildered
clumsy
confused
constrained
disgusted
disliked

displeased
dissatisfied
distrustful
disturbed
doubtful
foolish
futile
grief
helpless

hindered
impaired
impatient
imprisoned
lost
nauseated
offended
pained
perplexed

puzzled
ridiculous
sickened
silly
skeptical
speechless
strained
suspicious
swamped

tormented
touchy
troubled
ungainly
unlucky
unpopular
unsatisfied
unsure
weary

Fear—Anxiety

afraid
agitated
alarmed
anxious
apprehensive
bashful
dangerous
desperate

dreading
eerie
embarrassed
fearful
frantic
frightened
hesitant
horrified

insecure
intimidated
jealous
jittery
jumpy
nervous
on edge

overwhelmed
panicky
restless
scared
shaky
shy
strained

tense
terrified
timid
uncomfortable
uneasy
upset
worrying

The Reading Teacher's Book of Lists, Fourth Edition, © 2000 by John Wiley & Sons, Inc.

Inability—Inadequacy

anemic
ashamed
broken
catatonic
cowardly
crippled
defeated
defective
deficient
demoralized
disabled
exhausted
exposed
fragile
frail
harmless
helpless
impotent
inadequate
incapable
incompetent
ineffective
inept
inferior
insecure
meek
mummified
naughty
powerless
puny
shaken
shaky
shivering
sickly
small
strengthless
trivial
unable
uncertain
unfit
unimportant
unqualified
unsound
useless
vulnerable
weak

Joy—Elation

amused
blissful
brilliant
calm
cheerful
comical
contented
delighted
ecstatic
elated
elevated
enchanted
enthusiastic
exalted
excellent
excited
exuberant
fantastic
fit
funny
gay
glad
glorious
good
grand
gratified
great
happy
hilarious
humorous
inspired
jolly
jovial
joyful
jubilant
magnificent
majestic
marvelous
overjoyed
pleasant
pleased
proud
relieved
satisfied
smiling
splendid
superb
terrific
thrilled
tremendous
triumphant
vivacious
witty
wonderful

Love—Affection—Concern

admired
adorable
affectionate
agreeable
altruistic
amiable
benevolent
benign
brotherly
caring
charitable
comfortable
congenial
conscientious
considerate
cooperative
cordial
courteous
dedicated
devoted
empathetic
fair
faithful
forgiving
generous
genuine
giving
good
helpful
honest
honorable
hospitable
humane
interested
just
kind
kindly
lovable
loving
mellow
mild
moral
neighborly
nice
obliging
open
optimistic
patient
peaceful
pleasant
reasonable
receptive
reliable
respectful
sensitive
sweet
sympathetic
tender
thoughtful
tolerant
trustworthy
truthful
understanding
warm
worthy

Quantity

ample	few	lots	paucity	scarcity
abundant	heavy	many	plentiful	skimpy
chock-full	lavish	meager	plenty	sparing
copious	liberal	much	profuse	sparse
dearth	light	numerous	scads	sufficient
empty	loads	oodles	scant	well-stocked

Sight—Appearance

adorable	crinkled	foggy	motionless	skinny
alert	crooked	fuzzy	muddy	smoggy
beautiful	crowded	glamorous	murky	sparkling
blinding	crystalline	gleaming	nappy	spotless
bright	curved	glistening	narrow	square
brilliant	cute	glowing	obtuse	steep
broad	dark	graceful	rotund	stormy
blonde	deep	grotesque	round	straight
bloody	dim	hazy	pale	strange
blushing	distinct	high	poised	ugly
chubby	dull	hollow	quaint	unsightly
clean	elegant	homely	shadowy	unusual
clear	fancy	light	shady	weird
cloudy	filthy	lithe	shallow	wide
colorful	flat	low	sheer	wizened
contoured	fluffy	misty	shiny	

Size

ample	elfin	immense	miniature	stupendous
average	enormous	large	minute	tall
behemoth	fat	little	petite	tiny
big	giant	long	portly	towering
bulky	gigantic	mammoth	prodigious	vast
colossal	great	massive	puny	voluminous
diminutive	huge	microscopic	short	wee
dwarfed	hulking	middle-sized	small	

Smell—Taste

acrid	fragrant	putrid	sour	sweet
antiseptic	fresh	ripe	spicy	tangy
bitter	juicy	rotten	stale	tart
choking	medicinal	salty	sticky	tasteless
clean	nutty	savory	strong	tasty
delicious	peppery	smoky	stuffy	

The Reading Teacher's Book of Lists, Fourth Edition, © 2000 by John Wiley & Sons, Inc.

Sound

bang	groan	melodic	screech	thud
booming	growl	moan	shrill	thump
buzz	harsh	mute	silent	thunderous
clatter	high-pitched	noisy	snarl	tinkle
cooing	hiss	purring	snort	voiceless
crash	hoarse	quiet	soft	wail
crying	hushed	raspy	splash	whine
deafening	husky	resonant	squeak	whispered
faint	loud	screaming	squeal	

Time

ancient	daylight	late	outdated	sunrise
annual	decade	lengthy	periodic	sunset
brief	dusk	long	punctual	swift
brisk	early	modern	quick	tardy
centuries	eons	moments	rapid	twilight
continual	evening	noon	short	whirlwind
crawling	fast	noonday	slowly	yearly
dawn	flash	old	speedy	years
daybreak	intermittent	old-fashioned	sporadic	young

Touch

boiling	dirty	grubby	shaggy	stinging
breezy	dry	hard	sharp	tender
bumpy	dusty	hot	silky	tight
chilly	filthy	icy	slick	uneven
cold	flaky	loose	slimy	waxen
cool	fluffy	melted	slippery	wet
creepy	fluttering	plastic	slushy	wooden
crisp	frosty	prickly	smooth	yielding
cuddly	fuzzy	rainy	soft	
curly	gooey	rough	solid	
damp	greasy	sandpapery	sticky	

The Reading Teacher's Book of Lists, Fourth Edition, © 2000 by John Wiley & Sons, Inc.

List 61. STORY STARTERS

Writer's block happens to even the best writers. If some students are sluggish starters, these may help. After a first draft is done, use List 60, Descriptive Words, to add detail and color to the story.

1. Smarty couldn't believe his eyes. The cage door had been left open! This was his big chance. He ruffled his feathers and decided . . .

2. The footprint was the biggest one Steven had ever seen. What had toes like that?

3. "Wait right there—don't move! I'm coming to get you! I'm coming!" the voice called urgently. Surprised, Gloria looked down and saw . . .

4. "This will show them," Jim thought as he hammered the last nail into place.

5. My brother Alex is fussy. He doesn't like many foods. So we experimented in the kitchen. That's how we discovered the prize-winning recipe for chocolate-covered . . .

6. Garrett hungrily opened his Super Hero's lunch box. Next to the apple he found . . .

7. Every season has its good points and its bad points. The best thing about winter is . . .

8. All the way back to the bike shop, Clayton thought about what his uncle had told him.

9. My life changed the day I discovered . . .

10. The family decided to move to the new place in March, but I didn't want to go because . . .

11. It was a very rainy day—too rainy to go outside to play. So Adam and Christopher decided to . . .

12. I remember. It all started in the middle of the week—Wednesday. That morning, I didn't feel quite well enough to go to school.

13. I stood on the sidewalk and looked up. The building, all glass and steel, looked enormous next to the little brick houses that lined the street. I felt proud that the building belonged to . . .

14. The queen looked down from her throne and scowled. "Get this thing away from me!" Immediately, the guards removed the . . .

15. The airplane landed gently, and Lee breathed a sigh of relief.

16. Only Jessica and Jaime knew about the little room behind the door in the big oak tree. They found it one day while they were in the woods looking for the raspberry patch. Jessica had leaned against the tree trunk and accidentally pushed the door open. What a surprise to find . . .

17. "What do you think it is?" the small purple woman asked. She poked me gently with her boot.

    "I don't know," replied her lavender friend. "I've never seen anything like this before. Do you think it's a toy?"

18. Some days seem to last longer than others. Especially when everything goes wrong. Take Friday, for example. The trouble started when I . . .

19. Grandpa's attic is full of old clothes and other stuff from long ago. My sisters and I like to go up there and make believe we are . . .

20. It's always frustrating to have to sit and wait for . . .

The Reading Teacher's Book of Lists, Fourth Edition, © 2000 by John Wiley & Sons, Inc.

21. The field behind the school was David's favorite place to go after school.

22. I looked around the room and noticed there was a new student in the class.

23. All of the girl's friends had very ordinary hobbies except for . . .

24. I'd give anything in the world to see . . .

25. As she held the leaking pipe in place, Lisa thought, "What is keeping Mike?"

26. I never thought it would be possible, but there I was . . .

27. Scott frowned again and began to climb to the top of . . .

28. If I didn't have my skates with me that day, I don't know what I would have done.

29. It was dark and cold. There were no more logs to burn. Meg and Marianne waited to be rescued. It was already two days since the accident. All they could think about was . . .

30. Our cat, Joss, sometimes is too smart for her own good. Take last Sunday . . .

31. Darin was lucky to get the summer job. He was happy working at the small company fixing computers. It paid pretty well and he was saving up for . . .

32. Jason played hard. This was the last game of the tournament and he wanted to win. He looked up and saw the ball. He . . .

33. Nick and Phil planned the day carefully. They had waited for this trip for weeks and nothing was going to spoil it.

34. It was so dark that Camille couldn't tell the difference when she closed her eyes. "How did I ever get in a mess like this?" she thought.

35. Only an hour ago, the huge room was bustling and noisy. Now it was silent. I felt kind of sad and lonely now that the guests were gone. But I had to get up and get started . . .

36. The train stopped suddenly. The door slid open with a screech. I couldn't believe my eyes. There in the doorway was . . .

37. Ryan was excited as he boarded the plane to visit his friend in California.

38. Sometimes a dog can be a person's best friend.

39. Jenn couldn't wait for winter to be over. This summer she would have lots of time to . . .

40. There seemed to be no way out of the big old house. Every door opened into another room . . .

41. Kathy finished the painting and began wiping her brushes. The life-like portrait seemed to be looking right at her. "This is weird," she thought. Just then . . .

42. Nancy's eyes opened wide as she exclaimed, "Where on earth did you get those . . . ?"

43. The street was quiet. Then a dull gray delivery truck chuffed and sputtered around the corner. As it groaned to a stop in front of #682, the door flung open.

44. Sandy couldn't pass up any opportunity to enter a contest.

45. Samantha began her routine slowly, aware that everyone was watching her every move.

46. A truck rattled down the empty street. It slowed and then pulled into the dark parking lot. The sign on the gate said "Fred's Parts and Service . . . A Division of New Work Human Industries."

47. By the time Ni Kim had walked halfway home from school, she realized that she had left her house key on the kitchen table that morning.

48. We watched in horror as Ben came running out of the boys' bathroom and bumped right into the two men carrying the . . .

49. It all started on Monday morning when several citizens of Tumbler City noticed that the sky didn't look quite right.

50. It seemed like the perfect day to spend at the beach. But not long after Marie and Chuck put their surfboards in the water . . .

51. There is nothing better than the feeling you get when you . . .

52. They were at the supermarket, in the freezer section, when it happened.

53. Not long after I'd knocked, the narrow green door squeaked open. Inside was . . .

54. It was the third day of the camping trip, and Anisa knew that she would go crazy if she got one more mosquito bite. She looked at her arms and legs.

55. Jose yawned, stretching his arms way over his head. "If I could only stay awake just a little longer," he thought. "Then I could finish . . . "

56. Alexis knew her father would be mad when he got the bill.

57. My sister is quite the scientist. Last week, for example, she cloned a . . .

58. Gloria read her shopping list for the fifth time, making sure she hadn't left anything off.

59. I gave my grandmother's bureau a shove and heard a small tick, like the sound of a piece of paper falling to the floor.

60. Tami pretended she was asleep, even though she could hardly control her excitement.

61. The waiting room was quiet. The only sound was the quiet hum of the water cooler in the corner. Then the door creaked open. "Come in, please," the woman with the tattoo said to me.

62. The year was 2010, and Janek had finally saved up enough binnets to buy a . . .

63. There were nine people in the room. Some were talking quickly to each other. Others sat quietly on the edge of folding chairs, waiting. This was the first meeting and soon they would decide on a name for their group.

64. The phone had been ringing all morning. Jackie finally stopped answering it after the 14th call. It had been like this ever since . . .

65. Watching the small monkeys was Michael's favorite part of the day at the zoo. When he left he wished he could have one for a pet. Was he surprised when he opened his backpack later at home!

66. Beth walked around the corner toward her house. It had been a hard day at school. There was a surprise history quiz and she knew that she hadn't done very well. On top of that, she had heard that Artie was planning a party and hadn't even invited her.

67. Kathryn found Nicole in front of Gerry's house. Her bike lay across the curb. She was holding a note from Gerry. It said to meet her on the back porch of the abandoned house at the end of Elm Street.

68. The directions on the box said, "Washes off with warm water." Alicia had been trying to wash it off for an hour. But it was still there. How could she explain why her face was . . .

The Reading Teacher's Book of Lists, Fourth Edition, © 2000 by John Wiley & Sons, Inc.

69. All of a sudden the lights on the control panel went out. No power. No power at all. How were we going to get back to base camp?

70. Josef was watching his team from the bench. He had to sit this game out because last week he . . .

71. Today the mayor is going to give me a medal for bravery. I never thought about being brave. It just happened. The little girl needed help and I was the only one there. I just had to . . .

72. The ball crashed through the window. Oh, no. Who's in trouble now?

73. The old farmer dug deeper in his garden. Thud. The shovel hit something hard. He dug some more. There in the dirt was a large wooden box. "What's in this?" the old man asked himself.

74. The young doctor looked down at me and said, "I have good news for you, Pat."

75. My heart was pounding. The coach was about to call the name of the most valuable player for the season. "The MVP trophy, this year, goes to . . ."

List 62. HE SAID/SHE SAID

Dialogue can bring a story to life, or it can put the reader to sleep. Here are lively alternatives to ho-hum "he said/she said" exchanges. Use these vocal verbs in place of "said" or use the vocal adverbs to describe just how "he said/she said." Working with dialogue is a simple but very effective way to improve your storytelling.

Vocal Verbs

added
admitted
advised
agreed
announced
answered
argued
asked
asserted
began
bellowed
blurted
called
cautioned
claimed
commented
complained
conceded
concluded
confessed
continued
cried
demanded
exclaimed
explained
gasped
groaned
insisted
interrupted
joked
lied
mentioned
moaned
mumbled
muttered
noted
objected
observed
ordered
quipped
remarked

replied
reported
responded
said
screamed
shouted
snapped
sobbed
stated
swore
taunted
teased
told
vowed
warned
whined
whispered
yelled

Vocal Adverbs

adamantly
admiringly
adoringly
angrily
anxiously
arrogantly
bashfully
brazenly
casually
cautiously
cheerfully
clearly
cowardly
coyly
curiously
cynically
decisively
defensively
defiantly
dramatically
eerily
energetically
fiendishly

flatly
formally
gaily
gleefully
gloomily
happily
harshly
hysterically
jealously
joyfully
joyously
loudly
lovingly
meanly
meekly
mysteriously
nervously
offensively
off-handedly
pensively
proudly
questioningly
quickly

quizzically
rapidly
sadly
sarcastically
selfishly
serenely
seriously
sheepishly
shyly
sleepily
softly
sternly
stoically
stubbornly
sullenly
tauntingly
teasingly
tenderly
thankfully
thoughtfully
unexpectedly
unhappily
wisely

List 63. SIMILES

A simile is a figure of speech that uses the word "as" or "like." Figures of speech are used like adjectives or adverbs. They modify or describe a person, place, thing, or action with a colorful and often visual term or phrase. Creative writers and poets make good use of these. The following are frequently used similes.

The Reading Teacher's Book of Lists, Fourth Edition, © 2000 by John Wiley & Sons, Inc.

Similes Using "As"

as bright as the noonday sun
as busy as a bee
as certain as death and taxes
as clear as a bell
as clear as day
as clear as the nose on your face
as cold as ice
as comfortable as an old shoe
as cool as a cucumber
as cuddly as a baby
as cute as a button
as dark as night
as deaf as a doorpost
as deep as the ocean
as dry as a bone
as fat as a pig
as flat as a pancake
as fresh as dew
as green as grass
as happy as a lark
as hard as nails
as hard as rock
as hungry as a bear
as innocent as a newborn baby
as light as a feather
as loud as thunder
as lovely as a rose
as meek as a lamb
as quick as a wink
as quiet as a mouse
as rough as sandpaper
as skinny as a rail
as slow as molasses in January
as sly as a fox
as smart as a whip
as smooth as glass

as soft as old leather
as soft as silk
as stiff as a board
as strong as an ox
as stubborn as a mule
as sweet as honey
as white as new fallen snow

Similes Using "Like"

acts like a bull in a china shop
chatters like a monkey
cheeks like roses
cry like a baby
drinks like a fish
eat like a pig
eat like it's going out of style
eats like a bird
eyes like stars
feel like two cents
fits like a glove
fought like cats and dogs
laugh like a hyena
moves like a snail
run around like a chicken with its head
   cut off
run like a deer
sing like a bird
sit there like a bump on a log
slept like a dog
sparkled like diamonds
spoke like an orator
stood out like a sore thumb
waddle like a duck
walk like an elephant
work like a dog
works like a charm

See also List 60, Descriptive Words; List 64, Metaphors; List 153, Common Word Idioms.

List 64. METAPHORS

Metaphors are figures of speech that compare two things, but do not use the words "like" or "as." These colorful phrases are used like adverbs or adjectives to describe persons, places, things, or actions. Students must learn not to take them literally but to enjoy them and to create their own. This list provides enough metaphors to get a lesson started.

The small boat was a ping pong ball bouncing around on the waves.

Viewed from the airplane, the rush hour traffic was an army of ants working its way slowly toward home.

There was no rush and so we sent the letter snail mail.

Michael clamed up and refused to say anything.

At a flick of a switch, the house came alive with music.

The car slowed as it approached the hairpin turn.

I work so hard during the day that I become a couch potato at night.

Her eyes lit up when she saw that her friend was safe.

The birch tree danced in the breeze.

The fog was a blanket covering the valley floor.

The stars were diamonds sparkling in the sky.

Her heart was overflowing with kindness.

She was so shy she kept her ideas bottled up inside her.

Mr. Mather's bark is worse than his bite.

The air conditioning was so strong that the room became an icebox.

That car is a dinosaur. It's time to get a new one.

The toddler was a clinging vine near his mother.

The children grew up near a lake and were fish in the water.

My mother gave me a real tongue lashing when she saw my poor grades.

The branches of the tree were fingernails scratching my bedroom window.

The class was so excited about the new project that they became a fountain of ideas.

The growing boy's stomach was a bottomless pit.

Her porcelain skin contributed to her beauty.

The young girl blossomed as she gained more confidence.

The sunset painted the sky with red and orange.

The white smoke rose lazily from the campfire.

His fingers danced over the keyboard as he played his favorite music.

My legs turned to rubber when I approached the end of the diving board.

The awful meal I ate at that restaurant became a rock in my stomach.

When it came to science, Mary was a walking encyclopedia.

The calculator became a crutch and he was unable to do simple computations without it.

The World Wide Web is an information highway leading to resources throughout the world.

The night is growing old and there is still so much to do.

The morning sun peeked over the horizon as we set out to go fishing.

The tired soldiers were robots marching home at the end of the day.

The Reading Teacher's Book of Lists, Fourth Edition, © 2000 by John Wiley & Sons, Inc.

List 65. NONDISCRIMINATORY LANGUAGE GUIDELINES

"Sticks and stones can break my bones, but words can never hurt me." Remember this childhood refrain? We knew, even at the age of six or seven, that it wasn't true and that name calling and taunts hurt. Now we know that even subtle, unintended biased or discriminatory words hurt students' self-esteem as well as their relationships with others. Make a conscious effort to use and teach nondiscriminatory language in class.

GENDER RELATED

Instead of	Use	Comment
The student chooses his assignments in this class.	The student chooses the assignments in this class.	Avoid gender-specific pronouns (his, her)
	Students choose their assignments in this class.	Use plural form.
	The assignments in this class are chosen by the students.	Rewrite to avoid gender reference.
Man's scientific discovery is limited only by his diligence.	Scientific discovery is limited only by our diligence.	Rewrite, using first-person plural.
Man has . . . Mankind has . . .	People have . . . (humanity, human beings, humankind, the average person)	Use inclusive group words.
Manpower	Personnel, staff, workers, employees	Use inclusive group words.
Each participant should bring his own gear.	Participants should bring their own gear.	Use plural form.
The nurse will explain it to her patients.	Nurses will explain it to their patients.	Use plural; avoid the stereotype.
The male nurse said . . .	The nurse said . . .	Use inclusive term; no added gender words.
The child suffers from lack of mothering.	The child suffers from lack of nurturing (lack of parenting).	Use inclusive nonstereotype.
The chairman said . . .	The chairperson said . . . (chair, moderator, leader)	Avoid gender-specific term.
Dear Sir:	Dear Director: (Colleague, Editor, Service Manager)	Use title, avoid gender-specific term.

The Reading Teacher's Book of Lists, Fourth Edition, © 2000 by John Wiley & Sons, Inc.

Language use regarding gender is slowly changing. It might be fine for a woman to be a "benefactor" or a "patron," instead of a "benefactress" or a "patroness"; but if she gives a party, she will probably still be a "hostess."

Titles of royalty have hardly changed at all, for example:

king	queen
prince	princess
duke	duchess
lord	lady

But we have a woman "governor," not "governess." First names also continue to reflect gender, for example:

Paul	Pauline
Don	Donna
Edward	Edwina
Julius	Julia
Henry	Henrietta

However, many first names are used for either sex, though sometimes with a different spelling:

Billy	Billie
Terry	Terrie
Gene	Jean

Some other words rigidly adhere to the gender. For example, we never call a man whose wife has died a "widow," but a widower. Other words have become gender free because the occupation is regularly performed by both sexes:

nurse	pilot
bartender	accountant
attorney	lifeguard

DISABILITY RELATED

Instead of	Use	Comment
The handicapped	Persons with disabilities	Emphasis on people, not disability.
The AIDS victim	Person with HIV	Emphasis on person; avoid sensationalism.
The deaf use . . .	Deaf people use . . .	People are not the disability.
The deformed child The crippled child	The child who has a cleft lip, etc.	Avoid emotion-laden terms.
The wheelchair-bound boy	The boy who uses a wheelchair	Avoid emotion-laden terms.
The insane	People with mental illness	Emphasis on people.
The special student	The student with a disability	Avoid vague or euphemistic terms.

The Reading Teacher's Book of Lists, Fourth Edition, © 2000 by John Wiley & Sons, Inc.

List 66. BASIC SENTENCE PATTERNS

Parts of speech are put together to form sentences. The list of basic sentence patterns and variations shows the most common arrangements of words. Remember that every sentence must have at minimum a noun (or pronoun) and a verb. This is sometimes called a subject and a predicate.

N/V	noun/verb	*Children sang.*
N/V/N	noun/verb/noun	*Bill paid the worker.*
N/V/ADV	noun/verb/adverb	*Ann sewed quickly.*
N/LV/N	noun/linking verb/noun	*Arthur is President.*
N/LV/ADJ	noun/linking verb/adjective	*Chris looks sleepy.*
N/V/N/N	noun/verb/noun/noun	*Chuck gave Marie flowers.*

Variations of Basic Sentence Patterns

Affirmative to Negative—*It is raining./It is not raining.*

Affirmative to Question—*The bottle is empty./Is the bottle empty?*

Use of "there"—*A man is at the door./There is a man at the door.*

Request—*You mow the grass./Mow the grass.*

Active to Passive—*The dog chased the fox./The fox was chased by the dog.*

Possessive—*Robert owns this car./This is Robert's car.*

Prepositional phrase added—*This is Robert's car in the garage.*

Adverbial phrase added—*Birds fly quietly together.*

Present to Past—*I live in Chicago./I lived in Chicago.*

Simple Past to Progressive Past—*I live in Chicago./I was living in Chicago.*

Past to Future—*I lived in Chicago./I will live in Chicago.*

Certain to Uncertain—*I will do it./I might do it.*

See also List 67, Build a Sentence; List 150, Parts of Speech.

List 67. BUILD A SENTENCE

Select one from each column.

Who? (subject noun)	What? (verb predicate)	Why? (prepositional phrase)	When? (adverb)	Where? (object)
A boy	climbed into an airplane	for a vacation	last summer	in New York
The shark	looked everywhere	to find his mother	in 2020	on the moon
A big dump truck	slid		during the game	outside my house
The monster	laughed	to get a million dollars	next year	in a cave
	swam			on a farm
My dad	dove	for fun	today	under a rock
A rattlesnake	swung on a rope	because he was on fire	at midnight	next to a lion
Maria	fell	to fall in love	forever	100 feet beneath the ocean
Mickey Mouse	yelled loudly		before breakfast	in bed
A tiny ant	flew	for an ice cream cone	always	on top of a tree
			500 years ago	at the circus
The train	ran fast	to build a house	right now	in front of the city hall
Iron John	jumped	to fight the enemy	in a month	in a corn field
A beautiful princess	kicked		after school	behind the stove
	couldn't stop	to get to school	in an hour	in space
			yesterday	downtown
A large bird	slithered	to be kissed	during the war	inside an egg
My good friend	crawled			in Africa
				out West
A teacher	hopped on one foot	for a coat of paint	at dawn	on a tropical island
		because it was made		

Feel free to add more words to make your sentence read better or add interest. You can leave out anything except a subject and a verb. Make your own Build-a-Sentence chart using a theme like a monster, earthquake, or family. Also, try adding adjectives to your sentences (usually between the articles "the," "an," or "a" and the subject/noun).

See also List 66, Basic Sentence Patterns; List 150, Parts of Speech.

The Reading Teacher's Book of Lists, Fourth Edition, © 2000 by John Wiley & Sons, Inc.

List 68. PUNCTUATION GUIDELINES

This list will help students review the use of punctuation marks. Refer to it as part of your proofreading practice. Post an enlarged copy on the wall where students can see it during their writing activities.

<u>Symbol</u>	<u>Name</u>	<u>When used</u>
•	**Period**	1. At the end of a statement or command sentence. *Birds fly.*
		2. At the end of a command sentence. *Go home.*
		3. After most abbreviations. *Mr. Co. Ave.*
?	**Question Mark**	1. At the end of a question sentence. *Who is he?*
		2. To express doubt. *He ate 14 doughnuts?*
!	**Exclamation Point**	1. To show strong emotion with a word. *Great!*
		2. To show strong emotion with a sentence. *You're the best!*
" "	**Quotation Marks**	1. To show a direct quote. *She said, "May I help you?"*
		2. To set off a title of a short poem. *He read "A Visit from Saint Nicholas."*
		3. To imply sarcasm or someone else's use of a term. *The "hero" was not at home.*
'	**Apostrophe**	1. To form the possessive. *Bill's bike*
		2. In contractions, to show missing letters. *Isn't*
		3. To form the plurals of symbols. *Two A's*
'	**Comma**	1. To separate items in a series. *One, two, three*
		2. To separate things in a list. *bread, milk, cheese*
		3. To separate parts of a date. *February 22, 2000*
		4. After the greeting in a friendly letter. *Dear Gerry,*
		5. After the closing in a letter. *Sincerely,*
		6. To separate the city and state in an address. *New York, NY*
		7. To separate a name and a degree title. *Jenn Stock, M.D.*
		8. Between inverted names. *Smith, Joe*
		9. In written dialogue between the quotation and the rest of the sentence. *She said, "Stop it." "Ok," he replied.*
		10. Between more than one adjective or adverb. *The big, bad wolf.*
		11. To set off a descriptive or parenthetical word or phrase. *Tina, the announcer, read her lines.*
		12. Between a dependent and independent clause. *After the game, we went home.*

13. To separate independent clauses. *I like him, and he likes me.*

14. To set off incidental words. *I saw it, too. Naturally, I went along. Oh, I didn't see you.*

( )   **Parentheses**

1. To show supplementary material. *The map (see below) is new.*

2. To set off information more strongly than with commas. *Joe (the first actor) was ready.*

3. In numbering or lettering a series. *Choices: (a) a game or (b) a song; two steps: (1) Open the door. (2) Step in.*

:   **Colon**

1. To introduce a series. *He has three things: a pen, a book, and a backpack.*

2. To show a subtitle. *The book: How to read it.*

3. To separate clauses. *The rule is this: Keep it simple.*

4. After a business letter greeting. *Dear Ms. Turner:*

5. To separate hours and minutes or to show ratio. *10:15 A.M. 3:1 ratio*

;   **Semicolon**

1. To separate sentence parts more strongly than a comma. *November was cold; January was freezing.*

2. To separate sentence parts that contain commas. *He was tired; therefore, he took a nap.*

—   **En Dash**

To show period of time or space between. *2000–2005, Chicago–Boston*

—   **Em Dash**

To show the insertion of descriptive information. *Carla—the tallest student—held the flag.*

. . .   **Ellipsis**

1. To show that words have been left out. *The boy . . . was not at home . . . but his mom answered the phone.*

2. To show a pause for suspense or to heighten mood. *The announcer called out, "The winner is . . . Chris."*

•   **Bullet**

To show the items in a list.
Things to do on Saturday
- *Go swimming*
- *Visit Uncle Chuck*
- *Clean my room*

The Reading Teacher's Book of Lists, Fourth Edition, © 2000 by John Wiley & Sons, Inc.

List 69. WRITEABILITY CHECKLIST

The following is a list of suggestions for writing materials that are on an easy readability level. You can also use this as a readability checklist.

Vocabulary
- ❏ Avoid large and/or infrequent words. (submit—send)
- ❏ For high-frequency words use lists such as the Carroll, Davies, Richman word list or 3000 Instant Words. (See List 14, Instant Words.)
- ❏ For meaning lists, use *Living Word Vocabulary.*
- ❏ Avoid words with Latin and Greek prefixes. (See Lists 23 and 24.) (implement—carry out)
- ❏ Avoid jargon. (terms known in only one field)
- ❏ Okay to use technical words but make sure to define them and, if possible, give an example when you use them for the first time.

Sentences
- ❏ Keep sentences short on the average. For adults, keep average sentence below fifteen words.
- ❏ Avoid splitting sentence kernel (embedding).
- ❏ Keep verb active (avoid nominalizations).
- ❏ Watch out for too many commas. (See List 68, Punctuation Guidelines.)
- ❏ Semicolons and colons may indicate need for new sentence.

Paragraphs
- ❏ Keep paragraphs short on the average.
- ❏ One-sentence paragraphs are permissible at times.
- ❏ Indent and line up lists. (Keep lists out of paragraph.)

Organization
- ❏ Suit organization plan to topic and your purpose.
- ❏ Try to use SER—Statement, Example, Restatement.
- ❏ Use subheads.
- ❏ Use signal words. (See List 96, Signal Words.)
- ❏ Use summaries.
- ❏ Watch cohesion and use signal words. (See List 96.)

Personal Words
- ❏ Use personal pronouns, but not too many. (*Example:* I, you)
- ❏ Use personal sentences. (*Example:* 1. Sentences directed at reader, "You should . . . " 2. Dialogue sentences, "Dick said, 'Hello.'")

The Reading Teacher's Book of Lists, Fourth Edition, © 2000 by John Wiley & Sons, Inc.

For further information, see the chapter "Writeability: The principles of writing for increased comprehension" in *Readability, Its Past, Present, and Future.* Published by the International Reading Assn., Newark, DE.

Imageability

❏ Use more concrete or high imagery words.

❏ Avoid abstract or low imagery words.

❏ Use vivid examples.

❏ Use similes and metaphors. (See List 63, Similes, and List 64, Metaphors.)

❏ Use graphs whenever appropriate. (See List 194, Taxonomy of Graphs.)

Referents

❏ Avoid too many referents (*Example:* it, them, they). Replace some referents with nouns or verbs.

❏ Avoid too much distance between noun and referent.

❏ Don't use referent that could refer to two or more nouns or verbs.

Motivation

❏ Select interesting topics.

❏ Select interesting examples.

❏ Write at level that is a little below your audience. (See List 80, Readability Graph.)

The Reading Teacher's Book of Lists, Fourth Edition, © 2000 by John Wiley & Sons, Inc.

List 70. PROOFREADING CHECKLIST—ELEMENTARY

Check

- ❏ It says what I wanted it to say.
- ❏ Every sentence is a complete thought. (Contains a subject and a verb.)
- ❏ No words are missing.
- ❏ Every sentence begins with a capital letter.
- ❏ Every sentence has an end mark.
- ❏ Every word is spelled correctly.
- ❏ I checked the verb forms I used.
- ❏ I checked the pronouns I used.
- ❏ I checked all punctuation marks.
- ❏ I indented the first line of every paragraph.
- ❏ My writing is neat and can be read.
- ❏ I used interesting words instead of the most common ones.
- ❏ If it is a letter, it has the correct format.
- ❏ If it is a story, it has an interesting title.

List 71. PROOFREADING CHECKLIST—INTERMEDIATE

Content

Did I:

- ❏ Stick to my topic?
- ❏ Use good sources for information?
- ❏ Use enough sources for information?
- ❏ Organize my information carefully? (sequence, logical order, Q/A, main idea/supporting details, thesis statement/arguments, etc.)
- ❏ Check my facts?
- ❏ Consider/use graphs, tables, charts for data?
- ❏ Consider my readers and select words to catch their interest? to help them understand? to create images in their minds? to help them follow the sequence?
- ❏ Use sufficient detail and description?

Format

Did I:

- ❏ Choose an appropriate title?
- ❏ Use quotations correctly?
- ❏ Use headings and subheadings?
- ❏ Label graphs, charts, and tables?
- ❏ Include a list of resources or bibliography?
- ❏ Number the pages?
- ❏ Include my name, class, and date?

Mechanics

Did I:

- ❏ Check sentences for completeness and sense?
- ❏ Check for consistent verb tense?
- ❏ Check for consistent point of view?
- ❏ Check for subject–verb agreement?
- ❏ Check for proper use of pronouns?
- ❏ Check all spelling?
- ❏ Check for end marks and other punctuation?
- ❏ Check for capital letters and underlining?
- ❏ Check for paragraph indentations?
- ❏ Check legibility?

The Reading Teacher's Book of Lists, Fourth Edition, © 2000 by John Wiley & Sons, Inc.

List 72. PROOFREADING MARKS

Helping students develop essays, short stories, term papers, or other writing goes more smoothly when you use proofreading symbols. Introduce these early in the school year and use them throughout. The time and space saved may be devoted to comments on content and encouragement.

Notation in Margin	How Indicated in Copy	Explanation
¶	true. The best rule to follow	New paragraph
⌒	living room	Close up
#	Mary had a	Insert space
⌒	Mary had a lamb little	Transpose
sp	There were 5 children.	Spell out
cap	mary had a little lamb.	Capitalize
lc	Mary had a little Lamb.	Lower case
ℓ	The correct procedure	Delete or take out
stet	Mary had a little lamb.	Restore crossed-out word(s) (let stand as before corrected)
little	Mary had a lamb.	Insert word(s) in margin
⊙	Birds fly	Insert a period
⋏	Next the main	Insert a comma
BF	Mary had a little lamb.	Boldface
ital	Mary had a little lamb.	Italicize
u.s.	Mary had a little lamb.	Underline (or underscore)

See also List 70, Proofreading Checklist—Elementary; List 71, Proofreading Checklist—Intermediate; List 73, Teacher's Correction Marks.

List 73. TEACHER'S CORRECTION MARKS

ab	abbreviation problem	**pass**	misuse of passive voice
agr	agreement problem	**pr ref**	pronoun reference problem
amb	ambiguous	**pun**	punctuation needed or missing
awk	awkward expression or construction	**reas**	reasoning needs improvement
cap	capitalize	**rep**	unnecessary repetition
case	error in case	**RO**	run-on
cp	comma problem	**shift**	faulty tense shift
cs	comma splice	**sp**	incorrect spelling
d	inappropriate diction	**thesis**	improve the thesis
det	details are needed	**trans**	improve the transition
dm	dangling modifier	**TX**	topic sentence needed (or improved)
dn	double negative	**u**	usage problem
frag	fragment	**uw**	unclear wording
ital	italics or underline	**v**	variety needed
lc	use lower case	**VAG**	vague
mm	misplaced modifier	**VE**	verb error
num	numbers problem	**VT**	verb tense problem
^	insert	**w**	wordy
¶	new paragraph needed	**wc**	better word choice
‖	faulty parallelism	**WM**	word missing
,	insert comma	**ww**	wrong word

The Reading Teacher's Book of Lists, Fourth Edition, © 2000 by John Wiley & Sons, Inc.

See also List 70, Proofreading Checklist—Elementary; List 71, Proofreading Checklist—Intermediate; List 72, Proofreading Marks.

List 74. HANDWRITING CHARTS

Have you ever needed a handwriting chart for a student and couldn't quickly locate one? The Zaner–Bloser and D'Nealian manuscript and cursive alphabet charts are here to help you out in just such a situation.

Zaner–Bloser Manuscript Alphabet

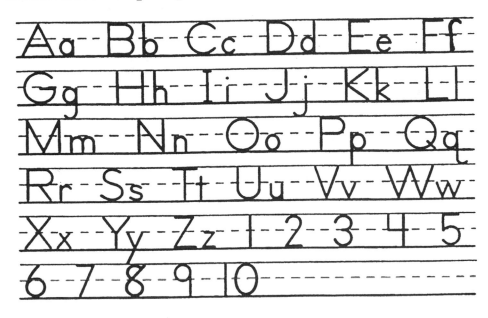

Zaner–Bloser Cursive Alphabet

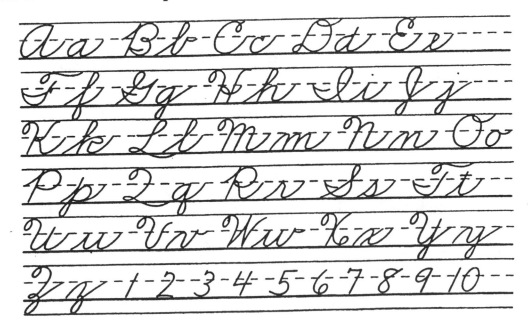

The Reading Teacher's Book of Lists, Fourth Edition, © 2000 by John Wiley & Sons, Inc.

D'Nealian® Manuscript Alphabet

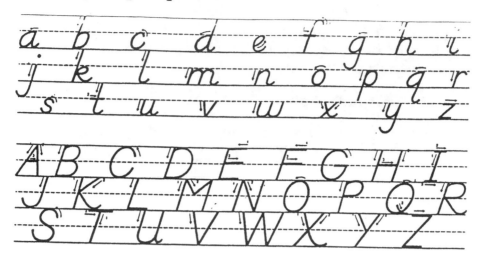

D'Nealian® Cursive Alphabet

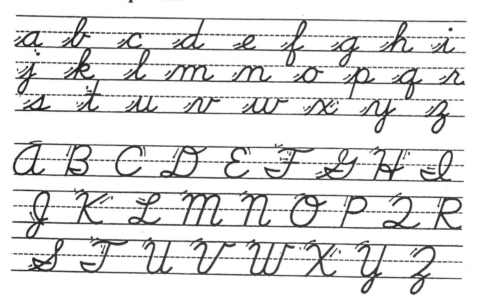

D'Nealian® Numbers

The Reading Teacher's Book of Lists, Fourth Edition, © 2000 by John Wiley & Sons, Inc.

7

INSTRUCTION

List 75. GOOD IDEAS
FOR READING TEACHERS

Teachers get some of the best advice from other teachers. Here are some suggestions from a wide range of reading specialists and researchers.

1. Integrate reading into the curriculum; integrate the language arts.
2. Use a variety of teaching methods and strategies.
3. Give plenty of reading practice for fluency and automaticity.
4. Use formal and informal assessment and diagnosis.
5. Use good reading materials: literature, expository, and variety.
6. Teach phonics and decoding, especially for beginners.
7. Develop vocabulary, both general and in subject areas.
8. Emphasize comprehension.
9. Pay attention to individual differences; tackle problems early.
10. Theory is important: schema, goals, emergent literacy, text structure, motivation, and success.
11. Have students read a passage and restate it in their own words—a simple, but important technique.
12. Preview difficult vocabulary before asking students to read a passage; discuss the words and related words. Have students keep a log of new words and their meanings.
13. Work on fluency. Have students read a short, not too difficult passage aloud. Count the errors and mark the time in seconds. Point out errors, discuss, and have the student reread and try to improve the time and error rate. Repeat for four or five readings. Gradually move to longer, more difficult passages.
14. Match students' reading material to their reading level using standardized test scores and readability formulas. If neither are available, have the student read aloud a passage from a book. If he or she averages more than one error for every 20 words, the book is too difficult.
15. Encourage and reward practice. Musicians, sports teams, artists, and readers all need practice to improve their skills. Don't worry about students reading materials that are too easy or on unconventional subjects. Worry only if they are not reading.
16. Write every day. Reading and writing are related. Improving one improves the other. Include at least some writing every day and lots of writing some days.
17. Focus on spelling. Improving word knowledge and recognition helps reading. Target high-frequency words, subject vocabulary lists, and words students misspelled in assignments. Use spelling lessons as an opportunity to review phonics.
18. Keep interest high. Nothing works better than interest and motivation. Have fun in reading class with jokes, humorous writing, and word play of all sorts. Find out students' interests and help them find books they'll love to read.

See also List 6, Phonic Awareness; List 81, Teaching with Newspapers; List 83, One Hundred Ways to Praise; List 92, Games and Methods for Teaching.

The Reading Teacher's Book of Lists, Fourth Edition, © 2000 by John Wiley & Sons, Inc.

List 76. ACTIVITIES FOR LANGUAGE DEVELOPMENT

Many children love acting. With these activities they can have some fun and learn a few words at the same time.

1. In One Place—Make Your Body:

wiggle	collapse	expand	hang
wriggle	shake	contract	slouch
squirm	rock	curl	droop
stretch	sway	uncurl	sink
bend	bounce	rise	tumble
twist	bob	lurch	totter
turn	spin	lean	swing
flop	whirl	sag	

2. From Place to Place—Make Your Body:

creep	hop	meander	stalk
crawl	tramp	limp	race
roll	hustle	hobble	plod
walk	stride	stagger	amble
skip	prance	scramble	sprint
run	strut	march	slink
gallop	stroll	scurry	dodge
leap	saunter	trudge	

3. Make Your Legs and Feet:

kick	stamp	trample	mince
shuffle	tap	tip-toe	stumble
skuff	drag	slip	

4. Make Your Face:

smile	wink	yawn	wince
frown	gape	chew	grimace
sneer	scowl	stare	squint
pout	grin	glare	blink
leer	smile		

5. Make Your Hands:

open	grasp	snatch	pinch
close	clap	pluck	poke
clench	scratch	beckon	point
grab	squeeze	pick	tap
stroke	wring	slap	clasp
poke	knead	pat	rub

6. Make Your Arms and Hands:

pound	reach	thrust	throw
strike	wave	lift	fling
grind	slice	stir	catch
sweep	chop	weave	whip
cut	push	clutch	grope
beat	pull	dig	punch

7. Pantomime or Dramatize:

yawning	speaking	hiccupping	twittering
sighing	cooling	wheezing	crowing
groaning	calling	murmuring	lowing
moaning	chuckling	muttering	squalling
grunting	rustling	sputtering	neighing
growling	snoring	whistling	shinnying
howling	whimpering	hissing	rattling
roaring	wailing	cackling	clanging
bellowing	shouting	trilling	ringing
screaching	laughing	hooting	honking
screaming	sneezing	creaking	popping
crying	snickering	braying	clicking
sobbing	tittering	whispering	buzzing
gasping	giggling	singing	purring
shrieking	sniffing	humming	ticking
whining	panting	croaking	chirping
mumbling	coughing	barking	squeaking

8. Dramatize These Moods:

fear	boredom	despair	contempt
pain	wonder	hope	reluctance
rage	generosity	pity	admiration
joy	reverence	hate	delight
sorrow	jealousy	love	anticipation
loneliness	envy	compassion	impatience
satisfaction	resentment	horror	happiness
frustation	pride	disgust	doubt
contentment	shame	surprise	greed
discontentment	repentence	gratitude	
anxiety	resignation	gaiety	

9. Dramatize These Activities:

work	study
play	fight
worship	build
destroy	celebrate
harvest	plant

10. Represent:

cat	bee
dog	seagull
caterpillar	mosquito
apple tree	any living thing

List 77. WAYS TO DEFINE A WORD

Following is a list of traditional and nontraditional ways to define a word. You may want to try some of these the next time you give your students a word definition assignment.

Formal Definition

word = A word is a sound or group of sounds that has meaning and is an independent unit of speech.

Definition by Example

phoneme = An example of a phoneme is the /p/ in "pin."

Definition by Description

rectangle = A rectangle is a geometric shape that has four straight line sides and four right angles.

Definition by Comparison

moon = The moon looks like a lighted disk in the sky (simile).
moon = The moon is a lighted ball in the sky (metaphor—note similes use "like" or "as").

Definition by Contrast

occupation = You might call it just a job, but I call it an occupation.

Definition by Synonym

consent = We want your consent that you agree to everything.

Definition by Antonym

dead = He wasn't dead, he was very much alive.

Definition by Apposition

(a meaning put in parentheses or set off by commas)
plaintiff = The plaintiff (person bringing suit) spoke to the judge first.
mango = The mango, the fruit that tastes something like a blend of peach and pineapple, is his favorite dessert.

Definition by Origin

telescope = The word telescope comes from the root "tele," which means "far," and the root "scope," which means "view."

Denotation and Connotative Meanings

The denotation meaning is the dictionary definition and is similar to most of the definition types listed above. The connotation meaning involves the feeling that surrounds the word. Note the differences in these words:

    prison—house of correction
    bum—unemployed person
    moron—mentally handicapped
    fat—overweight, heavy

See also List 25, Synonyms; List 26, Antonyms; List 27, Greek and Latin Roots.

The Reading Teacher's Book of Lists, Fourth Edition, © 2000 by John Wiley & Sons, Inc.

List 78. MULTIPLE INTELLIGENCES AND READING

Howard Gardner increased our understanding of the nature of intelligence by arguing that it is not simply a matter of how smart someone is, but more a matter of *how* he or she is smart. Teachers have long respected individual differences in learning and expression and have worked to provide a range of instructional activities that allow students to learn and demonstrate their understanding in a variety of ways. This list provides examples of activities linked to each of Gardner's eight kinds of intelligence.

Verbal/Linguistic (probably the most common teaching and learning strategies; focuses on ability to read, write, and understand through the use of words)

Dictated stories

Outlines

Written summaries or precis writing

Written reports

Debates

Daily oral "news reports"

Poetry

Journals and logs

Sequenced directions

Oral reports

Essays and reaction papers

Panel discussions

Word-a-day

Dramatic reading

Visual/Spatial (ability to think and understand through pictures, diagrams, and the arrangements of objects within a picture, diagram, map, etc.)

Find pictures to represent ideas

Design a logo or icon

Build a model

Sequence pictures to illustrate change

Design ideographs to tell a story

Make a video to tell a story/report

Draw pictures to illustrate concept or things

Color, underline, highlight to emphasize

Construct a mobile showing interrelations

Follow pictograms to construct an object

Make a photo-collage on a topic

Select format, type, materials for purpose

Body/Kinesthetic (ability to use the body for expression, for skilled action, for accomplishing tasks, for creating)

Act out/dramatize an event

Use papier-mâché, other media to express

Grow and observe plant development

"Simon Says"

Cooking experiences

Science experiments

Show through pantomime

Show a process through dance (e.g., growth)

Choreograph movement to problem-solve

Use bodies, movement, materials to weave

Perform precision drill routines

Dissection

Math manipulatives

Make facial expressions to demonstrate emotional states

Interpersonal (ability to get along with others and work together for common purposes)

Buddy learning

Reciprocal learning

Peer editing

Simulations and role play

Team competitions

Peer tutoring

Team research projects

Interviewing

Games for two or more

Class clubs

Logical/Mathematical (ability to use logic and mathematical processes to represent and manipulate ideas)

Categorize information

Compare and contrast

Create equations/rules for process/concept

Interpret data to support arguments

Use analogies, metaphors to explain

Extrapolate trends from historic data

Recognize anomalies, missing pieces

Develop flow charts, organization charts

Use formulas to compute answers

Distinguish facts from opinions

Use math processes to problem-solve

Recognize cause-and-effect relationships

Musical (ability to recognize and respond to rhythm, rhyme, tone, and other musical elements; to compose, perform, respond to musical compositions)

Listen to and appreciate rap, chants

Represent feelings with music

Create lyrics to tell story/express idea

Select music for multimedia presentation

Perform a set musical composition

Choral reading in parts

Respond to moods created by instruments

Relate musical style to social/historical idea

Sing alone or in groups

Perform an improvised musical composition

Intrapersonal (ability to know the self, to be aware of own thoughts, motivations, goals, principles, strengths and weaknesses)

Make and follow a plan

Diaries/journals/logs

Being aware of/explaining own actions

Appreciating self growth

Track own progress in learning

Create family tree and history

Develop school/personal growth portfolio

Prepare for a long-term goal

Estimate time/effort for personal activity

Metacognitive awareness during learning

Accurate self-evaluation of work/effort

Articulation of reasons for choosing hero

Link career options to personal qualities

Make scrapbook of photos/memorabilia

Environmental (ability to recognize, differentiate, appreciate objects and events in the natural world; attention to and appreciation of environment, including its natural systems)

Care for a pet

Collect and classify leaves

Experiment with simple machines

Observe and track weather for patterns

Keep an ant farm

Photograph/video one location in four seasons

Learn about and join a recycling project

Keep a log of nature's impact on daily life

The Reading Teacher's Book of Lists, Fourth Edition, © 2000 by John Wiley & Sons, Inc.

List 79. CHARACTERISTICS OF NARRATIVE AND EXPOSITORY TEXT

Pre-reading and early reading experiences help students develop frameworks for dealing with narratives. Most students, by the time they are learning to read, are sufficiently familiar with "Once upon a time"—they recognize it as the beginning of a fairy tale. But many other characteristics and conventions of text are not so familiar. Use this list to discuss differences between narrative and expository text.

Narrative (Stories)	Expository (Explanations)
Many based on common events from life	Often about topics not known
Familiarity makes prediction easier	New information makes prediction harder
Familiarity makes inferences easier	New information makes inferences harder
Key vocabulary often known	Key vocabulary often new
Simple vocabulary	Multisyllabic vocabulary, roots + affixes
Cause and effect known	Cause and effect not known
Concrete, real concepts	Abstract concepts
People oriented	Thing or subject oriented
Dialogue makes text less concept dense	Facts make text more concept dense
Stories can have personal meaning	Explanations have impersonal meaning
May give insight for own life/interest	May have no relation to own life/interest
Purpose is to entertain or share experience	Purpose is to explain or persuade
Chronological structure	Structure varies: definition/example; cause and effect; sequence of steps; main idea/details; examples/generalization
Simple concepts	Complex concepts
Familiar story types	Presentation varies; few recognizable types

See also List 45, Genre.

The Reading Teacher's Book of Lists, Fourth Edition, © 2000 by John Wiley & Sons, Inc.

List 80. READABILITY GRAPH

The Readability Graph is included on the next page so you will have it on hand when you need it. Use it to help judge the difficulty level of the materials your students use so that you can better match reading selections to students' reading abilities.

1. Randomly select three sample passages and count out exactly 100 words beginning with the beginning of a sentence. Count proper nouns, initializations, and numerals.

2. Count the number of sentences in the hundred words estimating length of the fraction of the last sentence to the nearest 1/10th.

3. Count the total number of syllables in the 100-word passage. If you don't have a hand counter available, an easy way is to put a mark above every syllable over one in each word, and then when you get to the end of the passage, count the number of marks and add 100. Small calculators also can be used as counters by pushing numeral "1," then push the "+" sign for each word or syllable when counting.

4. Enter graph with *average* sentence length and *average* number of syllables; plot a dot where the two lines intersect. The areas where a dot is plotted will give you the approximate grade level.

5. If a great deal of variability is found in syllable count or sentence count, putting more samples into the average is desirable.

6. A word is defined as a group of symbols with a space on either side; thus, "Joe," "IRA," "1945," and "&" are each one word.

7. A *syllable* is defined as a phonetic syllable. Generally, there are as many syllables as vowel sounds. For example, *stopped* is one syllable and *wanted* is two syllables. When counting syllables for numerals and initializations, count one syllable for each symbol. For example, *1945* is four syllables, and *IRA* is three syllables, and & is one syllable.

Example

	SYLLABLES	SENTENCES
1st hundred words	124	6.6
2nd hundred words	141	5.5
3rd hundred words	<u>158</u>	<u>6.8</u>
AVERAGE	141	6.3

READABILITY 7th GRADE (see dot plotted on graph)

The Reading Teacher's Book of Lists, Fourth Edition, © 2000 by John Wiley & Sons, Inc.

See also List 69, Writeability Checklist.

GRAPH FOR ESTIMATING READABILITY–EXTENDED

BY EDWARD FRY, PROFESSOR EMERITUS, RUTGERS UNIVERSITY

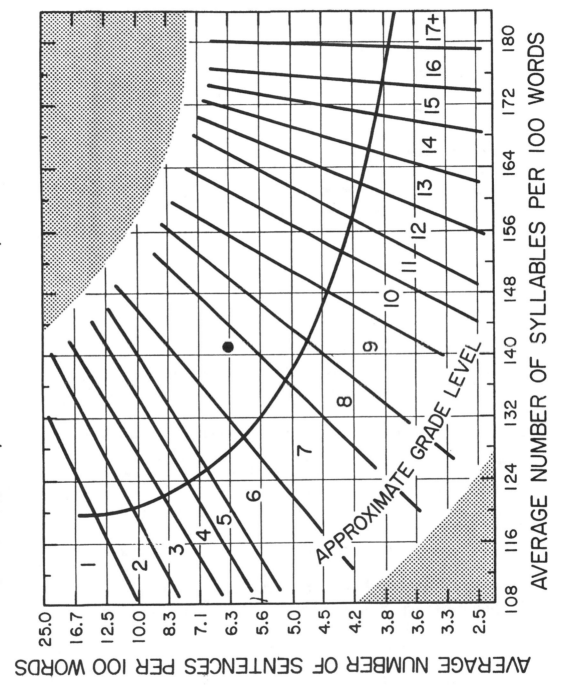

AVERAGE NUMBER OF SYLLABLES PER 100 WORDS

AVERAGE NUMBER OF SENTENCES PER 100 WORDS

APPROXIMATE GRADE LEVEL

List 81. TEACHING WITH NEWSPAPERS

Newspapers—whether delivered to your home in the morning or available 24 hours a day online—are our link to current events, local news, community happenings, and much more. They record history as it happens. One mark of a literate society is the rate of newspaper readership. In reading classrooms, newspapers offer unlimited opportunities for high interest, purposeful, natural reading activities. The list below will get you started.

Primary

- Circle words that begin with the target letter.
- Make an alphabet book—cut out pictures for words that begin with each letter of the alphabet.
- Find words and pictures that belong to a category: food, home, people, community helpers, fun, sports, animals, work, clothing, buildings.
- Compare prices of food or other current sale items.
- Find people from different countries; post the pictures around a world map and connect the photos by colored yarn to the countries.
- Find pictures (comics, ads, or news) that show a feeling (happy, sad, frightened, proud, etc.).
- Find pictures (comics, ads, or news) that show a concept (sharing, learning, teamwork, etc.).
- Find words that have a target ending (-ed, -ing, -ly, -tion, -ment, -ish).
- Find money words and symbols.
- Find long words for the class to divide into syllables.
- Make a pictograph with all the faces in today's newspaper. Which group had more: male/female? young/old?
- Add pictures/headline words to word walls on nouns, verbs, adjectives, adverbs, prepositions.
- Read a suitable comic strip together; "white out" the dialogue, duplicate, and have students create new dialogue for the pictures.
- Glue suitable comic strips to tagboard, cut into frames, and have students put in proper order.
- Read comic strip with a group. Discuss sequence, what changes in language and in the pictures.
- For a month, track the temperature on a graph.
- For a month, track the number of sunny, cloudy, foggy, snowy, rainy days in a table or in a graph.
- For a five-game period, track the number of runs made by the class's favorite teams; add them; compare; make tables; make pictographs; make scatter graphs.
- Using a grocery ad, list all the items that cost less than $1.00; less than $.50.
- Discuss movie ads—what they portray, what appeals and doesn't; adult or kids movie, topic, genre (mystery, adventure, thriller, war, etc.).

See also List 75, Good Ideas for Reading Teachers.

The Reading Teacher's Book of Lists, Fourth Edition, © 2000 by John Wiley & Sons, Inc.

Elementary/Intermediate

- Nominate "words of the week" that students find in the newspaper in these categories: best verb, best noun, best adjective, funniest sounding, longest, hardest to spell. Vote on nominations and post each week's winners on a word wall.

- Make a list of all the different activities and events scheduled for the upcoming weekend in town—include music, dance, movies, plays, fairs, concerts, festivals, etc.

- Find a news event that happened in another country; find 10 interesting facts about that country in almanacs, encyclopedias, web sites, books. Post the fact sheet with the news story for the class to read.

- In teams, make a list of all the different abbreviations you can find in 15 minutes; then define them. Get one point for each abbreviation; two for each correct definition.

- Find four news items about government, three articles about people, two articles about business, two articles about different sports.

- Divide a bulletin board with yarn. On one side students post news stories about "good news" and on the other, "bad news."

- Read the want ads and find three jobs that do not require a college education and three that do.

- Track news for a week to identify problems facing the state. Do research on the top problems and present information about causes and proposed solutions to the class.

- Draft a letter to the editor about a problem facing students in your town.

- Find the highest/lowest selling price for a one-family house advertised in your town.

- In teams, write on-the-road journals for politicians who are campaigning; include city and state, group addressed or met with, topics. Compare after a week.

- Make a list of all the countries mentioned in the newspaper during one week. Make a data table and bar graph of the results showing "where this week's news is happening."

- Classify types of front-page stories for one week.

- Collect interesting verbs from headlines.

- Using online versions of newspapers, track the weather for a week for New York, Los Angles, Washington, D.C., and your town.

- Collect headlines from front pages of three newspapers (local, state, national) for a week; discuss importance of stories.

- Compare headlines on major news story from different parts of the country (use online versions of the paper).

- Read about the same international news story in three newspapers from different countries. Discuss similarities and differences.

- Scavenger hunt for news story, human interest story, obituary, editorial, graph or chart, feature, schedule, ad, classified, comics, political cartoon.

- Have each student pick a state; track the high and low temperatures for its capital city; find the range and averages for a month; create individual and group data tables; summarize by categorizing states with similar temperature patterns.

- Scavenger hunt for newspaper parts: banner, box, byline, caption, column, credit line, dateline, editorial, flag, headline, jump, lead, masthead, news service, obituary.

The Reading Teacher's Book of Lists, Fourth Edition, © 2000 by John Wiley & Sons, Inc.

List 82. ORAL READING ACTIVITIES

Choral Reading. Group oral reading. It allows advanced readers to lead and delayed readers to follow. Also excellent for poetry.

Glossing. The teacher reads aloud slowly and accurately with good sentence tunes. Teacher "glosses" by stopping occasionally to explain a word, phrase, or idea. Students just listen or listen and follow along in their books.

Official Announcer. Appoint a student each day to read announcements, bulletins, student writings, short selections, continuing story, and so forth. Announcer may prepare and seek help from teacher or another student.

Radio Program. Small group takes parts and reads play or radio script into tape recorder for class or parent presentation.

Overviewer. Student reads aloud subheads, key words, and/or key sentences in a text before class studies it. Excellent in science or social studies.

Flash Cards. Students try to read word or phrase on flash cards the fastest, most accurate, or in turn.

Play Reading. Like radio program except students read play parts for live performance.

Singing. Read lyrics while learning new song. This is also great for ESL or learning foreign language. Good for stutterers.

Games. A number of board games and other games like Trivial Pursuit™ require players to read a word, set of directions, or questions aloud.

Formal Speech. Student writes a speech for an occasion or learning unit and reads it to a group. May be part of a speech contest.

Find the Answer. Teacher asks a question, student reads aloud just the part of the text that answers the question. This activity aids comprehension improvement and generates good discussions.

Joke of the Day. Read aloud a joke or humerous selection.

Letter. Read a letter sent or received by the class.

Author's Chair. Read aloud a story that is being written to obtain group feedback.

Word Wall. Read aloud known words listed on word walls or on the chalkboard.

See also List 47, Old and New Favorite Books to Read Aloud; List 92, Games and Methods for Teaching; List 99, Sentence Tunes.

List 83. ONE HUNDRED WAYS TO PRAISE

Be free with praise for even minor successes; it will encourage greater ones. Be careful, however. Never be phony and never praise when it isn't deserved; you will lose your credibility and the value of future praise.

Awesome!

Loved it!

Fantastic!

You're a great team member.

You showed you're a leader on this!

You're quite an expert.

Very informative.

I can tell you were very careful with this.

You really caught on!

Be sure to share this—it's great!

I like your choice of words.

Great style!

This is very well organized.

Very convincing!

Good use of details.

You've really mastered this.

Excellent beginning!

That's really nice.

That's clever.

You're right on target.

Thank you!

Wow!

That's great!

Very creative.

Very interesting.

I like the way you're working.

Good thinking.

That's an interesting way of looking at it.

Now you've figured it out.

Keep up the good work.

You've made my day.

You're on the ball today.

This is something special.

That's quite an improvement.

Much better.

Keep it up.

That's the right answer.

Exactly right!

You made me smile.

You're a Rising Star!

You're on the right track now.

This is quite an accomplishment.

I like the way you've tackled this assignment.

Way to go!

That's coming along nicely.

You've shown a lot of patience with this.

You've really been paying attention.

It looks like you've put a lot of work into this.

You've put in a full day today.

This is prize-winning work.

I like your style.

Pulitzer-Prize-winner in training.

Your work has such personality.

That's very perceptive.

This is a moving scene.

Your remark shows a lot of sensitivity.

Clear, concise, and complete!

A well-developed theme!

You are really in touch with the feeling here.

A splendid job!

You're right on the mark.

Good reasoning.

I can tell you really understand this.

You made an important point here.

Very artistic!

Outstanding!

This is a winner!

Superb!

Superior work.

Super!

Great going!

Where have you been hiding all this talent?

I knew you could do it!

Good job.

What neat work!

You really outdid yourself today.

That's a good point.

The Reading Teacher's Book of Lists, Fourth Edition, © 2000 by John Wiley & Sons, Inc.

239

That's a very good observation.

That's certainly one way of looking at it.

This kind of work pleases me very much.

Congratulations! You got ____ correct today.

That's right. Good for you.

Terrific!

Your parents will be proud of your work.

That's an interesting point of view.

You've got it now.

Nice going.

You make it look so easy.

This shows you've been thinking.

You're becoming an expert at this.

Beautiful.

I'm very proud of your work today.

Excellent work.

Very good. Why don't you show the class?

The results are worth all your hard work.

You've come a long way with this one.

Marvelous.

Very fine work.

I like the way you've handled this.

That looks like it's going to be a good report.

The Reading Teacher's Book of Lists, Fourth Edition, © 2000 by John Wiley & Sons, Inc.

List 84. INTEREST INVENTORY—PRIMARY

Whether choosing read-aloud books, interdisciplinary themes, or trying to reach and develop students' special interests and talents, interest inventories are a great help. For students not yet able to write their answers, use the inventories during your individual conference time with students and record their responses.

1. My favorite color is _____.

2. My favorite food is _____.

3. My favorite toy is _____.

4. My favorite game is _____.

5. My favorite story is _____.

6. My favorite sport to play is _____.

7. My favorite TV show to watch is _____.

8. My favorite person to play with is _____.

9. I like to collect _____.

10. I like to go to _____.

11. I like to learn about _____.

12. I like stories about _____.

13. I like to read about _____.

14. I have a pet named _____. It is a _____.

15. Things I like to do at school: _____.

16. Things I like to do at home: _____.

17. Things I like to do by myself: _____.

18. Things I like to do with friends: _____.

19. I go to the library.   Yes   No

20. I have a library card.   Yes   No

21. I like to read.   Yes   No

22. I read books at home.   Yes   No

23. I read magazines at home.   Yes   No

List 85. INTEREST INVENTORY— ELEMENTARY/INTERMEDIATE

Knowing students' interests, preferences, and activities helps you plan instruction that builds on strengths, prior knowledge, and natural enthusiasm. This information also helps you suggest research topics, good books, and project themes. Use this inventory as a getting-to-know-you activity the first week of school.

1. What are your two favorite school subjects? _____ and _____

2. What do you like best about school? _____

3. What do you like least about school? _____

4. What do you do after school? _____

5. What do you like to read? (*circle answers*)

    Stories about young people   Sports stories   Mysteries

    Stories about animals   Fables/Folktales   Biographies

    Stories about real people and events Adventures   How-to-do-it books

    Real science stories   Science fiction   Fantasy

    Poetry   None

6. What part of the newspaper do you read (at least sometimes)? (*circle answers*)

    Headlines   Sports   Comics   News   Letters to Editor

    Advertisements   Classified Ads   Advice (like Dear Abby)   Fashion

    Movie and Concert Reviews   Feature stories   Editorials   None

7. What magazines do you read? _____

8. What are your hobbies? _____

9. What places have you visited that you liked a lot? _____

10. Circle the things you like:

    Working alone   Working with a friend   Reading   Doing projects

    Using the library   Using the computer   Explaining things   Writing

    Drawing/Art   Listening to music   Playing an instrument

11. What is your favorite sport to play? _____

12. Have you played on a team?   Yes   No   Sport _____

13. What is your favorite sport to watch? _____

14. TV programs I regularly watch are _____.

15. Computer games I play are _____.

16. Three words that describe you: _____

The Reading Teacher's Book of Lists, Fourth Edition, © 2000 by John Wiley & Sons, Inc.

List 86. STUDENT/GROUP PROJECT GUIDE

Name: _____   Today's date: _____

Project topic: _____   Date due: _____

Two things I/we want to learn: (1) _____

(2) _____

Related ideas and words to look up: _____

_____

_____

INFORMATION SOURCES:

❑ almanac
❑ art
❑ biographical dictionary
❑ biographies
❑ CD-ROMs
❑ CDs or audiotapes
❑ Dictionary
❑ e-mail to expert
❑ encyclopedia

❑ experiment
❑ history books
❑ interviews
❑ magazines
❑ maps/atlas
❑ microscopic slides
❑ museum exhibits
❑ music
❑ newspapers

❑ nonfiction books
❑ photographs
❑ posters
❑ reference books
❑ speeches
❑ thesaurus
❑ video clips/tapes
❑ video disks (DVD)
❑ web sites

WAYS TO ORGANIZE INFORMATION:

Text

❑ order of events
❑ sequence
❑ category/subcategories
❑ comparison/contrast
❑ cause and effect
❑ questions and answers
❑ logical order
❑ main idea/details
❑ before and after

Graphics

❑ timeline
❑ flow chart
❑ tables
❑ graphs
❑ cause-and-effect diagram
❑ fact sheet
❑ tree diagram
❑ outline, word web, or story map
❑ photos/drawings or charts

PROJECT PRESENTATION WILL INCLUDE:

- ❏ demonstration
- ❏ picture essay
- ❏ exhibit of artifacts
- ❏ model
- ❏ photo sequence
- ❏ play
- ❏ speech
- ❏ audiotape with poster
- ❏ powerpoint slides

- ❏ photocollage
- ❏ diorama
- ❏ library display
- ❏ music and/or dance
- ❏ press release
- ❏ poetry
- ❏ videotape
- ❏ travel brochure
- ❏ animation

PROJECT SCHEDULE AND CHECKLIST: DATE

- ❏ I have planned my project.   _____
- ❏ I have discussed my project with my teacher and we agree.   _____
- ❏ I have located the information and materials I need.   _____
- ❏ I have reviewed the information, and I have selected the best sources.   _____
- ❏ I have enough information to complete the project I planned.   _____
- ❏ I have read and organized my information in notes and other ways as planned.   _____
- ❏ I have made a first draft of my report or other presentation materials.   _____
- ❏ I have edited and revised my first draft.   _____
- ❏ I have completed all the parts of my project.   _____
- ❏ I have proofread all the written materials.   _____
- ❏ I have practiced my oral presentation.   _____

The Reading Teacher's Book of Lists, Fourth Edition, © 2000 by John Wiley & Sons, Inc.

List 87. WORKING IN TEAMS

A person can do and understand many things, but no person has enough knowledge and skill to understand and do everything. Working in teams will help you learn more and solve complex problems in school and out. Before starting to work, decide who will have each of the jobs described below. Change jobs every time you start a new team project so that everyone has an opportunity to try each job.

Team Manager

- Describes the task or problem to the team, including what product or result is required.
- Explains the outcome that the teacher will use to judge whether the team is successful and keeps track of the team's progress toward the goal.
- Monitors the team's work to be sure it stays on target.

Organizer

- Schedules meetings, if they are not during class.
- Gets materials the group will need.
- Returns materials after use.
- Organizes and is responsible for clean-up.
- Arranges for computer time, AV equipment, etc.

Researcher

- Checks facts, computations, and other information.
- Locates library and other reference materials.
- Skims background materials and makes brief summary presentations to the team.
- Keeps log of sources and bibliographic information.

Member

- Suggests ideas in brainstorming and problem solving.
- Shares knowledge and skills related to the task.
- Criticizes ideas, not people.
- Stays on task.
- Does a fair share of the work.

Charter

- Creates flowcharts, diagrams, timelines, and other visual presentations of the problem and the solution.

Scribe

- Writes down brainstorming ideas, checking that the written statements match the team members' ideas.
- Records steps in the team's process or activities.
- Records the team's discoveries and answers.
- Drafts the report of the team's work.

Editor

- Checks the draft report for accuracy and completeness.
- Does final report and gives copies to team members and the teacher.

Presenter

- Gives an oral presentation of the team's work.
- Prepares video and/or audiotape presentation, if used.

The Reading Teacher's Book of Lists, Fourth Edition, © 2000 by John Wiley & Sons, Inc.

List 88. TEAMWORK RULES

Teamwork means working together to achieve a shared goal. These rules will help your teamwork work:

- Respect all teammates.
- Disagree without being disagreeable.
- Take turns speaking; don't interrupt.
- Be on time and prepared for meetings.
- Offer to share your special skills; for example, artistic talent, computer skills, typing.
- Share ideas; if you find or know something that will help a teammate, pass it on.
- Speak loudly enough to be heard by your group, but not so loudly that you disturb other teams.
- Don't give up or go off on your own project.
- Ask for help if you are stuck or forgot something.
- Don't decide by voting; figure out the right answer.

List 89. REPORT CARD HELPS

These euphemisms might stand you in good stead at report-card time or for parent interviews. They might also take some of the puffery out of some reports you may have to read. Students enjoy euphemisms; share some of these with your class and have them add to the list.

BLUNT TRUTH	EUPHEMISM
Lies	Shows difficulty in distinguishing between imaginary and factual material.
Is a klutz	Has difficulty with motor control and coordination.
Needs nagging	Accomplishes task when interest is constantly prodded.
Fights	Resorts to physical means of winning his or her point or attracting attention.
Smells bad	Needs guidance in development of good habits of hygiene.
Cheats	Needs help in learning to adhere to rules and standards of fair play.
Steals	Needs help in learning to respect the property rights of others.
Is a wiseguy (or -gal)	Needs guidance in learning to express himself or herself respectfully.
Is lazy	Requires ongoing supervision in order to work well.
Is rude	Lacks a respectful attitude toward others.
Is selfish	Needs help in learning to enjoy sharing with others.
Is gross	Needs guidance in developing the social graces.
Has big mouth	Needs to develop quieter habits of communciation.
Eats like a pig	Needs to develop more refined table manners.
Bullies others	Has qualities of leadership, but needs to use them more constructively.
Is babyish	Shows lack of maturity in relationships with others.
Hangs out	Seems to feel secure only in group situations; needs to develop sense of identity and independence.
Is disliked by others	Needs help in developing meaningful peer relationships.
Is often late	Needs guidance in developing habits of responsibility and punctuality.
Is truant	Needs to develop a sense of responsibility in regard to attendance.

List 90. ACTIVITIES FOR TUTORS

Reading tutors are often volunteers with little or no previous experience in teaching reading. That's OK, there are plenty of good things that they can do to help a child or an adult read better. Here are some of them.

Read to the Student

Students of all ages, even adults, like to listen to stories. Note the success of audiotapes for adults.

- Make it a little more of a lesson by having student retell the story or part of it in his or her own words.

- Discuss the story, its setting, similar stories, or similar real-life situations. Get the student to contribute to the discussion.

- Discuss interesting words and those with which the student might not be familiar.

Diagnostic Listening

Have the student read a story and listen very carefully.

- If the student is making a lot of mistakes, get an easier book. As a general rule of thumb, when reading orally the student should make less than one mistake in 20 words.

- Help the student with correct pronunciation. Sometimes just tell the student the difficult word.

- Sometimes help the student to figure out the word by seeing what word would make sense in that sentence, or by sounding it out using the first letter or initial sound as a clue.

- Encourage the student's reading by lots of praise. Sometimes the tutor takes a turn reading.

Silent Reading

Many beginning students will simply not read on their own. It is not a waste of time for the tutor to ask the student to read silently and wait while it is being done. Helping the student to develop silent reading habits is very important.

- Tell the student you are available to help with difficult words or to understand a difficult sentence.

- Check up on comprehension by asking questions. Ask a variety of comprehension questions. (See List 95, Comprehension Questions.)

- Help the student select a variety of different kinds of reading materials: short stories, book-length stories, jokes, comics, poems, factual stories from newspapers, or easy encyclopedias.

The Reading Teacher's Book of Lists, Fourth Edition, © 2000 by John Wiley & Sons, Inc.

Encourage Writing

Reading and writing are often practiced together.

- Have the student write something every day.

- Write a variety of things such as a continuing story or diary, a summary of a story just read, and/or a letter to a relative or friend.

- Write a rough draft first (using any kind of spelling or grammar).

- Check spelling, grammar, and punctuation.

- Sometimes have the story rewritten.

Encouragement

Everybody needs encouragement. Beginning readers need a lot.

- One of the best forms of encouragement is success in learning. Therefore, make your lessons or individual tasks easy enough and short enough that the student really experiences success.

- Use a lot of praise. Praise a correct reading. Praise a good retelling. Praise a good question, etc.

- Show progress over time. Save some writing samples periodically to show the student that stories just written are longer or better. Reread some easier material.

- Select stories or material that is interesting. Use an interest inventory to find student interests. (See Lists 84 and 85.) Assign a fun book to be read at home. Help the student to read something wanted, or write something needed.

- Don't get discouraged yourself. Be patient. It takes a long time to develop good reading and writing skills so don't expect immediate success. But every little bit helps. Every hour is important. Have a set schedule for lessons. Teaching someone how to read is very, very important.

See List 75, Good Ideas for Reading Teachers; List 82, Oral Reading Activities; List 92, Games and Methods for Teaching.

List 91. FIFTY READING TIPS
FOR PARENTS

Parents are important partners in the reading life of children. They can instill in their children a love of books and delight in wordplay, develop pre-reading skills, and help them become accomplished independent readers. Here are 50 ways parents can be partners in beginning reading and literacy education.

1. Read to your child every day. It's never too early to start, and the popularity of books-on-tape proves we never outgrow the enjoyment of being read to.

2. Recite or sing nursery rhymes and children's songs often, even to very young children.

3. Read and reread books without words, predictable books, rhyming books, and picture books to young children. Rereading helps develop memory for the story line, awareness of rhyme, and many other prereading skills.

4. Give your "junk mail" to children to pretend read.

5. Point to the words as you read; after a time, have your child point as you read.

6. Use the pictures in books to help your child understand the story. Have your child point to details in the pictures to highlight them.

7. Let your child "read" you the pictures in a familiar picture book. Ask questions: Why? What happens next? Then what? Where did it go?

8. Help preschoolers make their own books by picking out pictures in discarded magazines to cut-and-paste into "books." Some book ideas: a yellow book (all things yellow), a happy book, a pretty book, a sleepy book, a hungry book.

9. Use the pictures in books to expand your child's vocabulary. Provide synonyms for words he/she knows. (Sometimes we call that a . . . .)

10. Help your child organize knowledge by reviewing related words. (What other train words can you think of? Food words? Feeling words?)

11. Take your child to Story Time at your local library or bookstore—sharing books with other children increases enjoyment and connects children in a different social setting.

12. Encourage your child's personal response to stories. Ask "Do you think that was a good idea? Would you want to do that, too?"

13. Provide paper and pencils and encourage your child to pretend write while you are writing a shopping list, paying bills, writing greeting cards.

14. Introduce your child to different kinds of art through a selection of picture books: photos, line drawings, watercolor impressionism, cartoons, etc.

15. When reading to your child, stop periodically and talk about what has happened so far. Ask the child to tell what he/she thinks will happen next, then read to find out.

16. Help your child get a library card in his/her own name as early as your library allows.

17. Help develop attention and memory using books with lots of repetition by pausing for your child to supply the repeated word.

The Reading Teacher's Book of Lists, Fourth Edition, © 2000 by John Wiley & Sons, Inc.

The Reading Teacher's Book of Lists, Fourth Edition, © 2000 by John Wiley & Sons, Inc.

18. Use a book to begin a conversation about a difficult life topic like a trip to the hospital, the birth of a sibling, divorce, the death of a grandparent.

19. Treat books as though they are special. Your child will also.

20. Offer choices for your read-aloud time: Which would you like today? A story about a family on a trip, or a story about a boy and his new friend?

21. Read with expression to help communicate meaning as well as hold interest.

22. Give books as presents or to commemorate a special event.

23. Start your child's use of reference books early with a picture dictionary.

24. Set an example as an avid reader. Let your child see you reading a book, magazine, the newspaper.

25. Pick a letter for the day. Draw a large one, then have your child find more of them on a page from a discarded magazine. The child can mark it with a highlighter.

26. Make a Halloween costume for your child based on his/her favorite book character.

27. Make rebus recipe cards (using small pictures and diagrams) and help your child make a favorite snack by reading the recipe. Some are available on the Web or in bookstores.

28. Talk to your child about the parts of a book. Give them names: front cover, title, spine, table of contents.

29. Encourage response to stories by providing different kinds of art materials and ideas for creating after-reading artwork; for example, fingerpaint, paper-plate masks, sponge paintings, potato stamps.

30. Take favorite books or books on tape in the car, on vacation, to grandparents' homes, wherever you travel. Children's travel restlessness is often easy to overcome with a familiar favorite story.

31. Encourage and respond to children's interests by helping them pick out books on special topics; for example, pets, dinosaurs, bugs, horses, building things, how things work.

32. Use new sights and experiences as teaching tools for new words. Explain new things, tell stories about new places, tell the names of new objects and their uses.

33. Discuss the difference between real and make believe. Can animals talk like people do? Are there really magic stones?

34. Use a book character as the theme for a birthday party.

35. Use similes to help define a new concept. This helps bridge something your child knows to understanding something new. "It's like a train but it has . . . "

36. Tell a humorous story from your childhood and have your child illustrate it.

37. Help your child recognize cereal names and other common food stuff and help read the labels in the supermarket.

38. Show your child how to act out a character's part with a finger puppet. Then both of you take parts and tell the story together through your finger puppets.

39. Show how useful words can be. Label common objects in the child's room. Put his/her name on some belongings, a coat hook, book shelf, etc.

40. Try tongue twisters, hink pinks, and other wordplay games in the car as you travel, even on short trips. (See Section 13, Word Play Fun.)

41. Encourage your child to "read" signs for favorite fast-food restaurants, stop signs, stores, etc.

42. Ask your child to tell you a story and then write it (or use a word processor) in large print. Read it back pointing to the words. Have child read it back with you. Ask him/her to pick out key words like names, places, etc., if child is able.

43. Help child focus on the sounds that begin or end a word. Ask "What other word starts like Sam?" Give two words; one that starts with the sound and one that does not. Have the child pick. Later have the child suggest a word that begins with the same sound.

44. Play "Before and After" for a familiar sequence. For example: "Do you put your shoes on before or after your socks? Do you get a bowl before or after you pour your cereal?" Have the child ask you before and afters also.

45. Ask your child to help write the family shopping list. Together consult the supermarket ads in the newspapers and point out the names of fruit, vegetables, and other items that will be on the list.

46. Play OK/NoWay: Tell your child to listen carefully to what you say, then make up sentences, including some that make no sense. After each sentence, the child says "OK or No Way!" For example: John sleeps in a bed. (OK) Mary put her toys away in the lamp. (No Way!)

47. Keep a weather chart with your child. On a calendar, have child draw a symbol for the day's weather: sun, raindrops, snowflakes, clouds.

48. Tape record some favorite books so you can "read" to your child, even if you are not home or busy.

49. Show interest and delight in stories and books; tell which are your favorites and why. Ask which are your child's favorites and why.

50. Talk about a story, asking your child to recall facts (What did the bear do?) and to make inferences (Why did he put on his mittens? How can you tell?).

The Reading Teacher's Book of Lists, Fourth Edition, © 2000 by John Wiley & Sons, Inc.

See List 75, Good Ideas for Reading Teachers; List 82, Oral Reading Activities; List 90, Activities for Tutors; List 92, Games and Methods for Teaching.

List 92. GAMES AND METHODS FOR TEACHING

The games and methods for instruction listed here are suggestions for class activities that will help students learn many of the lists or words presented in this book.

1. Pairs. A card game for two to five players. Five cards are dealt to each player, and the remainder of the deck is placed in the center of the table. The object of the game is to get as many pairs as possible. There are only two cards alike in each deck. To play, the player to the right of the dealer may ask any other player if he or she has a specific card, for example, "Do you have *and*?" The player asking must hold the mate in his or her hand. The player who is asked must give up the card if he or she holds it. If the first player does not get the card asked for, he or she draws one card from the pile. Then the next player has a turn at asking for a card. If a player can't read his or her own card, the player may show the card and ask any other player how to read it.

If the player succeeds in getting the card asked for, either from another player or from the pile, he or she gets another turn. As soon as the player gets a pair he or she puts the pair face down in front of him or her. The player with the most pairs at the end of the game wins. *Note:* A deck of 50 cards (25 pairs) is good for two to five players. This game works well with an Instant Word list of 25 words with each word on two cards (see List 14). It can also work well with homophones (List 16) or any association in this section.

2. Bingo. Played like regular Bingo except that the players' boards have 25 words in place of numbers. Children can use bits of paper for markers, and the caller can randomly call off words from a list. Be certain when making the boards that the words are arranged in a different order on each card. Use with 25 Instant Words or any 25 words. Caller can write each word called on the board to help players learn to read the words.

the	of	it	with	at
a	can	on	are	this
is	will	you	to	and
your	that	we	as	but
be	in	not	for	have

The Reading Teacher's Book of Lists, Fourth Edition, © 2000 by John Wiley & Sons, Inc.

3. Board Games. Trace a path on posterboard. Mark off one-inch spaces. Write a word in each space. Students advance from Start by tossing dice until one reaches the finish line. Students must correctly pronounce (or give the meaning or sample use) of the word in the square. Use three pennies if you don't have dice; shake and advance number of squares for heads up.

4. Contests. Students, individually or as teams, try to get more words in a category than anyone else. For example, the teacher may start the contest by giving three homographs. The students try to amass the longest list of homographs. There may be a time limit.

5. Spelling. Use the list words in spelling lessons or have an old-fashioned spelling bee. See Lists 122 through 125 or Instant Words.

6. Use Words in a Sentence. Either orally or written. Award points for the longest, funniest, saddest, or most believable sentence.

7. Word Wheels. To make a word wheel, attach an inner circle to a larger circle with a paper fastener. Turn the inner wheel to match outer parts. This is great for compound words, phonograms, or matching a word to a picture clue. Sliding strips do the same thing.

8. Matching. Make worksheets with two columns of words or word parts. Students draw a line from an item in column A to the item in column B that matches (*prefix* and *root, word* and *meaning,* two synonyms, etc.). Matching also can be done by matching two halves of a card that has been cut to form puzzle pieces. See Association Pairs on page 257 for suitable lists of paired words.

9. Flash Cards. The word or word part is written on one side of a card. The teacher or tutor flashes the cards for the student to read instantly. Cards also can be shuffled and read by the student. Cards also can be used in sentence building, finding synonyms and antonyms, and the Concentration game.

WORD RACE

Toss three pennies, move marker X number of heads. Read the word you land on.

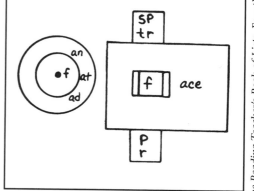

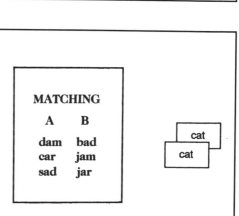

MATCHING

A	B
dam	bad
car	jam
sad	jar

The Reading Teacher's Book of Lists, Fourth Edition, © 2000 by John Wiley & Sons, Inc.

10. Hidden Words (or Word Search Puzzle). To make a word search puzzle, write words horizontally, vertically, or diagonally on a grid (graph paper is fine), one letter per box. Fill in all the other boxes with letters at random. Students try to locate all of the target words. When they find a word, they circle it.

11. Concentration. To play Concentration, use one-sided flash cards or any card with a word or symbol written on one side. Cards must be in pairs (duplicate) such as two identical cards or an association pair. Shuffle four or more pairs (more for older or advanced students) and place cards face down, spread out randomly over a table surface. The player may pick up any two cards and look at them. If they are a pair, he or she keeps them; if they are not, the cards must be put back in exactly the same place from which they came. The trick is to remember where different cards are located while they are sitting on the table face down so that when you pick up one card, you remember where its pair is located. Players take turns, and the object is to accumulate the most cards. Learning is needed to know what cards are pairs, for example, and which definition matches which card or any association pair.

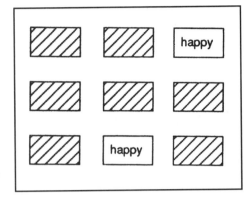

12. Association Cards. For students who don't want to fool around with games, a useful learning device is to develop a set of association pair cards with the word on one side and its definition on the other side. The student first studies both sides of a set of cards; then the student goes through a stack of cards reading the words and attempting to recall the definition. If correct, he or she puts the card into the "know pile"; if incorrect or the student can't remember, the card is studied and put into the "don't-know pile." Next, the "don't-know pile" is sorted once more into "know" and "don't-know." This process is complete when all cards are in the "know pile"; unfortunately, there is also something called forgetting, so the stack of cards should be reviewed at later intervals, such as a few days later and a few weeks later. Students should not attempt to learn (associate) too many new (unknown) cards at one time, or learning will become boring. But as long as motivation is high and learning is occurring, this is an excellent learning and study technique. Primary students can use picture nouns; older students, List 27, Greek and Latin Roots.

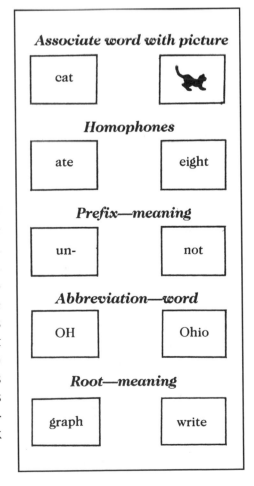

13. Tutoring. A teacher and a student, or a tutor and a student, or even two students can use these double-sided association pair cards in many ways. The tutor holds up one card, and the student calls off the associated definition. Students can take turns, have contests, win prizes, and so on.

14. Testing. Although it is often overused, testing is also a powerful learning motivator and teaching device. Done kindly and thoughtfully, testing can cause a lot of learning to occur in a classroom or tutoring situation. A technique of testing is to assign a set of association pairs to be learned (using any game or technique) and then test the results. Some teachers assign short daily tests that accumulate points or cause movement on a big chart. Other teachers give weekly tests and assign numeral or percent grades; these are shown to parents, or the five best papers are posted on a bulletin board. Part of the learning occurs because the students are motivated to study and because the students get feedback or knowledge or the results as to whether they know or don't know something. Hence, the corrected papers should be returned, or the students should trade papers and correct for more immediate and sometimes better knowledge of results.

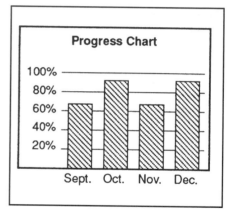

Testing also gives feedback to the teacher or tutor so that the teacher can regulate the amount of new learning (number of words) to be learned next or the amount needing review. It also can help the student to individualize and to give some students more and other students less to be learned.

15. Computer-Aided Instruction (CAI). Use computers to provide instruction, drills, and tests. CAI programs teach vocabulary both in and out of context, different types of comprehension, and subject content reading. CAI uses many elements of programmed instruction, such as small steps (limited from content), clear objectives, careful sequencing, active student response, immediate feedback on correctness, and often branching and recordkeeping. Most teachers buy programs already made, but it is possible to develop your own on a CAI program with the aid of a utility program in which the teacher inserts only desired content. The *Reading Teacher's Book of Lists* has excellent content for CAI programs.

16. Association Pairs. This is a table of items to be associated or learned together. We are calling them association pairs because they are often taught by association learning. The following association pairs can be used in developing games such as Concentration and Association, and in creating programs for computer-aided instruction.

USE THESE PAIRS FOR GAMES AND LESSONS

LIST NUMBER	ASSOCIATION PAIR
16	Word—Homophone (bare–bear)
18	Homograph—Definition (stoop–bend down; stoop–porch)
19	Word look-alike or sound-alike word (coma–comma)
36	Measurement term—Abbreviation (mm–millimeter)
36	Measurement term—Numerical relation (kilometer–1,000 meters)
25	Word—Synonym (see–look)
26	Word—Antonym (back–front)
114	First three words in analogy—Last word (story:read::song:sing)
154	Idiom root word—three or four usages (do–do away, do out of, do well)
155	Clipped word—Full word (pop–popular)
167	Portmanteau word—Full words (brunch–breakfast + lunch)
131	Contraction—Full words (she'd–she would)
179	Acronym—Full words (CB–citizens band)
33	Borrowed word—Origin (pasteurize–Louis Pasteur)
31	Foreign word—Translation (origin) (bonjour–good day, French)
28	-Ology word—Definition (cryptology–codes)
143	Computer term—Definition (bug–error)
29	-Phobia word—Definition (agoraphobia–open places)
27	Greek root—Meaning (graph–write)
27	Latin root—Meaning (duct–lead)
23	Prefix—Meaning (anti–against)
24	Suffix—Meaning (-ee–one who, ex. payee)
24	Suffix—Grammar (-s–plural)
8	Illustrating word or example word—Phoneme (at–short A)
100	Propaganda technique
194	Graph term—Example (bar graph)
107	Key object—Number (five–15)
150	Part of speech—Definition (noun–name of person, place)
151	Irregular verb present—Past (am–was)
151	Irregular verb present—Past participle (am–been)
46	Literary term—Definition (ballad–long narrative poem)
174	State abbreviation—Full name (CA–California)
176	Common abbreviation—Full term (Aug.–August)
182	Alphabet—Manual alphabet or Morse Code (B–. . .)
38	Symbol—Verbal equivalent (+–plus)
72	Proofreading symbol—Explanation (¶ –New paragraph)
187	Arabic number—Roman numeral (12–XII)
190	Library classification symbol—Area description (D–General History)
20	Collective Nouns—Animal (gaggle–geese)

17. Humor. Don't overlook the good effects of humor on learning. Both children and adults love word games and jokes. Many jokes use homophones and homographs. For example, "What is an outspoken hot dog? A frank frank." See List 163, Hink Pinks and Jokes. Children also like to draw humerous pictures of idiomatic expressions such as "It's raining cats and dogs" or "She's a ball of fire." Try a few Wacky Wordies (List 172).

18. Word Walls. Word walls help students recognize and recall new vocabulary and aid spelling and independent reading and writing skills. When teaching a new topic, make collections of related words and list them on a wall or chalkboard. Have students suggest additional words to add. Here are some categories of words that make good word walls.

Common nouns: bugs, stores, signs, places, drinks, sports, clothing, flowers, animals, oceans, colors, holidays, community helpers, family members, foods, transportation

Language categories: parts of speech, phonograms, phonics rules, suffixes, prefixes, homophones, contractions, spelling demons

Association categories: anger words, happy words, taste words, book words, camping words, adventure words, school words, feeling words

19. Kids' Book of Lists. Kids can categorize and list, too. Have students make booklets of their lists. Make a Kids' Book of Lists as a final project for a theme unit, or just for fun. Here are some categories to use:

Seven salty foods

Eight things to take to camp

Six TV shows about families

Twelve "strange" words

Five uses for a rubber band

Seven things most kids do better than most adults

Six things a nurse needs to know how to do

Six events that could make you late for school

Eight things you do well

Six things you can do after school

20. Honing Homophone Skills. Remember: (1) a computer's Spell Check will not detect homophone errors; (2) you learn to distinguish between homophones by paying attention to them. Here are some ways to hone students' homophone skills:

- Have some fun: Both you and students can develop homophone-based riddles and jokes. "What is a large animal without its fur?" (a bare bear) "An insect relative?" (an ant aunt)

- Proofread and correct sentences. "Please drink sum milk." "Turn write at the end of the street."

- Make flash cards. Put one of a homophone pair on each side. Student sees one side and tries to spell the other. Discuss meaning of both and use in sentences.

- Make playing cards for Go Fish, Concentration, or Rummy-type games.

- Make worksheets for student practice. Complete the homophone pair: sell _____. Select the correct word: Dogs have (for/four) legs.

- Make a Bingo or crossword game in which half of a pair of homophones is provided.

- Make spinner or dice board games based on homophone pairs.

- Have an old-fashioned spelling bee with homophones.

- Find homophones in other materials—social studies, art, math. Have classroom teams compete to see which term finds the most.
- Make a word wall of homophones. Discuss them for two minutes every day. Add a new one daily.

21. Vocabulary Stretching. Work on building vocabulary every day. Encourage students to use new words in speech and writing. Do not criticize misuse or near misses—praise the attempt. Constantly point out new words in every subject—art, science, social studies. Use the new and important words in your own speech and check students' knowledge in quizzes. Teach word roots and their origins. Put related words on the board or a word wall. Lead from a known word to an unknown word.

For example: *tele*vision → *tele*scope → *tele*metry. Encourage wide reading: stories, newspapers, encyclopedia, directions, poetry, songs. Use a variety of techniques, including the tried and true (like games and flash cards) and the new ones (like computer simulations).

See also List 75, Good Ideas for Reading Teachers; List 82, Oral Reading Activities; List 161, Jump Rope Rhymes—Choral; List 162, Anagrams.

8

COMPREHENSION AND STUDY SKILLS

List 93. COMPREHENSION SKILLS

Reading comprehension skills refer to a wide range of understandings and abilities competent readers develop over time. This list includes many traditional terms found in scope and sequence charts for reading texts and textbooks about reading instruction.

Identify details
Recognize stated main idea
Follow directions
Determine sequence
Recall details
Locate reference
Recall gist of story
Label parts
Summarize
Recognize anaphoric relationships
Identify time sequence
Describe a character
Retell story in own words
Infer main idea
Infer details
Infer cause and effect
Infer author's purpose, intent
Classify, place into categories
Compare and contrast

Draw conclusions
Make generalizations
Recognize paragraph (text) organization
Predict outcomes
Recognize hyperbole and exaggeration
Experience empathy for character
Experience emotional reaction to text
Judge quality/appeal of text
Judge author's qualifications
Recognize facts and opinions
Apply understanding to new situation
Recognize literary style
Recognize figurative language
Identify mood
Identify plot and story line
Detect use of propaganda techniques
Appreciate mental imagery
Illustrate using other media
Judging usefulness of text

Observable Comprehension Products

Students demonstrate their comprehension in many ways. This is a sample list of observable performance indicators that can be used to evaluate comprehension.

- *Recognizing:* underlining; multiple-choice items; matching; true/false statements

- *Recalling:* writing a short answer; filling in blanks;, flash card Q&A

- *Paraphrasing:* retelling in own words; summarizing; providing similes, metaphors

- *Classifying:* grouping components; naming clusters; completing comparison table; ordering components on a scale

- *Following directions:* completing steps in a task; using a recipe; constructing something

- *Visualizing:* graphing; drawing a map; illustrating; making a timeline; creating a flow chart

- *Fluent reading:* accurate pronunciation; phrasing; intonation; dramatic qualities

Other Comprehension Factors

THE READER
Age, IQ
Education
Background, SES
Out-of-school experiences
Fatigue, Health

READER'S PURPOSE
Find out content, Learn
Study for test
Get general idea quickly
Recreation
Goals, Rewards

TIME
Delay, Need to remember
Immediate post test, Action

ENVIRONMENT
Classroom, Home
Distractions
Light, Noise, Chair

TYPE OF MATERIAL
Fiction, Stories
Expository articles, Textbooks
Advertisements
Forms, Poetry
Different subjects (for example, social studies, science)

READABILITY
Difficulty level
Clear writing
Personal words
Legibility, Imagery

LENGTH
Sentence, Paragraph
Chapter, Book

GRAPHS
Comprehend illustrations
Bar charts, Maps, Tables

The Reading Teacher's Book of Lists, Fourth Edition, © 2000 by John Wiley & Sons, Inc.

See also List 95, Comprehension Questions; List 98, Comprehension Thesaurus; and List 103, Study Skills Checklist.

List 94. COMPREHENSION STRATEGIES

Students' success in understanding what they read depends on many factors, including the active reading and learning strategies they use before, during, and after reading. During guided reading lessons, build competency in one or more of these strategies until students develop independence in their application to new texts. Help students recognize which strategies work best with narratives or expository material.

BEFORE-READING STRATEGIES
Organize
- Gather everything you need (text, paper, highlighter, pen, Post-its®, dictionary, assignment pad).
- Check the assignment. (Most reading assignments are two parts: read and remember for discussion; read text and prepare for class; read and remember for quiz; read and tell others; read and use the information; read and take notes; read and write a reaction; read and answer questions.)
- Set aside enough time to complete the assignment or a particular part of the assignment.

Tune in to the task
- Think about what you already know about the subject or story.
- Think about the special directions you were given about the assignment.
- Think about what you will need to notice/remember in order to do the post-reading assignment (details, main ideas, summary, story line, characters, your opinion, etc.).
- Check to see how the author organized her/his writing (chapters? headings? dialogue? numbered steps? texts + drawings or pictures?).
- Think about what you expect to find out by reading and why.

Set up for success
- Make a KWL chart (know, what to learn, learned).
- Read the questions at the end so you'll recognize the answers when you get to them.
- Start a word web for the reading.

DURING-READING STRATEGIES
Find and mark
- Use a Post-it® to mark the paragraph in which you found an answer to one of your questions.
- Add important words to your word web.
- Write down the page number where you found important information.

If the book is yours:
- Highlight an answer or important information when you see it.
- Put a check mark in the margin next to important information.
- Underline key new words.

The Reading Teacher's Book of Lists, Fourth Edition, © 2000 by John Wiley & Sons, Inc.

Keep track of progress

- "Talk" to the author. (Imagine saying "OK, I got that, I like this part, I wouldn't do it that way," or whatever else you might say if the author was there with you as you read.)
- When you notice that you're telling the author that it doesn't make sense, go back to a part that did and reread.
- Add a Post-it® where you really liked what you read.
- Add a Post-it® where the reading was difficult for you.

AFTER-READING STRATEGIES

Review the reading

- Check back on all marked sections.
- Add to your word web.
- Retell a short version of the story or text in your own words.
- Reread any parts that you marked because they were difficult.
- Think about your feelings for the story or text. (Was it interesting? Did you like it? Was it easy to follow? Did it help you learn?)

Use what you've read

- Use the marked pages or sections to answer questions.
- Fill in the KWL chart.
- Write your reaction to the story/text.
- Create an outline or notes from the important information and key words.
- Make a vocabulary/spelling list of new words.
- Write questions to research later on the same topic.
- Think about how this story/information is like what you have read before.
- Teach part of what you learned to a classmate.
- Rate the reading material's difficulty: too easy, just right, too hard.
- Rate the reading material's interest: very interesting, OK, not very interesting.
- Rate the amount you learned: learned a lot, learned some, learned very little.

See also List 75, Good Ideas for Reading Teachers; List 93, Comprehension Skills; List 95, Comprehension Strategies.

The Reading Teacher's Book of Lists, Fourth Edition, © 2000 by John Wiley & Sons, Inc.

List 95. COMPREHENSION QUESTIONS

Here are some question types to help you add variety to your questioning. These questions can be adapted for use with any prose. Examples of each question type are based on the story of Cinderella.

Vocabulary
1. Questions to help students understand the meaning of a particular word. For example: *What does the word **jealous** mean? What did the stepsisters do that shows they were jealous?*
2. Questions to help students understand words used in the text in terms of their own lives. For example: *Have you ever known someone who was jealous? Have you ever been jealous? Why?*
3. Questions to help students understand multiple meanings of words. For example: *What does **ball** mean in this story? Can you think of any other meaning of the word **ball**?*

Pronoun Referents
4. Questions to help students understand what or who some pronouns refer to and how to figure them out. For example: *In the second sentence of the third paragraph, who does **she** refer to? How do you know?*

Causal Relations
5. Questions to help students recognize causal relations stated directly in the text. For example: *Why were Cinderella's stepsisters jealous of Cinderella?*
6. Questions to help students recognize causal relations not directly stated in the text. For example: *Why did the stepmother give Cinderella extra work to do on the day of the ball?*

Sequence
7. Questions to help students understand that the sequence of some things is unchangeable. For example: *What steps did the Fairy Godmother follow in order to make a coach for Cinderella? Could the order of these steps be changed? Why or why not?*
8. Questions to help students understand that the sequence of some things is changeable. For example: *What chores did Cinderella do on the day of the ball? Could she have done some of them in a different order? Why or why not?*

Comparison
9. Questions to encourage students to compare things within the text. For example: *How did the behavior of the stepsisters differ from the behavior of Cinderella?*
10. Questions to encourage students to compare elements of the story with elements of other stories. For example: *In what ways are the stories of Cinderella and Snow White similar? In what ways are they different?*

The Reading Teacher's Book of Lists, Fourth Edition, © 2000 by John Wiley & Sons, Inc.

11. Questions to encourage students to compare elements of the story with their own experiences. For example: *If you were in Cinderella's place, how would you have acted toward your stepsisters? Is this similar or different from the way Cinderella acted?*

Generalizing

12. Questions to encourage students to generalize from one story to another. For example: *Are most heroines of fairy tales as kind as Cinderella? Give some examples to support your answer.*

13. Questions to encourage students to generalize from what they read to their own experiences. For example: *Can we say that most stepmothers are mean to their stepchildren? Why or why not?*

Predicting Outcomes

14. Questions to encourage students to think ahead to what may happen in the future. For example: *After Cinderella's beautiful dress changes back to rags, what do you think happens?*

Detecting Author's Point of View

15. Questions to help students detect the author's point of view. For example: *What is the author's opinion of the stepsisters and what makes you think this? Support your answer with examples from the story.*

The Reading Teacher's Book of Lists, Fourth Edition, © 2000 by John Wiley & Sons, Inc.

See also List 93, Comprehension Skills; List 94, Comprehension Strategies; List 98, Comprehension Thesaurus.

List 96. SIGNAL WORDS

These are words that the author uses to tell us how to read. Signal words help us to understand how information is organized and provide clues about what is important. Teach signal words one group at a time. Give your students a few examples from a category and have them add others as they run across them in their reading. In terms of a schema theory, signal words tell the reader about the enabling schema, story grammar, or structure. Note that signal words are independent of the content; they can be used with any kind of article or story.

1. Continuation Signals (*Warning—there are more ideas to come.*)

and	also	another
again	and finally	first of all
a final reason	furthermore	in addition
last of all	likewise	more
moreover	next	one reason
other	secondly	similarly
too	with	

2. Change-of-Direction Signals (*Watch out—we're doubling back.*)

although	but	conversely
despite	different from	even though
however	in contrast	instead of
in spite of	nevertheless	otherwise
the opposite	on the contrary	on the other hand
rather	still	yet
while	though	

3. Sequence Signals (*There is an order to these ideas.*)

first, second, third	A, B, C
in the first place	for one thing
then	next
before	now
after	while
into (*far into the night*)	until
last	during
since	always
o'clock	on time
later	earlier

4. Time Signals (*When is it happening?*)

when	immediately	now	before
lately	already	little by little	after
at the same time	final	after awhile	earlier
once	during	later	during

5. Illustration Signals (*Here's what that principle means in reality.*)

for example	specifically	like
for instance	to illustrate	just as
such as	much alike	
in the same way as	similar to	

6. Emphasis Signals (*This is important.*)

a major development	it all boils down to
a significant factor	most of all
a primary concern	most noteworthy
a key feature	more than anything else
a major event	of course
a vital force	pay particular attention to
a central issue	remember that
a distinctive quality	should be noted
above all	the most substantial issue
by the way	the main value
especially important	the basic concept
especially relevant	the crux of the matter
especially valuable	the chief outcome
important to note	the principal item

7. Cause, Condition, or Result Signals (*Condition or modification is coming up.*)

because	if	of
for	from	so
while	then	but
that	until	since
as	whether	in order that
so that	therefore	unless
yet	thus	due to
resulting from	consequently	without

8. Spatial Signals (*This answers the "where" question.*)

between	below	about	left	alongside
here	outside	around	close to	far
right	over	away	side	near
near	in	into	beside	inside
middle	next to	beyond	north	outside
east	on	opposite	over	along
south	there	inside	in front of	against
under	these	out	behind	
across	this	adjacent	above	
toward	west	by	upon	

The Reading Teacher's Book of Lists, Fourth Edition, © 2000 by John Wiley & Sons, Inc.

9. Comparison-Contrast Signals (*We will now compare idea* **A** *with idea* **B.**)

and	or	also	similarly
too	best	most	on the other hand
either	less	less than	instead of
more than	same	better	as opposed to
even	then	half	in contrast to
much as	like	analogous to	
but	different from	still	
yet	however	although	
opposite	rather	while	
though			

10. Conclusion Signals (**T***his ends the discussion and may have special importance.*)

as a result	consequently	finally	at last
from this we see	in conclusion	in summary	nevertheless
hence	last of all	therefore	thus

11. Fuzz Signals (**I***dea is not exact, or author is not positive and wishes to qualify a statement.*)

almost	if	looks like
maybe	could	some
except	should	alleged
nearly	might	reputed
seems like	was reported	purported
sort of	probably	

12. Nonword Emphasis Signals

exclamation point (!)

<u>underline</u>

italics

bold type

subheads, like *The Conclusion*
   indentation of paragraph
graphic illustrations
numbered points (1, 2, 3)
very short sentence: *Stop war.*
"quotation marks"

See also List 66, Basic Sentence Patterns.

The Reading Teacher's Book of Lists, Fourth Edition, © 2000 by John Wiley & Sons, Inc.

List 97. USING LANGUAGE TO SUPPORT COMPREHENSION

Knowledge of grammar and the workings of our language are powerful comprehension tools. But not all students recognize just how useful they are in a learning solution. Use this "story" and list of questions to demonstrate the impact of word order in sentences: noun, adjective and adverb markers; verb forms; and plural spellings, and punctuation.

For a long time, Haro, the nimp fizbin, was the only fizbin in the zot. Every midsee, he would cond and ren, cond and ren, cond and ren. Then one midsee, Haro was zommed! There, in the middle of the parmon, was the nimpest fizbin and she was conding and renning just like Haro. Haro was so arky! He dagged up to the nimpest fizbin and chared. Soon Haro and the nimpest fizbin, Bindy, were ponted. Then every midsee, they conded and renned abatly in the parmon of the zot.

1. Who was Haro?

2. What did he do every midsee?

3. How do you think Haro felt in the beginning of the story? Why?

4. What words helped show his feelings?

5. Where was Bindy when Haro first saw her?

6. What was she doing?

7. How did Haro act when he saw her?

8. How do you think Haro felt at the end of the story? What changed his feelings?

9. How are Haro and Bindy the same?

10. How are they different?

11. List four things that a fizbin can do.

12. Which is larger, the zoyt or the parmon?

13. Add a new sentence to tell what happened later.

14. If you could rewrite the story, what words would you use instead of:

fizbin	midsee
cond	ren
zommed	arky
abatly	zot

The Reading Teacher's Book of Lists, Fourth Edition, © 2000 by John Wiley & Sons, Inc.

See also List 94, Comprehension Strategies; List 95, Comprehension Questions.

List 98. COMPREHENSION THESAURUS

Here is a Comprehension Thesaurus with which you can generate an astounding ten thousand eighty-seven (that's 10,087) different comprehension terms! Impress your principal by using a different one every day for the next 56 years. Although this list is mainly "tongue in cheek," it does make a point about the confusing multiplicity of comprehension terminology and jargon that some educators use. While polishing up your "educationese," remember there are also really good comprehension ideas here.

Directions: Select any term from Part A and link it with any term in Part B to form a Reading Comprehension Skill. (See List 163, Doublespeak, for another phrase generator.)

The Reading Teacher's Book of Lists, Fourth Edition, © 2000 by John Wiley & Sons, Inc.

PART A: THE ACTION

Getting	Organizing	Providing
Identifying	Outlining	Reading (for)
Understanding	Using	Following
Classifying	Locating	Previewing
Recalling	Retelling	Apprehending
Selecting	Reasoning (about)	Determining
Finding	Interpreting	Working (with)
Recognizing	Comprehending	Visualizing
Summarizing	Demonstrating	Thinking (about)
Grasping	Applying	Thinking critically
Drawing	Obtaining	Getting excited (about)
Evaluating	Predicting	Dealing (with)
Relating	Contrasting	Judging
Paraphrasing	Proving	Translating
Comparing	Anticipating	Synthesizing
Transforming	Internalizing	Checking
Clarifying	Sifting	Deriving
Specifying	Inferring	Integrating
Matching	Referring (to)	Actively responding (to)
Criticizing	Drawing	Describing
Analyzing	Making	Questioning
Noting	Concluding	Verbalizing
Perceiving	Forecasting	Processing
Extending	Extrapolating	Encoding
Restating	Foreshadowing	Learning
Reacting (to)	Producing (from memory)	

PART B: THE CONCEPT

Main ideas	Ambiguous statements	Climax
Central thoughts	Mood	Outcome
Author's purpose	Tone	Objective ideas
Author's intent	Inference	Subjective ideas
Point of view	Inference about author	Events
Thought units	Conjecture	Interactions

Story content
Details
Supporting details
Essential details
Specifics
Specific facts
Inferences
Wholes and parts
Conclusions
Propositions
Propositional relationships
Schema
Schemata
Constructs
Meanings
Scenarios
Scripts
Sense
Classifications
Categories
Multiple meanings
Connotations
Denotations
Causal relations
Sequence
Sequence of events
Sequence of ideas
Chronological sequence
Trends
Seriation
Anaphora
Associations
Facts
Deep structure
Analogies
Figurative language
Metaphors
Similes

Information
Text information
Important things
Humor
Directions
Trends
Goals
Aims
Principles
Generalizations
Universals
Abstractions
Abstract ideas
Structures
Judgments
Literary style
Elements of style
Elements
Imagery
Mental imagery
Cause and effect
Organization
Story line
Story problem
Plot
Plot structure
Time of action
Types of literature
Context
Affective content
Answers
General idea
Facts
Concepts
Relationships
Lexical relationships
Textual relationships
Written works

Relevancies
Semantic constraints
Linguistic constraints
Convictions
Inclinations
Characterization
Personal reaction
Effects
Comparisons
Time
Event-to-time relationship
Tense
Propaganda
Flashbacks
Repetitive refrain
Personification
Answers to questions
Directly stated answers
Indirectly stated answers
Extended answers
Various purposes
Validity
Antecedents
References
Experiences
Vicarious experiences
Concrete experiences
Concepts
Familiar concepts
Unfamiliar concepts
Vocabulary
Vocabulary in context
Word meaning
Terminology
Descriptions
Criteria
Attributes
Content

The Reading Teacher's Book of Lists, Fourth Edition, © 2000 by John Wiley & Sons, Inc.

See also List 93, Comprehension Skills.

List 99. SENTENCE TUNES

If you have a doubt that changing the way you say something can change the meaning, this example should convince you. Your students will enjoy playing with this sentence and should be able to create their own multi-tuned sentences. The changes in meaning are due to what are called *supersegmental phonemes*. A phoneme is a speech sound that changes the meaning. A supersegmental phoneme is one that has an additional change to the typical phoneme—in this case, inflection/stress—that affects meaning. Besides being interesting, this change in meaning as a result of inflection is an important characteristic of English that needs to be explicitly taught, particularly to students for whom English is a new or developing language.

Directions: Read the sentences below, emphasizing or stressing the bold word to change the meaning of the sentence.

I did not say you stole my red hat.   (Someone else said it.)

I **did** not say you stole my red hat.   (Strong indignant denial of saying it)

I did **not** say you stole my red hat.   (Strong denial of saying it)

I did not **say** you stole my red hat.   (I implied it, but I didn't say it.)

I did not say **you** stole my red hat.   (I wasn't talking about you.)

I did not say you **stole** my red hat.   (You did something else with it.)

I did not say you stole **my** red hat.   (You stole someone else's.)

I did not say you stole my **red** hat.   (You stole one of another color.)

I did not say you stole my red **hat**.   (You stole something else that was red.)

Try the same shifting of emphasis with these sentence and discuss the results.

Tom didn't push George first.

I didn't tell Mom you spent the dollar.

Ana didn't lose the book.

You weren't asked to go to the store.

See also List 82, Oral Reading Activities.

The Reading Teacher's Book of Lists, Fourth Edition, © 2000 by John Wiley & Sons, Inc.

List 100. PROPAGANDA TECHNIQUES

These persuasion devices are often used in advertising and political campaigning. Teach your students to be critical readers and listeners by being alert to these attempts to mold their choices and viewpoints.

Bandwagon. Using the argument that because everyone is doing it, you should, too. *Last year 30 million winners switched to AIR-POPS athletic shoes. Isn't it time you did, too?*

Card Stacking. Telling only one side of the story as though there is no opposing view. *This tape is especially designed to give the best audio playback money can buy.* (No mention is made that the tape wears out very quickly and is expensive.)

Exigency. Creating the impression that your action is required immediately or your opportunity will be lost forever. *Saturday and Sunday only! It's your last chance to get a really great deal on Camp jeans.*

Flag Waving. Connecting the person, product, or cause with patriotism. *I drink foreign beer? Never! I drink Bot Beer—American all the way.*

Glittering Generality. Using positive or idealistic words based on a detail or minor attribute to create an association in the reader's mind between the person or object and something that is good, valued, and desired. *Ron's been on the varsity team for all four years—you couldn't find a better team player or a more sportsmanlike young man.*

Innuendo. Causing the audience to become wary or suspicious of the product, person, or cause by hinting that negative information may be kept secret. *Other products claim they can handle the big, grimy, once-a-year cleaning jobs like a garage floor. Think what they will do to the no-wax finish on your kitchen floor where your baby plays.*

Name Calling. Using negative or derogatory words to create an association in the reader's mind between the person or object and something that is bad, feared, or distasteful. *Do you really want a mob-linked mayor?*

Plain Folks. Using a person who represents the "typical" target of the ad to communicate to the target audience the message that because we are alike and I would use/buy/believe this, you should, too. *If you're a sinus sufferer like I am, take extra-strength Azap. It helps me. It'll help you, too.*

Prestige Identification. Showing a well-known person with the object, person, or cause in order to increase the audience's impression of the importance or prestige of the object, person, or cause. *We treat our hotel guests like stars (the ad shows a celebrity walking into the hotel).*

Red Herring. Highlighting a minor detail as a way to draw attention away from more important details or issues. *The XT399—the only sports car available in 32 "eye-catching" colors.*

Snob Appeal. Associating the product, person, or cause with successful, wealthy, admired people to give the audience the idea that if they buy or support the same things, they will also be one of the "in-crowd." *There really isn't a better racket (man in tennis clothes holding a racket in front of a very elegant country club building).*

The Reading Teacher's Book of Lists, Fourth Edition, © 2000 by John Wiley & Sons, Inc.

Testimonial. Using the testimony or statement of someone to persuade you to think or act as he or she does. *I'm a doctor, and this is what I take when I have a headache.*

Transfer. Linking a known personal goal or ideal with a product or cause in order to transfer the audience's positive feelings to the product or cause. *Buy Pino in the biodegradable box and help end water pollution.*

See also List 93, Comprehension Skills.

List 101. STORY GUIDE

Name _____   **Date** _____

Title _____

Author _____

Theme

Main Characters (name and description)
    1.
    2.
    3.
    4.

Setting
    Time:
    Place:

Problem or Conflict

Action Sequence

Solution

See also List 102, SQ3R Study Guide; List 105, Graphic Organizers.

The Reading Teacher's Book of Lists, Fourth Edition, © 2000 by John Wiley & Sons, Inc.

List 102. SQ3R STUDY GUIDE

Name _____   **Date** _____

Title _____

SQ3R stands for Survey, Question, Read, Recite, Review.

Survey (clues from the title, headings, pictures, graphs, charts, tables, captions, and words in bold or italic print)

This will be about:

I will probably learn:

My questions (based on headings or at end of each page)
1.
2.
3.
4.

Read and Recite (These are the answers I found.)
1.
2.
3.
4.
5.

Review (Looking at the headings or my questions, I will think about what I read. I will answer my questions silently without rereading.)

See also List 101, Story Guide; List 105, Graphic Organizers.

List 103. STUDY SKILLS CHECKLIST

Mastering these study skills will enable students to succeed at any grade level, in any subject. Integrate instruction in these skills during subject matter classes, applying each skill to the texts, resources, and needs of the class. Review them monthly and have students reflect on their progress. Remember, skills develop through practice.

Preparing to study

❑ Writing down assignments and due dates in a calendar/assignment book

❑ Planning and managing time—how much and when

❑ Creating a study space where there are few distractions

❑ Gathering the things needed before starting to study—references, supplies

❑ Monitoring what works: taking notes, outlining, timelines, story maps, word webs, etc.

Reading with a purpose

❑ Using KWL—list of what you **k**now, **w**ant to learn, and have **l**earned

❑ Determining a purpose for reading

❑ Fitting the approach—skimming, scanning, careful reading—to the purpose

❑ Fitting reading speed to the purpose

❑ Monitoring understanding while reading

❑ Using strategies to correct misunderstanding/lack of understanding

❑ Recognizing facts and opinions

❑ Recognizing author's bias

❑ Judging author's credentials

❑ Judging relevance of material to assignment

❑ Recognizing the use of propaganda techniques

Using your textbooks and other resources

❑ Using the parts of the book: table of contents; introduction; headings and sub-headings; chapter summary; chapter/unit review questions; chapter/unit vocabulary lists; glossary; appendices; index

❑ Recognizing organizational patterns: chronological order; thematic; simple/complex; cause/effect; comparison/contrast

❑ Understanding graphics, tables, graphs, and charts

❑ Using a map, diagram, timeline

Learning new vocabulary

❑ Using context

❑ Using the glossary, standard and special dictionaries

❑ Noting special or new meanings for familiar words

❑ Recognizing author's techniques to highlight key words

❑ Using roots and affixes

❑ Using signs and symbols

The Reading Teacher's Book of Lists, Fourth Edition, © 2000 by John Wiley & Sons, Inc.

Gathering and organizing information

❏ Underlining key ideas
❏ Taking notes from text
❏ Outlining text
❏ Summarizing text
❏ Categorizing information
❏ Organizing your information
❏ Making a table, chart, timeline, or graph
❏ Listening skills
❏ Taking notes from lectures, multimedia presentations
❏ Using the online library catalogs and library classification systems
❏ Doing a basic online search for information on the Internet
❏ Using multimedia reference materials: CD-ROMs, video discs, videotapes, CDs
❏ Identifying your sources (quoting, writing footnotes, listing bibliographic information)

Learning from texts and other resources

❏ Using SQ3R study technique
❏ Using a study guide
❏ Creating a story map, timeline, word web, matrix, database
❏ Using mnemonic devices

Preparing written assignments

❏ Organizing research notes
❏ Answering the questions asked
❏ Developing an outline
❏ Writing a first draft
❏ Using tables, graphs, timelines, and other graphics as support
❏ Editing/proofreading the draft and final version

Preparing for and taking tests

❏ Reviewing text, study guides, text notes, and class notes
❏ Creating a list of potential test questions to use as a self-quiz
❏ Knowing key test words
❏ Becoming testwise
❏ Pacing yourself during a test
❏ Knowing you know—developing sense of when you know "enough"

See also List 102, SQ3R Study Guide.

The Reading Teacher's Book of Lists, Fourth Edition, © 2000 by John Wiley & Sons, Inc.

List 104. TIME-PLANNING CHART

A time-planning chart is a standard study skills tool. This is a practical one, just in case you don't have one readily available for your students. Use it to encourage leisure reading and studying.

STUDY, READING, WORK, RECREATION SCHEDULE

	Mon.	Tues.	Wed.	Thurs.	Fri.	Sat. Sun.
Study Period During School Day						A.M.
After School Afternoon						P.M.
Early Evening						
Late Evening						

Directions: Fill in every square with one or two of the following activities:

1. STUDY: Homework assignments, activity related to courses you are taking.
2. READING: Reading primarily books for your pleasure, or, at most, supplemental or extra-interest material for course you are taking.
3. WORK: Work that you do outside of school for pay, or at home.
4. RECREATION: Talking to friends, watching TV, sports, goofing around.

See also List 103, Study Skills Checklist; List 194, Taxonomy of Graphs.

The Reading Teacher's Book of Lists, Fourth Edition, © 2000 by John Wiley & Sons, Inc.

List 105. GRAPHIC ORGANIZERS

You can often improve a student's comprehension of a story or a subject by having the student draw a graphical representation. This list of story graphs contains only suggestions; most of them can be made larger and more complex. These graphs can be used in many other subjects, such as science or history. They can be used by writers in planning stories or expository articles. They are also excellent for note-taking and studying.

Spider Map

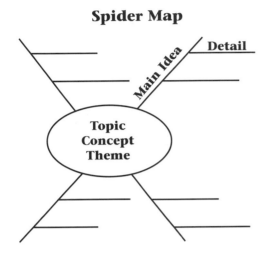

Used to describe a central idea: a thing (a geographic region), process (meiosis), concept (altruism), or proposition with support (experimental drugs should be available to AIDS victims). Key frame questions: What is the central idea? What are its attributes? What are its function?

Series of Events Chain

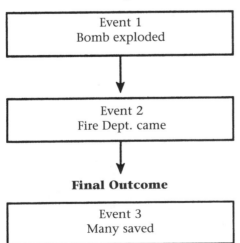

Used to describe the stages of something (the life cycle of a primate); the steps in a linear procedure (how to neutralize an acid); a sequence of events (how feudalism led to the formation of nation states); or the goals, actions, and outcomes of a historical figure or character in a novel (the rise and fall of Napoleon). Key frame questions: What is the object, procedure, or initiating event? What are the stages or steps? How do they lead to one another? What is the final outcome?

Continuum Scale (Timeline)

1950	1960	1970	1980	1990

Born   Moved to N.Y.   Wrote book

Low - - - - - - - - - - - Mid - - - - - - - - - - - High

Used for timelines showing historical events or ages (grade levels in school), degrees of something (weight), shades of meaning (Likert scales), or ratings scales (achievement in school). Key frame questions: What is being scaled? What are the endpoints? Multiple timelines can show relationship of two or more simultaneous events, like one line for Presidents and one line for Wars.

Compare/Contrast Matrix (Spreadsheet)

	Maria	Sally
Attribute 1 Friendliness	Liked everybody	Liked only a few people
Attribute 2 Dependability	Always on time	Missed school often
Attribute 3		

Used to show similarities and differences between two things (people, places, events, ideas, etc.). Key frame questions: What things are being compared? How are they similar? How are they different? Spreadsheets can be enlarged to contain many rows and columns.

The Reading Teacher's Book of Lists, Fourth Edition, © 2000 by John Wiley & Sons, Inc.

A **Semantic Feature Analysis** or grid can also be used to show which features or classes have things in common with a plus sign or not in common with a minus sign.

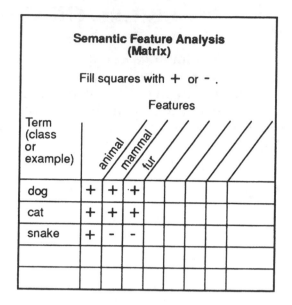

A **Structured Overview** is another type of map similar to the first simple Semantic Map that shows clusters of ideas, terms, or features.

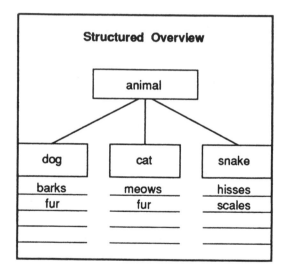

A **Venn Diagram** is often used in mathematics, but can easily be used with words and ideas to show features in common between two different concepts.

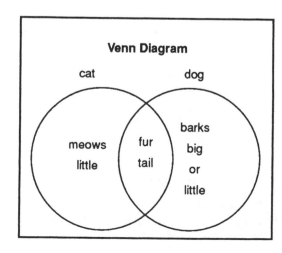

Problem/Solution Outline

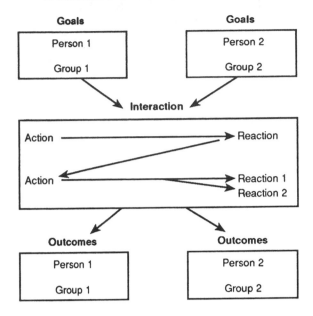

Problem

Who	Germany
What	Started World War II
Why	Gain territory

Solution

Attempted Solutions	Results
1. Attack France	1. Won
2. Attack Russia	2. Lost

Lost war

End Result

Human Interaction Outline

Used to represent a problem, attempted solutions, and results (the national debt). Key frame questions: What was the problem? Who had the problem? What attempts were made to solve the problem? Did those attempts succeed?

Used to show the nature of an interaction between persons or groups (European settlers and Native Americans). Key frame questions: Who are the persons or groups? What were their goals? Did they conflict or cooperate? What was the outcome for person or group?

Network Tree

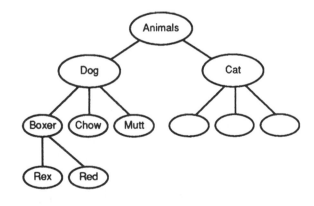

Fishbone Diagram

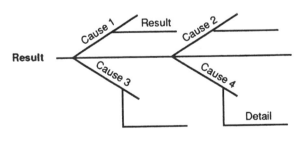

Used to show causal information (causes of poverty), a hierarchy (types of insects), or branching procedures (the circulatory system). Key frame questions: What is the superordinate category? What are the subordinate categories? How are they related? How many levels are there?

Used to show the causal interaction of a complex event (an election, a nuclear explosion) or complex phenomenon (juvenile delinquency, learning disabilities). Key frame questions: What are the factors that cause X? How do they interrelate? Are the factors that cause X the same as those that cause X to persist?

Another more formal **Class/Example Map** can show hierarchy relationship plus related features or properties. These Class/Example Maps are useful for teaching vocabulary, "thinking skills," and complex relationships in many subjects.

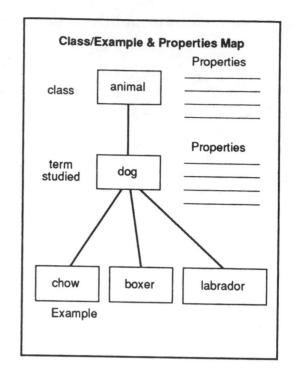

A **Coordinate Class Example Map** not only shows a hierarchy relationship but contrasts two similar or different terms, both of which belong to the same class and have some features or properties in common and some features that are different. Both contrasted terms have different examples.

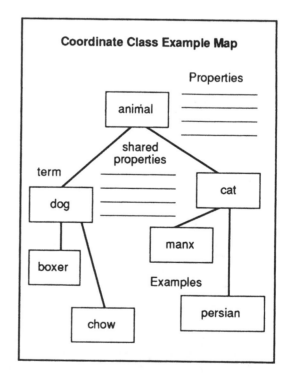

Cycle. Used to show how a series of events interact to produce a set of results again and again (whether phenomena, cycles of achievement and failure, the life cycle). Key frame questions: What are the critical events in the cycle? How are they related? In what ways are they self-reinforcing?

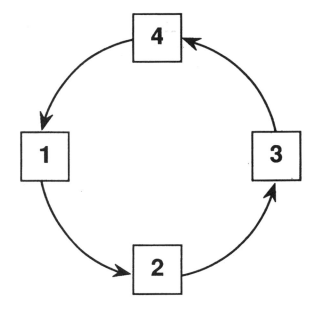

Semantic Mapping. There are a number of ways to make some of the ideas in stories or expository text graphically visible. These are sometimes called Semantic Maps or Cognitive Maps, Webbing, or a number of other terms. They are also excellent for developing or enriching vocabulary.

A simple **Semantic Map** might have a term, title, or vocabulary word in the middle and four clusters or areas of related terms.

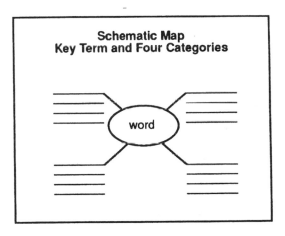

See also List 82, Oral Reading Activities; List 101, Story Guide; List 194, Taxonomy of Graphs.

The Reading Teacher's Book of Lists, Fourth Edition, © 2000 by John Wiley & Sons, Inc.

List 106. MEMORY AIDS

Here are some techniques that are useful in memorizing. Show your students how to use these techniques when they study for your tests.

1. **Study actively.** You are more likely to remember material if you write it or say it out loud than if you merely read it or hear it.

2. **Make sure you understand.** If you understand what you're trying to learn, you'll find that you can remember it better and for a longer period of time.

3. **Associate new information with old.** When learning something new, try to compare it with something similar that you are already familiar with.

4. **Make up examples.** When learning general principles, try to make up examples of your own. In addition to helping you remember the principle better, this will also help you check your understanding. If you're not sure that your example is correct, check it with your teacher.

5. **Visualize what you're trying to learn.** This can involve creating a mental image or drawing a graph (a timeline to help with time sequences, a hierarchical chart for organizations or family trees, etc.) (See List 194, Taxonomy of Graphs, for other ideas.)

6. **Group items into categories.** If you have to learn a long list of things, try to group similar items together. For example, to memorize a shopping list you would want to group vegetables together, meats together, dairy products, and so on.

7. **Be selective.** Most of the time you will not be able to memorize every detail, and if you try you may end up learning almost nothing. Concentrate on general concepts and a few examples to go with each. Pay particular attention to information the teacher indicates is important. Teachers frequently send signals to help you identify what is most important (information written on the chalkboard, or repeated several times orally, or prefaced by statements such as "You should know this.") (See List 96, Signal Words.)

8. **Space your study sessions.** You are more apt to remember material if you study over several days rather than in one crash session.

9. **Use key words.** For example, to learn this list of suggestions for improving your memory, pick out a key word for each suggestion and then learn just the key words. To learn items 1 through 9, you might choose the following key words: active, understand, associate, examples, visualize, group, selective, space, key words.

10. **Learn how many items are on the list.** When learning lists, make sure you learn the number of items on the list. For example, in item 9, it is not enough to learn the key words. You also should learn that there are nine items. This will aid you in recalling all the items.

The Reading Teacher's Book of Lists, Fourth Edition, © 2000 by John Wiley & Sons, Inc.

11. **Rhymes and sayings can be helpful.** For example, how many of us can remember the number of days in the months without:

> Thirty days has September,
> April, June, and November;
> All the rest have thirty-one,
> Excepting February alone,
> Which has just four and twenty-four,
> And every leap year one day more.

12. **Use alliteration.** Repeating initial sounds can be helpful in remembering information. For example, to remind sailors entering a harbor to keep the red harbor light on their right, they learn:

> Red to right returning

13. **Try acrostics.** Sometimes you can use the first letter of a list of words to form another word or sentence. These are referred to as acrostics and are similar to acronyms (see List 179, Acronyms and Initializations). For example, "ROY G. BIV" can help us remember the colors of the spectrum: Red, Orange, Yellow, Green, Blue, Indigo, and Violet.

14. **Exaggerate.** This is especially helpful when you are using visualization. Try to make your images big, colorful, and with lots of details. This will make them interesting and easier to remember.

15. **Have confidence.** Don't go around saying, "I can't remember names." You can if you try.

16. **Use a mnemonic device.** This is very useful when memorizing a list of anything. (See List 107, Mnemonic Device.)

List 107. MNEMONIC DEVICE

This mnemonic device has actually been known for centuries. It is still impressive as a study technique. Done with a bit of showmanship, it will also provide great entertainment. Your students can impress their parents by memorizing a list of twenty objects in just a few minutes (after they study and learn the mnemonic device).

The following is (1) an interesting trick with which the students can interest and amuse their friends, (2) a serious experiment in psychology that clearly demonstrates the power of associative learning, and (3) a useful skill that can sometimes help the student to remember a long and not necessarily related list of facts (useful in passing some examinations and in going to the grocery shop).

First, let us give an example of how the trick might be done in school. The student asks his or her friends to call out slowly a list of objects—any objects. The friends call out "clock–chair–hammer," and so on. Often a friend will write them down on the chalkboard so that the others will not forget them: "1. clock; 2. chair; 3. hammer." The student does not look at the chalkboard. After twenty objects, or however many the students decide, someone calls a halt and immediately announces that he or she has memorized all the objects and can call them out in any order—forward, backward, every other way—in fact, he or she can tell them the number of any object (without looking at the board). The friends say that they do not believe the student; one of them asks, "What is number three?" The student immediately replies, "Hammer." Then after a few such questions, the student demonstrates complete mastery by calling off the whole list either forward or backward.

Now, almost anyone can do this trick, once he or she knows how. The secret lies in memorizing a set of "key objects." You must first take a little time to memorize (make mental associations between) a "key object" and the number. For example, the key object for number one is "sun" and the key object for number two is "shoe," and so on (see list on the following page). You must learn the association between the key object and the number so well that whenever you say "one" to yourself you visualize "sun." You should easily be able to learn the first ten key objects and their numbers in a short learning session on the first day, ten more the next day, and so on. After you have learned the key objects well, you are ready to do the trick. When the first friend calls out the word "clock" as the first item for you to memorize, you must mentally picture a "clock" next to a "sun," which is your key object for number 1. After you have made a clear mental picture of a clock next to a sun, you then allow the next friend to call out a second item to be memorized, such as "chair"; you then mentally picture a chair with your key object, a shoe, sitting on it. You control the rate at which your friends can call out names of objects; at first, you will go rather slowly, but after you have done the trick a few times you can go more rapidly.

The Reading Teacher's Book of Lists, Fourth Edition, © 2000 by John Wiley & Sons, Inc.

KEY OBJECTS

1. Sun
2. Shoe
3. Tree
4. Door
5. Hive
6. Sticks
7. Heaven (an angel)
8. Gate
9. Sign
10. Pen

11. Elephant
12. Twig
13. Throne
14. Fort
15. Fire
16. Silver coin
17. Sea
18. Apron
19. Knife
20. Baby

There are several important learning principles involved in this trick that also apply to other learning. One is the "mental visualization"—it is a powerful factor in memory and can be developed with relatively little practice. Another important factor is self-confidence; if you say beforehand "I can't do it" you probably won't be able to. Self-confidence is also important during the trick, for you must concentrate only on the object to be remembered; you cannot worry about "Did I learn the first three things?" Exaggeration of mental pictures, making them large, brightly colored, or even purposefully distorted, will often aid memory.

This type of memorizing is not a new discovery. It was well known by the ancient people of both Greece and India.

The key objects have been chosen to take advantage of another learning principle—that of rhyming. The first ten objects all have an end-rhyme with the name of the number. The second ten objects all begin with the same sound as the name of the number, except for 20, where a rough rhyme is used to avoid confusion with 12. If you wish to extend the list of objects to 50 or 100, or to change any of the suggested list, you can choose any key objects that you wish. The important thing is that they be easily visualized and never change.

See also List 105, Graphic Organizers; List 106, Memory Aids.

The Reading Teacher's Book of Lists, Fourth Edition, © 2000 by John Wiley & Sons, Inc.

List 108. SKIMMING ILLUSTRATION

This illustration gives a good picture of skimming. In order for students to become proficient at skimming, they need lots of practice. Twice a week for half a year isn't too much.

Usually the first paragraph will be read at average speed all the way through. It often contains an introduction or overview of what will be talked about.

Sometimes, however, the second paragraph contains the introduction or overview. In the first paragraph, the author might just be "warming up" or saying something clever to attract attention.

Reading a third paragraph completely might be unnecessary but ... ... the main idea is usually contained in the opening sentence ... ... topic sentence ... ...

Besides the first sentence, the reader should get some but not all the detail from the rest of the paragraph ... ... names .... date ... ...

This tells you nothing ... ...hence, sometimes the main idea is in the middle or at the end of the paragraph.

Some paragraphs merely repeat ideas ... ...

Occasionally the main idea can't be found in the opening sentence. The whole paragraph must then be read.

Then leave out a lot of the next paragraph ... ...to make up time ... ...Remember to keep up a very fast rate ... ... 800 w.p.m.. ... ...

Don't be afraid to leave out half or more of each paragraph ... ...

Don't get interested and start to read everything ... ...skimming is work ... ...

Lowered comprehension is expected ... ... 50% ... ... not too low ... ...

Skimming practice makes it easier ... ... gain confidence ... .

Perhaps you won't get anything at all from a few paragraphs ... ... don't worry ... ...

Skimming has many uses ... ... reports ... ... newspapers ... ... supplementary ... ... text ... ... The ending paragraphs might be read more fully as often they contain a summary.

Remember that the importance of skimming is to get only the author's main ideas at a very fast speed.

The Reading Teacher's Book of Lists, Fourth Edition, © 2000 by John Wiley & Sons, Inc.

See also List 75, Good Ideas for Reading Teachers.

List 109. PROBLEM-SOLVING GUIDE

Use this three-step guide to solve problems when working alone or in problem-solving teams.

1. Understand the problem by:
- Stating the problem in your own words.
- Visualizing the problem.
- Acting out the problem.
- Drawing a diagram, flowchart, or picture of the problem.
- Making a table, Venn diagram, or graph of the problem.
- Looking for patterns in the problem.
- Comparing it with another problem you have solved.
- Listing everything you know about it.
- Thinking about its parts, one at a time.

2. Propose and try solutions by:
- Using logical reasoning.
- Brainstorming alternatives.
- Writing an equation.
- Choosing an operation and working it through.
- Estimating and checking the results.
- Working backward from the product or result.
- Linking a solution to each part of the problem.
- Solving problems within the problem.
- Evaluating and sorting the information you have.
- Organizing the information in a grid or matrix.
- Eliminating solutions that don't work.
- Solving a simpler version of the problem first.

3. Check the results by:
- Filling in an information matrix.
- Redoing the computation with a calculator.
- Creating a flowchart or visual of the answer.
- Dramatizing the result.
- Comparing the results with the estimates made earlier.
- Using the results on a trial basis.
- Monitoring the effects of the results over time.
- Checking the answer with a reference source.
- Having another team or the teacher critique the result.

See also List 110, Test-taking Strategies.

The Reading Teacher's Book of Lists, Fourth Edition, © 2000 by John Wiley & Sons, Inc.

9
ASSESSMENT

List 110. TEST-TAKING STRATEGIES

Teaching these strategies should help make your students "test wise" and improve their performance on essay and objective tests. Although a few students may use these strategies on their own, most will need instruction and encouragement.

General

- If you have a choice of seats, try to sit in a place where you will be least disturbed (e.g., not by a door).

- When you first receive the test, glance over it, noting the types of questions and the numbers of points to be awarded for them.

- Budget your time, making sure you allow sufficient time for the questions that are worth the most points.

- Read directions carefully. Underline important direction words, such as *choose one, briefly,* and so on.

- Start with the *easiest questions.*

- Be alert for information in some questions that may provide help with other more-difficult questions. If you find such information, be sure to note it before you forget.

Objective Tests

- Before you start, find out if there is a penalty for guessing and if you can choose more than one answer.

- Read the questions and all possible answers carefully.

- Be especially careful about questions with the choices of *all of the above* and *none of the above.*

- Underline key words and qualifiers such as *never, always,* and so on.

- Answer all of the questions you know first.

- Make a mark next to those you can't answer so you can go back to them later.

- After you complete the questions you know, go back and reread the ones you didn't answer the first time.

- If you still can't answer a question the second time through, here are some strategies to try:

  1. For a multiple-choice item, read the question; then stop and try to think of an answer. Look to see if one of the choices is similar to your answer.

  2. Start by eliminating those answers that you know are *not* correct and then choose among the remaining alternatives.

  3. Read through all the answers very carefully and then go back to the question. Sometimes you can pick up clues just by thinking about the different answers you have been given to choose from.

4. Try paraphrasing the question and then recalling some examples.

5. For a multiple-choice item, try reading the question separately with each alternative answer.

- If there is no penalty for guessing, make sure you answer all questions, even if you have to guess blindly.

- If there is a penalty for guessing, you usually should guess if you can eliminate one of the choices.

- If you have time, check over the exam. Change an answer only if you can think of a good reason to do so. Generally, you're better off if you stick with your first choice.

Essay Tests

- Read through all the questions carefully.

- Mark the important direction words that tell you what you're to do: *compare, trace, list,* and so on.

- Number the parts of the question so you don't forget to answer all of them.

- Take time to try to understand what the question is asking. Don't jump to conclusions on the basis of a familiar word or two.

- As you read through the questions, briefly jot down ideas that come into your mind.

- Briefly outline your answers before you begin to write. Refer back to the question to be sure your answer is focused on the question.

- As you write, be careful to stick to your outline.

- If possible, allow generous margins so you can add information later if you need to.

- Don't spend too much time on one question that you don't have time for other questions.

- If you have time, proofread what you have written. This is a good time to double-check to make sure you have answered all parts of the questions.

- If you run short of time, quickly outline answers to the questions that remain. List the information without worrying about complete sentences.

Quantitative Tests

- Read the questions carefully to make sure you understand what is being asked.

- Do the questions you are sure of first.

- Budget your time to allow for questions worth the most points.

- Don't just write answers. Make sure to show your work.

- As you work out answers, try to do it neatly and to write down each step. This helps you avoid careless mistakes and makes it possible for the tester to follow your work. It may make the difference between partial credit and no credit for a wrong answer.

- Check your answer when you finish to make sure it makes sense. If it doesn't seem logical, check again.

The Reading Teacher's Book of Lists, Fourth Edition, © 2000 by John Wiley & Sons, Inc.

- If you are missing information needed to calculate an answer, check to see if it was given in a previous problem or if you can compute it in some way.

- Check to see if you have used all the information provided. You may not always need to, but you should double-check to be sure.

- If you have time, go back and check your calculations.

List 111. IMPORTANT MODIFIERS

These are easy words, but ones sometimes skipped over by inattentive readers. Failure to pay attention to these modifiers can result in a wrong answer, even though the student actually knows the right answer. One way to help avoid this is to teach your students to underline these words as they take tests.

all	good	none
always	invariably	often
bad	less	seldom
best	many	some
equal	more	sometimes
every	most	usually
few	never	worst

List 112. ALTERNATIVE ASSESSMENT TECHNIQUES

Standardized tests, criterion-referenced tests, diagnostic tests, cloze exercises, unit tests, worksheets—these are some of the assessment tools frequently used in evaluating reading proficiency. The following four alternative assessment techniques build on classroom activities to provide insight to student learning.

1. Retellings

After students read a story or have one read to them, ask them to retell it as if they were telling it to a friend who never heard it before. It is important to let students know in advance that they will be asked to do this. To analyze the retelling quantitatively, use a checklist of important elements in the story (setting, plot, resolution, etc.) and assign a score for each. Qualitative evaluation focuses on students' deeper understanding of the story and ability to generalize and interpret its meaning. This type of evaluation can be noted in the form of comments at the bottom of the checklist. Retellings can be done individually or in groups. Teacher prompts may be required to help lead some students through the story.

2. Portfolios

Portfolios are systematic collections of student work over time. These collections help students and teachers assess student growth and development. It is essential that students develop a sense of ownership about their portfolios so they can understand where they have made progress and where more work is needed.

Portfolio Content. The content of portfolios will vary with the level of the student and will depend on the types of assignments they are given in class. In addition to completed reports, poems, letters, and so forth, portfolios often contain first and second drafts. Reading logs and audiotape recordings can also be included. As portfolios are assembled, it is important that students keep them in a place where they have easy access to them. Students should be encouraged to browse through their portfolios and share them with classmates.

Criteria for Selecting Items for Portfolios. Although almost all work may initially be included, portfolios can quickly become unmanageable if they are too large. Portfolios that will form the basis for assessment can be assembled at the end of each term and at the end of the school year. A specific number of items for inclusion (often five or six) and criteria for selecting them should be agreed to by the teacher and students. Some examples of criteria are: stories/reports that were favorites; papers that represent the best work; work that shows progress; assignments that were the most difficult. In making selections, students should be encouraged to consult with classmates.

Evaluation of Portfolios. Portfolio evaluation often occurs at three levels: the student, the student's peers, and the teacher. For each piece selected, students may be asked to describe briefly why they chose it, what they learned, and what their future goals are. Students can also be asked to prepare an overall evaluation of their portfolio.

Classmates are frequently enlisted in portfolio evaluation. Their evaluation can focus on what they see as the special strengths of the portfolio, their personal response to some item in the portfolio, and a suggestion of one thing their classmate could work on next.

The Reading Teacher's Book of Lists, Fourth Edition, © 2000 by John Wiley & Sons, Inc.

The Reading Teacher's Book of Lists, Fourth Edition, © 2000 by John Wiley & Sons, Inc.

Portfolio evaluation by the teacher should build on that of the student's and peer's. Although the teacher evaluation may result in a grade, it is important that an opportunity be found for discussion with the student. This discussion should culminate in agreement on future goals.

Although not a part of the formal evaluation process, it is helpful, particularly for elementary school children, for parents to review the portfolios. Portfolios can be sent home or they can be reviewed at the time of the parent–teacher conferences. It is essential that teachers take steps to help parents understand that their role should be to provide encouragement and that they should focus on the positive and not be critical.

3. Reading Logs

Have students keep a log of all their independent reading at school and at home. The log should include works completed and works started but not completed. In addition to the name of the book (article, etc.) and author, the log should include personal reactions to the selection. Periodic discussions of these logs will provide insight on how the student is developing as an independent reader and suggest ways in which the teacher can give added encouragement. These logs can be placed in students' portfolios.

4. Checklists

Checklists can be completed by both readers and students. For example, a checklist can be used by a teacher to assess word and letter knowledge. The first step is to develop a list of the concepts to be tested. The student is then asked to demonstrate understanding of these concepts using a real book. The teacher uses the checklist to identify those concepts that have been mastered and those that need futher work.

Students can use checklists to review their own work. Teachers and students can prepare a list of specific skills that need to be worked on (for example, a capital letter at the beginning of each sentence), and students can then use this list to check their own work.

See also List 70, Proofreading Checklist—Elementary; List 73, Proofreading Checklist—Intermediate; List 95, Comprehension Questions.

List 113. ENGLISH LANGUAGE ARTS STANDARDS

Standards for English Language Arts broadly articulate common expectations for the English language arts outcomes of instructional programs. They imply common understanding of what we know about reading and learning and about factors that contribute to developing a full range of literacy skills. The standards below are from the National Council of Teachers of English and the International Reading Association. Most states have developed standards, curriculum frameworks, and related assessment protocols which are available from their state departments of education.

Standards for the English Language Arts

1. Students read a wide range of print and nonprint texts to build an understanding of texts, of themselves, and of the cultures of the United States and the world; to acquire new information; to respond to the needs and demands of society and the workplace; and for personal fulfillment. Among these texts are fiction and nonfiction, classic and contemporary works.

2. Students read a wide range of literature from many periods in many genres to build an understanding of the many dimensions (e.g., philosophical, ethical, aesthetic) of human experience.

3. Students apply a wide range of strategies to comprehend, interpret, evaluate, and appreciate texts. They draw on their prior experience, their interactions with other readers and writers, their knowledge of word meaning and of other texts, their word identification strategies, and their understanding of textual features (e.g., sound–letter correspondence, sentence structure, context, graphics).

4. Students adjust their use of spoken, written, and visual language (e.g., conventions, style, vocabulary) to communicate effectively with a variety of audiences and for different purposes.

5. Students employ a wide range of strategies as they write and use different writing process elements appropriately to communicate with different audiences for a variety of purposes.

6. Students apply knowledge of language structure, language conventions (e.g., spelling and punctuation), media techniques, figurative language, and genre to create, critique, and discuss print and nonprint texts.

7. Students conduct research on issues and interests by generating ideas and questions, and by posing problems. They gather, evaluate, and synthesize data from a variety of sources (e.g., print and nonprint texts, artifacts, people) to communicate their discoveries in ways that suit their purpose and audience.

8. Students use a variety of technological and information resources (e.g., libraries, databases, computer networks, video) to gather and synthesize information and to create and communicate knowledge.

9. Students develop an understanding of and respect for diversity in language use, patterns, and dialects across cultures, ethnic groups, geographic regions, and social roles.

The Reading Teacher's Book of Lists, Fourth Edition, © 2000 by John Wiley & Sons, Inc.

10. Students whose first language is not English make use of their first language to develop competency in the English language arts and to develop understanding of content across the curriculum.

11. Students participate as knowledgeable, reflective, creative, and critical members of a variety of literacy communities.

12. Students use spoken, written, and visual language to accomplish their own purposes (e.g., for learning, enjoyment, persuasion, and the exchange of information).

From: National Council of Teachers of English/International Reading Association @ www.ncte.org/

List 114. ANALOGIES

Analogies are used for teaching and testing. The key is to determine the relationship of the first pair of words and then find a second pair of words that has the same relationship. For example, "in" is to "out" as "hot" is to "_____." (In the notation used below, this is written: "in : out :: hot :   .") Since "out" is the opposite of "in," the answer is "cold," which is the opposite of "hot." Below are some common types of analogies and several examples for each.

Antonyms

open : close :: up : down
serious : comical :: happy : sad
fiction : fact :: love : hate
large : small :: laugh : cry
waive : require :: transparent : opaque

Synonyms

back : rear :: under : below
near : close-by :: thin : slim
find : discover :: danger : peril
divide : separate:: flat : level
right : correct :: terrify : frighten

Cause and Effect

tired : sleep :: hungry : eat
work : success :: study : learn
wash : clean :: fertilize : grow
happy : smile :: sad : cry
earthquake : destruction :: disease : fever

Sequence

breakfast : lunch :: afternoon : evening
pour : drink :: cook : eat
go : arrive :: flower : fruit
sleep : dream :: plant : harvest
cold : snow :: cloudy : rain

Numerical Relationship

three : six :: four : eight
two : three :: seven : eight
one : three :: four : six
four : two :: eight : four
nine : three :: twelve : four

Degree

pretty : beautiful :: warm : hot
intelligent : brilliant :: hungry : starving
simmer : boil :: brown : burn
dirty : filthy :: clean : spotless
interesting : fascinating :: nice : wonderful

Grammatical Relationship

she : her :: he : him
eat : ate :: sleep : slept
run : running :: talk : talking
apple : apples : goose : geese
he : his :: I : mine

Part–Whole Relationship

finger : hand :: page : book
room : house :: branch : tree
handle : cup :: eraser : pencil
hand : clock :: yolk : egg
lens : camera :: wheel : car

Member–Group Relationship

fish : school :: student : class
professor : faculty :: sister : sorority
soldier : regiment :: star : constellation
athlete : team :: state : country
senator : congress :: judge : court

Object–Action

hand : write :: bell : ring
sun : shine :: knife : cut
clock : tick :: foot : kick
lamp : light :: rooster : crow
baby : cry :: airplane : fly

The Reading Teacher's Book of Lists, Fourth Edition, © 2000 by John Wiley & Sons, Inc.

Object–Class

peach : fruit :: fork : silverware
poodle : dog :: chair : furniture
shirt : clothing :: ring : jewelry
arm : limb :: jazz : music
white : color :: triangle : shape

Object–Description

floor : hard :: test : difficult
food : delicious :: sky : blue
flower : fragrant :: child : cute
bed : comfortable :: tree : tall
honey : sticky :: ice : cold

Object–Place

bear : den :: bee : hive
bird : sky :: fish : sea
car : garage :: stove : kitchen
computer : office :: tractor : farm
money : wallet :: hammer : toolbox

Object–Use

book : read :: food : eat
car : travel :: milk : drink
stove : cook :: nose : breathe
piano : music :: ladder : reach
clown : laugh :: coat : warm

Object–User

crib : baby :: guitar : musician
library : student :: oven : baker
register : cashier :: ship : sailor
pool : swimmer :: racquet : tennis player
microscope : scientist :: gun : robber

MORE ANALOGIES

mother : aunt :: father : uncle
car : driver :: plane : pilot
green : color :: cinnamon : spice
coffee : drink :: hamburger : eat
arrow : bow :: bullet : gun
ceiling : room :: lid : pan
page : book :: Ohio : U.S.
glove : hand :: boot : foot
swim : pool :: jog : road
meat : beef :: fruit : apple
date : calendar :: time : clock
carpenter : house :: composer : symphony
soldier : regiment :: star : constellation
duck : drake :: bull : cow
cells : skin :: bricks : wall
paw : dog :: fin : fish
moon : earth :: earth : sun
tree : lumber :: wheat : flour
library : books :: cupboard : dishes
princess : queen :: prince : king
story : read :: song : sing
length : weight :: inches : pounds
one : three :: single : triple
blind : deaf :: see : hear
wrist : hand :: ankle : foot
engine : go :: brake : stop
glass : break :: paper : tear
book : character :: recipe : ingredient
sing : pleased :: shout : angry
penny : dollar :: foot : yard
cabin : build :: well : dig
temperature : humidity :: thermometer : hygrometer
left : right :: top : bottom
easy : simple :: hard : difficult

See also List 25, Synonyms; List 26, Antonyms; List 110, Test-taking Strategies.

The Reading Teacher's Book of Lists, Fourth Edition, © 2000 by John Wiley & Sons, Inc.

List 115. RUBRICS FOR WRITING—PRIMARY

Even very young writers need feedback in order to understand their writing strengths and the areas in which they can improve. "Good job" or "You can do better" do not provide enough information to enable them to focus on important aspects of good writing. Be sure to show students examples of work at each level and discuss them, so they can develop self-monitoring skills.

Name					Date
	Beginning 1	**Developing 2**	**Accomplished 3**	**Exemplary 4**	**Score**
Topic	Key word(s) near beginning	Main idea or topic in first sentence	Good main idea or topic sentence	Interesting, well-stated main idea/topic sentence	
Words	Related words or ideas mentioned	Some key words or related ideas included as details with meaning	Key related words and ideas used as details with meaning	Key related words and ideas used correctly; defined for reader; interesting choices of words	
Order	Ideas not ordered	Some order of main idea + details or sequence	Main idea + details or sequential, as appropriate	Good flow of ideas from topic sentence + details or sequence	
Sentences	Sentence fragments	Mostly complete sentences	Complete sentences	Complete sentences; variety	
Punctuation	Some punctuation	Most sentences have punctuation	Correct punctuation	Correct punctuation and variety	
Capital Letters	Upper and lower case not distinguished	Uses upper and lower case	Begins sentences with upper case	Correct use of case for beginning of sentence, names, etc.	
Spelling	Many spelling errors	Some spelling errors	Few spelling errors	No spelling errors	
Handwriting	Hard to read; not well formed	Mostly legible	Well-formed letters	Neat, easy to read, well formed	

The Reading Teacher's Book of Lists, Fourth Edition, © 2000 by John Wiley & Sons, Inc.

List 116. RUBRICS FOR WRITING— ELEMENTARY/INTERMEDIATE

Good writing is a complex accomplishment involving the organization of ideas, the select use of vocabulary, attention to readers and purpose, and the "mechanics" of grammar, spelling, punctuation and handwriting. Rubrics provide students information about the qualities and dimensions of good writing and feedback about their progress. Examples of written work at each of the four levels should be available. Develop rubrics with your students for special writing projects such as reports, short stories, or journals.

The Reading Teacher's Book of Lists, Fourth Edition, © 2000 by John Wiley & Sons, Inc.

Name			Date		
	Beginning 1	Developing 2	Accomplished 3	Exemplary 4	Score
Topic	Key word(s) near beginning	Main idea or topic in first sentence	Good main idea or topic sentence	Interesting, well-stated main idea/topic sentence	
Organization	Ideas not ordered	Some order of main idea + details or sequence	Main idea + details or sequential, as appropriate	Good flow of ideas from topic sentence + details or sequence	
Paragraphs	One paragraph or text divided but not by content	Supporting details mostly grouped into appropriate paragraphs	Ideas appropriately divided into paragraphs with supporting details	Strong paragraphs ordered to develop story or exposition	
Sentences	Mostly complete sentences; some fragments or run-on	Complete sentences; few run-on sentences	Complete sentences; no run-ons or fragments; some variety in length and type	No sentence errors; variety in length and type; sentence types relate to style of writing	
Vocabulary	Related words or ideas mentioned; limited basic vocabulary	Attempts to use new key words in description; goes beyond basic vocabulary	Uses new key/related words and ideas correctly; varies language	Uses new key/related words/ideas easily; colorful, interesting words suitable for topic and audience	
Grammar	Many errors in agreement, number, tense	Some errors in agreement, number, tense	Few errors in agreement, number, tense	No errors in agreement, number, tense	
Punctuation and Case	Several punctuation and case errors	Few punctuation and case errors	Minor errors in punctuation and case; variety used	Correct punctuation and case throughout; variety used	
Spelling	Many spelling errors	Some spelling errors	Few spelling errors	No spelling errors	
Handwriting	Hard to read; not well formed	Mostly legible	Well-formed letters	Neat, easy to read, well formed	

List 117. PRESENTATION RUBRICS

Studies on the exchange of knowledge and research have shown that peer teaching, reciprocal teaching, and even the age-old "show and tell" are valuable teaching and learning activities. Developing students' presentation skills aids knowledge integration, speaking skills, interdisciplinary and creative thinking, self expression, and self confidence. Students need support and instruction throughout the various stages in the development process. The preparation also helps develop time-management skills.

Name			Date		
	Beginning 1	**Developing 2**	**Accomplished 3**	**Exemplary 4**	**Score**
Preparation	Storyboard or outline incomplete; lacks props or resources	Storyboard or outline doesn't represent whole; resources and props few or inappropriate	Storyboard or outline complete; resources and props appropriate	Storyboard or outline complete and well organized; resources and props outstanding	
Content	Mentions key ideas; little evidence of understanding	Expresses key ideas; not fully at ease with concepts	Expresses key ideas and shows understanding	Key words and ideas correctly used; defined for reader; interesting choices of words	
Order	Ideas not ordered; audience has difficulty following	Some order of ideas; but jumps around	Logical sequence of presentation; audience can follow	Logical sequence, easy to follow; good overview and transitions	
Media, Graphics, and Props	Media, graphics, and props missing or do not add information	Media, graphics, and props tangential to text; minor value	Media, graphics, and props relate to text; add value or information	Media, graphics, and props relate, add information, help explain, keep interest	
Speaking	Hesitates, whispers; many "fillers"; poor eye contact	Some hesitation; some "fillers" but moves along; some eye contact, but reads mostly	Clear, good pace and pronunciation; good eye contact; checks notes	Clear, well paced, well modulated; good eye contact; well rehearsed, little need for notes	
Q&A	Defensive; frequent "don't know" shrugs	Some "I don't know's"; some defensiveness	Answers correctly with little hesitancy	Answers correctly; expands, explains	

The Reading Teacher's Book of Lists, Fourth Edition, © 2000 by John Wiley & Sons, Inc.

308

List 118. TEST AND WORKBOOK WORDS

These words are found in directions in workbook exercises and in tests. It is absolutely essential that students understand and pay close attention to them. These key words are perhaps most effectively taught in context. Each time you give students a test or a written exercise, point them out and review their meaning.

answer sheet	definition	name	reason
best	directions	next	rhyming
blank	does not belong	none of these	right
booklet	end	not true	row
check your work	error	opposite	same as
choose	example	pairs	sample
circle	finish	paragraph	second
column	following	passage	section
compare	go on to next page	print	stop
complete	item	probably	true
contrast	mark	put an X	underline
correct	match	question	wait for directions
cross out	missing	read	

List 119. ESSAY TEST WORDS

These words occur in essay test questions. In order for students to perform well on essay tests, they must understand the types of answers that these words require. When you give essay tests, try to use a variety of these words and take the opportunity to instruct the students on their meaning.

analyze	develop	interpret	relate
apply	diagram	justify	relationship
argue	differentiate	list	select
assess	discuss	mention	show how
categorize	distinguish	organize	significance
cause	draw conclusions	outline	solve
cite evidence	effect	paraphrase	specify
classify	enumerate	point out	state
compare	estimate	predict	suggest
construct	evaluate	propose	summarize
contrast	explain	prove	support
convince	formulate	provide	survey
create	general	rank	tell
criticize	generalize	react	trace
define	give an example of	reason	utilize
demonstrate	identify	recall	why
describe	illustrate	recommend	

See also List 96, Signal Words.

List 120. CLOZE VARIATIONS

Cloze is a sentence-completion technique in which a word (or part of a word or several words) is omitted and the student fills in the missing part. Cloze can be used as a test or drill of reading comprehension or language ability, as a research tool, or as a measure to estimate readability or passage difficulty.

To estimate the readability or difficulty level appropriate for instruction, one suggested criterion is that a student be able to fill in 35 to 44 percent of the exact missing words when every fifth word is deleted from a 250-word passage.

Cloze passages can be made easily by the teacher on any subject or any type of material. All you need to do is omit parts of the passage and ask the students to fill in the missing parts. Here is a list of some possible variations:

Passage Variations (different kinds of passage to start with)
- A. Content of Passage
  - (1) Science
  - (2) History
  - (3) Literature, etc.
- B. Difficulty of Passage
  - (1) Readability level
  - (2) Imageability
  - (3) Legibility
- C. Length of Passage
  - (1) Sentence
  - (2) Paragraph
  - (3) 500 words, etc.

Deletion Variations (different kinds of deletions or blanks)
- A. Mechanical—automatic or no judgment used in deletions
  - (1) Delete every *n*th word (5th, 10th, etc.).
  - (2) Randomized deletion but average every *n*th word.
- B. Selective—judgment used in selected deletions
  - (1) Delete structure words or content words only.
  - (2) Delete only one part of speech. (For example, nouns omitted.)
  - (3) Delete particular letters (blends, bound morphemes, prefixes, vowels, consonants, etc.).
  - (4) Delete only words or letters that best fit a particular skill objective.
- C. Size of Deletion
  - (1) One word, two words, etc.
  - (2) One letter, two letters, etc.

Cueing Variation (different prompts or hints)
- A. No cues
- B. Multiple choice (sometimes referred to as "Maze"). If this is used, distractor words (wrong choices) can be varied as follows:

The Reading Teacher's Book of Lists, Fourth Edition, © 2000 by John Wiley & Sons, Inc.

(1) Similar to correct answer in length or different.

(2) Similar or different in phonemes.

(3) Similar or different in meaning.

C. One or more letters, depending on how many letters have been deleted.

Administration Variations

A. Preparation

(1) Student reads complete passage (no blanks) before answering.

(2) Student listens to complete passage before answering.

(3) Student is given a brief introduction to passage.

(4) No preparation.

B. Answering

(1) Student reads passage and writes answers.

(2) Teacher reads passage orally and student writes answers.

(3) Teacher reads passage orally and student gives answers orally.

(4) Student told to guess or not to guess.

Scoring Variations

A. Score as correct only exact word, or score synonym as correct.

B. Correct spelling required or not required.

C. Self-correction, teacher correction, other-student correction.

D. Discuss answers or no discussion.

Uses of Cloze

A. *Test student's ability.* All students take the same cloze passage: students are ranked by number correct. Cloze scores can be assigned norms or grade levels.

B. *Measure readability of a passage.* A group of students takes two different cloze passages. The passage with the highest mean score is most readable. Some research indicates that a cloze score of 35 to 45 percent correct on a fifth-word random deletion indicates Independent Reading Level for that student (or group).

C. *Research.* Cloze is used in many types of language research. For example, ESL ability, knowledge or pronoun use, generating wrong answers for Maze, spelling, memory.

D. *Teaching.* Cloze passages are used for reading comprehension drills, subject content knowledge, language use, discussion starters, and much more.

Sample cloze passage. This is a fifth-word deletion often used for comprehension teaching or testing.

> Each night Mrs. Darling _____ upstairs, read a story _____ her three children, and put them to bed. _____ was the oldest of _____ Darling children, then John, _____ little Michael. They had _____ dog named Nana.

See also List 66, Basic Sentence Patterns; List 95, Comprehension Questions.

The Reading Teacher's Book of Lists, Fourth Edition, © 2000 by John Wiley & Sons, Inc.

List 121. TESTING TERMS

Most school districts give tests. Most teachers get the results of those tests. What do those test scores mean? How do you interpret them? One place to start is with an understanding of the terminology that test makers use. Familiarity with these terms will help you to explain test results to interested and sometimes anxious students and parents.

Achievement tests. Tests that measure how much students have learned in a particular subject area.

Aptitude tests. Tests that attempt to predict how well students will do in learning new subject matter in the future.

CEEB test scores. College Entrance Examination Board test scores. This type of score is used by exams such as the Scholastic Aptitude Test. It has a mean of 500 and a standard deviation of 100.

Correlation coefficient. A measure of the strength and direction (positive or negative) of the relationship between two things.

Criterion-referenced tests. Tests for which the performance of the test taker is compared with a fixed standard or criterion. The primary purpose is to determine if the test taker has mastered a particular unit sufficiently to proceed to the next unit.

Diagnostic tests. Tests that are used to identify individual students' strengths and weaknesses in a particular subject area.

Grade equivalent scores. The grade level for which a score is the real or estimated average. For example, a grade equivalent score of 3.5 is the average score of students halfway through the third grade.

Mean. The arithmetical average of a group of scores.

Median. The middle score in a group of ranked scores.

Mode. The score that was obtained by the largest number of test takers.

Normal distribution. A bell-shaped distribution of test scores in which scores are distributed symmetrically around the mean and where the mean, median, and mode are the same.

Norming population. The group of people to whom the test was administered in order to establish performance standards for various age or grade levels. When the norming population is composed of students from various sections of the country, the resulting standards are called *national norms*. When the norming population is drawn from a local school or school district, the standards are referred to as *local norms*.

Norm-referenced tests. Tests for which the results of the test taker are compared with the performance of others (the norming population) who have taken the test.

Percentile rank. A comparison of an individual's raw score with the raw score of others who took the test (usually this is a comparison with the norming population). This comparison tells the test taker the percentage of other test takers whose scores fell below his or her own score.

Raw score. The initial score assigned to test performance. This score usually is the number correct; however, sometimes it may include a correction for guessing.

The Reading Teacher's Book of Lists, Fourth Edition, © 2000 by John Wiley & Sons, Inc.

Reliability. A measure of the extent to which a test is consistent in measuring whatever it purports to measure. Reliability coefficients range from 0 to 1. In order to be considered highly reliable, a test should have a reliability coefficient of 0.90 or above. There are several types of reliability coefficients: *parallel-form* reliability (the correlation of performance on two different forms of a test), *test–retest* reliability (the correlation of test scores from two different administrations of the same test to the same population), *split-half* reliability (the correlation between two halves of the same test), and *internal consistency* reliability (a reliability coefficient computed using a Kuder–Richardson formula).

Standard deviation. A measure of the variability of test scores. If most scores are close to the mean, the standard deviation will be small. If the scores have a wide range, then the standard deviation will be large.

Standard error of measurement (SEM). An estimate of the amount of measurement error in a test. This provides an estimate of how much a person's actual test score may vary from his or her hypothetical true score. The larger the SEM, the less confidence can be placed in the score as a reflection of an individual's true ability.

Standardized tests. Tests that have been given to groups of students under standardized conditions and for which norms have been established.

Stanine scores. Whole number scores between 1 and 9 that have a mean of 5 and a standard deviation of 2.

True score. The score that would be obtained on a given test if that test were perfectly reliable. This is a hypothetical score.

Validity. The extent to which a test measures what it is supposed to measure. Two common types of validity are *content validity* (the extent to which the content of the test covers situations and subject matter about which conclusions will be drawn) and *predictive validity* (the extent to which predictions made from the test are confirmed by evidence gathered at some later time).

10
SPELLING

List 122. SPELLING DEMONS—ELEMENTARY

Those who study children's spelling errors and writing difficulties have repeatedly found that a relatively small number of words make up a large percentage of all spelling errors. Many commonly misspelled words are presented in this Spelling Demons list. Other lists in this book, such as Homophones, Instant Words, and Subject Matter Words, can also be used as spelling lists.

about	dairy	hour	quarter	teacher	vacation
address	dear	house	quit	tear	very
advise	decorate	instead	quite	terrible	wear
again	didn't	knew	raise	Thanksgiving	weather
all right	doctor	know	read	their	weigh
along	does	laid	receive	there	were
already	early	latter	received	they	we're
although	Easter	lessons	remember	though	when
always	easy	letter	right	thought	where
among	enough	little	rough	through	which
April	every	loose	route	tired	white
arithmetic	everybody	loving	said	together	whole
aunt	favorite	making	Santa Claus	tomorrow	women
awhile	February	many	Saturday	tonight	would
balloon	fierce	maybe	says	too	write
because	first	minute	school	toys	writing
been	football	morning	schoolhouse	train	wrote
before	forty	mother	several	traveling	you
birthday	fourth	name	shoes	trouble	your
blue	Friday	neither	since	truly	you're
bought	friend	nice	skiing	Tuesday	
built	fuel	none	skis	two	
busy	getting	o'clock	some	until	
buy	goes	off	something	used	
children	grade	often	sometime		
chocolate	guard	once	soon		
choose	guess	outside	store		
Christmas	half	party	straight		
close	Halloween	peace	studying		
color	handkerchief	people	sugar		
come	haven't	piece	summer		
coming	having	played	Sunday		
cough	hear	plays	suppose		
could	heard	please	sure		
couldn't	height	poison	surely		
country	hello	practice	surprise		
cousin	here	pretty	surrounded		
cupboard	hospital	principal	swimming		

317

List 123. SPELLING DEMONS—
INTERMEDIATE

Secondary students may misspell words on the elementary list of Demons, and as their writing is more advanced than the younger students, they may also have trouble with these Demons. If you use these for spelling lessons, don't assign too many at once—pick and choose some you know they need.

absence	approach	category	descend
absolutely	approximately	ceiling	describe
acceptable	arctic	celebrate	description
accidentally	argue	cemetery	desert
accommodate	arguing	certainly	despair
accompany	argument	character	develop
accurate	around	chief	difference
accustom	arrangement	cite	different
ache	assistance	college	dilemma
achieve	athlete	comfortable	diligence
acknowledgment	attempt	coming	dining
acquaintance	attendance	committed	disagreeable
acquire	author	committee	disappear
across	awful	comparative	disappoint
actually	awkward	complete	disastrous
address	balloon	concede	discipline
adolescent	banquet	conceive	discover
advantageous	bargain	condemn	discussion
advertisement	beautiful	conquer	disease
advice	before	conscience	dissatisfied
again	beginning	conscientious	divided
against	belief	conscious	doubt
aisle	believe	consider	dropped
all right	beneficial	continually	drowned
almost	benefited	control	effect
although	bicycle	controversial	eighth
always	biggest	controversy	eleventh
amateur	boundary	council	eligible
ambition	breathe	courageous	embarrass
among	brilliant	courteous	emigrate
amusing	Britain	criticism	endeavor
analyze	built	criticize	enough
ancient	bulletin	crowd	environment
announces	buried	dangerous	equipment
annually	bury	deceive	equipped
answered	business	decided	especially
anticipated	busy	decision	eventually
anxious	cafeteria	defense	evidently
apology	calendar	definitely	exaggerate
apparent	captain	definition	exceed
appearance	career	democracy	excellent
appreciate	carrying	dependent	except

318

The Reading Teacher's Book of Lists, Fourth Edition, © 2000 by John Wiley & Sons, Inc.

excitement
exercise
exhausted
exhibit
existence
expense
experience
explanation
extraordinary
extremely
familiar
fascinate
fascinating
favorite
fierce
finally
flies
foreign
formerly
fortunately
forty
forward
fourth
friend
gaiety
gauge
generally
genuine
government
grammar
grateful
grieve
guarantee
guard
guessed
guidance
guilty
handkerchief
happened
having
heard
height
heroes
hesitate
hindrance
honorable
hoping
humorous
hurrying
hypocrite
ignorant

imaginary
immediately
importance
impossible
incredible
independent
Indian
individual
innocent
intelligence
interest
interrupt
irrelevant
its
jealousy
judgment
knife
knowledge
laboratory
led
leisure
library
license
lieutenant
lightning
likely
listener
literature
lose
losing
luxury
magnificent
making
maneuver
marriage
mathematics
meant
medicine
mere
million
miniature
miscellaneous
mischief
mischievous
moral
muscle
mysterious
naturally
necessary
neither
niece

nonsense
noticeable
numerous
obedience
occasion
occasionally
occur
occurred
occurrence
occurring
often
omitted
opinion
opportunity
ordinary
paid
parallel
paralyzed
particular
performance
perhaps
permanent
permitted
personal
personnel
persuade
physical
picnicking
planned
pleasant
pledge
politician
portrayed
possess
possible
practical
precede
prefer
preferred
prejudice
preparation
prepare
prescription
prestige
prevalent
principal
principle
privilege
probably
procedure
profession

professor
prominent
pursue
quantity
quiet
realize
really
receipt
receive
recognize
recommend
referred
referring
relief
remember
renowned
repetition
representative
responsibility
responsible
restaurant
rhythm
running
sacrifice
safety
salary
sandwich
satisfactory
saucer
scene
schedule
scheme
science
seize
sense
sensible
separate
sergeant
serious
shining
shriek
siege
similar
sincerely
skiing
soldier
sophomore
source
speak
special
speech

stationary
stopped
straight
strength
stubborn
studying
substantial
subtle
succeed
success
sufficient
suggestion
summary
supersede
suppose

surprise
susceptible
swimming
system
technique
temperature
terrible
therefore
thief
thorough
tired
together
toward
tragedy
transferred

tremendous
tries
truly
twelfth
unnecessary
until
unusual
using
usually
vacant
vacuum
valuable
vegetable
vengeance
victim

villain
visible
waive
weigh
weird
woman
wrench
write
writing
written
yacht
yield

The Reading Teacher's Book of Lists, Fourth Edition, © 2000 by John Wiley & Sons, Inc.

See also List 122, Spelling Demons—Elementary; List 124, Spelling Demons—National Spelling Bee List.

List 124. SPELLING DEMONS—
NATIONAL SPELLING BEE LIST

Every May, Scripps Howard sponsors the National Spelling Bee in Washington, DC. The 227 contestants in 1992 were sponsored by 221 newspapers from all over the nation, as well as Guam, Mexico, Puerto Rico, and the Virgin Islands. Spellers must be under 16 and not have progressed in school beyond the eighth grade.

For 54 finalists in the 1992 National Spelling Bee, a chance for the championship was lost by misspelling one of the following words. These are obviously the very hardest words. If you want a booklet, "Words of the Champions," of beginning, intermediate, and advanced words, you can write to Scripps Howard, National Spelling Bee, P.O. Box 5380, Cincinnati, OH 45202.

alpestrine	effaceable	knurl	obloquy	synod
anathema	emolument	lilliputian	opsimath	tendresse
beleaguer	epistrophe	linguipotence	ossuary	tralatitious
burgherly	exscind	lorgnette	paroxysm	trattoria
cabochon	famulus	loupe	pellagra	trousseau
cappuccino	gentian	lycanthrope	pylorus	usurpation
catechism	grogram	mademoiselle	requital	venireman
condign	habiliment	marquee	rescissory	vitiate
crinoline	immolate	nacelle	serigraph	wainwright
diptych	ingenue	nefarious	sinecure	zwciback
doughty	jodhpur	nonpareil	sorbefacient	

These 31 words were the last words given in each of the years from 1969 to 1992 at the Scripps Howard National Spelling Bee. They were all spelled correctly, thereby determining the national championship.

1969—interlocutory	1977—cambist	1985—milieu	1993—kamikaze
1970—croissant	1978—deification	1986—odontalgia	1994—antediluvian
1971—shalloon	1979—maculature	1987—staphylococci	1995—xanthosis
1972—macerate	1980—elucubrate	1988—elegiacal	1996—vivisepulture
1973—vouchsafe	1981—sarcophagus	1989—spoliator	1997—euonym
1974—hydrophyte	1982—psoriasis	1990—fibranne	1998—chiaroscurist
1975—incisor	1983—purim	1991—antipyretic	1999—logorrhea
1976—narcolepsy	1984—luge	1992—lyceum	

List 125. SPELLING DEMONS—WISEGUYS

Try using these as examples of the utility of syllabication for pronouncing new words.

Antidisestablishmentarianism: State support of the church.

Supercalifragilisticexpialidocious: Mary Poppins says it means "good."

Pheumonoultramicroscopicsilicovolcanoconiosis: Lung disease cause by inhaling silica dust.

Floccinaucinhilipilification: Action of estimating as worthless.

List 126. SPELLING
TEACHING METHODS

Test–Study–Test Method

Since this book basically gives you the content, such as the Instant Words, Subject Words, or Phonograms, you must use your own methods to teach spelling. However, you might like a few suggestions based on experience and research on using the test–study–test method.

1. **Give a spelling test at the beginning of the week.** For example, you might give a spelling test of the 20 words to all your fourth graders or 5 to 10 words for first graders.

2. **Have the students correct their own papers.** Make sure they properly spell all the words they spelled incorrectly. During the first few weeks you should check their papers to see that they have both (1) found the words they misspelled, and (2) spelled them correctly. After a few weeks most students can do the self-correcting satisfactorily; however, there may be a few students who need frequent or continual supervision.

3. **Have the students carefully study the words that they missed,** paying careful attention to just the incorrect or missing letters, perhaps by circling the incorrect letter(s) and writing the word correctly from memory several times. See the *5-Step Word Study Method* below.

4. **Give a second spelling test on Wednesday.** Every student who gets either 100% or perhaps 90% (your choice) will not have to take the test again on Friday. They can read or write stories.

5. **A final test should be given on Friday** only for those students who did not score well on the Wednesday test. They should study just the words and letter(s) they missed. You can help them by pointing out phonics, syllabication, spelling patterns, suffix principles, or irregularities.

6. **Each student can keep a chart of final scores** achieved on his/her final spelling test (Wednesday or Friday).

5-Step Word Study Method

1. *Look* at the whole word carefully.
2. *Say* the word aloud to yourself.
3. *Spell* the word. (Say each letter to yourself.)
4. *Write* the word from memory. (Cover the word and write it.)
5. *Check* your written word against the correct spelling. (Circle errors and repeat the 5 steps.)

See also List 14, Instant Words; List 16, Homophones; List 19, Easily Confused Words.

The Reading Teacher's Book of Lists, Fourth Edition, © 2000 by John Wiley & Sons, Inc.

List 127. DOUBLE-LETTER SPELLING PATTERNS

Teachers often find it helpful to give a little explanation when they see a student making spelling errors. A common type of spelling error is failure to double a letter. The following spelling patterns might be helpful when used at the "teachable moment" in a classroom explanation.

Spelling Pattern 1: Syllabication

Many double letters are explained by syllabication. If a syllable ends in a consonant and the next syllable begins with the same consonant, a double letter occurs. For example:

TT	little = lit tle
LL	follow = fol low
FF	office = of fice
PP	supper = sup per
SS	missal = mis sal
CC	occur = oc cur
ZZ	blizzard = bliz zard
RR	hurry = hur ry
NN	penny = pen ny

Spelling Pattern 2: Compound Words and Prefixes

A variation of Pattern 1, Syllabication, is the doubling of letters in compound words or when adding prefixes. The general rule in compounding or adding prefixes is that both keep their full spelling. For example:

KK	bookkeeper = book+keeper
TT	cattail = cat+tail
SS	misspell = mis+spell
NN	unnatural = un+natural

Spelling Pattern 3: Vowel Digraphs

Two vowel digraphs OO and EE are a source of many double-letter spellings. For example:

OO	moon, room (long sound)
OO	look, cook (short sound)
EE	see, three (long E sound)

Spelling Pattern 4: Prefix A

The prefix A followed by a consonant often doubles the consonant. (The meaning of that prefix is "to or toward.") Take a look at these examples:

AC	accident, accord
AF	affluent, affix
AG	aggrandize, aggregate
AL	allege, alliance
AN	annex, annual
AP	applause, appeal
AR	arrest, arrive
AS	asset, associate
AT	attach, attire

The Reading Teacher's Book of Lists, Fourth Edition, © 2000 by John Wiley & Sons, Inc.

Spelling Pattern 5: Final Consonants F, L, and S

The letters F, L, and S are often doubled at the end of a word. For example:

F   cliff, off, staff
L   ball, mill, toll, dull
S   class, fuss, kiss

Spelling Pattern 6: Suffixes

Suffixes can be a bit confusing, but here is a basic doubling rule:

"You double the final consonant when the words end in a single consonant preceded by a single vowel and the suffix begins with a vowel."

Phyllis Fischer (1993) developed a nice mnemonic that she calls "1+1+1," which means when one vowel (1) is followed by one consonant (+1), you add (double) one consonant (+1).

Examples that follow the basic doubling rule (1+1+1):

run—running
big—bigger

See also List 13, Syllabication Rules; List 23, Prefixes; List 24, Suffixes; List 128, Spelling Rules for Adding Suffixes.

The Reading Teacher's Book of Lists, Fourth Edition, © 2000 by John Wiley & Sons, Inc.

List 128. SPELLING RULES FOR ADDING SUFFIXES

There are a number of special spelling rules for adding suffixes that change the form of a word (tense of a verb, part of speech) or the meaning (root word + suffix). Most of them are aids to pronouncing the new word; that is, they help make the transition of sounds within the word smoother. Focus on one rule at a time and use lots of examples. (See List 129, Plurals, for additional information on spelling rules for forming plurals.)

Basic rule for adding suffixes to change the verb form, compare adjectives, change a word to an adverb, or make a word plural: **Just add the suffix.**

want + s = wants	want + ing = wanting	want + ed = wanted
talk + s = talks	talk + ing = talking	talk + ed = talked
tall + er = taller	smart + er = smarter	slow + ly = slowly
tall + est = tallest	smart + est = smartest	quick + ly = quickly
chair + s = chairs	book + s = books	bill + s = bills

If a word ends in "e"
- If a word ends in "e," drop the final "e" if the suffix begins with a vowel.
  rose - rosy   dine - dining   name - named
- If a word ends in "e," keep the final "e" if the suffix begins with a consonant.
  safe - safely   care - careful   tire - tireless
- If a word ends in "e," keep the final "e" if it is preceded by a vowel.
  see - seeing

If a word ends in "y"
- If a word ends in "y," change the "y" to "i" if the "y" is preceded by a consonant.
  carry - carried
- If a word ends in "y," keep the "y" if it is preceded by a vowel. joy - joyful
- If a word ends in "y," keep the "y" if the suffix begins with "i." marry - marrying

If a word ends in "c"
- If a word ends in "c," add a "k" before a suffix beginning with an "e," "i," or "y."
  picnic - picnicking   panic - panicky

If a word ends in a single consonant
- If a one-syllable word ends in a consonant (or the final syllable is accented), double the final consonant. brag - bragged
- If a word ends in a single consonant (other than "x"), double the consonant. regret - regretting If the word ends in two consonants, do not double the final one. hard - harder
- If a word has a single vowel letter, double the final consonant. run - running If it has a two-letter vowel, do not double the consonant. rain - rained
- If a word ends in a single consonant and the suffix begins with a vowel, double the consonant. bag - bagged
- If a word ends in "le" and the suffix is "ly," drop the final "le" before adding the suffix. able - ably. But if the word ends in "l," leave the "l" before adding "ly." cool - coolly

See also List 13, Syllabication Rules.

The Reading Teacher's Book of Lists, Fourth Edition, © 2000 by John Wiley & Sons, Inc.

List 129. PLURALS

Mastery of these rules will help students in any grade. The irregular spellings must be memorized. Try a fast-paced spelling bee for practice.

Rules for forming plurals:

1. The plural form of most nouns is made by adding -s to the end of a word.

   chair—chairs   floor—floors
   president—presidents   desk—desks
   face—faces   drill—drills

2. If the word ends in -s, -sh, -ch, -x, or -z, the plural is formed by adding -es.

   boss—bosses   dish—dishes
   bench—benches   fox—foxes
   waltz—waltzes   tax—taxes

3. If the word ends in a consonant followed by -y, the plural is formed by changing the -y to -i and adding -es.

   city—cities   country—countries
   variety—varieties   candy—candies
   family—families   cherry—cherries

4. If the word ends in a vowel followed by -y, the plural is formed by adding -s.

   valley—valleys   turkey—turkeys
   key—keys   play—plays
   journey—journeys   boy—boys

5. The plurals of most nouns ending with -f or -fe are formed by adding -s.

   gulf—gulfs   belief—beliefs
   cuff—cuffs   roof—roofs
   cliff—cliffs   dwarf—dwarfs

6. Some words that end in -f or -fe are formed by changing the -f to -v and adding -es.

   knife—knives   wife—wives
   leaf—leaves   elf—elves
   thief—thieves   life—lives
   loaf—loaves   wolf—wolves
   half—halves   self—selves
   calf—calves

7. If the word ends in a consonant followed by -o, form the plural by adding -es.

   hero—heroes   potato—potatoes
   tomato—tomatoes   echo—echoes
   zero—zeroes   cargo—cargoes

See also List 13, Syllabication Rules.

The Reading Teacher's Book of Lists, Fourth Edition, © 2000 by John Wiley & Sons, Inc.

8. If the word ends in a vowel followed by -o, form the plural by added -s.

video—videos   radio—radios
studio—studios   patio—patios

9. To form the plural of a compound word, make the base noun, or second noun, plural.

brother-in-law—brothers-in-law   bucketseat—bucketseats
sandbox—sandboxes   passerby—passersby

10. Some words have irregular plural forms:

child—children   foot—feet
ox—oxen   mouse—mice
louse—lice   radius—radii
piano—pianos   Eskimo—Eskimos
sheep—sheep   tooth—teeth
trout—trout   deer—deer
salmon—salmon   woman—women
man—men   goose—geese
series—series   species—species
basis—bases   stimulus—stimuli
crisis—crises   medium—media
index—indices   criterion—criteria
solo—solos   auto—autos
axis—axes   focus—foci
oasis—oases   parenthesis—parentheses
die—dice   datum—data

11. Some words are used for both singular and plural meanings:

cod   deer   trout   sheep
moose   bass   corps   wheat
barley   mackerel   rye   series
traffic   dozen   fish   gross

The Reading Teacher's Book of Lists, Fourth Edition, © 2000 by John Wiley & Sons, Inc.

List 130. CAPITALIZATION GUIDELINES

Review these guidelines with your students and provide practice exercises for problem areas. Give "proofreading" assignments to help students become sensitive to the proper use of upper-case letters.

- Capitalize the pronoun I.

  I often sleep late on weekends.

- Capitalize the first word of any sentence.

  Kittens are playful.

- Capitalize the first word and all important words in titles of books, magazines, newspapers, stories, etc.

  The Lion, the Witch, and the Wardrobe

- Capitalize names of specific people, events, dates, and documents.

  Eunice Jones, Toronto, Fourth of July, Thanksgiving, September, the Constitution

- Capitalize the names of organizations and trade names.

  Ford Motor Company, Tide detergent

- Capitalize titles of respect.

  Mr. Cox, Ms. Blake, Judge Rand

- Capitalize names of races, languages, religions, and deity.

  Caucasian, Spanish, Catholic, the Almighty, Jehovah

- Capitalize the first word in a direct quotation.

  Ann inquired, "Where is the suntan lotion?"

- Capitalize abbreviations and acronyms, all or part.

  U.S., UNESCO, CA, St., Mr.

The Reading Teacher's Book of Lists, Fourth Edition, © 2000 by John Wiley & Sons, Inc.

See also List 66, Basic Sentence Patterns; List 68, Punctuation Guidelines; List 70, Proofreading Checklist—Elementary; List 71, Proofreading Checklist—Intermediate; List 167, Portmanteau Words.

List 131. CONTRACTIONS

Contractions substitute an apostrophe for a letter or letters. You will find the grouping of contractions a good teaching strategy.

am	is, has	would, had	have	will	not
I'm	he's	I'd	I've	I'll	can't
	she's	you'd	you've	you'll	don't
are	it's	he'd	we've	she'll	isn't
you're	what's	she'd	they've	he'll	won't
we're	that's	we'd	could've	it'll	shouldn't
they're	who's	they'd	would've	we'll	couldn't
who're	there's	it'd	should've	they'll	wouldn't
	here's	there'd	might've	that'll	aren't
let	one's	what'd	who've	these'll	doesn't
let's		who'd	there've	those'll	wasn't
		that'd		there'll	weren't
				this'll	hasn't
				what'll	haven't
				who'll	hadn't
					mustn't
					didn't
					mightn't
					needn't

See also List 13, Syllabication Rules; List 19, Easily Confused Words; List 167, Portmanteau Words.

The Reading Teacher's Book of Lists, Fourth Edition, © 2000 by John Wiley & Sons, Inc.

List 132. COMPOUND WORDS

Compound words are made by the joining of two whole words. The joined words may be two nouns (watermelon, handcuff), two non-nouns (takeoff, checkup), or a noun and a non-noun (blackbird, sunrise). When they form a compound word, the two words do not always keep the same meaning as they had as separate words (brainstorm, shoelace). Some paired words are treated like compound words but use a hyphen between the two words (trade-off, knock-knee) or have a blank space between them (time clock, pinch hitter).

There are many compound words built on a common base word forming meaning families. For example, here are some members of the "house" family: birdhouse, clubhouse, doghouse, farmhouse, firehouse, greenhouse, schoolhouse, warehouse. Here are some members of the "some" family: somebody, someday, somehow, someone, someplace, something, sometimes, somewhat, somewhere.

afternoon	basketball	daydream
airborne	bathroom	daylight
airline	bedroom	daytime
airmail	bedspread	doorbell
airplane	birdhouse	doorknob
airport	birthday	downpour
airtight	blackbird	downstairs
anchorperson	blackboard	drawbridge
another	blueprint	driveway
anybody	boyfriend	dugout
anyone	brainstorm	earring
anyplace	breakfast	earthquake
anything	broadcast	earthworm
anyway	bulldog	everybody
anywhere	burnout	everyday
applesauce	buttermilk	everyone
audiotape	campfire	everything
backache	cannot	everywhere
backboard	carpool	eyeball
backbone	chalkboard	fingernail
backbreaking	checkup	firefighter
backfire	classmate	fireplace
background	clipboard	fireproof
backpack	cockpit	firewood
backyard	cookbook	fireworks
ballpark	copyright	flashback
ballroom	cowboy	flashlight
barefoot	crosswalk	folklore
baseball	cupcake	football

The Reading Teacher's Book of Lists, Fourth Edition, © 2000 by John Wiley & Sons, Inc.

forever
frostbite
gentleman
girlfriend
goldfish
grandchildren
grandfather
grandmother
grandparent
grapefruit
grasshopper
haircut
hamburger
handcuff
handlebar
haystack
headache
headlight
headquarters
headset
herself
highway
hilltop
himself
homemade
homesick
homework
however
indoor
infield
inside
into
itself
jellyfish
keyboard
keypal
landlord
leftover
lifeboat
lifeguard
lightheaded
lighthouse
lightweight
lipstick
loudspeaker

maybe
meanwhile
moonlight
motorcycle
myself
network
newscast
newspaper
nightgown
nobody
notebook
oatmeal
online
ourselves
outcome
outfield
outfit
outlaw
outline
outside
outstanding
overalls
overcoat
overlook
overpass
pancake
paperback
payoff
peanut
peppermint
pinball
pinpoint
playground
playmate
ponytail
popcorn
postcard
quarterback
quicksand
railroad
rainbow
raincoat
rattlesnake
rawhide
redwood

Rollerblade
runway
sailboat
sandpaper
scarecrow
screwdriver
seacoast
seafood
seagull
seaport
seashell
seaside
seaweed
seesaw
shipwreck
shoelace
shortstop
showdown
showoff
showroom
sidewalk
silverware
skateboard
skyscraper
snowball
snowfall
snowflake
snowman
snowplow
snowstorm
softball
somebody
someday
somehow
someone
someplace
something
sometimes
somewhat
somewhere
spotlight
starfish
stepfather
stepmother
strawberry

suitcase
sundown
sunflower
sunlight
sunrise
sunset
sunshine
sunstroke
suntan
sweatshirt
sweetheart
takeoff
teammate
textbook
Thanksgiving
themselves
thunderstorm
timeline
timeout
timetable
tiptoe

today
toenail
together
toothbrush
touchdown
tryout
tugboat
turnpike
turtleneck
undercover
underground
undertake
uproot
upset
upstairs
uptown
videotape
vineyard
wastebasket
watercolor
waterfall

waterfront
watermelon
weatherman
weekend
wheelchair
whenever
whirlpool
wholesale
windmill
windpipe
windshield
windsurfing
wingspan
wiretapping
without
woodland
woodpecker
wristwatch
yourself

List 133. SPELLING GAME

Here's a spelling game your students might like to do in their spare time. If they do, have them make up other similar games using other letters (and a dictionary). If you would like a little book of these games, see *Games Make Alpha-Betics Fun* by John Dean and Karol Hicks.

AN "F PLUS" PAPER

1. F plus one letter: a music note
2. F plus two letters: cost; charge
3. F plus two letters: not many
4. F plus three letters: after three comes . . .
5. F plus three letters: to locate
6. F plus three letters: froth
7. F plus four letters: fictitious story
8. F plus four letters: before second
9. F plus four letters: case for a picture
10. F plus four letters: defect; flaw; misdeed
11. F plus five letters: celebrated, distinguished
12. F plus five letters: group of related people
13. F plus five letters: delicately
14. F plus five letters: to secure
15. F plus five letters: solidly; compactly
16. F plus six letters: untrue story
17. F plus six letters: used in swimming
18. F plus six letters: covered with water
19. F plus six letters: blooms
20. F plus six letters: other than one's own country
21. F plus six letters: cargo
22. F plus seven letters: after thirty-ninth
23. F plus seven letters: a heating fuel
24. F plus seven letters: celebration
25. F plus seven letters: having an elevated temperature
26. F plus seven letters: fleeing from danger or justice
27. F plus seven letters: the normal action of anything
28. F plus seven letters: Walt Disney movie; musical

1. ____fa____
2. _____
3. _____
4. _____
5. _____
6. _____
7. _____
8. _____
9. _____
10. _____
11. _____
12. _____
13. _____
14. _____
15. _____
16. _____
17. _____
18. _____
19. _____
20. _____
21. _____
22. _____
23. _____
24. _____
25. _____
26. _____
27. _____
28. _____

ANSWERS

1. fa
2. fee
3. few
4. four
5. find
6. foam
7. fable
8. first
9. frame
10. fault
11. famous
12. family
13. finely
14. fasten
15. firmly
16. fiction
17. flipper
18. flooded
19. flowers
20. foreign
21. freight
22. fortieth
23. firewood
24. festival
25. feverish
26. fugitive
27. function
28. fantasia

The Reading Teacher's Book of Lists, Fourth Edition, © 2000 by John Wiley & Sons, Inc.

List 134. SPEECH PRONUNCIATION

Pronouncing words properly can be a great help in spelling them correctly. Furthermore, you can sometimes exaggerate the pronunciation, even distort it a bit, to emphasize what letter should be used. A further help in pronunciation sometimes is to pronounce the word syllable-by-syllable. Here are a few other pronunciation suggestions:

1. Watch out for confusing words that have similar but not identical sounds; for example, celery—salary; finally—finely.

2. Don't add syllables that aren't there; for example, athlete (not athelete); laundry (not laundery).

3. Don't skip syllables that are there; for example, chocolate (not choclate); probably (not probly).

4. Don't skip letter sounds that are there; for example, arctic (not artic); government (not goverment).

5. Don't reverse letters; for example, perform (not preform); tragedy (not tradegy).

6. Watch out for the schwa /ə/ or unaccented vowel sound. Because it causes a lot of errors in spelling lessons, it is often helpful to temporarily exaggerate the unaccented vowel letter (thereby making it not a schwa sound). Example: doll*a*r; spons*o*r; ben*e*fit; def*i*nite.

7. For purposes of mnemonics or memory devices, it is sometimes helpful to even use a temporary incorrect pronunciation; for example, "Wednesday" might be pronounced "Wed-nes-day."

8. Take a little extra time with ESL students to see that they are pronouncing all the spelling words correctly.

The Reading Teacher's Book of Lists, Fourth Edition, © 2000 by John Wiley & Sons, Inc.

11

THE

INTERNET

List 135. TIPS FOR SEARCHING THE INTERNET

The vast holdings of the Internet are just a click or two away . . . well, maybe not. Unless you master a few basic search techniques, you can spend a lot of valuable time surfing the net or weeding through hundreds of "matches" before you find what you are looking for. These tips will help you develop search expertise quickly.

1. **Bookmark or save as a favorite at least three search engine sites.** A search engine is a large data base that helps index the web pages and other sites on the Internet. No one search engine indexes the whole Internet; in fact, less than 15% of the sites are indexed by each one. See List 136 for recommendations and their URLs.

2. **Do a quick word web.** Jot down the search topic and related words including a category it is in, subcategories, type of information you are looking for, etc. For example, for "collective nouns" a word web might include: grammar, elementary, list. If the word has multiple meanings, add a few key words to distinguish the target from the others, such as: not farm, not agriculture. As you search note the words that helped most so you can use them if you need to use a second search engine.

3. **Use lower-case letters when entering your query.** Most search engines are case sensitive and will not give you matches for collective nouns if you queried Collective or Noun or COLLECTIVE NOUN.

4. **Use singular, not plural in your query.** A match is made when all of what you ask for is found. If your word has an -s, its singular form will not be counted as a match. Because the spelling of the singular is generally part of the plural, plurals will be found using the singular form.

5. **Use quotations marks to search for a specific phrase or multi-word term.** For example: "collective noun." Otherwise the search will find sites with either collective or noun but not those with the two words together.

6. **Use the plus (+) and minus (–) signs in your query.** The + and – signs show what to include or exclude from the search results. A search for *"collective noun" +grammar+elementary+list–farm–agriculture* has a much different result than just using "collective noun." (Note: Do not leave space after the + or – sign.) Also using the + with two (or more) words will find sites that contain both words, but not necessarily together as in a phrase.

7. **Use the * as a wildcard.** The * at the end of a word will enable you to find variants of the word, including plurals. For example, "white water raft*" will locate raft, rafts, rafter, rafters, rafting. This is a technique that expands the catch of your search.

8. **Look for titles.** Simple searches match your query to words anywhere in the site. To find sites that have your target word in the title, type title: followed by your topic. Here are two examples: *title:caldecott title:"Mother Goose"*

9. **Look for links.** Many of the best sites include links to other related web pages, chat groups, etc., and often these are most important or useful additional sites. To find links from one site to another, type link: then the URL of the site you already know. For example, this query is for links about technology and learning online: *link:www.techlearning.com/*

The Reading Teacher's Book of Lists, Fourth Edition, © 2000 by John Wiley & Sons, Inc.

List 136. SEARCH ENGINES FOR EDUCATORS

There are more than 150 million web pages out there and more are added every day. No single search engine can sort through it all. The search engines listed below are easy to use and net the best results for educational and general information searches. Yahooligans is especially good for students, but all are fairly easy to use once you've learned the basics. Be sure to check out List 135, Tips for Searching the Internet, to be on your way. Bookmark at least two search engines on your home and classroom computers. Consult the search engine site below, if you need a specialized search.

AltaVista Audio/Visual	//image.altavista.com/cgi-bin/avncgi
AltaVista Search	www.altavista.com
Argos (ancient and medieval times)	//eawc.evansville.edu/index.htm
Ask Jeeves	www.askjeeves.com
Clip Art Search Engines	www.webplaces.com/search/
Deja.Com (Newsgroup Search)	www.deja.com
Dogpile	www.dogpile.com
Excite	www.excite.com
Goggle Uncle Sam	www.google.com/unclesam
InfoSeek	www.infoseek.com
Liszt—The Mailing List Directory	www.liszt.com
Lycos	http://lycos.com
The White House	www.whitehouse.gov/
Thomas (Congress)	//thomas.loc.gov/
WebCrawler	http://webcrawler.com/
WebSeek: Image Catalog	www.disney.ctr.columbia.edu/webSEEk/ docs/web/web.htm
Yahoo!	www.yahoo.com/
Yahooligans	www.yahooligans.com

Directory of All Search Engines   www.allsearchengines.com

The Reading Teacher's Book of Lists, Fourth Edition, © 2000 by John Wiley & Sons, Inc.

List 137. COMMONLY-ASKED QUESTIONS ABOUT THE INTERNET

What is the Internet?

It consists of a network of computers connected worldwide that share information in all types of media and communicate directly with each other.

What can I do with the Internet?

Using the Internet tools, e-mail, Telnet, Gopher, FTP, and WWW, you can communicate by voice, text, or video anywhere in the world; locate and research archived or current information; and transfer files containing text or graphics.

What is needed to begin?

- a computer
- a modem
- a phone line
- communication software
- Internet account

Where do I get an account?

- University, college, or local school
- Freenets are found locally through the library, university, or state systems
- Department of Education in your state might provide accounts for teachers
- Local Internet providers may be found in local phonebooks
- Commercial providers: CompuServe, America Online, Prodigy, etc.

How do I begin using the Internet in my classroom?

- Enter the local number of your Internet provider and the settings for data bits, parity, stop bits, speed, and terminal emulation into your communication package.
- Your provider should provide you with instructions for logging on to the system. Every system is unique.
- You will need to remember your user name, password, and your unique Internet address.
- Create an Acceptable Use Policy for each user in your classroom. The contract among the teacher, parent, and student should establish use policies, unacceptable uses and consequences, and signatures of all parties.

Where do I start once I am connected?

- Use e-mail to join listservs or to send messages to individuals.
- Use FTP (File Transfer Protocol) to download or capture files on software.
- Use Gopher to view archived data in a menu-based format.

The Reading Teacher's Book of Lists, Fourth Edition, © 2000 by John Wiley & Sons, Inc.

- Use Telnet to log on to a remote computer and use that system's files and software. Most Telnet sites require that you have a registered user name in order for you to access their system.
- Use WWW (World Wide Web) to search and locate worldwide graphics, text, and audio in a hypertext format with a browser software program.

Do any web sites offer free teacher training?

There are many, but here are a couple you may want to try:

- **SchoolCity** (www.schoolcity.com), an online community for teachers, students, and parents, provides users with tools and information they need to harness the power of the Internet.
- **WebTeacher** (www.webteacher.org) covers e-mail, video conferencing, chat rooms, web page design, and Internet safety. WebTeacher leads you through lessons, online exercises, and activities when you select the topics and depth of knowledge you seek.

The Reading Teacher's Book of Lists, Fourth Edition, © 2000 by John Wiley & Sons, Inc.

List 138. WEB SITES FOR
READING INSTRUCTION

Need information about a basal reading program? New ideas for teaching prediction or plot? Lesson plans for reading instruction? The national standards for reading and literacy? These sites offer a broad range of instructional resources, including thematic units for cross-discipline literacy instruction and materials for gifted and struggling students. Links to scores of other resources for teaching all aspects of reading are included on many sites.

Reading Programs

Harcourt Brace	www.harcourtschool.com/
Houghton Mifflin	www.eduplace.com/catalog/rdg//
Macmillan/McGraw Hill	www.mmhschool.com/teach/reading/ mhreading/index.html
Open Court (SRA)	www.sra4kids.com
Scott Foresman/Addison Wesley	www.scottforesman.com/sfaw/
Silver, Burdett, Ginn/Scott Foresman	www.sbgschool.com/

Instructional Resources

AskERIC Virtual Library	http://ericir.syr.edu/Virtual/
Blue Web'n Applications Library	www.kn.pacebell.com/wired/bluewebn/
Busy Teachers' Web Site K–12	www.ceismc.gatech.edu/busyt/
CEC Lesson Plans	www.col-ed.org/cur/
Connections+	www.mcrel.org/resources/plus/
English Pavilion	http://pen.k12.va.us/Anthology/Pav/ LangArts/LangArts.html
Instructor Magazine	www.scholastic.com/Instructor/
Language Arts	www.csun.edu/~vceed009/languagearts.html
Linguistic Funland	www.tesol.net/tesltext.html
Reading Recovery	www.readingrecovery.org/
SCORE Language Arts	www.sdcoe.k12.ca.us/score/cla.html
Standards for Education	http://putwest.boces.org/Standards.html
Success for All	www.successforall.net/
Teacher's Resource Center	www.bdd.com/teachers/
Teaching PreK–8	www.TeachingK-8.com
Whole Language Umbrella	www.ncte.org/wlu/

The Reading Teacher's Book of Lists, Fourth Edition, © 2000 by John Wiley & Sons, Inc.

List 139. WEB SITES FOR WRITERS AND WORD LOVERS

Rhymes. Word histories. Help with research papers. Word puzzles and games. Places to publish student writing. Even a puzzlemaker for budding cruciverbalists. These web sites and their links are great for every student writer and word aficionado you know.

Words

English Homophone Dictionary	www.earlham.edu/~peters/writing/homophone.htm
English Teacher	www.theenglishteacher.org
The Etymology of First Names	www.engr.uric.ca/~mcampbel/etym.html
Fun With Etymology	www.compastnet.com/mrex/etymol.htm
Funbrain.com	www.funbrain.com/vocab/index.html
The Grammar Lady	www.grammarlady.com/
Intercultural E-Mail Classroom Connections	www.stolaf.edu/network/iecc
People's Names and What They Mean	www.zelo.com/firstnames
Puzzlemaker	www.puzzlemaker.com/
Rhyming Dictionary	www.cs.cmu.edu/~dougb/rhyme.html
Syndicate	http://syndicate.com
A Word a Day	www.wordsmith.org/awad/index.html
Word Central	www.wordcentral.com/dailybuzzword.html
WordPlay	http://homepage.interaccess./~wolinsky/word.htm
Wow Word of the Week	www.wowwords.com/

Writing

Inkspot for Young Writers	www.inkspot.com/young/
KidNews	www.vsa.cape.com/~powens/Kidnews3.html
KidPub	www.kidpub.org/kidpub/
Pitsco's Launch to Keypals	www.keypals.com/p/keypals.html
Poetry Gallery	www.kidlit@mgfx.com
The Quill Society	www.quill.net/
Researchpaper.com	www.researchpaper.com/
Virtual Presentation Assistant	www.ukans.edu/cwis/units/coms2/vpa/vap.html
Writing Den: Teacher's Guide	www.actden.com/writ_den/t-guide.htm
Writing Links	//andromeda.rutgers.edu/~jlynch/Writing/links.html

The Reading Teacher's Book of Lists, Fourth Edition, © 2000 by John Wiley & Sons, Inc.

List 140. WEB SITES FOR CHILDREN'S LITERATURE

These Internet sites offer an amazing array of useful and interesting information related to children's literature. The sites in the Authors section connect you with many favorite authors and illustrators and includes one where you can contact authors. The Literature section offers book lists, online versions of classics, as well as specialty sites such as Myths and Legends and Cinderella stories. The Books list includes children's book publishers and online bookstores. Most sites have links and many include instructional activities and much more.

Authors

Ask the Author	www.ipl.org/youth/AskAuthor/
Author & Illustration Links	www.cbcbooks.org/navigation/teaindex.htm
Authors and Illustrators on the Web	www.acs.ucalgary.ca/~dkgrown/authors.html
HarperCollins Authors	www.harperchildrens.com/index.htm
Into the Wardrobe: The CS Lewis Site	www//cslewis.DrZeus.net
Laura Ingalls Wilder Home Page	http://webpages.marshall.edu/~irby1/laura.html
Lewis Carroll Home Page Illustrated	www.cstone.net/library/alice/carroll.html
Mark Twain	http://etext.lib.virginia.edu/railton/index2.html
Winnie the Pooh Collection	www.penguinputnam.com/yreaders/pooh/winnie.htm

Literature

Aesop's Fables Online Exhibit	www.pacificnet.net/~johnr/aesop/
American Library Association	www.ala.org
Arthuriana	www.ncsu.edu/~spirko/arthur.html
Booktalks—Quick and Simple	www.concord.k12.nh.us/schools/rundlett/booktalks/
Carol Hurst's Children's Literature Site	www.carolhurst.com/
Children's Book Cooperative	www.soemadison.wisc.edu/ccbc/
Children's Book Council	www.cbcbooks.org/
Children's Literature	http://pages.hotbed.com/edu/wouldchuck/childlit.html
Children's Literature	www.childrenslit.com/
Children's Literature & Language Arts Resources	http://falcon.jmu.edu/~ramseyil/childlit.html
Children's Literature Web Guide	www.acs.ucalgary.ca/~dkbrown/index.html
Children's Literature—Resources for Teachers	www.ucalgary.ca/~dkbrown/rteacher.html
Cinderella Stories	www.ucalgary.ca/~dkbrown/cinderella.html
Cinderella Studies	www-dept.usm.edu/~engdept/cinderella/cinderella.html
Cyberkids	www.cyberkids.com/
Electric Library	www.elibrary.com/
Fairrosa Cyber Library	www.dalton.org/libraries/Fairrosa
Internet Public Library	www.ipl.org

Kid's Web—A WWW Digital Library for School Kids	www.kidvista.com/index.html
Kidzeen	www.cyberkids.com/issue10/
Lear, Limericks & Literature	www.castlemoyle.com/lear/learte/htm
The Little Red Riding Hood Project	www-dept.usm.edu/~engdept/lrrh/lrrhhome.htm
Multicultural Book Review	www.isomedia.com/homes/jmele/homepage.html
Mystery Readers Journal	www.murderonthemenu.com/mystery/
Myths and Legends	http://pubpages.unh.edu/~cbsiren/myth.html
New York Public Library	www.nypl.org/
Notable Children's Trade Books	www.ncss.org/resources/notable/home.html
The On-Line Books Page	www.cs.cmu.edu/Web/books.html
Online Mystery Database	www.mysteries.com
Project Bartleby Archive	www.bartleby.com
Tales of Wonder: Folk & Fairy Tales from Around the World	http://itpubs.ucdavis.edu/richard/tales/

Books

AddALL (searches and compares 41 bookstores)	www.bookarea.com
Amazon.com	www.amazon.com/
Barnes and Noble	www.barnesandnoble.com/
	www.bn.com
Books-a-Million	www.booksamillion.com
Borders' Children's Page	www.borders.com/
Publishers of Children's Books	www.acs.ucalgary.ca/~dkbrown/publish.html

The Reading Teacher's Book of Lists, Fourth Edition, © 2000 by John Wiley & Sons, Inc.

See also List 48, Award-Winning Children's Books; List 191, Publishers of Reading Materials and Tests.

List 141. KIDS' ZINES

Zines are online counterparts for magazines (see Kids' Magazines, List 55). These online versions are accessible to many students with just a few mouse clicks. Their interactive nature is also very engaging. As with magazines, zines are a great source of high-interest material for reluctant and/or developing readers.

ABC Kids Gazette	www.eint.com/abagain/
American Girl	www.americangirl.com/homepage2.html
ClubZ!	www.club-z.com/index.html
CyberKids	www.cyberkids.com/
Daybreak	//daybreak.simplenet.com/contents.html
HiPMag Online	www.hipmag.org/
International Kids' Space	www.kids-space.org
Kids World Magazine	www.kidsworld-online.com/
MidLink Magazine	//longwood.cs.ucf.edu/~MidLink/
National Geographic Kids	www.nationalgeographic.com/kids/
National Geographic World	www.nationalgeographic.com/world/index.html
Sports Illustrated for Kids	www.sikids.com/index.html
Time for Kids	//pathfinder.com /TFK/index.html
WebINK Online	www.ipl.org/webink/
YES Mag	www.yesmag.bc.ca/

List 142. VIRTUAL REFERENCE LIBRARY

Every classroom (and every teacher) is just a click or two away from a world-class reference library. These sites and their links cover every school subject and then some. To make the most of these, bookmark the sites on your Internet browser so students will not have to type in the URLs.

Almanacs

CIA World Factbook	//odci.gov/cia/publications/factbook
Events & Calendars of the Day	//erebus.phys.cwru.edu/~copi/events.html
Information Please Almanac	www.infoplease.com
Literary Calendar	//litcal.yasuda-u.ac.jp/
The Old Farmers Almanac	www.almanac.com

Dictionaries

3-D Dictionary	http://207.136.90.76/dictionary/
A Web of On-Line Dictionaries	www.facstaff.bucknell.edu/rbeard/diction.html
Little Explorers Picture Dictionary	www.LittleExplorers.com/dictionary.html
Mirriam Webster Dictionary Online	www.m-w.com
Multilingual Picture Dictionary	www.EnchantedLearning.com/Dictionary.html
My Facts Page Dictionaries & Language Resources	www.refdesk.com/factdict.html
My Virtual Reference Desk	www.refdesk.com/
OneLook Dictionary	www.onelook.com
Online Dictionaries	www.dict.org
Online Dictionaries	www.dictionary.com
The Oxford English Dictionary OnLine	www.oed.com
Rhyming Dictionary	www.link.cs.cmu.edu/dougb/rhyme-doc.html

General Reference

AskERIC	http://ericir.syr.edu/
E-Conflict World Encyclopedia	www.emulateme.com/
The Human Languages Page	www.june29.com/HLP/
Internet Connections: Language Arts	http://neptune.k12.nj.us/tlef/lang.htm
Internet Library for Librarians	www.itcompany.com/inforetriever/dict_eng.htm
Internet Public Library Youth Division	www.ipl.org/youth
Liszt Directory of Newsgroups	www.liszt.com/news/
MapQuest	www.mapquest.com
PC Webopedia	www.pcwebopedia.com
Roget's Thesaurus.com	www.thesaurus.com
Study WEB	www.studyweb.com
The Universal Library	www.ul.cs.cmn.edu/

The Reading Teacher's Book of Lists, Fourth Edition, © 2000 by John Wiley & Sons, Inc.

Special Subject Reference

A&E Biographical Dictionary	www.biography.com
Artcyclopedia	www.artcyclopedia.com
Bartlett's Familiar Quotations	www.bartleby.com
Biographical Dictionary	www.s9.com:80/biography/
Encyclopedia Mythica	www.pantheon.org/mythica/
English Homophone Dictionary	www.earlham.edu/~peters/writing/ homofone.htm
Family Search	www.familysearch.com
FamilyTreeMaker's Genealogy Site	www.familytreemaker.com
Life Science Dictionary	http://biotech.icmb.utexas.edu/pages/ dictionary.html
SciCentral	www.scicentral.com/index.html
The Weather Channel	www.weather.com
Weather Glossary	www.weatherlabs.com
Whatis.com (Internet/computer terms)	www.whatis.com

The Reading Teacher's Book of Lists, Fourth Edition, © 2000 by John Wiley & Sons, Inc.

List 143. COMPUTER AND INTERNET TERMS

This is a list of the most commonly used computer and Internet terms, along with a brief definition for each. Since the use of computers and the Internet is becoming increasingly widespread in schools, homes, and the workplace, computer literacy is essential. This list provides a good start. Note that words used in definitions that are themselves defined in this list are in italics. See also List 144, E-mail, Chat, and Internet Acronyms.

abort	To stop a *program* or function before it finishes.
archive	To copy computer files onto a long-term storage device for safe keeping.
ASCII	American Standard Code for Information Interchange. A code for representing English letters as numbers, which makes it possible to transfer data from one computer to another.
backbone	The main cable that connects devices on a computer *network*.
bandwidth	The amount of data that can be transmitted in a fixed amount of time; e.g., *bits* per second.
baud rate	The speed at which a *modem* can transmit data.
bit	Binary digit. The smallest unit of information used by computers. Each bit can represent only two values: 0 or 1.
bookmark	To mark a *Web* address or document for later retrieval.
boot	To start a computer by loading the *operating system*.
browser	Computer *software* used to search the Web and display information.
bug	An error in the computer *software* or *hardware* that causes a malfunction.
byte	Groups of eight bits that can be used to represent numbers and letters of the alphabet.
CAD	Computer Aided Design. *Software* used especially by architects and engineers that allows them to manipulate pictorial representations on the display screen.
CAM	Computer Aided Manufacturing. The use of computer systems to assist in automated manufacturing.
CD-ROM	Compact Disk-Read Only Memory. A type of *compact disk* designed to have information read from it but not have information recorded on it.
chip	An extremely small piece of silicon on which thousands of electronic elements are implanted.
click	To tap a *mouse* button. "Click on" means to select an item on the screen by pointing the *cursor* at it and tapping the mouse button.
clip art	Electronic graphics, often part of a software package, and generally royalty-free, that can be inserted into a document.

compact disk	CD. A disk (or disc) with one or more metal layers used to store digital information that is read by a laser.
connectivity	The ability of a device or *software* to link with other devices or software.
cookie	Information that is given to a *Web* browser by a *server* to identify a user when the server is accessed in the future.
CPU	Central Processing Unit. The main unit in a computer that contains the *chip* that makes the computer operate. It can be thought of as the brains of the computer.
crash	A major failure in a computer resulting from a failure in the *hardware* or *software*.
cursor	A special symbol, usually blinking, that indicates where the next character will appear on the screen.
database	A computer file or collection of data.
debug	To find and remove errors from a *program*.
default	A value or setting that is preset by the manufacturer or *program* and remains until changed.
defragment	A process whereby scattered files on a *disk* are reorganized to make them contiguous and improve operating efficiency.
desktop	The primary display screen with *icons* representing programs, files, etc.
dial-up access	Connection to a computer by telephone and *modem*.
disk	A plate on which data can be encoded. See also *floppy disk* and *hard disk*.
disk drive	A device that reads and writes data to a *disk*.
DOS	Disk Operation System. A collection of programs that form the *operating system* for the *disk drives*. Often refers to the operating system developed by Microsoft, i.e., MS-DOS.
download	To copy a file, *program*, etc., from a main source such as the *Internet* or a *mainframe* computer to a local computer, printer, etc.
e-mail	Electronic mail, i.e., a message sent over a communication *network*.
ESC	Escape key on the computer keyboard
execute	To run a *program* or perform a command or function.
floppy disk	*Disks* designed to be removed from computers and thus are portable. These disks used to be in a sealed envelope and "flopped" when shaken. Now they are generally in a rigid shell.
freeware	*Software* given away by the author, often available over the *Internet*.
FTP	File Transfer Protocol. The protocol used on the *Internet* for sending files.
GIF	Graphics Interchange Format. A graphics file format used by the *Web* and other systems.
graphical interface	Allows the user to give the computer commands by pointing and activating *icons* on the computer screen.

hard disk	A rigid magnetic *disk* sealed inside the computer on which data can be stored.
hardware	The actual physical computer and other objects such as monitor, keyboard, printer, etc., that connect to it.
home page	The main page of a *web site*—often the first page accessed by visitors to the Web site.
HTML	HyperText Markup Language. The language used to create documents on the *World Wide Web.*
HTTP	HyperText Transfer Protocol. The way in which *World Wide Web* pages are transferred over the *Internet.*
hypermedia	An extension of *hypertext* that includes sound and graphics in addition to text.
hypertext	A system of writing and displaying text in which there are links that allow the reader to browse and find connections with related documents and text.
icon	A little picture appearing on the computer screen that represents something larger such as a *program,* object, or choice of action.
Internet	A large number of computer *networks* that are interconnected and make it possible for millions of computers throughout the world to communicate with each other.
intranet	A computer *network* accessible within an organization that uses *protocols* like those of the *Internet.*
kilobyte	KB. 1,024 bytes, or approximately one thousand *bytes.*
LAN	Local Area Network. A computer *network* confined to a limited area.
landscape	Printing or other printer *output* that is parallel to the long side of the paper.
laptop	A small, portable computer.
laser printer	High-speed, high-resolution printer that uses a laser beam to print.
listserv	A family of programs used to distribute messages to a list of members. Listservs usually are organized around a particular theme or interest. Members subscribe to a listserv in order to exchange information with people who share that interest.
local area network	See *LAN.*
log on	To access a computer system by providing a password or other identification.
log off	To terminate a session on a computer system.
mainframe	The largest computers to which terminals or *personal computers* may be linked.
memory	Storage area in the computer.
megabyte	MB. 1,048,576 bytes, or approximately one million *bytes.*
minimize	To shrink a *window* into an *icon.*
modem	Modulator–Demodulator. A device that makes it possible for a computer to send and receive data over a telephone line.
monitor	A screen for displaying computer information.

mouse	A small device connected to the computer that controls the movements of the *cursor*.
multimedia	The use of computers to present voice, video, and data in an integrated way.
multitasking	The ability to execute more than one task or program simultaneously in a *Windows* environment.
netiquette	Etiquette for posting messages on computer networks, particularly the *Internet*.
network	Two or more computers linked together.
notebook	A lightweight and portable computer. See also *laptop*.
NT	See *Windows NT*.
off-line	Not connected.
online	Turned on and connected.
operating system	The program that performs the most basic tasks of a computer such as recognizing data from the keyboard, sending data to the display screen or other peripheral device, organizing files, etc.
output	Anything that comes out from the computer.
password	A series of characters that is kept secret and allows the user to gain access to files, computers, etc.
personal computer	PC. A micro computer that has its *central processing unit* etched onto a single *chip*. This is the most common type of computer in use today. In recent years PCs have become extremely powerful.
PC	*Personal computer.*
pixel	A picture element. A single point in a graphic.
program	A series of instructions that tell a computer what to do.
protocol	Any set of rules that allows different computers to communicate with each other accurately and reliably.
purge	To remove or delete unneeded files.
RAM	Random Access Memory. The most common type of memory found in most computers.
read-only	Capable of being displayed but not modified or deleted.
ROM	Read Only Memory. Computer memory on which basic low-level *programs* have been prerecorded.
save	To copy data from a temporary to a more permanent storage area in a computer so that it can be accessed at a later time.
screen saver	A small *program* that takes over a display screen when it has not been used for a preset amount of time. Often displays decorative patterns.
search engine	A *program* that searches for information on the *World Wide Web*.
server	A computer or other device that manages resources on a *network*.
shareware	Software that is readily available, often over the *Internet*, that allows you to try it out with the understanding that if you decide to keep it, you will pay for it.

SMTP	Simple Mail Transfer Protocol. A *protocol* for sending *e-mail* messages between *servers* on a *network*.
software	Computer *programs* and accompanying documentation.
spreadsheet	*Software* used for working with data (both words and numbers) in rows and columns.
upload	Transmit information from a computer to a *mainframe* or *network*.
username	A name used to gain access to a computer.
virus	Computer code that is introduced to the computer from an outside source without the user's knowledge and causes problems.
Web	See *World Wide Web*.
Webmaster	An individual who manages a *web site*.
web page	A document on the *World Wide Web*.
web site	A collection of interrelated *web pages*.
window	An enclosed rectangular area on a display screen.
Windows	*Multitasking* software that creates a *graphical interface* environment that allows the user to divide the computer screen into multiple *windows* and to move freely among them.
Windows NT	A *32-bit operating system* that supports *multitasking*.
word processor	Computer *software* used to produce and edit text.
World Wide Web	WWW. A *hypermedia* system on the *Internet* that makes it possible to browse through information.
WYSIWYG	What You See Is What You Get. Computer *software* that shows on the display screen exactly what you will get when you print.
ZIP	A popular way of compressing data so that it takes less computer memory.

The Reading Teacher's Book of Lists, Fourth Edition, © 2000 by John Wiley & Sons, Inc.

List 144. E-MAIL, CHAT, AND INTERNET ACRONYMS

This list of special acronyms will help you keep Internet communications flowing—in e-mail, chat rooms, and discussion groups. They communicate a lot with very few key-strokes, keeping your dialogue fast paced, informal, and clear.

AAMOF	as a matter of fact	MHOTY	my hat's off to you
AFAIK	as far as I know	NH	nice hand
AKA	also known as	NRN	no reply necessary
ASAP	as soon as possible	OIC	oh, I see
BBFN	bye bye for now	OK	okay
BFN	bye for now	OTOH	on the other hand
BRB	be right back	PMFJI	pardon me for jumping in
BTW	by the way	PMJI	pardon my jumping in
BYKT	but you knew that	PS	post script
CMIIW	correct me if I'm wrong	ROF	rolling on the floor
EOL	end of lecture	ROTFL	rolling on the floor laughing
FAQ	frequently asked question(s)	RSN	real soon now
FC	fingers crossed	SITD	still in the dark
FITB	fill in the blank	SMS	split my sides
FWIW	for what it's worth	SNAFU	situation normal: all fouled up
FYI	for your information	SOHF	sense of humor failure
GG	good game	SPAM	stupid persons' advertisement
HAND	have a nice day	SWAK	sealed with a kiss
HTH	hope this helps	TAH	take a hint
IAC	in any case	TIA	thanks in advance
IAE	in any event	TIC	tongue in cheek
IDK	I don't know	TPTB	the powers that be
IIRC	if I recall correctly	TTFN	ta ta for now
IMCO	in my considered opinion	TTYL	talk to you later
IMHO	in my humble opinion	TWIMC	to whom it may concern
IMNSHO	in my not-so-humble opinion	TYVM	thank you very much
IMO	in my opinion	WRT	with respect to
IOW	in other words	WYSIWYG	what you see is what you get
IYKWIM	if you know what I mean	YMMV	your mileage may vary
JM2C	just my 2 cents	YWIA	you're welcome in advance
LOL	laughing out loud		

List 145. EMOTICONS

Getting your ideas across on the Internet—in e-mail, chat rooms, or discussion groups—is helped by the use of emoticons that let your readers know how you feel about things. The word "emoticon" is a portmanteau formed by combining the words *emotion* and *icon*. They are formed using regular letters and symbols on the computer keyboard. Although they are also called "smileys," they represent a wide range of feelings.

:-)	happy	:-()	bored
;-)	playful, winking	:-(	sad, unhappy, upset
:-<	miserable, frowning	:-D	laughing, joking
:-|	indifferent, who cares?	:-X	it's a secret, lips are sealed
(-:	left-handed writer	%-)	cross-eyed, exhausted
8-)	wearing sunglasses	::-)	wearing regular glasses
B-)	wearing dark-rimmed glasses	8:-)	girl, woman
:-)>==	boy, man	:-{)	has a mustache
:'-(	crying	:-/	confused, not sure, skeptical
:-#	wearing braces	:-o	talking
|-D	laughing out loud	:-O	shouting
:-0	uh-oh!	:-@	screaming
:-&	tongue tied	:-]	grinning
|-O	yawning	:-P	sticking tongue out
|-I	sleeping	:-[	frowning, miserable
:->	smirk, joking, devilish	:-{}	wearing lipstick
{:-)	wearing a toupee	*<:-)	Santa or partygoer
*.o)	clowning around	[ ] **	hugs & kisses
{{{}}}	thinking it over	0 :-)	angel, angelic
[:-]	robot	<:-)	dunce
[:-)	wearing earphones	<:3)~	mouse
3:]	pet, cat, dog, cow	8 :-)	wizard
$-)	greedy	:-*	kiss
@--)--	flower, rose	<()(—)<<	fish
:-)X	wearing a bow tie	(:::[ ]:::)	bandaid
@(*0*)@	koala bear		

The Reading Teacher's Book of Lists, Fourth Edition, © 2000 by John Wiley & Sons, Inc.

12
ESL/LANGUAGE

The Reading Teacher's Book of Lists, Fourth Edition, © 2000 by John Wiley & Sons, Inc.

List 146. SPEECH SOUND DEVELOPMENT

Oral speech sounds (phonemes) develop slowly over five or six years. Here is a chart showing the age at which 75 percent of children had mastered each spoken phoneme.

CONSONANTS

IPA*	Conventional	INITIAL Age	MEDIAL Age	FINAL Age
m		2	2	3
n		2	2	3
ŋ	(ng) sing	—	3	nt"
p		2	2	4
b		2	2	3
t		2	5	3
d		2	3	4
k		3	3	4
g		3	3	4
r		5	4	4
l		4	4	4
f		3	3	3
v		5	5	4
θ	(th voiceless) thin	5	nt	nt
ɣ	(th voiced) this	5	5	nt
s		5	5	5
z		5	3	3
ʃ	(sh) shoe	5	5	5
ʒ	(zh) measure	nt	5	nt
h		2	nt	—
w		5	nt	—
j	(y) yes	2	2	—
tʃ	(ch) chief	4	5	4
dʒ	(j) just	4	4	6

VOWELS AND DIPHTHONGS

IPA	Conventional		Age
i	Long E	Me	2
ɪ	Short I	Is	4
ɛ	Short E	Met	3
æ	Short A	At	4
ʌ	Short U	Up	2
ə	Schwa	Alone	2
ɑ	Broad A	Father	2
ɔ	Broad O	Off	3
ʊ	Short OO	Look	4
u	Long OO	Moon	2
ju	Long U	Use	3
ou	Long O	Go	2
au	Ou	Out	3
eɪ	Long A	May	4
aɪ	Long I	Ice	3
ɔɪ	OI	Boy	3

CONSONANT BLENDS

Blend	Age	Blend	Age
pr-	5		
br-	5		
tr-	5		
dr-	5	sl-	6
kr-	5	sw-	5
gr-	5	tw-	5
fr-	5	kw-	5
θr-	6	-ŋk	4
pl-	5	-ŋg	5
bl-	5	-mp	3
kl-	5	-nt	4
gl-	5	-nd	6
fl-	5	spr-	5
-ld	6	spl-	5
-lk	5	str-	5
-lf	5	skr-	5
-lv	5	skw-	5
-lz	5	-ns	5
sm-	5	-ps	5
sn-	5	-ts	5
sp-	5	-mz	5
st-	5	-nz	5
-st	6	-ŋz	5
sk-	5	-dz	5
-ks	5	-gz	5

*IPA stands for International Phonetic Alphabet. **Not tested.

See also List 134, Speech Pronunciation.

List 147. ENGLISH SOUNDS NOT USED IN OTHER LANGUAGES

Some sounds are used in English, but are not parts of other languages. Students whose primary language is not English may have difficulty pronouncing words that use these sounds. To master them, students will need to practice recognizing the sounds in words they hear, then pronouncing the sounds.

LANGUAGE	ENGLISH SOUNDS NOT USED IN THE LANGUAGE					
Spanish	dg	j	sh	th	z	
Chinese	b	ch	d	dg	g	oa	sh
	<u>s</u>	th	<u>th</u>	v	z	
French	ch	ee	j	ng	oo	th	<u>th</u>
Greek	aw	ee	i	oo	schwa	
Italian	a	ar	dg	h	i	ng	th
	<u>th</u>	schwa				
Japanese	dg	f	i	th	<u>th</u>	oo	v
	schwa					

List 148. PROBLEM ENGLISH SOUNDS FOR ESL STUDENTS

Some English sounds are difficult for students whose primary language is not English. It will help to practice pronouncing these sounds in initial, medial, and final positions in English words. Use the words in Lists, 8, 9, and 10 for practice.

LANGUAGE	PROBLEM SOUNDS								
Spanish	b	d	dg	h	j	m	n	ng	r	sh
	t	th	v	w	y	z	s-clusters		
	end clusters								
Chinese	b	ch	d	dg	f	g	j	l	m	n	ng
	ō	sh	<u>s</u>	th	<u>th</u>	v	z	l-clusters		
	r-clusters								
French	ā	ch	ē	h	j	ng	oo	oy	s	th
	<u>th</u>	<u>s</u>	schwa						
Italian	a	ar	dg	h	i	ng	th	<u>th</u>	v	schwa
	l-clusters		end clusters						
Japanese	dg	f	h	i	l	th	<u>th</u>	oo	r	sh
	<u>s</u>	v	w	schwa	l-clusters		r-clusters		
Korean	b	l	ō	ow	p	r	sh	t	<u>th</u>
	l-clusters		r-clusters						

See also List 82, Oral Reading Activities; List 134, Speech Pronunciation.

For further information, consult *The ESL Teacher's Book of Lists* (Prentice-Hall, 1993) by Jacqueline Kress.

The Reading Teacher's Book of Lists, Fourth Edition, © 2000 by John Wiley & Sons, Inc.

List 149. STUDENTS' LANGUAGE BACKGROUND

According to the Census Bureau, for nearly 14% of the U.S. population over the age of five—some 31.9 million people—English is not the language they speak at home. This may seem surprising because 25.2 million of these individuals (79%) not only speak their native language but speak English well or very well. Children in many of these households develop competence in both languages as they grow up. In contrast, a nationwide study conducted by the U.S. Department of Education identified the language groups of students who are limited English proficient (LEP). The first table below shows the top twenty languages spoken in American homes. The second table shows the most common language groups of LEP students. Spanish is by far the most frequently spoken other language in either category, accounting for 54% of the non-English home language use and 73% of the language backgrounds of limited English proficient students.

The Reading Teacher's Book of Lists, Fourth Edition, © 2000 by John Wiley & Sons, Inc.

Languages Spoken at Home

1. Spanish	6. Tagalog	11. Japanese	16. Yiddish
2. French	7. Polish	12. Greek	17. Laotian
3. German	8. Korean	13. Arabic	18. Persian
4. Italian	9. Vietnamese	14. Hindi	19. Creole
5. Chinese	10. Portuguese	15. Russian	20. Armenian

Language Groups of LEP Students

1. Spanish	6. Korean	11. Creole	16. Chinese
2. Vietnamese	7. Laotian	12. Arabic	17. Mandarin
3. Hmong	8. Navajo	13. Portuguese	18. Farsi
4. Cantonese	9. Tagalog	14. Japanese	19. Hindi
5. Cambodian	10. Russian	15. Armenian	20. Polish

For additional information, visit the U.S. Census Bureau web site at: www.census.gov or the National Center for Bilingual Education's web site at: www.ncbe.gwu.edu

List 150. PARTS OF SPEECH

Over the centuries that English has been spoken and written, patterns of word usage have developed. These patterns form the grammar or syntax for the language and govern the use of the eight parts of speech.

Noun. A word names a person, place, thing, or idea. It can act or be acted upon.
Examples:
> Roger, Father McGovern, bowlers, cousins, neighborhood, Baltimore, attic, Asia, Newark Airport, Golden Gate Bridge, glove, class, triangle, goodness, strength, joy, perfection

Pronoun. A word that is used in place of a noun.
Examples:
> he, you, they, them, it, her, our, your, its, their, anybody, both, nobody, someone, several, himself, ourselves, themselves, yourself, itself, who, whom, which, what, whose

Adjective. A word that is used to describe a noun or pronoun, telling what kind, how many, or which one.
Examples:
> green, enormous, slinky, original, Italian, some, few, eleven, all, none, that, this, these, those, third

Verb. A word that shows physical or mental action, being, or state of being.
Examples:
> swayed, cowered, dance, study, hold, think, imagine, love, approve, considered, am, is, was, were, has been, seems, appears, looks, feels, remains

Adverb. A word that is used to describe a verb, telling where, how, or when.
Examples:
> quietly, lovingly, skillfully, slyly, honestly, very, quite, extremely, too, moderately, seldom, never, often, periodically, forever

Conjunction. A word that is used to join words or groups of words.
Examples:
> and, or, either, neither, but, because, while, however, since, for

Preposition. A word used to show the relationship of a noun or pronoun to another word.
Examples:
> across, below, toward, within, over, above, before, until, of, beyond, from, during, after, at, against

Interjection. A word that is used alone to express strong emotion.
Examples:
> Heavens! Cheers! Oh! Aha! Darn!

See also List 66, Basic Sentence Patterns; List 67, Build a Sentence.

The Reading Teacher's Book of Lists, Fourth Edition, © 2000 by John Wiley & Sons, Inc.

List 151. IRREGULAR VERB FORMS

Most rules have exceptions, and exceptions can cause problems. Here is an extensive list of verbs and their principal parts that do not follow the regular pattern. (Regular verbs form the past or past participle by simply adding *d* or an *ed*. For example: *call, called, has called*.)

Present	Past	Past Participle*
am	was	been
are (pl.)	were	been
beat	beat	beaten
begin	began	begun
bend	bent or bended	bent or bended
bet	bet	bet
bite	bit	bitten
bleed	bled	bled
blow	blew	blown
break	broke	broken
bring	brought	brought
build	built	built
burst	burst	burst
catch	caught	caught
choose	chose	chosen
come	came	come
cost	cost	cost
creep	crept	crept
cut	cut	cut
dig	dug	dug
dive	dived or dove	dived
do	did	done
draw	drew	drawn
dream	dreamed or dreamt	dreamed or dreamt
drink	drank	drunk
drive	drove	driven
eat	ate	eaten
fall	fell	fallen
feed	fed	fed
feel	felt	felt
fight	fought	fought
fly	flew	flown
forbid	forbade	forbidden
forget	forgot	forgotten
forgive	forgave	forgiven
freeze	froze	frozen

*Note: The past participle also needs one of the following verbs: was, has had, is.

361

Present	Past	Past Participle
get	got	got or gotten
give	gave	given
go	went	gone
grow	grew	grown
grind	ground	ground
hang	hung or hanged	hung
has	had	had
hear	heard	heard
hide	hid	hidden
hold	held	held
hurt	hurt	hurt
is	was	has been
keep	kept	kept
kneel	kneeled or knelt	kneeled or knelt
know	knew	known
lay	laid	laid
leap	leaped or leapt	leaped or leapt
leave	left	left
lend	lent	lent
let	let	let
lie	lay	lain
light	lit	lit
lose	lost	lost
make	made	made
mean	meant	meant
mow	mowed	mowed or mown
put	put	put
read	read	read
ride	rode	ridden
ring	rang	rung
rise	rose	risen
run	ran	run
saw	sawed	sawed or sawn
say	said	said
see	saw	seen
sell	sold	sold
set	set	set
sew	sewed	sewed or sewn
shake	shook	shaken
shed	shed	shed
shine	shined or shone	shined or shone
shoot	shot	shot
show	showed	shown or showed
shrink	shrank or shrunk	shrunk

Present	Past	Past Participle
shut	shut	shut
sing	sang	sung
sink	sank	sunk
sit	sat	sat
sleep	slept	slept
slide	slid	slid
sow	sowed	sowed or sown
speak	spoke	spoken
spend	spent	spent
spin	spun	spun
spit	spit	spit
split	split	split
spread	spread	spread
spring	sprang or sprung	sprung
stand	stood	stood
steal	stole	stolen
stick	stuck	stuck
sting	stung	stung
strike	struck	struck
string	strung	strung
swear	swore	sworn
sweat	sweat or sweated	sweat or sweated
sweep	swept	swept
swim	swam or swum	swum
swing	swung or swang	swung
take	took	taken
teach	taught	taught
tear	tore	torn
tell	told	told
think	thought	thought
throw	threw	thrown
understand	understood	understood
wake	woke or waked	woken or waked
wear	wore	worn
weave	wove	woven
weep	wept	wept
wet	wet	wet
win	won	won
wind	wound	wound
write	wrote	written

See also List 66, Basic Sentence Patterns.

The Reading Teacher's Book of Lists, Fourth Edition, © 2000 by John Wiley & Sons, Inc.

List 152. PROVERBS

Proverbs are common, wise, or thoughtful sayings that are short and often applicable to different situations. Every culture and language has its own, from the ancient Chinese Confucian "A picture is worth a thousand words" to the American "A stitch in time saves nine." You and your students might enjoy adding to this collection. Proverbs can also be used as prompts for writing assignments, or you may want to ask your students to complete the end of a proverb. Don't be surprised if the result is humorous. For example, one teacher reported that her first grader completed "A penny saved is . . . " with "not much."

Relationships

A friend in need is a friend indeed.

Absence makes the heart grow fonder.

All's fair in love and war.

Better to have loved and lost than never to have loved at all.

Familiarity breeds contempt.

Good fences make good neighbors.

If you can't beat them, join them.

Like father, like son.

Love will find a way.

Marry in haste, repent at leisure.

Misery loves company.

Short visits make long friends.

Action and Determination

A faint heart never won a fair lady.

A quitter never wins and a winner never quits.

A rolling stone gathers no moss.

A stitch in time saves nine.

Actions speak louder than words.

All things come to those who wait.

Confession is good for the soul.

He/She who hesitates is lost.

He/She who sits on the fence is easily blown off.

If you can't stand the heat, get out of the kitchen.

If you want something done, ask a busy person.

Leave no stone unturned.

Make hay while the sun shines.

Never put off 'til tomorrow what you can do today.

No pain, no gain.

Sometimes you have to run just to stay in place.

Strike while the iron is hot.

When the going gets tough, the tough get going.

Where there's a will, there's a way.

Caution

Better safe than sorry.

Don't cross the bridge until you come to it.

Forewarned is forearmed.

Haste makes waste.

Learn to walk before you run.

Look before you leap.

Waste not, want not.

Encouragement

Every cloud has a silver lining.

The darkest hour is just before the dawn.

The first step is the most difficult.

Appearances

Beauty is in the eye of the beholder.

Beauty is only skin deep.

The grass is always greener on the other side.

You can't tell a book by its cover.

Good Deeds

Charity begins at home.

Civility costs nothing.

Do right and fear no one.

Do unto others as you would have them do unto you.

Give credit where credit is due.

The Reading Teacher's Book of Lists, Fourth Edition, © 2000 by John Wiley & Sons, Inc.

Great oaks from little acorns grow.

One good turn deserves another.

To err is human; to forgive, divine.

Two wrongs don't make a right.

Words

A picture is worth a thousand words.

A soft answer turneth away wrath.

A tongue is worth little without a brain.

A word spoken is not an action done.

Ask a silly question and you get a silly answer.

Ask no question and hear no lies.

Bad news travels fast.

Brevity is the soul of wit.

Sticks and stones may break my bones but names can never hurt me.

Still waters run deep.

The pen is mightier than the sword.

The squeaky wheel gets the grease.

There's many a slip between cup and lip.

Animals

A bird in the hand is worth two in the bush.

Birds of a feather flock together.

Curiosity killed the cat.

Don't change horses in midstream.

Don't count your chickens before they're hatched.

Let sleeping dogs lie.

One camel doesn't make fun of another camel's hump.

The early bird catches the worm.

When the cat's away, the mice will play.

You can lead a horse to water but you can't make it drink.

You can't teach an old dog new tricks.

Money

A fool and his/her money is soon parted.

A penny saved is a penny earned.

All that glitters is not gold.

Early to bed, early to rise makes a man/woman healthy, wealthy, and wise.

He/She who pays the piper calls the tune.

Lend your money and lose your friend.

Money burns a hole in your pocket.

They who dance must pay the fiddler.

Time is money.

Food

An apple a day keeps the doctor away.

Don't cry over spilt milk.

Half a loaf is better than none.

He/She who would eat the fruit must climb the tree.

Honey catches more flies than vinegar.

The apple never falls far from the tree.

The proof of the pudding is in the eating.

There's no such thing as a free lunch.

Too many cooks spoil the broth.

You can't have your cake and eat it too.

Miscellaneous

A good beginning makes a good ending.

A house divided cannot stand.

A hovel on the rock is better than a palace on the sand.

A little knowledge is a dangerous thing.

A rising tide lifts all boats.

A watched pot never boils.

Adversity makes strange bedfellows.

All good things come to an end.

An idle brain is the devil's workshop.

Beggars can't be choosers.

Better late than never.

Different strokes for different folks.

Don't get mad—get even.

Everybody's business is nobody's business.

Experience is the father/mother of wisdom.

Fact is stranger than fiction.

Fool me once, shame on you. Fool me twice, shame on me.

For every joy there is a price to be paid.

He/She gives twice who gives quickly.

He/She who lives by the sword, dies by the sword.

If it isn't broken, don't fix it.

If the shoe fits, wear it.

If you're not part of the solution, you're part of the problem.

Imitation is the sincerest form of flattery.

Many hands make light work.

Never is a long time.

Out of sight, out of mind.

People who live in glass houses shouldn't throw stones.

Politics make strange bedfellows.

The best laid plans of mice and men often go astray.

The best things come in small packages.

The bigger they are, the harder they fall.

The hand that rocks the cradle rules the world.

The nut doesn't reveal the tree it contains.

The shoemaker's children always go barefoot.

Two heads are better than one.

What goes around, comes around.

You can have too much of a good thing.

You cannot get blood from a stone.

The Reading Teacher's Book of Lists, Fourth Edition, © 2000 by John Wiley & Sons, Inc.

See also List 153, Common Word Idioms; List 154, Idiomatic Expressions.

List 153. COMMON WORD IDIOMS

Many idioms are formed around common words. Use this list as a starter for exploring American idioms.

all	all along, all at once, all but, all ears, all eyes, all hours, all in all, all out, all over, all set, all systems go, all there, all thumbs, all wet
back	back down, back out, back up, back and forth, back off, back street, backseat driver, back to the salt mines
beat	beat around the bush, beats all, beat down, beat it, beat the band, beat the bushes, beat someone to the punch, beat up
blow	blow a fuse, blow hot and cold, blow your own horn, blow out, blow one's mind, blow one's lines, blow over, blow the whistle, blow up, blow the lid off
break	break down, break in, break into, break one's promise, break out, break the ice, break the news, break up, break even, break ground, break one's heart, break one's neck, break through
bring	bring about, bring around, bring down the house, bring (something) home to one, bring home the bacon, bring in, bring off, bring on, bring one to do something, bring out, bring up
burn	burn one's bridges, burn one's fingers, burn out, burn rubber, burn the candle at both ends, burn the midnight oil, burn up
call	call a halt, call a spade a spade, call attention to, call for, call forth, call in, call names, call on, call out, call up, call a strike, call it quits, call it a day, call the shots, call to order
catch	catch cold, catch fire, catch on, catch one's breath, catch one's eye, catch up
come	come about, come again, come alive, come a long way, come back, come by, come clean, come across, come around, come down on, come in for, come into, come into your own, come off, come off it, come out, come to pass, come up, come up to, come upon, come-on, come over, come to, come through, come to think of it
cut	cut across, cut corners, cut in, cut out, cut someone out, cut out for, cut up, cut into, cut off, cut the mustard
do	do away with, do justice for, do for, do in, do someone proud, do out of, do up, do well by someone, do without, do the honors, do away with
eat	eat away, eat humble pie, eat crow, eat like a bird, eat like a horse, eat dirt, eat someone out of house and home, eat your heart out, eat your words, eat your hat, eat out of your hand, eat it up
fall	fall by the wayside, fall down, fall flat, fall for, fall in with, fall out, fall over each other, fall short, fall through, fall behind, fall back on, fall over backwards, fall head over heels
get	get along, get at, get away with, bet back at, get carried away by, get even with, get in with, get into, get on, get on someone's nerves, get your back up, get someone's goat, get out of, get over, get the better of, get the hang of, get up, get wind of, get across, get ahead, get around to, get cracking, get lost, get off the ground, get one's feet wet, get the ax, get the show on the road, get up and go

The Reading Teacher's Book of Lists, Fourth Edition, © 2000 by John Wiley & Sons, Inc.

367

give	give a damn, give away, give in, give of, give out, give up, give a hand, give oneself up, give up the ship
go	go all out, go by, go down, go easy, go far, go for, go in for, go into, go off the deep end, go on, go one better, go out, go over, go to the dogs, go with, go without, go ahead, go back on a promise, go broke, go fly a kite, go haywire, go it along, go like clockwork
hang	hang around, hang on, hang out, hang up, hang in there, hang ten
have	have it both ways, have it coming, have it in for someone, have it out with someone, have a heart, have had it, have it made
hit	hit your stride, hit the books, hit the ceiling, hit the roof, hit the hay, hit the sack, hit the headlines, hit the high points, hit the nail on the head, hit upon, hit bottom, hit and run, hit it off, hit the road, hit the jackpot, hit the spot, hit the bull's eye
hold	hold a candle to, hold forth, hold on, hold down, hold back, hold everything, hold your fire, hold out, hold up, hold the fort, hold your own
keep	keep a straight face, keep company, keep on, keep your head, keep your head above water, keep your word, keep the pot boiling, keep the wolf from the door, keep up, keep up appearances, keep up with, keep it down, keep one's chin up, keep one's nose clean, keep track, keep one's fingers crossed
lay	lay a finger on someone, lay aside, lay down one's life, lay down the law, lay hands on, lay it on, lay off, lay your hand on something, lay yourself open to, lay out, lay up, lay low, lay to rest
let	let off steam, let on, let your hair down, let sleeping dogs lie, let the cat out of the bag, let up, let down, let go of
look	look down on, look down your nose at, look for, look into, look out, look up, look up to someone, look after, look back, look over
make	make a move, make a play for, make certain, make something do, make ends meet, make fun of, make good, make haste, make heads or tails of something, make believe, make a point, make friends, make sense of, make it, make out, make over, makeshift, make sure, make the fur fly, make the grade, make up, make up for, make up your mind, make up to
play	play at something, play down, play fast and loose, play havoc with, play hooky, play into someone's hands, play on, play second fiddle, play the devil, play the fool, play the game, play by ear, play along with, play off, play possum, play the field, play up to, play with fire
pull	pull a fast one, pull off, pull your weight, pull strings, pull through, pull to pieces, pull together, pull up, pull the wool over your eyes, pull up stakes, pull rank, pull together, pull the rug out from under
put	put away, put an end to, put in one's place, put one's foot down, put it on the map, put someone on, put to bed, put to use, put down, put forward, put in for, put off, put on, put your cards on the table, put out, put right, put two and two together, put up, put up with
run	run across, run into, run away, run down, run afoul of, run in, run out of, run over, run ragged, run rings around, run through, run the risk of, run away with, run short, run wild

The Reading Teacher's Book of Lists, Fourth Edition, © 2000 by John Wiley & Sons, Inc.

see   see about, see eye to eye, see into, see through, see to, see daylight, see off, see red, see to it

sit   sit on, sit on the fence, sit out, sit pretty, sit tight, sit up, sit back, sit-in, sit tight

take   take aim, take after, take a bath, take advantage of, take in, take by surprise, take by storm, take effect, take a back seat, take a powder, take care, take it easy, take someone for, take for granted, take heart, take ill, take in, take issue, take it from me, take it hard, take it into your head, take it out on someone, take something lying down, take note of, take off, take on, take your time, take out, take over, take the cake, take to heart, take the trouble, take it upon yourself, take a breath

throw   throw a curve, throw one's hat in the ring, throw the book at, throw cold water on, throw a fit, throw a party, throw in the sponge, throw light on, throw off, throw one's weight around, throw out, throw up

turn   turn a cold shoulder to, turn color, turn off, turn one's stomach, turn the clock back, turn the tide, turn thumbs down, turn over a new leaf, turn a deaf ear, turn down, turn in, turn loose, turn on, turn your head, turn out, turn over, turn the tables on someone, turn to, turn turtle, turn up

See also List 60, Descriptive Words; List 154, Idiomatic Expressions.

List 154. IDIOMATIC EXPRESSIONS

Idiomatic expressions cannot be understood from the literal meanings of their words. Instead, these colorful phrases must be "translated." Idiomatic expressions are often used in conversation and informal writing; however, most are not suitable for formal writing. Students who are learning the English language find idiomatic expressions particularly troublesome. Teach the expressions just as you would teach single vocabulary words.

Amanda was happy she was on the last leg of her long trip home.

I could tell by the expression on his face that he had something up his sleeve.

After winning the championship, the soccer team got the red-carpet treatment.

There wasn't much work to do and so we sat around shooting the breeze.

Classical music isn't my cup of tea.

Jim was so tired he decided to call it a day.

She stuck her neck out and ended up losing her job.

Nan bent over backwards to please her mother.

Nunzio bought the used bicycle for a song.

Although Susan paid a lot for her new stereo, it turned out to be a lemon.

Liz was so grouchy we knew she had gotten up on the wrong side of the bed.

The young couple was really struggling to make ends meet.

After receiving a good report card, I felt like a million dollars.

Because he was such a good student, Alan's teacher went to bat for him when it came time for giving the award for best student.

She was so angry with me that she jumped down my throat.

You could tell by his beautiful garden that he had a green thumb.

She was skating on thin ice when she promised to get all A's on her report card.

Even though he was taking vitamins, Jonathan caught a bad cold.

Nikoli was down in the dumps after losing the game.

Anthony lost his temper for no reason.

When she finally admitted that she had made a mistake, it was a relief to get it off her chest.

He was so young, he was hardly wet behind his ears.

The solution to the problem was as plain as the nose on his face.

The new movie was for the birds. I could barely stand to stay until the end.

She was so serious I couldn't get her to crack a smile.

You could count on her to dot all the i's and cross all the t's.

Once we got the ball rolling, everyone joined in.

He was so excited about his new basketball shoes that he was on cloud nine.

Althea drove a hard bargain and ended up with a good deal.

He didn't know the ropes and there was no one willing to help him.

Jason has tennis on the brain.

We each coughed up five dollars and bought her a gift.

We were all excited about getting to see the hot new video.

Learning to use the new software was a piece of cake.

We all need to stick together.

Unfortunately, money talks.

The Reading Teacher's Book of Lists, Fourth Edition, © 2000 by John Wiley & Sons, Inc.

He paid through the nose for those front-row seats.

I can't go to the movies today but I'll take a rain check.

The fact that I can't remember his name is really eating me.

If you can just hang on a little longer, I'm almost ready to leave.

All the students in the school were pretty much in the same boat.

Drop me a line when you arrive.

The young girl stole the spotlight.

There's only a slim chance he will make the team.

I hear through the grapevine that Nancy has won first prize.

It was getting dark and so we decided to call it a day.

They were running neck and neck in the election.

She's so slow it takes her forever and a day to answer the phone.

The team really stuck together and ended up winning.

Kim Li's new car hugged the road as it took the curve.

I got cold feet when it came my time to make my speech.

He was mistaken and so I set him straight.

The solution to my problem finally dawned on me.

He was dead to the world the minute he hit the bed.

I have to get up early, so it's time to hit the hay.

The Reading Teacher's Book of Lists, Fourth Edition, © 2000 by John Wiley & Sons, Inc.

See also List 153, Common Word Idioms.

List 155. CLIPPED WORDS

These are words that have been shortened or clipped by common use, as in *sub* for *submarine*. This shortening is called Zipf's Principle and is well known in the study of languages.

ad	advertisement	memo	memorandum
auto	automobile	miss	mistress
bike	bicycle	mod	modern
burger	hamburger	movie	moving picture
bus	omnibus	mum	chrysanthemum
bust	burst	pants	pantaloons
cab	cabriolet	pen	penitentiary
canter	Canterbury gallop	pep	pepper
cent	centum	perk	percolate
champ	champion	perk	perquisite
chemist	alchemist	phone	telephone
clerk	cleric	photo	photograph
coed	coeducational student	pike	turnpike
con	convict	plane	airplane
copter	helicopter	pop	popular
cuke	cucumber	prof	professor
curio	curiosity	prom	promenade
deb	debutante	ref	referee
doc	doctor	scram	scramble
dorm	dormitory	specs	spectacles
drape	drapery	sport	disport
exam	examination	stat	statistics
fan	fanatic	stereo	stereophonic
flu	influenza	still	distill
fridge	refrigerator	sub	submarine
gab	gabble	tails	coattails
gas	gasoline	taxi	taxicab
grad	graduate	teen	teenager
gym	gymnasium	tie	necktie
hack	hackney	trig	trigonometry
iron	flatiron	trump	triumph
lab	laboratory	tux	tuxedo
limo	limousine	typo	typographical error
lube	lubricate	van	caravan
lunch	luncheon	varsity	university
margarine	oleomargarine	vet	veteran
mart	market	vet	veterinarian
math	mathematics	wig	periwig
mend	amend	zoo	zoological garden

The Reading Teacher's Book of Lists, Fourth Edition, © 2000 by John Wiley & Sons, Inc.

See also List 176, Common Abbreviations.

List 156. WORDS WITH MULTIPLE MEANINGS

Many words have several meanings. Here are some of the more common ones.

arms
He placed the child in her mother's *arms*.
The rebels needed to buy *arms* to fight the war.

ball
The *ball* rolled under the table.
The women wore their prettiest dresses to the *ball*.

bank
You can cash your check at the *bank*.
We had a picnic on the *bank* of the river.

bark
Did you hear the dog *bark*?
The *bark* on the old tree is dry and brittle.

bat
A *bat* flew from the barn and frightened me.
The children played with the *bat* and ball.

bit
Jenn checked the *bit* in the horse's mouth.
I *bit* into the apple.
It will take just a *bit* longer.

blow
The wind began to *blow*, and the leaves fell.
The *blow* to his head knocked the fighter out.

bridge
We crossed the *bridge* over the Raritan River.
Bridge is a card game for four people.

case
She put her eyeglasses in their *case*.
The lawyer won her first *case*.

compound
The soldiers surrounded the enemy *compound*.
A *compound* sentence is made of two clauses.

count
The duke, *count*, and earl received awards.
The child is learning to *count* from one to ten.

cue
The actor missed his *cue* and did not say his line.
He held the *cue* steady and aimed at the eight-ball.

date
Bill asked Sally for a *date*.
Today's *date* is March 28.

fair
The weather was *fair* on the day of the race.
The judge's decision was *fair*.
We went on the rides at the *fair*.

fan
David is a baseball *fan*; he never misses a game.
It's very warm; please, turn on the *fan*.

file
Put your papers in the *file*.
The children marched in a single *file*.
The prisoner used a *file* to cut the metal bar.

firm
When he finished college, he joined a law *firm*.
Apples should be *firm*, not soft.

fold	*Fold* your paper in half. The girl took care of the sheep in the *fold*.
game	It sounded exciting, so I was *game* to try it. Poker is his favorite card *game*.
hide	The belts were made from the *hide* of a cow. I usually *hide* the gifts for the children's birthdays.
grave	There was no laughter on the *grave* occasion. The coffin was lowered into the *grave*.
hold	The sailors put their supplies into the ship's *hold*. *Hold* the string or the balloon will drift away.
jam	I tried to *jam* one more coat into the full closet. We put strawberry *jam* on our toast. We were stuck in a traffic *jam* for an hour.
kind	What *kind* of ice cream do you like? She was always *kind* and gentle.
last	I hope this will *last* until Tuesday. The *last* time I saw her she was very thin.
like	A briefcase is *like* a bookbag. I *like* fudge cookies.
line	We stood in *line* to get tickets. Write your name on the *line*.
long	I *long* to go to a quiet beach. How *long* is the story?
mean	What did you *mean* when you said that? He was *mean* and unkind. We calculated the *mean* score for the two teams.
mine	The silver ore is brought out of the *mine* in carts. Put you chair next to *mine*.
miss	*Miss* Sims is the new biology teacher. I will *miss* you when you move to the city.
net	The fish were caught in the *net*, not on hooks. After we paid the taxes, our *net* pay was $300.
pen	The pigs live in a *pen*. Sign your name with this *pen*.
present	John was absent on Friday, not *present*. For her birthday, Jill received a *present* from Kaneesha.
press	The editor and other members of the *press* took notes. Ask the tailor to *press* this skirt. *Press* the button to start the machine.
rare	I like my steak *rare*, not well done. Only three people have ever owned this *rare* coin.
rest	Anna will do the *rest* of the shopping. After the long walk up the hill, I wanted to *rest*.

The Reading Teacher's Book of Lists, Fourth Edition, © 2000 by John Wiley & Sons, Inc.

The Reading Teacher's Book of Lists, Fourth Edition, © 2000 by John Wiley & Sons, Inc.

second	There are sixty *seconds* in a minute. I was *second* today, but tomorrow I might be first.
sole	I ordered the *sole* for lunch because I like fish. He was the *sole* survivor of the crash. There was a hole in the *sole* of his shoe.
spell	The child learned to *spell* his name. The witch put a magic *spell* on the tree.
stable	Put the horses in the *stable*. He may leave the hospital if his breathing is *stable*.
stick	The glue was dried, and the stamp would not *stick*. We collected *sticks* and leaves for the fire.
story	This is a five-*story* building. Tell the children a bedtime *story*.
temple	He took two aspirin for the pain in his *temple*. The men walked to the *temple* to pray.
tick	*Ticks* are insects that spread Lyme's disease. Can you hear the clock *tick*?
tire	I never *tire* of hearing my favorite music. I had a flat *tire* on my new car.
vault	The athlete *vaulted* the six-foot barrier with ease. The actress put her diamond jewelry in the *vault*.
wake	Be quiet or you will *wake* the baby. The waves in the *wake* of the speedboat were very high.
well	I feel very *well* today. The boy put the bucket into the *well* to get water.
will	The lawyer wrote a *will* for the old man before he died. I *will* see the man tomorrow, not today.
yard	A *yard* is equal to thirty-six inches. We had a picnic in the *yard*.

See also List 16, Homophones; List 18, Homographs and Heteronyms.

375

List 157. DAILY LIVING WORDS

Words are all around us. Those listed below are part of the American daily living experience. Use these words in literacy education for new and native speakers of English, students with special educational needs, and young students. Check students' comprehension of key survival words like "flammable," "acid," and "combustible."

accident
acid
admission
alarm
ambulance
apartment
ATM
bakery
bank
beauty shop
breakfast
bus
bus stop
cab
cable
cafeteria
cancel
car
cash
caution
cell phone
charge
check
child
children
church
cigarettes
clean
cleaners
close door
closed
closet
clothes
cold
cold drinks
collect
combustible
confidential
computer
coupon
credit cards
customer service

danger
day care
delicatessen
delivery
dentist
deposit
destination
diner
dinner
directions
discount
do not bend
do not drink
do not place near heat
do not swallow
doctor
don't walk
down
driver
drug store
drugs
dryer
due
east
electric
elevator
emergency
employer
enter
entrance
exit
explosives
fast food
female
fire
fire escape
fire exit
fire hose
firefighter
first aid
first class
flammable

follow signs
food
fragile
free
fuel
garage
gas
gentlemen
glass
grocery store
hair salon
handle with care
hardware
harmful if swallowed
help
help wanted
hospital
hot
hotel
husband
information
insert coins
job
keep off
keep out
keep refrigerated
ladies
laundry
lease
license number
lights
local
lost
lunch
M.D.
male
manager
map
married
medicine
Miss
money

The Reading Teacher's Book of Lists, Fourth Edition, © 2000 by John Wiley & Sons, Inc.

money order
Mr.
Mrs.
Ms.
newspapers
no admittance
no smoking
no trespassing
north
northbound
notice
nurse
one way
open
operator
order
out
out of order
oxygen
parking
passengers
payment
pedestrians
perishable
phone
pick-up
poison
police
post office
press
price

private
public parking
pull
push
quiet
radio
railroad
receipt
refund
rent
repair service
reservations
reserved
rest rooms
restaurant
rinse
sale
sales tax
schedule
school
self-service
sick
size
skills
smoking prohibited
south
southbound
spouse
stairs
stairway
state

stop
store
straight ahead
subway
supermarket
supper
swim at your own risk
tax
telephone
television
this way
ticket
timetable
toll
total
train
train station
use other door
walk
warm
warning
wash
watch your step
water
weekday
west
wife
withdrawal
women
work

See also List 158, Travel Words; List 159, Application Words; List 160, Work Words.

List 158. TRAVEL WORDS

Traveling is part of earning a living, visiting friends, exploring the world. Many students eagerly look forward to the day they will qualify for a driver's license. Mastering this list will help students pass the test and navigate the roadways.

alternate route
bike route
bridge freezes before road
bridge may be slippery
bridge out
cattle Xing
caution
children crossing
congested ahead
construction ahead
curve
dangerous curve
dangerous intersection
dead end
deer Xing
detour
dip
divided highway
do not block
do not drive
do not enter
do not pass
emergency parking only
end one way
entrance
exit
express lane
expressway
falling rock
four-way stop
freeway
fuel
gasoline
go slow
hidden driveway
highway ends
hill—trucks use lowest gear
hospital zone
information center
inspection
insurance

intersection
interstate
junction
keep right (left)
lane ends
left lane must turn
local traffic only
low clearance
mechanic on duty
men working
merge
merging traffic
minimum speed
motor vehicle
narrow bridge
no idling
no left (right) turn
no motorcycles
no parking
no passing zone
no right turn on red
no shoulder
no standing
no stopping
no thoroughfare
no trucks
no turns
no U turn
north
not a through street
one way
parkway
pass with care
pedestrian crossing
private road
railroad crossing
ramp
rest area
resume speed
roadside table
route

runaway truck ramp
safe speed
school crossing
school zone
service area
signal ahead
slippery when wet
slow ahead
slow traffic keep right
soft shoulder
speed limit 60 mph
steep grade
tailgate
through traffic keep right
tow-away zone
traffic ahead
truck crossing
turnpike use next exit
two-way traffic ahead
visitor's center
winding road
wrong way
yield

The Reading Teacher's Book of Lists, Fourth Edition, © 2000 by John Wiley & Sons, Inc.

See also List 157, Daily Living Words; List 159, Application Words; List 160, Work Words.

List 159. APPLICATION WORDS

Filling out applications for special programs, jobs, and services is part of everyone's life. This list will help students be ready to fill-in-the-blanks confidently. These words are a must for older language learners as well.

Elementary

address	date of birth	male	P.M.
age	driver's license	Miss	previous
A.M.	education	month/day/year	primary
applicant	elementary school	mother	print
attending	emergency	Mr.	rent
awards	employer	Mrs.	resident
beginner	father	Ms.	school
birth certificate	female	municipality	sex
birth date	first choice	name (last, first)	signature
brother(s)	health insurance	next of kin	sister(s)
carefully	height	nickname	Social Security
children	high school	notification	number
citizen	home	own	state
city	honors	per week	telephone
college	husband	permanent	weight
country	in full	personal	wife
county	language	phone	work
current	list	physician	year
date	location		ZIP Code

Intermediate

ability to learn	exemptions	license plate	shift
academic history	experience	list in order	sick leave
application	extension	maiden name	signature
apply in person	fringe benefits	married	single
available immedi-	full-time	mature	Social Security card
ately	graduated	NOK (next of kin)	Social Security
bonus	health plan	overtime	number
certificate	health provider	part-time	special skills
chronological	hobbies	passport	status
claim form	human resources	pension plan	temporary
compensation	identification	permanent	trainees
department	immigration	personal day	union
dependents	incentive	personal statement	vacation
divorced	income	personnel	visa
DOB	inexperienced	preference	vita
dues	insurance	prior experience	voluntary
earn	interns	references	volunteer
eligible	internships	résumé	widow
employment	landlord	salary	widower
equal opportunity	license	seniority	withholding
ethnicity			work history

See also List 157, Daily Living Words; List 158, Travel Words; List 160, Work Words.

The Reading Teacher's Book of Lists, Fourth Edition, © 2000 by John Wiley & Sons, Inc.

List 160. WORK WORDS

These meaningful words and phrases help adults and adolescents improve their reading and writing skills so they can obtain better employment.

DANGER WORDS I

Acid
Caution
Combustible
Danger
High Voltage
Keep Out
Live Power Supply
Radioactive
Explosives
Do Not Close
Do Not Drink
Do Not Place Near Heat
Electrical Outlet
Extend Hose Completely
  Before Opening Valves
Flammable
For Fire Use Only
Fuel
Gas
Harmful if Swallowed
No Admittance
No Trespassing
Oxygen
Poison
Private Property
Stop
Walk
Warning

DANGER WORDS II

Alarm
Arrested
Aspirin
Break Glass
Close Door
Danger Below This Line
Do Not Use
Down

Emergency Exit Only
Fire Escape
Fire Hose
For Burns
Hot
No Smoking
Not for Electrical Fire
One Way
Open Door Out
Pedestrians
Proceed at Your Own Risk
Railroad (R.R.)
Smoking Prohibited
Swim at Your Own Risk
This Way Out

DANGER WORDS III

Blasting
Keep Away
Danger—Slow
Do Not Clean or Oil
  Machinery While in
  Motion
Do Not Close Switch
Do Not Get off While in
  Motion
Do Not Open Valve
Do Not Operate Without
  Guards
Do Not Stand Up
Do Not Use This Machine
Do Not Wear Loose
  Clothing or Gloves
  Around Machines
Don't Stand Above This
  Line
Equipment Must Not Be
  Taken Within 10' of
  Electric Lines
Fire Exit Only

Break Glass
Open Door
Keep Fingers out of Meat
  Grinder—Use Tamper
Keep Your Hands and Arms
  Within Sides of Car
Only Regular Machine
  Operator Allowed to Use
  Machine
Open Truck
Report Dangerous
  Conditions at Once
Stairway
Stay Clear of Moving Cars
Stop—Blow Horn
Proceed with Caution
This Is an Empty Elevator
  Shaftway
Truck Crossing
Watch Out for Persons
  Below
Your Eyes Are Priceless—
  Wear Proper Protection

ROAD SIGNS I

Children Crossing
Divided Highway Ends
Do Not Drive
Do Not Enter
Do Not Pass
Driveway Ahead
Keep Right
Left Lane Must Turn Left
Low Clearance 10 Feet
Low Shoulder
Merging Traffic
Minimum Speed
No Left Turn
Pass with Care
Railroad Crossing

The Reading Teacher's Book of Lists, Fourth Edition, © 2000 by John Wiley & Sons, Inc.

Safe Speed 15 mph
School Crossing
School Zone
Shoulder Work Ahead
Slippery When Wet
Slow Ahead
Slow Traffic
Keep Right
Soft Shoulder
Two-Way Traffic Ahead
Yield

ROAD SIGNS II

Bridge May Be Slippery
Dead End
Detour Ahead
End Construction
End One Way
Express Lane
Highway Ends
Narrow Bridge
No Thoroughfare
No Trucks
No Turns
Pavement Ends
Ramp
Roadside Table
Route
Signal Ahead
Signal Set for 35 mph
Speed Zone Ahead
Speed Limit 50 mph
Through Traffic Keep Right
Traffic Ahead
Truck Crossing
Trucks Use Right Lane
Turnpike Use Next Exit

SIGNS I

Alcohol
Burns
Do Not Close
Do Not Smoke
Drinking Water

Enter
Falling Rock
First Aid
Gentlemen
Glass
Information
Keep Refrigerated
Key
Ladies
Men
Not Allowed
Not Permitted
Out of Order
Perishable
Reset Safety Switch
Shut Off Valve
Turn Bottom
Walk on Left
Water
Women

SIGNS II

Bus
Cab
Do Not Bend
East (E.)
Elevator
Follow Signs
Fragile
Handle with Care
Keep Door Closed
Keep Flat
Lay Flat
Men Working
No Exchange
North (N.)
Passengers
Pull
Push
This End Up
This Side Up
Turn Off Engine
Use No Hooks
Watch for Signal

Watch Your Step
West (W.)

SIGNS III

All the Way Down
Apply Pressure
Automatic
Call
Cleaners
Cold
Cool
Delivery
Deposit a Quarter and
   Dime or Two Nickels
Deposit 10¢ in Coin
Dimes Only
Entrance Gate
Fold Back
Hospital Zone
Inch
Insert Coins
No Storage
Operator
Per Couple
Press Button
Self-Service
Straight Ahead
Use Other Door
Wash
Warm

SIGNS IV

Bath
Check Your Valuables
Cook
Customer Must Present
   Identification
Fifth Floor
Fold on Dotted Line
Free
Inside Front Cover
Lights
Lock Door
Main Door
Lobby

The Reading Teacher's Book of Lists, Fourth Edition, © 2000 by John Wiley & Sons, Inc.

Next Counter
Next Exit
Notice
Not Responsible
Damaged Merchandise
Please Do Not Touch
Public Parking
Refrigerator
Reset Cycle
Take Your Seat
Tear at Perforations
Tickets
Toll
Use Key

SIGNS V

Bakery
Beauty Shop
Breakfast Being Served
Cafeteria
Cleaners
Closet
Dance
Delicatessen
Dentist
Discount Drugs
Garage
Hardware
Laundry
M.D.
Nurse
Pick Up
Purchase Price
Repair Service
Rinse
Sale
Tavern
Taxi
Telephone
Tobacco
Wash

WANT ADS I

Ability to Learn
Apply in Person

Available Immediately
Beginner
Call
Certificate
Department
Eligible
Employment
Evening (Eve.)
Inexperienced
License
Manager
Mature
Office (Off)
Over 21 Years of Age
Personnel
Phone
Post Office Box (P.O.)
Trainees

WANT ADS II

Assemblers
Assist
Attendant
Automotive Machine
Cook
Counterman
Driver
Factory (Facty)
Food Service Helper
Hospital
Janitor
Maid
Maintenance
Painters
Production Workers
Rotating Shift
Second Relief
Stock Man
Trucking
Warehouseman
Waitress

WANT ADS III

Blue Cross
Blue Shield

Bonus
Company Benefits
Compensation
Earn
Equal Opportunities
Fringe Benefits
Forty-Hour Week
Full Time
Incentive Plan
Life Insurance
Overtime
Paid Vacation
Part Time
Pension Plan
Per Hour
Positions
Sick Leave
Steady Income
Working Conditions

GROCERY AND DRUG I

Aspirin
Bayer
St. Joseph
Baby Food
Baking Powder
Bread
Butter
Cellophane
Cereal
Chocolate
Corn
Crackers
Dozen
Eggs
Flour
Gallons
Jello
Juice
Junior
Laxatives
Margarine
Net Weight
Noodles
Orange

Ounces (oz)
Pancake Mix
Peas
Pepper
Strained

GROCERY AND DRUG II

Pint
Potatoes
Pounds (lbs)
Quart (qt)
Rice
Salt
Sanitary Napkins
Sausage
Shortening
Soap
Soda
Soup
String Beans
Sugar
Tablespoon
Tablets
Teaspoon
Tincture of Iodine
Tincture of Mercury
Tissues
Turkey
Vanilla
Vegetable Oil
Vegetables
Vinegar

MENUS

Cheeseburger
Chicken Noodle
Grilled Cheese
Ham and Cheese
Hamburger
Hoagies
Meat Ball
Pork Roll
Steak
Tuna
Vegetable

Beans
Chicken
Choice of Two Vegetables
Cole Slaw
Fish and Chips
French Fries
Mashed Potatoes
Peas
Pizza
Pork Chops
Roast Beef
Turkey
Coffee
Cola
Iced Tea
Milk
Milk Shake
Tea

INCOME TAX

If Filing Joint Return
First Names
Middle Initials
Spouse's
Check One
Married Filing Joint Return
Married Filing Separately
Enter Total Wages
Tips
Interest
Dividends
Total Income Tax from Tax Table
Total Federal Income Tax Withheld
Larger Than
Balance Due
Refund
Dependent's Support
Amount Furnished
If Filing 100% Write "All"
Sign Here
Both Must Sign
Initials—Middle
Interest

Joint Return
Larger Than
Married
Withholding Allowances
Attached Certificate
Deductions Allowed
Exemptions
Itemized Deductions

CREDIT TERMS

Badge
Bank Balance
Business Phone
Extension
Checking Account
Contract Expires
Draft Status
Driver's License
Excluding Overtime
Finance Company
Account
Furniture Value
Address of School
How Long
Insurance Coverage
Landlord
List Your Debts
Creditors
Live with My Parents
Loan Value
Mortgage Balance
Purchase Price
Registration Number
Take-Home Pay

HOSPITAL

Accident
Admissions
Aerosol
Ambulance
Cancel
Dispensary
Disposal Plastic Syringe
Drain
Glass Cans

Hospital
In Laboratory
Local
Manual
Nurse
Oxygen
Pick-up
Physician
Seamstress
Slop
Storeroom
Steam
Vinyl Plastic
Ward
Water Level
X-ray

AIRPORT

Aircraft Landing Zone
Air Express
Air Freight
Concourse
Direct Line
Do Not Use Near Unit
Grease or Oil
Equipment Operators
   Check Fuel and Engine
   Oil Before Placing
   Machine in Operation
Final Destination
Flight Leaves
Flight Number
Ground Transportation
If in Doubt Contact Your
   Supervisor
Keep Cart 4 Feet from
   Airplane
Keep Within Yellow Lines
Moving Aircraft Proceed
   with Caution
Never Use Oxygen as
   Compressed Air
No Carrying Lighted
   Materials Beyond This
   Point
This P.I.V. Controls
   Sprinklers

Warning! These are
   Instantaneous Switches—
   Do Not Hold Push Button

TRUCKING I

Bags
Barrels
Bill of Lading (B/L)
Bottles
Bundles
Cartons
Case (Cs)
Commodities Rate
Consigner
Consignor
Crate
Delivery Number
Destination
Dispatcher
Don't Tailgate
Drums
Explosives
**Class A,B,C
Fiber Drums
F.O.B. (Free on Board)
Look Before Backing

TRUCKING II

C.O.D. (Collect on Delivery)
First Class Rates
Gross Load
Gross Weight
Kegs
L/T/1 (Less Than
   Truckload)
Livestock
Number Pieces
Paid Insurance
Pails
Prepaid
Pro Number
Protective Signature Service
Received in Good
   Condition
Second Class Rates
Shipper

Storage
Tailgate
Total Due
Vehicle Number

CONSTRUCTION

Acetone
Caution—Keep Walking
   Paths Clear
Caution—Only Regular
   Operator Allowed to Use
   This Machine
Cement
Men Working Above
Riding on This Forbidden
This Means You
Employees Only Allowed
   Past This Point
Fuse
Heater Room
Kerosene
Lock
Mortar Cement
Negative
Panel
Pile All Materials Properly
Positive
Projecting Nails Cause
   Accidents—Bend Them
   Over
Replace Guards and
   Barriers Immediately
Solvent
Stop Machines Before
   Cleaning or Adjusting
This Hoist for Materials
   Only—Do Not Ride
Warning—Stop Machines
   Before Clearing Jams or
   Repairing
Wear Your Hard Hat
Wire

SALES

Bill of Lading
Cash
Charge

The Reading Teacher's Book of Lists, Fourth Edition, © 2000 by John Wiley & Sons, Inc.

C.O.D. (Collect on
Delivery)
Collect
Do Not Write in Above
Space
Due
F.O.B. (Free on Board)
Invoice
Item
License Number
Price Includes Tax
Quantity (Qty)
Rate
Received by
Received in Good
Condition
Sales Tax
Sold by
Sold to
Total

LUMBER I

Base
Bevel
Birch
Cedar
Colonial
Common
Crosscuts
Crown
Dowel
Drip Cap

FAS 1 (Front and Sideboards
Clear on 1 Side)
FAS 2 (Front and Sideboards
Clear on 2 Sides)
Fencing
Fir
Flat Grain
Hemlock
Jambs
Knotty Pine
Mahogany
Mldg. (Moulding)

LUMBER II

Nutmeg
Oak
Panels
PCS (Pieces)
Pine
Ply
Rail
Ranch Trim
Rips
S 2 5 (Surface 2 Sides)
S 4 S (Surface 4 Sides)
Shoe
Siding
Sill
Spruce
Square Feet (Sq. Ft.)
Standard
Sterling

Vertical Grain
Walnut

TELEPHONE

Phone
Telephone
Directory
Area Code
Local Call
Long Distance
Information
Directory Assistance
Exchange
Person-to-Person
Dial
Dial Tone
Assistance
Emergency Call
Deposit 25¢
Business Office
Operator
Repair Service
White Pages
Yellow Pages
Classified Directory
Location
Day Rate
Evening Rate
Night Rate
Collect Call
Telegram
Credit Card

See also List 157, Daily Living Words; List 158, Travel Words; List 159, Application Words.

List 161. JUMP-ROPE RHYMES—CHORAL

Jump-rope rhymes or street poems are fun. Nearly every youngster knows at least some of these. Many are learned at camp and in after-school programs and activities. Use jump-rope rhymes to discuss cadence, rhyme, rhythm, and the uses of chants in our culture.

A Horse, a Flea, and Three Blind Mice

A horse, a flea, and three blind mice,
Sat on a curbstone shooting dice.
The horse, he slipped and fell on the flea.
The flea said, "Whoops, there's a horse on me."
The flea, he slipped and fell on the mice
And no one knows what became of the dice.

All in Together, Girls

All in together, girls; never mind the weather, girls.
Tell me when your birthday is; just jump in:
January, February, March, April, May, June, July,
August, September, October, November, December.
All in together girls; never mind the weather, girls.
Tell me when your birthday is: just jump out
1, 2, 3, 4, 5, 6, 7, 8, 9, 10, 11, 12, 13, 14, 15,
16, 17, 18, 19, 20, 21, 22, 23, 24, 25, 26, 27, 28, 29, 30, 31

Cinderella

Cinderella, dressed in yellow, went upstairs to kiss a fella.
Made a mistake and kissed a snake.
How many stitches did it take?
1, 2, 3, 4, 5, etc.

I Like Coffee

"I like coffee, I like tea, I'd like (name) to come in with me."
(Repeat, with the first person leaving, and second person picking a name.)
I like coffee, I like tea,
I like the boys and the boys like me.
Yes, no, maybe so; Yes, no, maybe so, etc.

Doctor, Doctor

Doctor, doctor, can you tell, what will make poor Anna well?
Is she sick and going to die? That would make poor Tommy cry.
Tommy, Tommy, don't you cry. You will see her by and by.
Dressed in pink or white or blue, waiting at the church to marry you.

Ice Cream Soda

Ice cream soda, cherry on top! Who's your new friend? I forgot.
A, B, C, D, E, etc. (instead of new friend, could be boyfriend, best friend, girlfriend)

The Reading Teacher's Book of Lists, Fourth Edition, © 2000 by John Wiley & Sons, Inc.

Last Night, the Night Before

Last night, the night before, my old friend took me to the candy store.
He bought me an ice cream, he bought me some cake,
Then he brought me home with a belly ache.
Mama, Mama, I feel sick. Call the doctor quick, quick, quick!
Doctor, Doctor will I die?
No you won't, you're bound to survive!

Lemon Lime

Lemon lime, be on time,
1, 2 (first person jumps in and out); 3, 4 (the next person jumps in and out), etc.

Miss Mary Mack

Miss Mary Mack, Mack, Mack; All dressed in black, black, black
With silver buttons, buttons, buttons; All down her back, back, back.
She asked her mother, mother, mother; For 50 cents, cents, cents
To see the elephants, elephants, elephants; Jump over the fence, fence, fence.
They jumped so high, high, high; They reached the sky, sky, sky
And they didn't come back, back, back; 'Til the 4th of July, ly, ly!

School, School

School, school, and the golden rule
Spell your name and go to school.
(Person jumps and spells name, then continues to jump counting the grades 1–12)

Miss Polly Had a Dolly

Miss Polly had a dolly who was sick, sick, sick,
So she called for the doctor to be quick, quick, quick.
The doctor came with his bag and his hat,
And he knocked at the door with a rat-a-tat-tat.
He looked at the dolly and he shook his head,
And he said "Miss Polly, put her straight to bed."
He wrote out a paper for a pill, pill, pill,
"That'll make her better, yes it will, will, will!"

Teddy Bear, Teddy Bear

Teddy Bear, Teddy Bear, turn around.
Teddy Bear, Teddy Bear, touch the ground.
Teddy Bear, Teddy Bear, show your shoe.
Teddy Bear, Teddy Bear, that will do!
Teddy Bear, Teddy Bear, go upstairs.
Teddy Bear, Teddy Bear, say your prayers.
Teddy Bear, Teddy Bear, turn out the lights.
Teddy Bear, Teddy Bear, say good-night!

Miss Susie

Miss Susie had a steamboat, the steamboat had a bell
Miss Susie went to heaven, the steamboat went to . . .
Hello operator, give me number nine,
And if you disconnect me, I'll kick you from . . .
Behind the refrigerator there was a piece of glass
Miss Susie sat upon it and cut her little . . .
Ask me no more questions, tell me no more lies
The boys are in the bathroom zipping up their . . .
Flies are in the meadow, the bees are in the park
Miss Susie and her boyfriend are kissing in the . . .
Dark is like a movie, a movie's like a show
A show is like a TV screen and that is all . . .
I know I know my mother, I know I know my pa
I know I know my sister has an alligator bra.

Not Last Night but the Night Before

Not last night but the night before,
Twenty-four robbers came knocking at my door.
I asked them what they wanted, and this is what they said:
We want to see your sister do the splits, splits, splits.
We want to see your brother do the twist, twist, twist.
We want to see the baby turn around, round, round.
And we want to see you touch the ground, ground, ground.
Now that it was over, it wasn't such a chore,
The twenty-four robbers went running out the door.

See also List 92, Games and Methods for Teaching.

The Reading Teacher's Book of Lists, Fourth Edition, © 2000 by John Wiley & Sons, Inc.

13
WORD PLAY FUN

List 162. ANAGRAMS

Anagrams—words formed by rearranging the letters of another word—are fun and they help students pay close attention to spelling and spelling patterns.

Primary

act—cat	flow—wolf	ring—grin
aide—idea	god—dog	sink—skin
ape—pea	mars—rams	slip—lips
are—ear	meat—team	tab—bat
arm—ram	meats—steam	tar—rat
bare—bear	nap—pan	tea—eat
beak—bake	night—thing	urn—run
best—bets	note—tone	use—sue
boss—sobs	ours—sour	war—raw
café—face	pat—tap	was—saw
care—race	pea—ape	wed—dew
case—aces	pear—reap	who—how
earth—heart	pins—spin	won—now
fast—fats	pots—spot	yap—pay

Elementary/Intermediate

avenge—Geneva	limped—dimple	panels—Naples	skills—kills
balm—lamb	loin—lion	parks—sparks	snail—nails
blot—bolt	looted—Toledo	pools—spool	sober—robes
blow—bowl	lump—plum	ports—sport	soil—oils
brag—grab	march—charm	posts—stops	solo—Oslo
chum—much	mash—hams	races—cares	spray—prays
coal—cola	meals—males	reap—pear	stack—tacks
counts—Tuscon	meals—Salem	reef—free	stick—ticks
diagnose—San Diego	mean—mane	robed—bored	stops—posts
diary—dairy	melon—lemon	rock—Cork	strip—trips
domains—Madison	moist—omits	room—moor	study—dusty
dottier—Detroit	more—Rome	ropes—pores	team—meat
fired—fried	needs—dense	saint—stain	ticks—stick
fringe—finger	nerved—Denver	sales—seals	tooled—Toledo
hasten—Athens	none—neon	salts—lasts	votes—stove
iced—dice	nude—dune	salvages—Las Vegas	waits—waist
inch—chin	ocean—canoe	sharp—harps	wasps—swaps
keen—knee	pace—cape	shrub—brush	wells—swell
lamp—palm	pairs—Paris	siren—rinse	west—stew
last—salt	pale—leap	skids—disks	what—thaw

The Reading Teacher's Book of Lists, Fourth Edition, © 2000 by John Wiley & Sons, Inc.

Advanced

an aisle—is a lane
atom—bomb
considerate—care is noted
conversation—voices rant on
a decimal point—I'm a dot in place
departed this life—He's left it, dead; R I P
dormitory—dirty room
dynamite—may end it
eleven plus two—twelve plus one
Fourth of July—joyful fourth
gold and silver—grand old evils
HMS Pinafore—name for ship
limericks—slick rime
monasteries—Amen stories

a near miss—an air miss
the earthquakes—that queer shake
the Morse Code—here come dots
the nudist colony—no untidy clothes
the public art galleries—large picture halls, I bet
old England—golden land
restaurant—runs a treat
saintliness—least in sins
Semolina—is no meal
signature—a true sign
Statue of Liberty—built to stay free
the tennis pro—he in net sport
Valentine poem—pen mate in love
Year Two Thousand—a year to shut down!

The Reading Teacher's Book of Lists, Fourth Edition, © 2000 by John Wiley & Sons, Inc.

See also List 92, Games and Methods for Teaching; List 165, Onomatopoeia.

List 163. DOUBLESPEAK

Here's something both you and your students can enjoy. Select in any order one word from Column A, one from Column B, and one from Column C. Now copy them on scratch paper in the order they were selected.

A	B	C
1. social	1. involvement	1. objectives
2. perceptual	2. motivation	2. activity
3. developmental	3. accelerated	3. curriculum
4. professional	4. cognitive	4. concept
5. homogeneous	5. effectiveness	5. evaluation
6. interdependent	6. maturation	6. processes
7. exceptional	7. integration	7. approach
8. instructional	8. orientation	8. articulation
9. individual	9. guidance	9. utilization
10. sequential	10. creative	10. resources
11. environmental	11. culture	11. adjustment
12. incremental	12. relationship	12. capacity

EXAMPLES: (A-10) sequential, (B-1) involvement, (C-2) activity;
(A-3) developmental, (B-4) cognitive, (C-7) approach

Now that you have the hang of it, enjoy your new status by sprinkling a few common words between the phrases like this:

> Social involvement objectives in today's schools are realized by combining an accelerated developmental curriculum with professional effectiveness utilization and creative instructional evaluation.

> The motivation of interdependent activity in an environmental adjustment culture is not easy when one takes into account the perceptual maturation processes of the individual.

> The utilization of instructional guidance resources will enable students to employ a sequential orientation approach to social integration.

After you have mastered this creative incremental approach to educationalese (also called "jargon") you will realize that happiness is social effectiveness through concept articulation. Infectious, isn't it?

See List 98, Comprehension Thesaurus, for additional terms and jargon.

If you are interested in Doublespeak, you might enjoy the book *Doublespeak* by William Lutz (Harper Row, 1981); also, the *Committee on Public Doublespeak,* NCTE, 1111 Kenyon Road, Urbana, IL 61801 publishes the *Quarterly Review of Doublespeak,* edited by William Lutz.

Used with permission from William Lutz.

List 164. HINK PINKS AND JOKES

Word games and jokes help to increase vocabulary and verbal fluency. Some word games such as Hink Pinks also help to increase phoneme awareness. Besides that, they are fun! Use a few of these for starters, then make up some of your own. *Hint:* The list of example words in List 8 will help you.

What is a single speech machine?	*lone phone*
What is an uncovered seat?	*bare chair*
What is a library burglar?	*book crook*
What is a strong beautiful plant?	*power flower*
What is an entrance to a shop?	*store door*
What is a boring singing?	*long song*
What is a skyway to heaven?	*air stair*
What is a weak bird?	*frail quail*
What is a container for wood fasteners?	*nail pail*
What is a resting place for ducks?	*quack rack*
What is an unhappy father?	*sad dad*
What is an old marine mammal?	*stale whale*
What is a chicken enclosure?	*hen pen*
What is a beach party-giver?	*coast host*
What is a hip place of learning?	*cool school*
What is a journey by boat?	*ship trip*
What is bad air in a swamp?	*bog smog*
What is a fat behind?	*plump rump*
What is a closed-up shack?	*shut hut*
What is a beginning prophet?	*new guru*
What is a house mortgage?	*home loan*
What is a skinny hotel?	*thin inn*
What is a cheap medieval soldier?	*tight knight*

Hink Pinks have one-syllable word answers, but the more advanced Hinky Pinkies have two-syllable word answers, and Hinkety Pinketys have three-syllable answers.

Hinky Pinkies

What do you call a rabbit that tells jokes?	*funny bunny*
What do you call a dog that fell in the river?	*soggy doggie*
What is sunshine in the high mountains?	*alpine sunshine*
What is a student who doesn't like to pay?	*cheapskate classmate*

Hinkety Pinketys

What is a love affair?	*affection connection*
What do rich people eat off of?	*millionaire dinnerware*

The Reading Teacher's Book of Lists, Fourth Edition, © 2000 by John Wiley & Sons, Inc.

JOKES

Knock knock.
Who's there?
Doris.
Doris who?
Doris locked, that's why I knocked.

Knock knock.
Who's there?
Olive.
Olive who?
Olive across the street.

Knock knock.
Who's there?
Police.
Police who?
Police stop telling these silly knock-knock jokes.

Waiter, there is a fly in my soup.
That's all right, sir, he won't drink much.

Waiter, what's this fly doing in my soup?
I believe he is doing the backstroke, miss.

Waiter, this soup is terrible. Please call the manager.
He won't drink it either, sir.

Patient: Doctor, my little brother is really crazy. He thinks he is a chicken.
Doctor: How long has this been going on?
Patient: About six years.
Doctor: Good heavens. Why have you waited so long to come for help?
Patient: Because we needed the eggs.

Why did the doctor take her eye chart into the classroom?
Because she wanted to check the pupils.

See also List 168, Riddles.

The Reading Teacher's Book of Lists, Fourth Edition, © 2000 by John Wiley & Sons, Inc.

List 165. ONOMATOPOEIA

Onomatopoeic words, borrowed from sounds, resemble the sound they refer to; for example, a cow *moos*. These words are favorites with poets and comic-strip writers. Entertainers love them, and children's authors use them regularly. Your students will enjoy them and probably add some to this list. If you have a class with students from several different language backgrounds, an interesting, and sometimes humorous, multicultural lesson is to compare the sounds animals make in different languages.

ah choo	cluck	hoot	rat a tat	twang
arf arf	conk	howl	rattle	tweet
	coo	huff n puff	ring	twitter
baa	crack	hum	ring a ling	
bang	crackle	hurrah	rip	varoom
bark	crash		roar	
beep	creak	jabber	rumble	whack
blabber	crinkle	jangle	rush	whir
bleat	croak	jingle	rustle	whish
blink	crunch			whiz
bong	cuckoo	kerchoo	screech	whoop
bonk		klomp	shriek	whoopee
boo	ding a ling	knock	sigh	woof woof
boom	ding dong		sizzle	wow
bow wow	drip	meow	slurp	
bray	drop	moan	smack	yahoo
bump		moo	smash	yikes
burp	eek	murmur	snap	
buzz			sniffle	zap
	fizz	neigh	snort	zing
caw	flip flop		splash	zip
cheep		oink	splat	zonk
chirp	giggle	oops	sputter	zoom
choo choo	gong	ooze	squeak	
chug	grate		squeal	
clang	grind	patter	squish	
clank	groan	ping	stomp	
clap	growl	pitter patter	swish	
clash	grunt	plop		
clatter		pop	tick tock	
click	hee haw	pow	thud	
clink	hiccup	purr	thump	
clip clop	hiss		tinkle	
clomp	honk	quack	toot	

See also List 162, Anagrams.

The Reading Teacher's Book of Lists, Fourth Edition, © 2000 by John Wiley & Sons, Inc.

List 166. PALINDROMES

Palindromes are words or sentences that read the same way forward and backward. They are enjoyed by people of all ages who like to have some fun with words. Your students will likely come up with several more.

Word Palindromes

Anna	eye	mum	refer
bob	gag	noon	reviver
civic	gig	nun	rotor
deed	Hannah	Otto	sees
did	kayak	peep	solos
dud	level	pop	SOS
ere	madam	racecar	toot
eve	mom	radar	tot

Sentence and Phrase Palindromes

A man, a plan, a canal, Panama!

Able was I ere I saw Elba

Cigar? Toss it in a can. It is so tragic.

Did Hanna say as Hanna did?

Don't nod.

Flee to me remote elf.

Live evil.

Ma handed Edna ham.

Madam I'm Adam.

May a moody baby doom a yam?

Name no one man.

Net ten.

Never odd or even.

No lemons, no melons.

Now sir, a war is won.

Nurses run.

Rats star.

Red root put up to order.

Red rum, sir, is murder.

"Reviled did I live," said I, "as evil I did deliver."

Rise to vote sir.

Roy, am I mayor?

Sages use gas.

So, Ida, adios!

Stab bats.

Step on no pets.

Stressed desserts.

Too bad I hid a boot.

Top spot.

Was it a car or a cat I saw?

Was it a rat I saw?

We sew.

The Reading Teacher's Book of Lists, Fourth Edition, © 2000 by John Wiley & Sons, Inc.

Words That Read Differently Backward and Forward

These words are often used in forming phrase palindromes.

bats	lager	parts	stab
but	laid	peek	star
cod	lain	peels	step
deer	lap	sleek	stool
deliver	leg	pets	stop
dennis	Leon	pools	stops
desserts	live	pot	strap
dial	loots	pots	stressed
doc	may	rat	stun
doom	mood	rats	tang
dot	mug	reed	taps
draw	nail	regal	tar
drawer	naps	reviled	ten
emit	net	reward	time
evil	no	saw	Tod
flag	Noel	sinned	ton
gel	not	slap	top
gnat	now	sleep	tub
golf	nuts	sloop	ward
gum	on	span	was
keels	pal	spat	won
keep	pals	spots	yam

The Reading Teacher's Book of Lists, Fourth Edition, © 2000 by John Wiley & Sons, Inc.

See also List 162, Anagrams.

List 167. PORTMANTEAU WORDS

Alice, in *Alice in Wonderland,* asks Humpty Dumpty what "slithy" (from the Jabberwocky) means. He tells her that it means "lithe" and "slimy." "You can see there are two meanings packed into one word." *Portmanteau* is French for suitcase. The words in the comprehensive list below are called "portmanteau words" because they have two parts that are folded into one, just as the two parts of a suitcase fold into one piece of luggage. Your students will have fun with these, and understanding the derivations of the words will enhance their comprehension. They may even enjoy making up portmanteau words of their own and quizzing each other on how they were derived.

The Reading Teacher's Book of Lists, Fourth Edition, © 2000 by John Wiley & Sons, Inc.

autobus	automobile + bus	flop	flap + drop
bash	bang + smash	flounder	flounce + founder
because	by + cause	flunk	flinch + funk
bit	binary + digit	flurry	flutter + hurry
bleep	blankout + beep	flush	flash + gush
blimp	B + limp	fortnight	fourteen + nights
blotch	blot + botch	galumph	gallop + triumph
blurt	blow + spurt	gasohol	gasoline + alcohol
boost	boom + hoist	gerrymander	Gerry + salamander
brash	bold + rash	gimp	game + limp
brunch	breakfast + lunch	glimmer	gleam + shimmer
caplet	capsule + tablet	glitterati	glitter + literati
cellophane	cellulose + diaphane	glitz	glamour + ritz
chocoholic	chocolate + alcoholic	glob	globe + blob
chortle	chuckle + snort	glop	goo + slop
chump	chunk + lump	goodbye	God + be (with) + ye
clash	clap + crash	goon	gorilla + baboon
clump	chunk + lump	guestimate	guess + estimate
con man	confidence + man	hassle	haggle + tussle
daisy	day's + eye	hi-fi	high + fidelity
dancercise	dance + exercise	humongous	huge + monstrous
ditsy	dizzy + dotty	intercom	internal + communication
doddle	dodder + toddle	Internet	international + network
dumbfound	dumb + confound	Medicare	medicine + care
econometric	economic + metric	model	modulator + demodulator
electrocute	electronic + execute	moped	motor + pedal
emoticon	emotion + icon	motel	motor + hotel
farewell	fare + ye + well	motocross	motor + cross country
flabbergast	flap + aghast	motorcade	motor + cavalcade
flare	flame + glare	Muppet	marionette + puppet
flaunt	flout + vaunt	napalm	naphthene + palmitate

399

netiquette	network + etiquette	snazzy	snappy + jazzy
o'clock	of (the) + clock	sparcity	sparceness + scarcity
pang	pain + sting	splatter	splash + spatter
paratroops	parachute + troops	splurge	splash + surge
pixel	picture + element	squash	squeeze + crash
prequel	precede + sequel	squiggle	squirm + wriggle
prissy	prim + sissy	swipe	wipe + sweep
prod	poke + rod	tangelo	tangerine + pomelo
pulsar	pulsating + star	taxicab	taximeter + cabriolet
rubbage	rubbish + garbage	telecommuter	telecommunication + commuter
satisfice	satisfy + suffice	telethon	television + marathon
scrawl	scribble + sprawl	telsat	telecommunications + satellite
scrunch	squeeze + crunch		
scuzzy	scrummy + lousy	transistor	transfer + resistor
skort	skirt + short	travelogue	travel + monologue
skyjack	sky + hijack	twiddle	twist + fiddle
skylab	sky + laboratory	twinight	twilight + night
slang	slovenly + language	twirl	twist + whirl
slather	slap + lather	waddle	wade + toddle
slosh	slop + slush	workaholic	work + alcoholic
smash	smack + mash		
smog	smoke + fog		

See also List 131, Contractions; List 132, Compound Words.

List 168. RIDDLES

Youngsters love riddles and other kinds of word play. These riddles, like many other types of humor, rely on the definitions of key words. The word play makes good use of a word's denotation (literal definition), connotation (special meaning in context), or one of a word's multiple meanings. Word play helps students focus on details, shades of meaning, and figurative language. *Teaching suggestion:* Write one riddle question on the chalkboard each day. Pick a student to read and answer it. Have a contest—Let a student write one of his or her riddles on the board, and you try to answer it. Let class vote for the best riddle.

The Reading Teacher's Book of Lists, Fourth Edition, © 2000 by John Wiley & Sons, Inc.

Where do fish sleep? *in water beds*

What do you call a burning jacket? *a blazer*

Which is faster, hot or cold? *hot because you can catch a cold*

What never gets locked out? *a piano; it has 88 keys*

What kind of room has no windows? *a mushroom*

What do you call a horse that stays up very late? *a nightmare*

What question did the owl ask the turtle about the winner of the race? *Who? Who?*

What do you get if you put a dog in the oven? *a hot dog*

What do computers eat? *computer chips*

What kind of house is always hot? *a firehouse*

Why did the boy close the refrigerator door quickly? *because he saw the salad dressing*

Where do fish keep their money? *in the River Bank*

What is the quietest sport? *bowling because you can hear a pin drop*

What did one eye say to the other eye? *between you and me something smells*

Why is a river rich? *because it has two banks*

What must you pay when you go to school? *attention*

When is a door not a door? *when it is ajar*

Who sleeps with his shoes on? *a horse (horseshoes)*

What should you do to fall asleep faster? *try sleeping on the edge of the bed, you'll drop off soon*

Where do frozen ants come from? *Antarctica*

Where do dogs refuse to shop? *at flea markets*

What sounds better the more you beat it? *a drum*

Why did the robber take a bath? *so he could make a clean get away*

What kind of house weighs the least? *a lighthouse*

Why did the puppy take a nap? *because he was dog tired*

What kind of key won't work in the lock? *a monkey*

How was your dog's birthday party? *it was a howling success*

What did the car have on its toast this morning? *traffic jam*

Where do big black birds hang out? *at crowbars*

When is a car not a car? *when it turns into a driveway*

What runs around the garden without moving? *a fence*

What happened when the frog parked its car in a "no parking" zone? *it was toad away*

Why is it hard to catch a refrigerator? *because it's always running*

Why was Cinderella thrown off the baseball team? *because she ran away from the ball*

What did one wall say to the other wall? *I'll meet you at the corner*

Why is 10 afraid of 7? *because 7, 8, 9*

What kind of bird goes "Bang Bang"? *a fire quacker*

What goes tick-tick, woof-woof? *a watch dog*

Where do cows go on vacation? *Moo York*

What do you get if you cross a cat and a lemon? *a sour puss*

What do you get if you cross a centipede and a parrot? *a walkie-talkie*

What year do frogs like best? *leap year*

What did the judge give the thief who stole the calendar? *twelve months*

What does an eagle like to write with? *a bald point pen*

What is an outspoken hot dog? *a frank frank*

What is a writing instrument used in jail? *a pen pen*

What is bought by yard and worn by the foot? *a carpet*

The Reading Teacher's Book of Lists, Fourth Edition, © 2000 by John Wiley & Sons, Inc.

See also List 164, Hink Pinks and Jokes.

List 169. CHILDREN'S HUMOR: WHAT KIDS SAY

Humorists, comedians, and pundits often bemoan the work involved in being funny. Yet, as all teachers know, kids do it innocently and without a moment's effort. Here is a collection of children's answers, observations, and thoughts that prove the point.

- The difference between a green light and a red light? The color.
- Beethoven wrote music even though he was deaf. He was so deaf he wrote loud music.
- Lindberg is the capital of Germany.
- It is always darkest before Daylight Savings Time.
- Superglue is forever.
- One of the main causes of dust is janitors.
- The red-brick wall was the color of brick-red crayon.
- Ancient Egypt was inhabited by mummies.
- Beethoven expired in 1827 and later died of this.
- Her vocabulary was as bad as, like, whatever.
- The people who followed the Lord were called the 12 opossums.
- Maybe Cain wouldn't have killed his brother Able if they had their own rooms. It works for my brother and me.
- What people live in the Po Valle? Po people.
- History called them Romans because they moved around a lot.
- When you smell an odorless gas, it is probably carbon monoxide.
- The future of "I give" is "I take."
- Climate lasts all the time, but weather lasts just a few days.
- Sir Francis Drake circumcised the world with a 100-foot clipper.
- Dear God: I want to live 900 years like that guy in the bible.
- Terminal illness: getting sick at the airport.
- A myth is a female moth.
- Spelling doesn't madder.
- In Pittsburgh, they make iron and steal.
- Julius Caesar extinguished himself on the battlefield.
- At the bottom of Lake Michigan is Chicago.
- I can wait to fall in love—fourth grade is hard enough.
- No, it's not a right angle—it's a left angle.
- H_2O is hot water, CO_2 is cold water.
- The sun never set on the British Empire because the British Empire is in the East and the sun sets in the West.
- Imports are ports very fair inland.
- Dear God: Are you really invisible or is that just a trick?
- When you breathe, you inspire. When you do not breathe, you expire.
- Never trust your dog to watch your food.

403

- In the Olympic games, Greeks ran races, jumped, hurled biscuits, and threw java.
- Denver is just below the "o" in Colorado.
- Marie Curie worked at the Sore Bun in Paris.
- If today was a fish, I'd throw it back in.
- Involuntary muscles are not as willing as voluntary ones.
- Who draws the lines around the countries?
- The spinal column is a long bunch of bones. The head sits at the top and you sit at the bottom.
- The population of London is a bit too thick.
- I'd explain it to you, but your brain would explode.
- Socrates died from an overdose of wedlock—after his death his career suffered a dramatic decline.
- A fossil is an extinct animal. The older it is, the more extinct it is.
- Moses went up to Mount Cyanide to get the Ten Commandments.
- The general direction of the Alps is up.
- Hot lather comes from volcanoes. When it cools, it turns into rocks.
- In some rocks we find the fossil footprints of fishes.
- Ever stop to think and forget to start again?
- Instead of having people die and having to make new ones, why doesn't God just keep the ones he already has?
- Live teddy bears are best.
- Love is the most important thing in the world, but baseball is pretty good, too.
- It's not a good idea to hide puppies in your closet for a whole week.
- The earth makes a resolution every 24 hours.
- You know when you know, you know?
- Ever jump out of bed and miss the floor?
- When driving through fog, use your car.
- The four seasons are salt, pepper, mustard, and ketchup.
- If you didn't get caught, did you really do it?
- Why is "abbreviation" such a long word?
- Water is melted steam.
- It works better if you plug it in.

The Reading Teacher's Book of Lists, Fourth Edition, © 2000 by John Wiley & Sons, Inc.

See also List 171, Murphy's Law and Others.

List 170. TONGUE TWISTERS

Tongue twisters are great fun. Try a different one each week. Tongue twisters are great practice for auditory awareness, sound discrimination, and articulation. They can be especially helpful for students who are learning English as a second language. Many of these tongue twisters are used by actors and announcers as elocution exercises.

Repeaters (Try saying these three times quickly.)

A regal rural ruler	Pug puppy
Baboon bamboo	Red leather, yellow leather
Cheap ship trips	Smashed shrimp chips
Crisco crisps crusts	Three free throws
Girl gargoyle, guy gargoyle	Tiny orangutan tongues
Greek grapes	Toy boat
Knapsack strap	Truly plural
Lemon liniment	Urgent detergent
Peggy Babcock	

One Liners

A box of mixed biscuits, a mixed biscuit box.

A noisy noise annoys an oyster.

An icehouse is not a nice house.

Andy ran from the Andes to the Indies in his undies.

Black bugs bleed black blood.

Do drop in at the Dewdrop Inn.

Even Edith eats eggs.

Five minutes to eight, not five minutes to wait.

For fine fish phone Phil.

Friday's Five Fresh Fish Specials.

Give me some ice, not some mice.

How much wood would a woodchuck chuck if a woodchuck could chuck wood?

Is there a pleasant peasant present?

Lesser leather never weathered lesser wetter weather.

Lesser weather never weathered lesser wetter leather.

Lot lost his hot chocolate at the loft.

Mrs. Smith's Fish Sauce Shop.

Seven silly Santas slid on the slick snow.

Seven silly swans swam silently seaward.

She sells seashells by the seashore, and the shells she sells are seashells.

Sheep shouldn't sleep in a shack. Sheep should sleep in a shed.

Silly Sally slid down a slippery slide.

Six sharp smart sharks.

Six sick snakes sit by the sea.

Six thick thistle sticks.

Strong sharks sink ships.

Ten tiny tin trains toot ten times.

That bloke's back brake-block broke.

The big black-backed bumblebee.

The cat catchers can't catch caught cats.

The myth of Miss Muffet.

The sheik's sixth sheep's sick.

The summer school, not a summer's cool.

The sun shines on shop signs.

Thin sticks, thick bricks.

Three free thugs set three thugs free.

Which witch wished which wicked wish?

Whistle for the thistle sifter.

Stories

A big black bug bit a big black bear and the big black bear bled blood.

A big bug bit the little beetle but the little beetle bit the big bug back.

A flea and a fly flew up in a flue. Said the flea, "Let us fly!" Said the fly, "Let us flee!" So they flew through a flaw in the flue.

A tree toad loved a she-toad that lived up in a tree. She was a three-toed tree toad, but a two-toed toad was he.

Betty Botter had some butter. "But," she said, "this butter's bitter. If I bake this bitter butter, it would make my batter bitter."

Fuzzy Wuzzy was a bear, Fuzzy Wuzzy had no hair. Fuzzy Wuzzy wasn't fuzzy, was he?

I thought a thought. But the thought I thought wasn't the thought I thought I thought.

On two thousand acres, too tangled for tilling, where thousands of thorn trees grew thrifty and thrilling, Theophilus Twistle, less thrifty than some, thrust three thousand thistles through the thick of his thumb!

Once upon a barren moor there dwelt a bear also a boar. The bear could not bear the boar. The bear thought the boar a bore. At last that bear could bear no more of that boar that bored him on the moor and so one morn' he bored that boar. That boar will bore the bear no more.

Our Joe wants to know if your Joe will lend our Joe your Joe's banjo. If your Joe won't lend our Joe your Joe's banjo, our Joe won't lend your Joe our Joe's banjo when our Joe has a banjo!

Two witches bought two wrist watches, but which witch wore which wrist watch?

Unique New York, you need New York, you know you need unique New York.

Whether the weather is hot. Whether the weather is cold. Whether the weather is either or not. It is whether we like it or not.

See also List 134, Speech Pronunciation; List 146, Speech Sound Development.

The Reading Teacher's Book of Lists, Fourth Edition, © 2000 by John Wiley & Sons, Inc.

List 171. MURPHY'S LAW AND OTHERS

Murphy's Law and other principles might amuse or bemuse you. Some have a little jab of truth in them. Society is governed by certain immutable laws and principles. Murphy's Law, though, of somewhat doubtful authorship, is nonetheless real. Ask any engineer, mechanic, office manager, or computer programmer.

Both the Peter Principle and Parkinson's Law were developed by very real college professors, and both are explained somewhat seriously in full books.

The other principles given here are sometimes original and sometimes borrowed from the common folklore. Use them and amuse them as needed. Both you and your students might like to add to this important list of real-life observations for fun and profitable insight.

Murphy's Law: If anything can go wrong, it will (and at the worst possible moment.)

Corollaries

The other line always moves faster.

The race isn't always to the swift or the battle to the strong, but that's the way to bet.

When in doubt, use a bigger hammer.

If you play with anything long enough, you'll break it.

If everything seems to be going fine, you've probably overlooked something.

Nature always sides with the hidden flaw.

Peter Principle: In a hierarchy every employee tends to rise to his or her level of incompetence.

Corollaries

All useful work is done by those who have not yet reached their levels of incompetence.

Cream rises until it sours.

Parkinson's Law: Work expands to fill time available for its completion.

Corollaries

An administrator wants to multiply subordinates, not rivals.

Administrators make work for each other.

Fry's Observation: The more challenging the kid, the less he or she will be absent.

Kling's Axiom: Any simple idea can be worded in a complicated way.

See also List 169, Children's Humor: What Kids Say.

The Reading Teacher's Book of Lists, Fourth Edition, © 2000 by John Wiley & Sons, Inc.

Miscellaneous

No matter how hard you teach a thing, some student is certain not to learn it.

Trouble never comes at a convenient time.

Everything takes longer than you think.

The greater the hurry, the slower the traffic.

No amount of careful planning will ever beat dumb luck.

A good theory might be worth a thousand words, but that won't make it any more practical.

School budgets are always cut in a manner so as to create the most disruption.

There are three kinds of lies: white lies, damned lies, and statistics.

Extracurricular activities sometimes are neither extra nor curricular.

One person's exuberance is the next person's annoyance.

Principals may come and principals may go, but the secretary will run the school regardless.

You can plan anything you like; just don't expect it to happen that way.

Things don't get lost, but they sometimes are carefully put away in some strange places.

People who ask for just a minute of your time don't have very accurate watches.

There's got to be a way to eliminate the last few days of school.

Just when you are sure kids are no good, one of them will do something nice for you.

Maybe a school could exist without heat, light, and water, but take away the copier and it would have to close down.

If Saint Peter uses multiple-choice tests, we are all in for trouble.

Whoever said the worst students aren't creative? Look at their excuses.

Don't fix it if it is not baroque.

These are the good old days of the next generation.

Kids are the only future the human race has.

You can't have everything; where would you put it?

Nobody notices big errors.

Any change looks terrible at first.

Everybody who does not work has a scheme that does.

The Reading Teacher's Book of Lists, Fourth Edition, © 2000 by John Wiley & Sons, Inc.

List 172. WACKY WORDIES

A. The object in solving is to discern a familiar phrase, saying, cliché, or name from each arrangement of letters and/or symbols. For example, box 1a depicts the phrase "just between you and me." Box 1b shows "hitting below the belt." The puzzles get more diabolical as you go.

The Reading Teacher's Book of Lists, Fourth Edition, © 2000 by John Wiley & Sons, Inc.

	a	b	c	d	e	f
1	you just me	belt hitting	lo head heels ve	V I O L E T s	A B E D U M R	agb
2	cry m i l k	·–⊂ ⋛ʊ·–↵	Symphon	ǝlddɐǝuᴉd cake	arrest you're	timing tim ing
3	O TV	night fly	S T I N K	injury + insult	r o rail d	my own heart a person
4	at the · of on	dothepe	wear long	strich grôound	lu cky	the market
5	worl	the x way	word YYY	search and	go off coc	no ways it ways
6	oholene	t o e earth h	ooo circus	1 at 3:46	late nᴇᵥer	get a word in
7	let gone gone be gone gone	a chance n	O MD BA PhD	wheather	world world world world	lo ose
8	lines reading lines	chicken	y fireworks	L D Bridge	pace k̶	danc t e s c etno

Reprinted from *Games* magazine (19 West 21st St., New York, NY 10010). Copyright © 1979, 1981 Playboy Enterprises, Inc.

B. The object in solving is to discern a familiar phrase, saying, cliché, or name from each arrangement of letters and/or symbols. For example, box 1a depicts "sleeping on the job." Box 1b shows a "cornerstone." Sounds easy, but wait until you see the others.

	a	b	c	d	e	f
1	sleeping job	s t one	jink jink jink	g n i t t da wn e g	Roger	escape
2	right = right	house prairie	goodbye	milk	c c garage r r	c o m i c
3	L u e c l i	clou	ieieceiie	neegr geren ngree regen	t i o n a i n l f	pölkä
4	MIRROR	momanon	clams she	ma√il	1.D 5.U 2.R 6.L 3.A 7.A 4.C	ca se case
5	TRN	ping willow	animation	sugar Please	ha̲i̲r̲	L v o R E E A T
6	bus	age a g e age	TU↑LOIPE̸S	m ce m ce m ce	eyebrows	ri poorch
7		morning	socket	TORTILLA	12safety345	s d r k i n house

The Reading Teacher's Book of Lists, Fourth Edition, © 2000 by John Wiley & Sons, Inc.

410

Reprinted from *Games* magazine (19 West 21st St., New York, NY 10010). Copyright © 1979, 1981 Playboy Enterprises, Inc.

C. The object in solving is to discern a familiar phrase, saying, cliché, or name from each arrangement of letters and/or symbols. For example, box 1a depicts the phrase "eggs over easy." Box 1b shows "Trafalgar Square."

	a	b	c	d	e	f
1	eggs / easy	T R A / F A L / G A R	told tales / told	e t t r i / k c i t p	new leaf (upside down)	sᴎky
2	price	L / +O / SS	swear / bible / bible / bible / bible	league	bridge / waᴛer	school
3	-attitude	hoppin	century (curved)	E RC / T O / N U	orseman	D / UC / K
4	set one's teeth	or O / or	bet one's / dollar	tpmerhao	what must (curved)	way yield
5	t / o 2 par / n	dictnry	rifle / rifle / rifle / rifle	PAINS	everything / pizza	L / Y / I / N / G / JOB
6	tr ial	prosperity (curved)	monkey O	busines	writers	moon sonata
7	power	mesnackal	Wilson (upside down)	pit	wheel / wheel / wheel / wheel drive	✓✓ ✓ / counter

black

D. The object in solving is to discern a familiar phrase, saying, cliché, or name from each arrangement of letters and/or symbols. For example, box 1a depicts "once over lightly." Box 1b shows "gossip column."

	a	b	c	d	e	f
1	once lightly	g o s s i p	~wave~ radio	c a p n t a i	noon good	bathing suit
2	ee ch sp	God nation ✳	✓ yearly	ses ame	d deer e r	hold second
3	r − i × s + k	pox	strokes *strokes* **strokes**	n p y o c m a	law of return₅	e a s p u a l
4	hou_{se}	age beauty	harm on y	encounters encounters encounters	breth	*hearted*
5	p a r t i c i p	**MAN** campus	momanon	ᴗld block	"Duty!" and beyond	day day
6	sigh	qonpſ	skating ice	inflat10n	g o s p e l	enemy enemy
7	to^{ngue} to^{ngue}	gettingitall	e a v e s	c m ɾ e a ban ana	e e q u a l s m c	aluminum

WACKIE WORDIES—ANSWERS

A

1a	Just between you and me
1b	Hitting below the belt
1c	Head over heels in love
1d	Shrinking violets
1e	Bermuda Triangle
1f	A mixed bag
2a	Cry over spilt milk
2b	Lying in wait
2c	*Unfinished Symphony*
2d	Pineapple upside-down cake
2e	You're under arrest
2f	Split-second timing
3a	Nothing on TV
3b	Fly-by-night
3c	Raise a big stink
3d	Add insult to injury
3e	Railroad crossing
3f	A person after my own heart
4a	At the point of no return
4b	The inside dope
4c	Long underwear
4d	Ostrich with its head in the ground
4e	Lucky break
4f	Corner the market
5a	World without end
5b	Way behind the times
5c	Word to the wise
5d	Search high and low
5e	Go off half-cocked
5f	No two ways about it
6a	Hole-in-one
6b	Down-to-earth
6c	Three-ring circus
6d	One at a time
6e	Better late than never
6f	Get a word in edgewise
7a	Let bygones be bygones
7b	An outside chance
7c	Three degrees below zero
7d	A terrible spell of weather
7e	World Series
7f	Cut loose
8a	Reading between the lines
8b	Chicken Little
8c	Fourth of July fireworks
8d	London Bridge
8e	Change of pace
8f	Square dance contest

B

1a	Sleeping on the job
1b	Cornerstone
1c	High jinks
1d	Getting up before the crack of dawn
1e	"Roger, over and out"
1f	Narrow escape
2a	Equal rights
2b	*Little House on the Prairie*
2c	Waving goodbye
2d	Condensed milk
2e	Two-car garage
2f	Stand-up comic
3a	Lucille Ball
3b	Partly cloudy
3c	"I before E except after C"
3d	Mixed greens
3e	Spiraling inflation
3f	Polka-dotted
4a	Full-length mirror
4b	Man in the moon
4c	Clams on the half-shell
4d	"The check is in the mail"
4e	Count Dracula
4f	Open-and-shut case
5a	No U-Turn
5b	Weeping willow
5c	Suspended animation
5d	"Pretty please with sugar on top"
5e	Receding hairline
5f	Elevator out of order
6a	Double-decker bus
6b	Middle-age spread
6c	"Tiptoe Through the Tulips"
6d	"Three Blind Mice" (without their i's)
6e	Raised eyebrows
6f	Steal from the rich and give to the poor
7b	Top of the morning
7c	Light socket
7d	*Tortilla Flat*
7e	Safety in numbers
7f	Round of drinks on the house

C

1a	Eggs over easy
1b	Trafalgar Square
1c	*Twice-Told Tales*
1d	Round-trip ticket
1e	Turn over a new leaf
1f	Pie in the sky
2a	*The Price is Right*
2b	Total loss
2c	Swear on a stack of Bibles
2d	Little League
2e	Bridge over troubled water

The Reading Teacher's Book of Lists, Fourth Edition, © 2000 by John Wiley & Sons, Inc.

2f	High school	1f	Topless bathing suit
3a	Negative attitude	2a	Parts of speech
3b	Shopping center	2b	One nation, under God, indivisible
3c	Turn-of-the-Century	2c	Yearly checkup
3d	Counterclockwise	2d	Open sesame
3e	Headless Horseman	2e	Deer crossing
3f	Sitting duck	2f	Hold on a second
4a	Set one's teeth on edge	3a	Calculated risk
4b	Double or nothing	3b	Smallpox
4c	Bet one's bottom dollar	3c	Different strokes
4d	Mixed metaphor	3d	Mixed company
4e	What goes up must come down	3e	Law of diminishing returns
4f	Yield right of way	3f	Round of applause
5a	Not up to par	4a	Split-level house
5b	Abridged dictionary	4b	Age before beauty
5c	Repeating rifle	4c	Three-part harmony
5d	Growing pains	4d	*Close Encounters of the Third Kind*
5e	Pizza with everything on it	4e	A little out of breath
5f	Lying down on the job	4f	Light-hearted
6a	Trial separation	5a	Dangling participle
6b	Prosperity is just around the corner	5b	Big man on campus
6c	Monkey around	5c	Man in the moon
6d	Unfinished business	5d	Chip off the old block
6e	Writer's cramp	5e	Above and beyond the call of duty
6f	*Moonlight Sonata*	5f	Day in and day out
7a	Power blackout	6a	No end in sight
7b	Between-meal snack	6b	Shadow of a doubt
7c	Flip Wilson	6c	Skating on thin ice
7d	Bottomless pit	6d	Double-digit inflation
7e	Four-wheel drive	6e	Spread the gospel
7f	Checkout counter	6f	Archenemies
		7a	Forked tongue
		7b	Getting it all together
D		7c	Eavesdropping
1a	Once over lightly	7d	Banana split with whipped cream topping
1b	Gossip column	7e	$E = mc^2$
1c	Short-wave radio	7f	Aluminum siding
1d	Captain Hook		
1e	Good afternoon		

The Reading Teacher's Book of Lists, Fourth Edition, © 2000 by John Wiley & Sons, Inc.

List 173. FUN NAMES

Chester Drawers

Mary Goround

Della Ware

Mark Time

Billie Club

Cherry Tree

Otto Knowbetter

Isiah Kanusee

June Moon

Odelia Anotherhand

Terry Cloth

Ann Chovy

Sandy Beach

Warren Peace

Mañuel Transmission

Rocky Shore

Norman Conquest

Pete Moss

Lynn Oleum

Polly Dent

Polly Esther

Dawn Early

Candy Cotton

Penny Wise

Will B. Livengood

Lorne Mowers

Jack B. Quick

Donna N. Blitzen

Bea Sharpe

Gracie Mansion

Ima Hogg

Ray On

The Reading Teacher's Book of Lists, Fourth Edition, © 2000 by John Wiley & Sons, Inc.

See also List 192, Popular Names.

14

ABBREVIATIONS, SYMBOLS, AND SIGNS

List 174. STATE ABBREVIATIONS AND CAPITALS

The official postal abbreviations and the traditional abbreviations are listed for each state. Some of the postal abbreviations are easy to remember, such as NY and FL. Others will take a bit of concentration to get straight, such as MI, MO, MS, MA, MT, and ME. The postal abbreviations generally are not followed by periods. Literate students need to know them just as they need to know how to spell the state names.

Full Name	New	Old	Capital
Alabama	AL	Ala.	Montgomery
Alaska	AK	Alaska	Juneau
Arizona	AZ	Ariz.	Phoenix
Arkansas	AR	Ark.	Little Rock
California	CA	Calif.	Sacramento
Colorado	CO	Colo.	Denver
Connecticut	CT	Conn.	Hartford
Delaware	DE	Del.	Dover
Florida	FL	Fla.	Tallahassee
Georgia	GA	Ga.	Atlanta
Hawaii	HI	Hawaii	Honolulu
Idaho	ID	Idaho	Boise
Illinois	IL	Ill.	Springfield
Indiana	IN	Ind.	Indianapolis
Iowa	IA	Iowa	Des Moines
Kansas	KS	Kans.	Topeka
Kentucky	KY	Ky.	Frankfort
Louisiana	LA	La.	Baton Rouge
Maine	ME	Me.	Augusta
Maryland	MD	Md.	Annapolis
Massachusetts	MA	Mass.	Boston
Michigan	MI	Mich.	Lansing
Minnesota	MN	Minn.	St. Paul
Mississippi	MS	Miss.	Jackson
Missouri	MO	Mo.	Jefferson City
Montana	MT	Mont.	Helena
Nebraska	NE	Nebr.	Lincoln
Nevada	NV	Nev.	Carson City
New Hampshire	NH	N.H.	Concord
New Jersey	NJ	N.J.	Trenton
New Mexico	NM	N.Mex.	Santa Fe
New York	NY	N.Y.	Albany
North Carolina	NC	N.C.	Raleigh
North Dakota	ND	N.Dak.	Bismarck
Ohio	OH	Ohio	Columbus

Full Name	New	Old	Capital
Oklahoma	OK	Okla.	Oklahoma City
Oregon	OR	Oreg.	Salem
Pennsylvania	PA	Pa.	Harrisburg
Rhode Island	RI	R.I.	Providence
South Carolina	SC	S.C.	Columbia
South Dakota	SD	S.D.	Pierre
Tennessee	TN	Tenn.	Nashville
Texas	TX	Tex.	Austin
Utah	UT	Utah	Salt Lake City
Vermont	VT	Vt.	Montpelier
Virginia	VA	Va.	Richmond
Washington	WA	Wash.	Olympia
West Virginia	WV	W.Va.	Charleston
Wisconsin	WI	Wisc.	Madison
Wyoming	WY	Wyo.	Cheyenne

Full Name	New/Old	Capital
District of Columbia	DC	Washington
Puerto Rico	PR	San Juan
Virgin Islands	VI	St. Thomas

The Reading Teacher's Book of Lists, Fourth Edition, © 2000 by John Wiley & Sons, Inc.

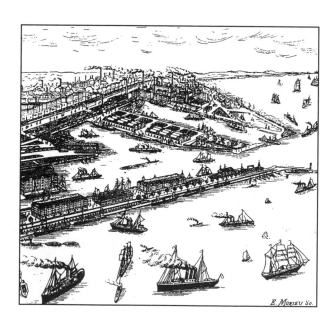

E. MORIEU Sc.

See also List 176, Common Abbreviations.

List 175. EDUCATION ABBREVIATIONS

The field of education has its share of abbreviations. Here are some widely known ones that you may find useful.

AAHPERD	American Alliance for Health, Physical Education, Recreation and Dance
AASA	American Association of School Administrators
AD/HD	Attention Deficit/Hyperactivity Disorder
AFT	American Federation of Teachers
AP	Advanced Placement
ASCD	Association for Supervision and Curriculum Development
CEC	Council for Exceptional Children
CEEB	College Entrance Exam Board
EH	Emotionally Handicapped
ERIC	Educational Resources Information Center
ESL	English as a Second Language
ETS	Educational Testing Service
GED	General Educational Development Test (high school equivalency test)
IEP	Individualized Education Plan
IRA	International Reading Association
LEP	Limited English Proficiency
LD	Learning Disabled
LDA	Learning Disabilities Association
LRE	Least Restrictive Environment
MENC	National Association for Music Education
MH	Mentally Handicapped
NAEA	National Art Education Association
NAEP	National Assessment of Educational Progress
NAESP	National Association of Elementary School Principals
NAEYC	National Association for the Education of Young People
NASSP	National Association of Secondary School Principals
NCATE	National Council for Accreditation of Teacher Education
NCEA	National Catholic Educational Association
NCES	National Center for Educational Statistics
NCPT	National Congress of Parents and Teachers
NCSS	National Council for the Social Studies
NCTE	National Council of Teachers of English
NCTM	National Council of Teachers of Mathematics
NEA	National Education Association
NSF	National Science Foundation
NSTA	National Science Teachers Association
SAT	Scholastic Aptitude Test

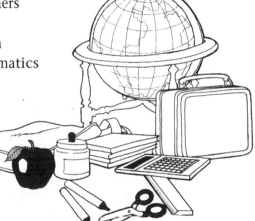

List 176. COMMON ABBREVIATIONS

Abbreviations are so widely used that it is important to know what the common ones stand for. In addition to being an advantage in reading comprehension, knowing and using abbreviations saves time, space, and energy when we write.

Streets and Roads

Blvd.	Boulevard
Dr.	Drive
St.	Street
Pkwy.	Parkway
Rd.	Road
Hwy.	Highway
Ln.	Lane

Titles

Dr.	Doctor
Esq.	Esquire
Hon.	Honorable
H.R.H.	Her (His) Royal Highness
Jr.	Junior
Pres.	President
Supt.	Superintendent
Rev.	Reverend
St.	Sister, Senior
Mr.	Mister
Mrs.	Mistress

Military Titles

Capt.	Captain
Lt.	Lieutenant
Col.	Colonel
Gen.	General
Sgt.	Sergeant

Degrees

B.A.	Bachelor of Arts
B.S.	Bachelor of Science
D.D	Doctor of Divinity
D.D.S.	Doctor of Dental Surgery
M.A.	Master of Arts
M.D.	Doctor of Medicine
Ph.D.	Doctor of Philosophy
Ed.D.	Doctor of Education
R.N.	Registered Nurse

Days of the Week

Sun., Sund.	Sunday
Mon.	Monday
Tues.	Tuesday
Wed.	Wednesday
Thur., Thur., Th.	Thursday
Fri., Fr.	Friday
Sat.	Saturday

Months of the Year

Jan.	January
Feb.	February
Mar.	March
Apr.	April
Jul.	July
Aug.	August
Sept.	September
Oct.	October
Nov.	November
Dec.	December

Parts of Speech

adj.	adjective
adv.	adverb
conj.	conjunction
n.	noun
prep.	preposition
v.	verb
art.	article
pn.	pronoun

Other Abbreviations

acct.	account
A.D.	Anno Domini (in the year of our Lord)
ad lib	ad libitum (improvise)
AKA	also known as
A.M.	ante meridiem (morning)

The Reading Teacher's Book of Lists, Fourth Edition, © 2000 by John Wiley & Sons, Inc.

amt	amount	H.M.S.	His (Her) Majesty's Ship
anon.	anonymous	hosp.	hospital
ans.	answer	hr	hour
arith.	arithmetic	ht	height
assn.	association		
assoc.	association	ibid.	ibidem (in the same place)
asst.	assistant	id.	idem (the same)
atty.	attorney	i.e.	id est (that is)
		illus.	illustration
bib.	bibliography	in.	inch
biog.	biography	Inc.	incorporated
B.C.	before Christ	incl.	including
bldg.	building	intro	introduction
C	centigrade	Jour.	Journal
cap.	capital		
cc	cubic centimeter	kg	kilogram
cert.	certificate		
chap.	chapter	lat.	latitude
Chas.	Charles	lb.	pound
cm	centimeter	long.	longitude
Co.	company		
conj.	conjunction	mag.	magazine
Corp.	corporation	masc.	masculine
cu	cubic	math	mathematics
		mdse.	merchandise
dept.	department	med.	medium
diam.	diameter	mgr.	manager
div.	division	min.	minute
doz.	dozen	misc.	miscellaneous
		ml	milliliter
ea.	each	mo.	month
ed.	edition	mph	miles per hour
e.g.	exempli gratia (for example)		
elec.	electric	neg.	negative
et al.	et alii (and others)	neut.	neuter
etc.	et cetera (and others)	no.	number
ex.	example		
		opp.	opposite
F	Fahrenheit	oz.	ounce
fem.	feminine		
fig.	figure	p.	page
freq.	frequency	pd.	paid
ft.	foot	pkg.	package
		pl.	plural
g	gram	P.M.	post meridiem (afternoon)
gal.	gallon	pop.	population
Gen.	General	pp.	pages
govt.	government	prin.	principal
		pt.	pint

qt.	quart	vet.	veterinarian, veteran
recd.	received	vocab.	vocabulary
ref.	referee; reference	vol.	volume
		vs.	versus
sci.	science		
sec.	second	wk.	week
sing.	singular	Wm.	William
sq.	square	wt.	weight
St.	Saint		
subj.	subject	yd.	yard
		yr.	year
tel.	telephone		
univ.	university		
USA	United States of America		

The Reading Teacher's Book of Lists, Fourth Edition, © 2000 by John Wiley & Sons, Inc.

See also List 174, State Abbreviations and Capitals; List 179, Acronyms and Initializations.

List 177. MEASUREMENT SYSTEM ABBREVIATIONS

CUSTOMARY MEASUREMENT SYSTEM

In the customary system of measurement, the reference unit used for length is the **inch**; the reference unit used for liquid capacity is the **ounce**. Inch rulers and yard sticks are used to measure length in the customary system.

Length

12 inches (12 in.)	equal	1 foot (1 ft.)
3 feet (3 ft.)	equal	1 yard (1 yd.)
220 yards (220 yds.)	equal	1 furlong (1 fur.)
8 furlongs (8 fur.)	equal	1 mile (1 mi.)

Liquid Capacity

8 fluid ounces (8 fl. oz)	equal	1 cup (1 c.)
2 cups (2 c.)	equal	1 pint (1 pt.)
16 fluid ounces (16 fl. oz)	equal	1 pint (1 pt.)
2 pints (2 pt.)	equal	1 quart (1 qt.)
32 fluid ounces (32 fl. oz.)	equal	1 quart (1 qt.)
4 quarts (4 qt.)	equal	1 gallon (1 gal.)
128 fluid ounces (128 fl. oz)	equal	1 gallon (1 gal.)

Mass Weight

16 ounces (16 oz.)	equal	1 pound (1 lb.)
2,000 pounds (2,000 lb.)	equal	1 ton (1 T.)

Area

144 square inches (144 sq. in.)	equal	1 square foot (1 sq. ft.)
9 square feet (9 sq. ft.)	equal	1 square yard (1 sq. yd.)
4,840 square yards (4,840 sq. yd.)	equal	1 acre (1 A.)

Volume

1,728 cubic inches (1,728 cu. in.)	equal	1 cubic foot (1 cu. ft.)
27 cubic feet (27 cu. ft.)	equal	1 cubic yard (1 cu. yd.)

METRIC SYSTEM

In the metric system of measurement, the reference unit used for length is the **meter**; the reference unit used for capacity is **liter**. Centimeter rulers and meter sticks are used to measure length in the metric system.

Length

10 millimeters (10 mm)	equal	1 centimeter (1 cm)
10 centimeters (10 cm)	equal	1 decimeter (1 dm)
100 millimeters (100 mm)	equal	1 decimeter (1 dm)
10 decimeters (10 dm)	equal	1 meter (1 m)
100 centimeters (100 cm)	equal	1 meter (1 m)
1,000 meters (1000 m)	equal	1 kilometer (1 km)

Liquid Capacity

10 milliliters (10 ml)	equal	1 centiliter (1 cl)
1,000 milliliters (1000 ml)	equal	1 liter (1 L)

Mass (Weight)

10 milligrams (10 mg)	equal	1 centigram (1 cg)
1,000 milligrams (1000 mg)	equal	1 gram (1 g)
1,000 grams (1000 g)	equal	1 kilogram (1 kg)
1,000 kilograms (1000 kg)	equal	1 metric ton (1 t)

Area

100 square millimeters (100 mm^2)	equal	1 square centimeter (1 cm^2)
10,000 square centimeters (10,000 cm^2)	equal	1 square meter (1 m^2)
10,000 square meters (10,000 m^2)	equal	1 hectare (1 ha)

Volume

1,000 cubic millimeters (1000 mm^3)	equal	1 cubic centimeter (1 cm^3)
1,000 cubic centimeters (1000 cm^3)	equal	1 cubic decimeter (1 dm^3)
1,000,000 cubic centimeters (1,000,000 cm^3)	equal	1 cubic meter (1 m^3)

METRIC CONVERSIONS

Customary System

		Metric System
1 inch	equals	2.5 centimeters
1 foot	equals	30 centimeters
1 yard	equals	0.9 meters
1 mile	equals	1.6 kilometers
1 pound	equals	0.45 kilogram
1 quart	equals	0.95 liter
1 gallon	equals	3.8 liters

Metric System

		Customary System
1 meter	equals	3.3 feet
1 hectare	equals	2.5 acres
1 centimeter	equals	0.4 inch
1 liter	equals	1.06 quarts
2 liter	equals	0.26 gallon
1 gram	equals	0.035 ounce
1 kilogram	equals	2.2 pounds

See also List 35, Math Vocabulary—Primary; List 38, Reading Math.

The Reading Teacher's Book of Lists, Fourth Edition, © 2000 by John Wiley & Sons, Inc.

List 178. OTHER MEASUREMENT ABBREVIATIONS

acre (ac.)	An area of 43,560 square feet.
Astronomical Unit (A.U.)	93,000,000 miles, the average distance of the earth from the sun.
Board Foot (fbm)	144 cubic inches (12 in. × 12 in. × 1 in.). Used for lumber.
Bolt (bo.)	40 yards. Used for measuring cloth.
BTU	British thermal unit. Amount of heat.
Carat (c)	200 milligrams. Used for weighing precious stones.
Chain (ch)	A chain 66 feet. Used in surveying.
Decibel (db)	Unit of relative loudness. One decibel is the smallest amount of change detectable by the human ear.
Fathom (fm.)	1 fathom = 6 feet.
Furlong (fur.)	1 furlong = 220 yards.
Gross (gr.)	12 dozen or 144.
Hand (hd.)	4 inches. Used for measuring the height of horses.
Hertz (Hz)	Unit for measurement of electromagnetic wave frequencies (equivalent to "cycles per second").
Horsepower (hp)	The power needed to lift 33,000 pounds a distance of one foot in one minute.
Karat (kt)	A measure of the purity of gold. 24 are pure gold. Sometimes spelled *carat*.
Knot (kn.)	Rate of speed of one nautical mile per hour.
League (L.)	Usually estimated at 3 miles.
Light Year (ly.)	5,880,000,000,000 miles the distance light travels in a vacuum in a year.
Magnum (Mg.)	Two-quart bottle.
Nautical Mile (nm)	1 mile (nautical) = 1.852 kilometers; 1.151 statute miles.
Pi (Π)	3.14159265+. The ratio of the circumference of a circle to its diameter.
Pica (pc.)	1/6 inch or 12 points. Used in printing.
Quire (qr.)	Used for measuring paper. Sometimes 24, but more often 25. There are 20 quires to a ream.
Ream (rm.)	Used for measuring paper, often 500 sheets.
Roentgen (R)	International unit of radiation produced by X-rays.
Score (sc)	20 units.
Sound, Speed of	Usually placed at 1.088 ft. per second.
Span	9 inches or 22.86 cm. End of the thumb and the end of the little finger when both are outstretched.
Township (T)	U.S. land measurement of almost 36 square miles.

See also List 37, Math Vocabulary—Intermediate.

The Reading Teacher's Book of Lists, Fourth Edition, © 2000 by John Wiley & Sons, Inc.

List 179. ACRONYMS AND INITIALIZATIONS

Everyone knows about TGIF, but what about MMB? Acronyms and initializations are used frequently in media and everyday communication. They are "shortcuts" that refer to multiword names and phrases. Both initializations and acronyms are formed from the first letters of the words they represent; however, they are pronounced differently. An initialization is pronounced using the letters that form it (e.g., ABC) whereas an acronym is pronounced as a word (e.g., AIDS). In both cases, periods signifying abbreviations are usually omitted. Entire dictionaries are now devoted to acronyms and a Web search will turn up more than you will ever need. This list includes commonly used acronyms and initializations. Acronyms are noted by *(acr)* following the definition. Additional computer-related acronyms and initializations can be found in List 143, Computer and Internet Terms, and List 144, E-mail, Chat, and Internet Acronyms.

ABC	American Broadcasting System
ADA	Americans with Disabilities Act
AIDS	Acquired immune deficiency syndrome *(acr)*
AKA	Also known as
ATM	Automated teller machine
ASAP	As soon as possible
AWOL	Absent without leave *(acr)*
BBC	British Broadcasting Corporation
BLT	Bacon, lettuce, and tomato
BMOC	Big man on campus
CBS	Columbia Broadcasting System
BTO	Big-time operator
CEO	Chief executive officer
CIA	Central Intelligence Agency
COD	Cash on delivery
CPA	Certified public accountant
DA	District attorney
DINK	Dual income no kids *(acr)*
DJ	Disk jockey
DOA	Dead on Arrival
EEOC	Equal Employment Opportunity Commission
EDP	Electronic Data Processing
EKG	Electrocardiogram
ERA	Equal rights amendment
ESL	English as a second language
EU	European Union
GNP	Gross national product
GPA	Grade point average
HIV	Human immunodeficiency virus
HMO	Health maintenance organization
HQ	Headquarters
IOU	I owe you
IQ	Intelligence quotient
IRA	International Reading Association; Irish Republican Army
IRS	Internal Revenue Service

The Reading Teacher's Book of Lists, Fourth Edition, © 2000 by John Wiley & Sons, Inc.

KISS	Keep it simple stupid *(acr)*
LASER	Light amplification by stimulated emission of radiation *(acr)*
MIA	Missing in action
MIT	Massachusetts Institute of Technology
MMB	Monday morning blues
MO	Modus operandi
MRI	Magnetic resonance imaging
MYOB	Mind your own business
NA	Not applicable
NAACP	National Association for the Advancement of Colored People
NASA	National Aeronautics and Space Administration *(acr)*
NATO	North Atlantic Treaty Organization *(acr)*
NBC	National Broadcasting System
NIMBY	Not in my backyard *(acr)*
PA	Public address
PBS	Public Broadcasting System
PDQ	Pretty darn quick
POW	Prisoner of war
PR	Public relations
PS	Post script
PTA	Parent–Teacher Association
RADAR	Radio detecting and range *(acr)*
RIP	Rest in peace
RSVP	Repondez s'il vous plait
RV	Recreational vehicle
SAT	Scholastic Aptitude Test
SCUBA	Self-contained underwater breathing apparatus *(acr)*
SNAFU	Situation normal: all fouled up *(acr)*
SONAR	Sound navigation ranging *(acr)*
SUV	Sports utility vehicle
SWAK	Sealed with a kiss *(acr)*
SWAT	Special weapons action team *(acr)*
TBA	To be arranged
TDD	Telecommunications device for the deaf
TEFLON	Tetrafloroethylene resin *(acr)*
TGIF	Thank God it's Friday
TLC	Tender loving care
TNT	Trinitrotoluene
TV	Television
UFO	Unidentified flying object
UN	United Nations
UPS	United Parcel Service
USA	United States of America
VCR	Video cassette recorder
VIP	Very important person
WASP	White Anglo-Saxon Protestant *(acr)*
ZIP	Zone Improvement Plan *(acr)*

List 180. DICTIONARY PHONETIC SYMBOLS

Dictionaries tell you how to pronounce words by using phonetic symbols. These are based on the Roman alphabet but add diacritical marks and special letter combinations. Although all dictionaries use similar phonetic symbols, they are not all identical. This list shows four of the more widely used sets of symbols.

PHONEMES	COMMON AND UNCOMMON SPELLINGS	PHONEMES	COMMON AND UNCOMMON SPELLINGS
ă	**A Short** h<u>a</u>t, pl<u>ai</u>d	f	**F** <u>f</u>at, e<u>ff</u>ort, lau<u>gh</u>, <u>ph</u>rase
ā	**A Long** <u>a</u>ge, <u>ai</u>d, <u>gao</u>l, <u>gau</u>ge, s<u>ay</u>, br<u>ea</u>k, v<u>ai</u>n, th<u>ey</u>	g	**G** <u>g</u>o, e<u>gg</u>, <u>gh</u>ost, <u>gu</u>est, catalo<u>gu</u>e
ā, er, ar, âr	**A** ("air" sound-diphthong) c<u>are</u>, <u>air</u>, <u>ear</u>, wh<u>ere</u>, p<u>ear</u>, th<u>eir</u>	h	**H** <u>h</u>e, <u>wh</u>o
		hw	**WH Digraph** <u>wh</u>eat
ä	**A Broad** <u>fa</u>ther, h<u>ear</u>t, s<u>er</u>geant	ĭ	**I Short** <u>E</u>ngland, b<u>ee</u>n, b<u>i</u>t, s<u>ie</u>ve, w<u>o</u>men, b<u>u</u>sy, b<u>ui</u>ld, h<u>y</u>mn
b	**B** <u>b</u>ad, ra<u>bb</u>it		
ch	**CH Digraph** <u>ch</u>ild, wa<u>tch</u>, righ<u>teo</u>us, ques<u>tio</u>n vir<u>tu</u>ous	ī	**I Long** <u>ai</u>sle, <u>ay</u>e, h<u>eigh</u>t, <u>eye</u>, <u>i</u>ce, l<u>ie</u>, b<u>uy</u>, sk<u>y</u>
d	**D** <u>d</u>id, a<u>dd</u>, fill<u>ed</u>	j	**J** bri<u>dg</u>e, gra<u>du</u>al, sol<u>di</u>er, tra<u>g</u>ic, exa<u>gg</u>erate, <u>j</u>am
ĕ	**E Short** m<u>a</u>ny, <u>ae</u>sthetic, s<u>ai</u>d, s<u>ay</u>s, l<u>e</u>t, br<u>ea</u>d, h<u>ei</u>fer, l<u>eo</u>pard, fr<u>ie</u>nd, b<u>u</u>ry	k	**K** <u>c</u>oat, a<u>cc</u>ount, <u>ch</u>emistry, ba<u>ck</u>, a<u>cq</u>uire, sa<u>cq</u>ue, <u>k</u>ind, li<u>qu</u>or
		l	**L** <u>l</u>and, te<u>ll</u>
ē	**E Long** C<u>ae</u>sar, qu<u>ay</u>, <u>e</u>qual, t<u>ea</u>m, b<u>ee</u>, rec<u>ei</u>ve, p<u>eo</u>ple, k<u>ey</u>, ma<u>chi</u>ne, bel<u>ie</u>ve, ph<u>oe</u>nix	m	**M** dra<u>chm</u>, paradi<u>gm</u>, ca<u>lm</u>, <u>m</u>e, cli<u>mb</u>, com<u>m</u>on, sole<u>mn</u>
		n	**N** <u>gn</u>aw, <u>kn</u>ife, <u>n</u>o, ma<u>nn</u>er, <u>pn</u>eumonia
ėr, ə, ûr	**R** (or short u plus R) st<u>er</u>n, p<u>ear</u>l, f<u>ir</u>st, w<u>or</u>d, j<u>our</u>ney, t<u>ur</u>n, m<u>y</u>rtle	ng	**NG Blend** i<u>n</u>k, lo<u>ng</u>, to<u>ngue</u>
		o, ə, ŏ	**O Short** w<u>a</u>tch, h<u>o</u>t

The Reading Teacher's Book of Lists, Fourth Edition, © 2000 by John Wiley & Sons, Inc.

PHONEMES	COMMON AND UNCOMMON SPELLINGS	PHONEMES	COMMON AND UNCOMMON SPELLINGS
ō	**O Long** b<u>eau</u>, y<u>eo</u>man, s<u>ew</u>, <u>o</u>pen, b<u>oa</u>t, t<u>oe</u>, <u>oh</u>, br<u>oo</u>ch, s<u>ou</u>l, l<u>ow</u>	u̇, u, o̽o̽	**U Short** w<u>o</u>lf, g<u>oo</u>d, sh<u>ou</u>ld, f<u>u</u>ll
ô, ȯ	**O Broad** <u>a</u>ll, Ut<u>ah</u>, t<u>au</u>ght, l<u>aw</u>, <u>o</u>rder, br<u>oa</u>d, b<u>ou</u>ght	ü, o͞o	**OO Long** man<u>eu</u>ver, thr<u>ew</u>, m<u>o</u>ve, sh<u>oe</u>, f<u>oo</u>d, y<u>ou</u>, r<u>u</u>le, fr<u>ui</u>t
oi, ȯi	**OI Diphthong** b<u>oi</u>l, b<u>oy</u>	v	**V** of, Ste<u>ph</u>en, <u>v</u>ery, fli<u>vv</u>er
ou, əu	**OU Diphthong** h<u>ou</u>se, b<u>ough</u>, n<u>ow</u>	w	**W** ch<u>oi</u>r, <u>qu</u>ick, <u>w</u>ill
p	**P** cu<u>p</u>, ha<u>pp</u>y	y	**Y** (consonant) opin<u>i</u>on, hallelu<u>j</u>ah, <u>y</u>ou
r	**R** <u>r</u>un, <u>rh</u>ythm, ca<u>rr</u>y	z	**Z** ha<u>s</u>, di<u>sc</u>ern, <u>sc</u>i<u>ss</u>ors, <u>X</u>erxes, <u>z</u>ero, bu<u>zz</u>
s	**S** <u>c</u>ent, <u>s</u>ay, <u>sc</u>ent, <u>sch</u>ism, mi<u>ss</u>	zh	**ZH** gara<u>g</u>e, mea<u>s</u>ure, divi<u>si</u>on, a<u>z</u>ure, bra<u>zi</u>er
sh	**SH Digraph** o<u>c</u>ean, ma<u>ch</u>ine, spe<u>ci</u>al, <u>s</u>ure, <u>sch</u>ist, con<u>sci</u>ence, nau<u>se</u>ous, p<u>sh</u>aw, <u>sh</u>e, ten<u>si</u>on, i<u>ss</u>ue, mi<u>ssi</u>on, na<u>ti</u>on	ə	**Schwa** <u>a</u>lone, fount<u>ai</u>n, mom<u>e</u>nt, pen<u>ci</u>l, c<u>o</u>mplete, cauti<u>ou</u>s, circ<u>u</u>s
t	**T** stoppe<u>d</u>, bough<u>t</u>, <u>t</u>ell, <u>Th</u>omas, but<u>t</u>on	**Diacritical Marks**	
th	**TH (voiceless)** <u>th</u>in	ôrder	(circumflex)
ŦH, <u>th</u>, t̸h	**TH (voiced)** <u>th</u>en, brea<u>th</u>e	ēqual	(macron)
		cañon	(tilde)
u, ə, ŭ	**U Short** c<u>o</u>me, d<u>oe</u>s, fl<u>oo</u>d, tr<u>ou</u>ble, c<u>u</u>p	naïve	(dieresis)
		façade	(cedilla)
		pu̇t	(single dot)
yü, yo͞o	**U Long** b<u>eau</u>ty, f<u>eu</u>d, qu<u>eue</u>, f<u>ew</u>, ad<u>ieu</u>, v<u>iew</u>, <u>u</u>se	attaché	(acute accent)
		à la mode	(grave accent)

See also List 1, Consonant Sounds; List 2, Vowel Sounds; List 8, Phonics Example Words.

The Reading Teacher's Book of Lists, Fourth Edition, © 2000 by John Wiley & Sons, Inc.

List 181. DIACRITICAL MARKING SYSTEM

The Diacritical Marking System (DMS) was an experimental teaching system that provided much phonic regularity to help beginning readers pronounce words. Diacritical marks are added to the text without altering the words' traditional spellings. If you want an interesting and challenging learning experience, have your students take any printed material and add these diacritical marks.

SHORT VOWELS & REGULAR CONSONANTS (no marks)

A	apple	F	fish	K	kitten	P	penny	U umbrella
B	Bill	G	girl	L	Linda	Q	queen (qu)	V valentine
C	cookies	H	hat	M	midnight	R	Rickey	W window
D	Daddy	I	Indian	N	nest	S	saw	X box (ks)
E	egg	J	jar	O	ox	T	table	Y baby
								Z zebra

LONG VOWELS (bar over)   Ā āpron   Ē ēar   Ī icĕ creăm   Ō Ōceán   Ū Ūnited States

---

SCHWA (comma over)   Á   É   'O   can also be used when any vowel, not a u, makes a short u sound. Examples:
ágo   énóugh   óthĕr   sóme frónt

LETTER Y   y in yes (consonant)   ȳ in mȳ (long vowel)   funny (Note y = E not marked)

DIPHTHONGS (underline both)   OI = boil   OY = boy   OU = out   OW = owl

---

BROAD O (A) (circumflex)   Â = âll   âwful   âuto   Ô = lông   ôr

---

LONG AND SHORT OO (one and two dots)

One Dot U or Short OO   U̇ = pu̇t   Ȯ = ġood

Two Dot U or Long OO   Ü = Jünĕ   Ö = roöm   Ë = nëw

R-CONTROLLED VOWELS (r acts as vowel)   AR far   AR vāry   IR fĭr   ER hĕr   UR fŭr

---

DIGRAPHS (underline)

SH shoĕ   CH chāïr   WH which   TH that (voiced)
TH thing (unvoiced)   NG sing   PH f phōnĕ

SECOND SOUNDS OF CONSONANTS (underline)

C (c = s) cent
S c = z is
G (g = j) gem

SILENT (slash)   cómĕ   rĭ g ht   hĕr

EXCEPTIONS (+ over)   womén   action   onĕ   stopped   of

The Reading Teacher's Book of Lists, Fourth Edition, © 2000 by John Wiley & Sons, Inc.

List 182. MANUAL ALPHABET

The manual alphabet shows one way in which deaf persons communicate. They also use a signing language that uses hand positions for whole words or concepts, and most can read lips to some extent.

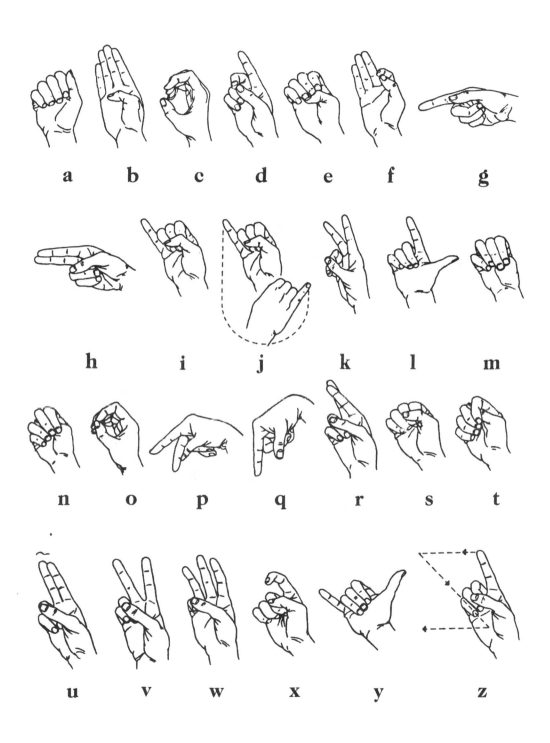

List 183. BRAILLE ALPHABET

Blind and visually impaired people learn to read the alphabet by feeling raised dots with their fingers.

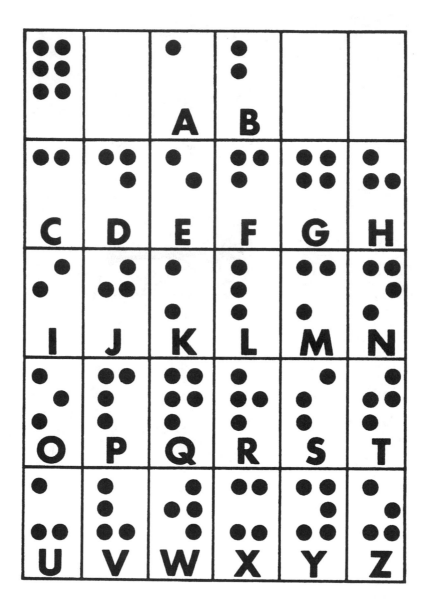

List 184. RADIO VOICE ALPHABET

This international alphabet is used by airplane pilots, ship personnel, ham radio operators, and many others who speak over the radio when they need to spell out words or give call letters.

Alfa	**H**otel	**O**scar	**V**ictor
Bravo	**I**ndia	**P**apa	**W**hiskey
Charlie	**J**uliett	**Q**uebec	**X**ray
Delta	**K**ilo	**R**omeo	**Y**ankee
Echo	**L**ima	**S**ierra	**Z**ulu
Foxtrot	**M**ike	**T**ango	
Golf	**N**ovember	**U**niform	

The Reading Teacher's Book of Lists, Fourth Edition, © 2000 by John Wiley & Sons, Inc.

List 185. MORSE CODE

The Morse Code is still used by some radio hams. With practice, it is possible for amateurs to use it to send flashlight messages.

A	.—	V	...—
B	—...	W	.——
C	—.—.	X	—..—
D	—..	Y	—.——
E	.	Z	——..
F	..—.	Á	.—.——
G	——.	Ä	.—.—
H	....	É	..—..
I	..	Ñ	——.——
J	.———	Ö	———.
K	—.—	Ü	..——
L	.—..	1	.————
M	——	2	..———
N	—.	3	...——
O	———	4	....—
P	.——.	5	.....
Q	——.—	6	—....
R	.—.	7	——...
S	...	8	———..
T	—	9	————.
U	..—	0	—————

,	(comma)	——..——
.	(period)	.—.—.—
?		..——..
;		—.—.—.
:		———...
/		—..—.
- (hyphen)		—....—
apostrophe		.————.
parenthesis		—.——.—
underline		..——.—

The Reading Teacher's Book of Lists, Fourth Edition, © 2000 by John Wiley & Sons, Inc.

436

List 186. NATIVE AMERICAN SYMBOLS

The earliest writings of the Native American Indians were those of signs and symbols. These symbols are also apparent in their handicraft and jewelry.

HORSE
Journey
MAN
Human Life
SUN RAYS
Constancy
LASSO
Captivity
THUNDERBIRD
Sacred Bearer of Happiness Unlimited
CROSSED ARROWS
Friendship
ARROW
Protection
ARROWHEAD
Alertness
FOUR AGES
Infancy, Youth, Middle and Old Age
CACTUS
Sign of the Desert
GILA MONSTER
Sign of the Desert
CACTUS FLOWER
Courtship
SADDLE BAGS
Journey
BIRD
Carefree, Lighthearted
LIGHTNING SNAKE
SNAKE
Defiance, Wisdom
THUNDERBIRD TRACK
Bright Prospects
DEER TRACK
Plenty Game
BEAR TRACK
Good Omen
RATTLESNAKE JAW
Strength
HEADDRESS
Ceremonial Dance

COYOTE TRACKS
RAIN CLOUDS
Good Prospects
LIGHTNING AND
LIGHTNING ARROW
Swiftness
DAYS AND NIGHTS
Time
MORNING START
Guidance
SUN SYMBOLS
Happiness
RUNNING WATER
Constant Life
RAINDROP—RAIN
Plentiful Crops
TEPEE
Temporary Home
SKY BAND
Leading to Happiness
MEDICINE MAN'S EYE
Wise, Watchful
MOUNTAIN RANGE
HOGAN
Permanent Home
BIG MOUNTAIN
Abundance
HOUSE OF WATER
FENCE
Guarding Good Luck
ENCLOSURE FOR
CEREMONIAL DANCES
EAGLE FEATHERS
Chief
WARDING OFF EVIL SPIRITS
PATHS CROSSING
PEACE
(broken arrow)
BUTTERFLY
Everlasting Life

List 187. ROMAN NUMERALS

We might have taken our alphabet from the Romans but, thankfully, we did not take their number system. Roman numerals are used for formal or decorative purposes, such as on clocks and cornerstones. For fun and learning, have every student write his or her date of birth in Roman numerals. Write the principal's birthday, too.

Roman	Arabic	Roman	Arabic
I	1	XX	20
II	2	XXI	21
III	3	XXIX	29
IV	4	XXX	30
V	5	XL	40
VI	6	XLVIII	48
VII	7	IL	49
VIII	8	L	50
IX	9	LX	60
X	10	XC	90
XI	11	XCVIII	98
XII	12	IC	99
XIII	13	C	100
XIV	14	CI	101
XV	15	CC	200
XVI	16	D	500
XVII	17	DC	600
XVIII	18	CM	900
XIX	19	M	1000
		MCMLXCIX	1999

Note: Roman Numerals have the following basic symbols:

I = 1   L = 50   M = 1000
V = 5   C = 100
X = 10   D = 500

A smaller symbol *before* a larger symbol means *subtract* the smaller amount, thus:

IX = 9   CM = 900   IL = 49   XXIX = 29

A smaller symbol *after* a larger symbol means *add* the small amount, thus:

XI = 11   LI = 51   XXVIII = 28
MC = 1100 XXXI = 31 LV = 55

List 188. TRAFFIC SIGNS

As international travel has become more common, the United States has adopted traffic signs that use pictures and symbols. These help overcome language barriers. Understanding traffic signs is important for safety for drivers and pedestrians.

Shapes have meaning. Diamond-shaped signs signify a warning; rectangular signs with the longer dimension vertical provide a traffic regulation; rectangular signs with the longer dimension horizontal contain guidance information; an octagon means stop; an inverted triangle means yield; a pennant means no passing; a pentagon shows the presence of a school; and a circle warns of a railroad crossing.

Regulatory Signs

Black and white signs are for posting regulations. Red signifies stop, yield or prohibition. The red circle with a diagonal slash always indicates a prohibited movement.

NO U TURN

NO LEFT TURN

NO RIGHT TURN

NO TRUCKS

KEEP RIGHT

**CENTER LANE
LEFT TURN ONLY**

Left turns may be allowed for traffic coming from opposing directions in the center lane of a highway. There are two types of signs used to identify these locations. One a word message and the other a symbol sign showing opposing left turn arrows with the word "Only."

ONLY

SPEED LIMIT 55

NO TURN ON RED

RIGHT TURN ON RED AFTER STOP

Turns are permitted in many States at traffic signals when the red traffic signal is on. There are two types of laws which permit this movement. One permits the turn only with posting of the sign "Right Turn on Red After Stop." The other law allows turns at any intersection unless specifically prohibited by displaying the sign "No Turn on Red."

The pennant-shaped warning sign supplements the rectangular regulatory, "Do Not Pass" sign. The pennant is located on the left side of the road at the beginning of the no-passing pavement marking.

NO PASSING ZONE

STOP

YIELD

WRONG WAY

DO NOT ENTER

DO NOT PASS

A "Restricted Lane Ahead" sign provides advance notice of a preferential lane which has been established in many cases to conserve energy by the use of high occupancy vehicles such as buses and carpools. The diamond symbol displayed on the sign is also marked on the pavement to further identify the controlled lane.

RESTRICTED LANE AHEAD

The Reading Teacher's Book of Lists, Fourth Edition, © 2000 by John Wiley & Sons, Inc.

Guide Signs

Green background signs provide directional information. Diagrams on some signs are being introduced to help motorists find the correct path through complicated interchange ramp networks. Roadside mileage markers will assist in trip planning and provide locational information. In addition mileage numbers (mile post numbers) are used to identify interchanges and exits. The number for an exit is determined from the nearest roadside mileage marker preceding the crossroad. Green signs also point the way of such items as trails for hiking and places for parking.

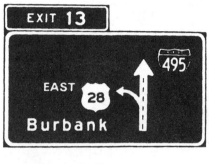

The brown background sign provides information pertaining to access routes for public parks and recreation areas.

Signs for Bicycles

Bicycles are used by many persons on portions of heavily traveled roadways. This mixing of bicycles and motor vehicles is extremely dangerous and wherever possible, separate facilities are being provided for the bicycles.

Service Signs

The blue color of these signs indicates that they provide direction to motorist service facilities. Word message signs generally are used to direct motorists to areas where service stations, restaurants, and motels are available. Logo signs are optional.

Signs in Construction Areas

The color orange has a special use. It appears on signs and barricades in construction and maintenance areas as a constant warning to motorists of possible dangers.

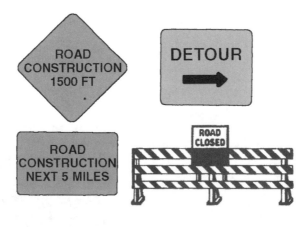

See also List 157, Daily Living Words; List 158, Travel Words.

The Reading Teacher's Book of Lists, Fourth Edition, © 2000 by John Wiley & Sons, Inc.

15
REFERENCE

List 189. READING ORGANIZATIONS AND JOURNALS

Reading and literacy education is dynamic and there is always something new to learn or share with reading colleagues. Keep abreast of research, trends, best practices, and promising innovations by being an active member of one or more professional associations in reading and by reading journals and publications in the field. The organizations have local and regional affiliates and sponsor national conferences. Their web sites have current information, links to reading sites, and much more.

Organizations

International Reading Association (IRA)
Box 8139
Newark, DE 19711
www.ira.org
Annual meeting, early May

National Reading Conference (NRC)
122 S. Michigan Ave.
Suite 1100
Chicago, IL 60603
www.oakland.edu/~mceneane/nrc/nrcindex.html
Annual meeting, early December

College Reading Association (CRA)
Gary L. Shaffer, Pub/Business Manager
113 Danny Drive, Apt. F
Carollton, GA 30117
//coe@.tsuniv.edu/cra/
Annual meeting, October

National Council of Teachers of English (NCTE)
1111 Kenyon Road
Urbana, IL 61801
www.ncte.org/
Annual meeting, mid-November

Journals

Many journals are available through membership in the reading associations listed above. Your school librarian can contact the associations for library subscription information. Visit *Reading OnLine*, the electronic journal of the International Reading Association, at www.readingonline.ort/about/welcome.index.

CRA Yearbook (CRA)

English Education (CEE/NCTE)

English Journal (NCTE)

Journal of Adolescent & Adult Literary (IRA)

Journal of Literacy Research (NRC)

Language Arts (NCTE)

Primary Voices (NCTE)

Reading Research & Instruction (CRA)

Reading Research Quarterly (IRA)

Reading Teacher (IRA)

Research in the Teaching of English (NCTE)

Talking Points (WLU/NCTE)

The Reading News (CRA)

Voice from the Media (NCTE)

IRA Past Presidents

1955–1956	William S. Gray	1960–1961	Mary C. Austin
1956–1957	Nancy Larrick	1961–1962	William D. Sheldon
1957–1958	Albert J. Harris	1962–1963	Morton Botel
1958–1959	George D. Spache	1963–1964	Nila Banton Smith
1959–1960	A. Sterl Artley	1964–1965	Theodore Clymer

1965–1966	Dorothy K. Bracken	1984–1985	Bernice E. Cullinan
1966–1967	Mildred A. Dawon	1985–1986	John C. Manning
1967–1968	H. Alan Robinson	1986–1987	Roselmina Indrisanoa
1968–1969	Leo C. Fay	1987–1988	Phylliss J. Adams
1969–1970	Helen Huus	1988–1989	Patricia S. Koppman
1970–1971	Donald L. Cleland	1989–1990	Dale Johnson
1971–1972	Theodore L. Harris	1990–1991	Carol Braun
1972–1973	William K. Durr	1991–1992	Judith Thelen
1973–1974	Millard H. Black	1992–1993	Marie M. Clay
1974–1975	Constance M. McCullough	1993–1994	Doris Roettger
1975–1976	Thomas C. Barrett	1994–1995	Susan Mandel Glazer
1976–1977	Walter H. MacGinitie	1995–1996	Dolores B. Malcolm
1977–1978	William Eller	1996–1997	Richard T. Vacca
1978–1979	Dorothy S. Strickland	1997–1998	John Pikulski
1979–1980	Roger C. Farr	1998–1999	Kathryn Ransom
1980–1981	Olive S. Niles	1999–2000	Carol M. Santa
1981–1982	Kenneth S. Goodman	2000–2001	Carmelita K. Williams
1982–1983	Jack Casssidy	2001–2002	Dona M. Ogle
1983–1984	Ira E. Aaron		

NRC Presidents

1952–1959	Oscar Causey	1988	M. Trika Smith-Burke
1960–1961	William Eller	1989	James Hoffman
1962–1964	George Spache	1990	Gerald Duffy
1964–1965	Albert Kingston	1991	Robert Tierney
1967–1968	Paul Berg	1992	Donna Alverman
1969–1970	Alton Raygor	1993	Rebecca Barr
1971	Wendell Weaver	1994	James Flood
1972–1974	Earl Rankin	1995	Jane Hansen
1974–1976	Edward Fry	1996	Richard Allington
1976–1978	Jaap Tuinman	1997	Kathryn H. Au
1978–1980	Harry Singer	1998	Martha R. Ruddell
1980–1982	Frank Greene	1999	Linda B. Gamdrell
1982–1984	Irene Athey	2000	Taffy E. Raphael
1985	Lenore Ringler	2001	Peter B. Mosenthal
1986	P. David Pearson	2002	Deborah R. Dillon
1987	Jerome Harste		

List 190. LIBRARY CLASSIFICATIONS

Most universities, research organizations, large public libraries, and, of course, the Library of Congress, use the Library of Congress classifications for organizing their book collections. Most school libraries and smaller public libraries use the Dewey Decimal System. Students should have at least a modest acquaintance with both systems.

The Reading Teacher's Book of Lists, Fourth Edition, © 2000 by John Wiley & Sons, Inc.

LIBRARY OF CONGRESS CLASSIFICATION

A   General Works
B   Philosophy and Religion
C   History of Civilization
D   General History
E–F History—Americas
G   Geography and Anthropology
H   Social Sciences
J   Political Science
K   Law
L   Education
M   Music
N   Fine Arts
P   Language and Literature
     PA   Classical Language and Literature
     PB–PH   Modern European Languages
     PJ–PL   Oriental Language and Literature
     PN   General Literature
     PQ   French, Italian, Spanish,
             Portugeuse Literature
     PR   English Literature
     PS   American Literature
     PT   German, Dutch, Scandinavian
             Literature
Q   Science
R   Medicine
S   Agriculture
T   Technology
U   Military Science
V   Naval Science
Z   Bibliography

SIMPLIFIED DEWEY DECIMAL SYSTEM

000	General Works
100	Philosophy and Psychology
200	Religion
300	Social Sciences
310	Statistics
320	Political Science
330	Economics
331	Labor Economics
331.3	Labor by Age Groups
331.39	Employed Middle-aged and Aged
340	Law
350	Administration
360	Welfare and Social Institutions
370	Education
380	Public Services and Utilities
390	Customs and Folklore
400	Philosophy
500	Pure Science
600	Applied Science
700	Fine Arts
800	Literature
900	History

Note: Libraries that use the Dewey Decimal System classify fiction by author's last name and it is usually divided into Adult Fiction and Children's Fiction. All the books in the library are listed in the "Card Catalog." Most books have 3 cards: an author card, a subject card, and a title card. Many libraries currently have their card catalog online.

List 191. PUBLISHERS OF READING MATERIALS AND TESTS

This list will be helpful when requesting current catalogs. For a list of all major U.S. publishers, including trade books for children, see *Literary Market Place*, which is published annually and can be found in most libraries.

Addison Wesley Longman
One Jacob Way
Reading, MA 01867

Advantage Learning Systems, Inc.
2911 Peach St.
Wisconsin Rapids, WI 54494

Allyn & Bacon
160 Gould Street
Needham Heights, MA 02194

Atheneum Books for Young Readers
1230 Avenue of the Americas
New York, NY 10020

Audio Bookshelf
174 Prescott Hill Rd.
Northport, ME 04849

Avon Books
1350 Avenue of the Americas
New York, NY 10019

Bantam Doubleday Dell
1540 Broadway
New York, NY 10036

Boyds Mill Press
815 Church St.
Honesdale, PA 18431

Broderbund Software
500 Redwood Blvd.
Novato, CA 94947

Celebration Press
One Jacob Way
Reading, MA 01867

Cobblestone Publishing Company
30 Grove St.
Peterborough, NH 03458

Computer Curriculum Corporation
1287 Lawrence Station Rd.
Sunnyvale, CA 94089

Continental Press
520 E. Bainbridge St.
Elizabethtown, PA 17022

Crabtree Publishing Company
350 Fifth Ave., Ste. 3308
New York, NY 10118

The Cricket Magazine Group
315 Fifth St.
Peru, IL 61354

Curriculum Associates Inc.
153 Rangeway Rd.
N. Billerica, MA 01862

Cuisenaire, Dale Seymour
10 Bank St.
P.O. Box 5026
White Plains, NY 10602

Disney Press
114 Fifth Ave.
New York, NY 10011

ERIC Clearinghouse on Reading, English,
 and Communication
Indiana University, Smith Research Center
2805 East 10th, Ste. 150
Bloomington, IN 47408

Farrar, Straus and Giroux
19 Union Square West
New York, NY 10003

Firefly Books
3680 Victoria Park Ave.
Willowdale, Ontario M2H 3K1
Canada

Goodyear Books
One Jacob Way
Reading, MA 01867

The Great Books Foundation
35 East Wacker Dr., Ste. 2300
Chicago, IL 60601

Grolier Classroom Publishing
Sherman Turnpike
Danbury, CT 06813

Harcourt Brace Educational Measurement
  Division
555 Academic Court
San Antonio, TX 78204

Harcourt Brace School Publishers
6277 Sea Harbor Dr.
Orlando, FL 32887

HarperCollins Children's Books
10 East 53 St.
New York, NY 10022

Highlights for Children
P.O. Box 269
Columbus, OH 43216

Henry Holt and Company
115 West 18 St.
New York, NY 10011

Holt, Rinehart and Winston
1120 South Capital of Texas Hwy.
Austin, TX 78746

Houghton Mifflin Company
222 Berkeley St.
Boston, MA 02116

Jamestown Publishers
4255 W. Touhy Ave.
Lincolnwood, IL 60646

Kendall/Hunt Publishing Company
4050 Westmark Dr.
Dubuque, IA 52002

Learning Well
1720 H. Belmont Ave.
Baltimore, MD 21244

Little, Brown and Company
Three Center Plaza
Boston, MA 02108

Longman
1185 Avenue of the Americas
New York, NY 10036

Macmillan/McGraw-Hill
1221 Avenue of the Americas
New York, NY 10020

McGraw-Hill School Division
1221 Avenue of the Americas
New York, NY 10020

Modern Curriculum
299 Jefferson Rd.
Parsippany, NJ 07054

William Morrow & Company
1350 Avenue of the Americas
New York, NY 10019

Richard C. Owen Publishers
P.O. Box 585
Katonah, NY 10536

Oxford University Press—Education
4525 Prime Pkwy.
McHenry, IL 60050

Penguin Putnam Inc.
375 Hudson St.
New York, NY 10014

Perfection Learning Corporation
1000 N. Second Ave.
Logan, IA 51546

Pocket Books/Simon & Schuster
1230 Avenue of the Americas
New York, NY 10020

Prentice Hall Direct
240 Frisch Ct.
Paramus, NJ 07652

Prentice Hall Higher Education
1 Lake Street
Upper Saddle River, NJ 07458

Prentice Hall School
1 Lake Street
Upper Saddle River, NJ 07458

Rigby
500 Coventry Ln., Ste. 200
Crystal Lake, IL 60014

Frank Schaffer Publications
23740 Hawthorne Blvd.
Torrance, CA 90505

Scholastic Inc.
555 Broadway
New York, NY 10012

Scott Foresman
1900 East Lake Ave.
Glenview, IL 60025

Dale Seymour Publications
10 Bank St., Ste. 880
White Plains, NY 10602

Silver Burdett Ginn
299 Jefferson Rd.
Parsippany, NJ 07054

Simon & Schuster Books
1230 Avenue of the Americas
New York, NY 10020

SRA/McGraw-Hill
250 Old Wilson Bridge Rd.
Worthington, OH 43085

Steck–Vaughn
4515 Seton Center Pkwy.
Ste. 300
Austin, TX 78759

Teacher Created Materials
6421 Industry Way
Westminister, CA 92683

Teacher Support Software
3542 NW 97th Blvd.
Gainesville, FL 32606

TIME for Kids
1271 Avenue of the Americas
New York, NY 10020

Touchphonics Reading Systems
4900 Birch St.
Newport Beach, CA 92660

Wadsworth Publishing
10 Davis Dr.
Belmont, CA 94002

Weekly Reader
P.O. Box 120023
Stamford, CT 06912

The Wright Group
19201 120th Ave. NE
Bothell, WA 98011

Zaner–Bloser
P.O. Box 16764
Columbus, OH 43216

The Reading Teacher's Book of Lists, Fourth Edition, © 2000 by John Wiley & Sons, Inc.

See also List 138, Web Sites for Reading Instruction.

List 192. POPULAR NAMES

Here is a list of the most frequently given names for births in the past year. Note that each unique spelling is also considered a unique name, even if both names sound the same—like Kaitlyn and Katelyn, or Brian and Bryan. They're still unique even if they represent the same name, like Alejandro and Alexander.

Female Names

1. Emily	35. Destiny
2. Samantha	36. Natalie
3. Madison	37. Jennifer
4. Ashley	38. Alexandra
5. Sarah	39. Amber
6. Hannah	40. Hailey
7. Jessica	41. Katherine
8. Alyssa	42. Kaitlyn
9. Alexis	43. Maria
10. Kayla	44. Katelyn
11. Abigail	45. Mary
12. Taylor	46. Shelby
13. Elizabeth	47. Andrea
14. Olivia	48. Sierra
15. Brianna	49. Vanessa
16. Victoria	50. Savannah
17. Emma	51. Allison
18. Megan	52. Erin
19. Rachel	53. Gabrielle
20. Amanda	54. Kimberly
21. Courtney	55. Sara
22. Nicole	56. Chloe
23. Lauren	57. Michelle
24. Jasmine	58. Sophia
25. Sydney	59. Breanna
26. Anna	60. Brooke
27. Morgan	61. Kathryn
28. Stephanie	62. Makayla
29. Julia	63. Jordan
30. Rebecca	64. Kaylee
31. Brittany	65. Mackenzie
32. Grace	66. Madeline
33. Haley	67. Melissa
34. Danielle	68. Christina

Male Names

1. Michael	35. Ethan
2. Jacob	36. Cameron
3. Matthew	37. Nathan
4. Christopher	38. Aaron
5. Joshua	39. Caleb
6. Austin	40. Cody
7. Nicholas	41. Steven
8. Tyler	42. Eric
9. Joseph	43. Luis
10. Andrew	44. Timothy
11. Daniel	45. Jason
12. Ryan	46. Adam
13. Brandon	47. Charles
14. Anthony	48. Isaac
15. David	49. Brian
16. William	50. Jesus
17. John	51. Richard
18. Zachary	52. Sean
19. Dylan	53. Gabriel
20. James	54. Bryan
21. Alexander	55. Jack
22. Justin	56. Jared
23. Jonathan	57. Juan
24. Jordan	58. Alex
25. Noah	59. Connor
26. Robert	60. Devin
27. Jose	61. Isaiah
28. Kyle	62. Antonio
29. Kevin	63. Carlos
30. Samuel	64. Elijah
31. Christian	65. Logan
32. Benjamin	66. Patrick
33. Thomas	67. Mark
34. Hunter	68. Jesse

Female Names

69. Marissa	85. Mariah
70. Paige	86. Riley
71. Sabrina	87. Angela
72. Alexandria	88. Kiara
73. Kelsey	89. Mikayla
74. Laura	90. Cassidy
75. Miranda	91. Erica
76. Molly	92. Veronica
77. Alexa	93. Autumn
78. Jacqueline	94. Cassandra
79. Jade	95. Diana
80. Bailey	96. Gabriella
81. Briana	97. Jenna
82. Caroline	98. Michaela
83. Katie	99. Alicia
84. Kylie	100. Faith

Male Names

69. Chase	85. Bradley
70. Cole	86. Brett
71. Luke	87. Bryce
72. Seth	88. Jackson
73. Angel	89. Adrian
74. Dakota	90. Brendan
75. Jeremy	91. Evan
76. Alejandro	92. Gavin
77. Ian	93. Paul
78. Jake	94. Tanner
79. Nathaniel	95. Tristan
80. Garrett	96. Dalton
81. Lucas	97. Devon
82. Victor	98. Kenneth
83. Stephen	99. Spencer
84. Trevor	100. Xavier

The Reading Teacher's Book of Lists, Fourth Edition, © 2000 by John Wiley & Sons, Inc.

See also List 173, Fun Names.

List 193. THE NORMAL DISTRIBUTION CURVE

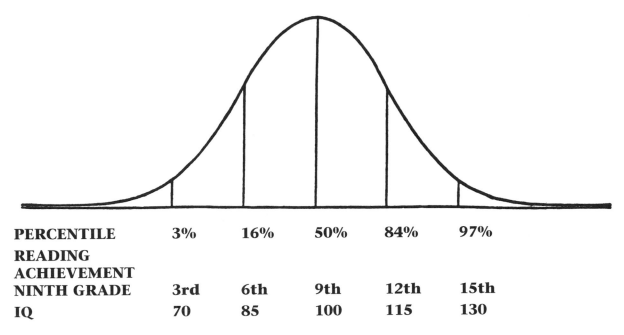

PERCENTILE	3%	16%	50%	84%	97%
READING ACHIEVEMENT NINTH GRADE	3rd	6th	9th	12th	15th
IQ	70	85	100	115	130

There is a strong but far from perfect correlation between Reading Achievement scores and IQ. In other words, on average a ninth grader with an IQ of 85 tends to read about at the sixth-grade level.

TYPICAL READING ABILITIES FOUND IN A FOURTH-GRADE CLASS

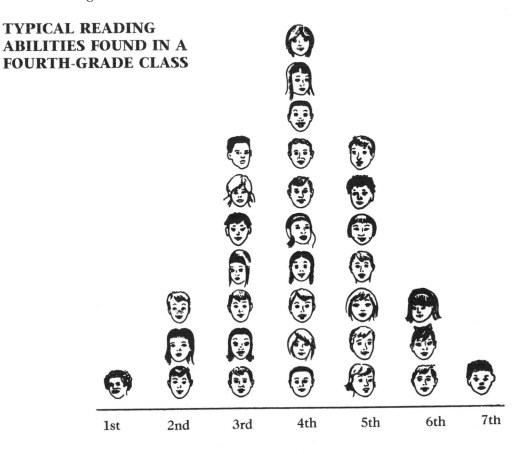

| 1st | 2nd | 3rd | 4th | 5th | 6th | 7th |

List 194. TAXONOMY OF GRAPHS

This is a simplified version of a more complete taxonomy of graphs. Its purpose is to show some of the varieties of graphical expression used by writers and read by readers. Teachers should encourage students to use graphs to express ideas and to supplement writing. Graph comprehension can be taught using many of the same questions used to teach paragraph comprehension (main idea, inference, sequence, etc.).

1. Lineal

    a. Simple   story

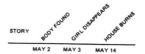

    b. Multiple   history

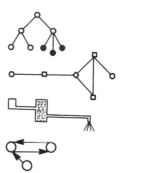

    c. Complex Hierarchy   organization

       Flow   computer

       Process   chemicals

       Sociogram   friendship

2. Quantitative

    a. Frequency polygon   growth

    b. Bar graph   production

    c. Scattergram   test scores

    d. Status graph   scheduling

    e. Pie graph   percentage

    f. Dials   clock

The Reading Teacher's Book of Lists, Fourth Edition, © 2000 by John Wiley & Sons, Inc.

From "Graphical Literacy" by Edward Fry. *Journal of Reading*, Feb. 1981. Also see "Theory of Graphs" ERIC, #ED 240/528.

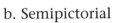

3. Spatial

a. Two dimensions
(single plane)   map   floor plan

b. Three dimensions
(multiplane)   relief map  math shapes

4. Pictorial

a. Realistic

b. Semipictorial

c. Abstract

5. Hypothetical

a. Conceptual

b. Verbal

6. Near Graphs

a. High verbal outline

    Main idea
    a. Detail
    b. Another detail

b. High numerical

Table	
25	4.2
37	6.1
71	7.3

c. Symbols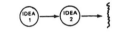

d. Decorative Design

See also List 105, Graphic Organizers.

455

Index

E

Easily confused words, 75-78
Education abbreviations, 422
Ellipsis, 216
E-mail acronyms, 353. *See also* Emoticons
Emoticons, 354
Emphasis, change in sentence meaning, 275
Employment words. *See* Application words,
    Want ad words
English language arts standards, 302-303
English sounds
    not used in other languages, 358
    problems for ESL students, 358
ESL (English as a Second Language)
    common word idioms, 367-369
    English sounds not used in other lan-
        guages, 358
    idiomatic expressions, 370-371
    problem English sounds for ESL students,
        358
    students' language background, 359
    words with multiple meanings, 373-375
    See also Application words, Daily living
        words, Jump-rope rhymes, Nonreversible
        word pairs, Travel words, Word origins,
        Work words
Essay test words, 309
Euphemisms. *See* Doublespeak, Report card
    helps
Exclamation point, 215
Expository text, characteristics of, 233

F

Fiction and nonfiction collections, 189-191
Final "E" Rule, 5
Fishbone diagram, 285
Flower names coined from people, 123
Food, proverbs about, 365. *See also* Grocery
    and drug words, Menu words
Foreign words, 114-116
French phrases, 117
Fun. *See* Children's humor, Fun names, Games
    and methods for teaching, Hinks pinks,
    Jokes, Jump-rope rhymes, Tongue
    twisters, Wacky wordies

G

Games for
    spelling, 333
    teaching, 253-259
Gardner, Howard, and multiple intelligences,
    231-233

G (continued)

Gender-neutral language. *See*
    Nondiscriminatory language guidelines
Genre, literature, 154
Geography vocabulary
    continents, 143
    intermediate, 142
    largest U.S. cities, 144
    oceans, 143
    population centers, 144
    primary, 141
    religions, 144
    rivers, 143
Geometry vocabulary
    elementary, 132
    intermediate, 133-135
German words, 115
Good ideas for reading teachers, 227
Grammar. *See* Capitalization guidelines, Parts
    of speech
Graph, readability, 234-235
Graphic organizers to improve comprehen-
    sion, 283-287
Graphs, taxonomy of, 454-455. *See also*
    Graphic organizers, Normal distribution
    curve
Greek
    -*ology* word family, 112
    -*phobia* word family, 113
    root words, 106-111
Grocery and drug words, 382-383
Group project guide, 243. *See also* Teams

H

Handwriting charts, 223-224
He said/she said, 208
Heteronyms, 65-74
High frequency words. *See* Instant words
Highway travel. *See* Traffic signs, Travel words
Hinks pinks, 394
Homographs, 65-74. *See also* Words with mul-
    tiple meanings
Homonyms. *See* Homophones, Homographs
Homophones, 55-63
    teaching suggestions, 64, 258-259
Hospital words, 383-384
Humor, children's, 403-404

I

Income tax words, 383
Indian (East) words, 114
Idiomatic expressions, 370-371. *See also*
    Nonreversible word pairs

Praise, ways to, 239-240
Predicates. *See* Sentence patterns, Verbs
Predictable books, 176-177
Prefixes, 85-92
    beginning, 85-86
    expressing numbers, 88-89
    for super-large numbers, 135
    for super-small numbers, 135
    intermediate to advanced, 86-88
    meaning categories, 88-92
Prepositional phrase, 214
Prepositions, definition, 360
Presentation rubrics, 308
Problem-solving guide, 293
Project guide, student/group, 243-244
Pronouns, definition, 360
Pronunciation, words with similar. *See* Easily
    confused words.
Proofreading
    checklist, elementary, 219
    checklist, intermediate, 220
    marks, 221
    See also Correction marks for teachers
Propaganda techniques, 276-277
Proverbs, 364-366
Publishers of reading materials and tests, 448-
    450
Punctuation guidelines, 215-216

Q

Question mark, 215
Questions, sentence pattern for, 213
Quotation mark, 215

R

Radio voice alphabet, 435
Readability graph, 234-235
Reading
    activities, oral, 238
    aloud, books for, 159-163
    and multiple intelligences, 231-233
    ideas for teaching, 227
    journals, 445
    logs, 301
    tips for parents, 250-252
    Web sites for instruction of, 341
    See also Comprehension, Story guide
Reading organizations
    list of, 445
    presidents of 445-446
Reference library, virtual, 346-347
Relationships, proverbs about, 364
Religions of the world, 144
Reluctant readers, books for, 182, 187

Report card helps, 247
Requests, sentence pattern for, 213
Retelling, 300
Riddles, 401-402. *See also* Jokes, Children's
    humor
Rimes. *See* Phonograms
Rivers of the world, major, 143
Road signs, 380-381
    traffic signs, 439-442
Roman numerals, 438
Roots, Greek and Latin
    less common, 108-111
    more common, 106-108
    See also -Cide, -Ology, -Phobia
Rubrics
    presentation, 308
    writing, elementary/intermediate, 307
    writing, primary, 306
Ruler
    phonics, 5-7
    plurals, 326-327
    suffixes, 325
    syllabication, 43
    teamwork, 246

S

Sales words, 384-385
Sanskrit words, 115
Schwa, 4, 7
Science vocabulary
    elementary, 145-146
    intermediate, 147-149
Science words from people's names, 122-123
Search engines for educators, 338
Searching the Internet, tips for, 337
Semantic
    feature analysis, 284
    mapping, 287
Semicolon, 216
Sentence, chart for building, 214
Sentence patterns, 213
Sentence tunes, 275
Short forms of words. *See* Clipped words
Signal words, 269-271. *See also* Essay test
    words, Modifiers in test questions
Sign language. *See* Manual alphabet
Signs, 381-382
    road, 380-381
    traffic, 439-442
Silent consonants, 3
Similes, 209
Size, prefixes used to describe, 89. *See also*
    Measurement
Skills. *See* Comprehension, Study skills
Skimming, 292

Tutors, activities for, 248-249

U

Urban areas, 144
Useful words, 47-82

V

Venn diagram, 284
Verbs
 definition of, 360
 in dialogue, 208
 irregular forms, 361-363
 math, 133
 suffixes, 96, 99
Virtual reference library, 346
Vocabulary building. *See* Antonyms, *-Cide*,
 Greek and Latin roots, *-Ology*, *-Phobia*,
 Prefixes, Suffixes, Synonyms, Ways to
 define a word
Vocabulary words. *See* Subject words, Section
 4.
Vowel sounds, 4
 double vowels, 6
 final "e" rule, 5
 sound determined by letter position, 7
 suggested teaching order, 9-10
Vowels in syllabication, 43

W

Wacky wordies, 409-414
Want ads, 382
Ways to define a word, 230
Web sites for
 children's literature, 343-344
 kids' zines, 345
 reading instruction, 341
 writers and word lovers, 342
 See also Virtual reference library
Word origins. *See also* -Cide, Clipped words,
 Foreign words, Greek and Latin roots,
 -Ology, *-Phobia*, Portmanteau words,
 Prefixes, Suffixes, Words borrowed from
 names
Word pairs, nonreversible, 82
Words borrowed from names, 121-124
Words, ways to define, 230
Words with multiple meanings, 373
Workbook words, 309

Working in teams, 245-246. *See also*
 Teamwork rules
Work words
 application, 379
 airport, 384
 construction, 384
 credit terms, 383
 danger, 380
 grocery and drug, 382-383
 hospital, 383-384
 income tax, 383
 lumber, 385
 menus, 383
 road signs, 380-381
 sales, 384-385
 signs, 381-382
 telephone, 385
 trucking, 384
 want ads, 382
 See also Daily living words, Travel words
Writers, Web sites for, 342
Writing, Section 6
 basic sentence patterns, 213
 build a sentence, 214
 descriptive words, 199-203
 he said/she said, 208
 nondiscriminatory language guidelines,
  211-212
 proofreading checklists, 219-221
 punctuation guidelines, 215-216
 rubrics for, elementary/intermediate, 307
 rubrics for, primary, 306
 story starters, 204-207
 writeability checklist, 217-218
 See also Contractions, Proofreading checklist, Proofreading marks, Spelling
  demons, Spelling rules and patterns,
  Syllabication rules, Capitalization guidelines
Writeability checklist, 217-218

Y

Yiddish words, 116

Z

Zaner-Bloser handwriting charts
 manuscript, 223
 cursive, 223
Zines for kids, 345
Zipf's Principle, 372